Self-determination and Minority Rights in China

Chinese and Comparative Law Series

VOLUME 7

The titles published in this series are listed at *brill.com/ccls*

Self-determination and Minority Rights in China

By

Linzhu Wang

BRILL
NIJHOFF

LEIDEN | BOSTON

Part of the material in this book has previously been published:
Linzhu Wang, *The Definition of Indigenous Peoples and Its Applicability in China*, 22:2 International Journal on Minority and Group Rights, 2015, pp. 232–258;
Linzhu Wang, *The Identification of Minorities in China*, 16:2 Asian-Pacific Law and Policy Journal, 2015, pp. 1–21.

Library of Congress Cataloging-in-Publication Data

Names: Wang, Linzhu, author.
Title: Self-determination and minority rights in China / by Linzhu Wang.
Description: Leiden ; Boston : Brill, [2019] | Series: Chinese and comparative law series, ISSN 2213-4875 ; volume 7 | Includes bibliographical references.
Identifiers: LCCN 2018041941| ISBN 9789004380561 | ISBN 9789004380578 (e-book)
Subjects: LCSH: Minorities–Civil rights–China. | Self-determination, National–China.
Classification: LCC JQ1506.M5 W36 2019 | DDC 323.151–dc23
LC record available at https://lccn.loc.gov/2018041941

Typeface for the Latin, Greek, and Cyrillic scripts: "Brill". See and download: brill.com/brill-typeface.

ISSN 2213-4875
ISBN 978-90-04-38056-1 (hardback)
ISBN 978-90-04-38057-8 (e-book)

This book is printed on acid-free paper and produced in a sustainable manner.

Contents

Acknowledgements

This book grew out of my doctoral thesis at Lancaster University. First, I would like to thank my doctoral supervisor, James Summers, for his guidance and encouragement throughout my years of study at Lancaster. I am thankful to Sigrun Skogly, who co-supervised the thesis, for her advice and support. My thanks also go to my Viva Voce examiners, Bill Bowring and James Sweeney, and the reviewers of my draft manuscript at Brill. Their critiques and comments are valuable to the formation of the final published piece. I would like to thank Sophia Kopela and André de Hoogh for their help and encouragement in my pursuit of academic career. I am also grateful for the financial support I received from Lancaster University Law School during 2010–2013, which enabled me to complete my doctoral studies and to present the research findings in this book at conferences and workshops. My gratitude and appreciation goes to John Pearson, Samantha Spence, Wu Zhiqin, Jia Yuanchi, Eileen Jones, and those who have helped me during this project. I am also thankful to everyone at Brill, in particular Anna Schmitt Nagelbach, Ingeborg van der Laan and Anitha Rajasekaran, for their assistance through the publication process. Lastly, I would like to give special thanks to my parents, Pan Guimei and Wang Xiaohui, to whom this book is dedicated, for their endless love, support and encouragement.

This book contains materials previously published. The details are as follows:

- Linzhu Wang, "The Definition of Indigenous Peoples and Its Applicability in China", 22:2 International Journal on Minority and Group Rights (2015), pp. 232–258. © International Journal on Minority and Group Rights, published by Brill. Reprinted with permission.
- Linzhu Wang, "The Identification of Minorities in China", 16:2 Asian-Pacific Law and Policy Journal (2015), pp. 1–21, blog.hawaii.edu/aplpj/files/2015/09/APLPJ_16_2_Wang.pdf, published by Asian-Pacific Law and Policy Journal. © Linzhu Wang.

Linzhu Wang
Southwest University of Political Science and Law
September 2018

Abbreviations

ACHPR	African Commission on Human and People's Right
CAT	Committee Against Torture
CEDAW	Convention on the Elimination of All Forms of Discrimination against Women
CERD	Committee on the Elimination of Racial Discrimination
CESCR	Committee on Economic, Social and Cultural Rights
CPC	Communist Party of China
CPCCC	Central Committee of the Communist Party of China
CRC	Convention on the Rights of the Child
GA	General Assembly
GAOR	General Assembly Official Records
GZAR	Guangxi Zhuang Autonomous Region
HRC	Human Rights Committee
ICCPR	International Covenant on Civil and Political Rights
ICERD	International Convention on the Elimination of All Forms of Racial Discrimination
ICESCR	International Covenant on Economic, Social and Cultural Rights
ICJ	International Court of Justice
IMAR	Inner Mongolia Autonomous Region
KMT/GMD	Chinese Nationalist Party (Kuomintang/Guomindang)
LPC	Local People's Congress
LPCSC	Standing Committee of the Local People's Congress
LPG	Local People's Government
NHAR	Ningxia Hui Autonomous Region
NPC	National People's Congress
NPCSC	Standing Committee of the National People's Congress
PLA	Chinese People's Liberation Army
REA	Regional Ethnic Autonomy
RMB/CNY	*Ren Min Bi* (Official Currency of the People's Republic of China)
ROC	Republic of China
SAR	Special Administrative Region
SCC	Standardised Chinese Characters
SEAC	State Ethnic Affairs Commission of China
TAR	Tibet Autonomous Region

UNESCO	United Nations Educational, Scientific and Cultural Organisation
UNDRIP	United Nations Declaration on the Rights of Indigenous Peoples
USSR	Union of Soviet Socialist Republics
VAT	Value Added Tax
XUAR	Xinjiang Uyghur Autonomous Region

Introduction

1 Aims and Scope

China's population, of 1.37 billion people, are officially classified into 56 ethnic groups, among which the Han account for approximately 91.51 percent and minorities constitute the remaining 8.49 percent.[1] According to the Chinese government, it is the Chinese people, composed of all of these ethnic groups, who determined to establish an independent state and exercise the right to freely determine their political status and pursue economic, social and cultural development.[2] The Constitution of the People's Republic of China (PRC) starts with the statement that the Chinese people of all nationalities[3] have jointly created a

---

1 The statistics are from the sixth national census in 2010. The Communiqué of the National Bureau of Statistics on Major Figures of the 2010 Population Census (No. 1), http://www.stats.gov.cn/tjsj/tjgb/rkpcgb/qgrkpcgb/201104/t20110428_30327.html, last accessed on 15/03/2018.

2 The 1982 Constitution (recently amended in 2018), Preamble; the Initial Report Submitted by China under Articles 16 and 17 of the International Covenant on Economic, Social and Cultural Rights (ICESCR), 2003, UN Doc. E/1990/5/Add.59, pp. 5–6, para.6; the Second Periodic Report Submitted by China under Articles 16 and 17 of the ICESCR, 2010, UN Doc. E/C.12/CHN/2, p. 5.

3 The term "*min zu*" in Chinese appears as two separate characters. In regard to ethnicity, "*min*" literally means "people" and "*zu*" equates to lineage/clan. As early as the Zhou dynasty (ca. 1046–256 B.C.), these two terms were used interchangeably, as both defined a group of people living in certain localities who shared common features—blood, history, way of living, customs, and so forth. After the introduction of the nation concept in 1903, the traditional ethnic groups began to be named the Han *minzu/zu* or Tibetan *minzu/zu*, alongside the new Chinese nation (*zhonghua minzu*). The usage of *minzu* in this sense is confusing, as it represents the Chinese nation on the one hand and refers to its constituent parts on the other. Therefore, how to accurately translate *minzu*, the constituent groups of the Chinese nation, has long been debated. Diverse translations, such as nationality, ethnicity, ethnic group, or *minzu* as it is, have been suggested. Following the Soviet tradition, *minzu* was used as the synonym of nationality within China until the 1990s. After the dissolution of the former socialist states, the State Nationality Affairs Commission of China became the State Ethnic Affairs Commission to avoid any possible political implications deriving from the concept of nationality. In the White Papers issued by the Information Office of the State Council, "ethnic minorities" and "regional ethnic autonomy" have gradually replaced the old terms "minority nationalities" (Human Rights in China, 1991) and "regional national autonomy" (Human Rights in China, 1991; Tibet-Its Ownership and Human Rights Situation, 1992; the Progress of Human Rights in China, 1995). Although the term "nationality" is still being used in practice, the official stance seems to prefer "ethnicity" or "ethnic group" as the translation of "*minzu*" in relation to China's minorities. As far as this book is concerned, "nationalities" and "ethnic groups" will be used interchangeably to refer to the constituent groups of the Chinese nation, e.g. the Han *minzu*, or

 | DOI:10.1163/9789004380578_002

culture of grandeur and finally become the masters of the country through their arduous struggles, which began in the 1840s.[4] In regard to Chinese minorities, a special Regional Ethnic Autonomy (REA) system has been designed and implemented to guarantee their participatory right on the basis of ethnic equality. The comprehensive legal system of China, as argued by the Chinese government, has effectively protected and promoted the rights of the minorities, and it can therefore be viewed as an appropriate mechanism through which the minorities can exercise the right to self-determination within the state.[5]

---

the Tibetan *minzu*. "Regional Ethnic Autonomy" and "Regional National Autonomy" are also used synonymously. See Huang Guangxue and Shi Lianzhu (eds), *Zhongguo de minzu shibie* [*The Ethnic Identification in China*] (Minzu chubanshe, 2005), pp. 1–2; Li Min and Wang Jian, *Shangshu yizhu* [*Commentaries to the Book of Documents*] (Shanghai guji chubanshe, 2004), pp. 399–400; Yang Bojun, *Chunqiu zuozhuan zhu* [*Commentaries to Spring and Autumn (annals) and Zuo' Tradition*] *Volume II* (Zhonghua shuju, 1995), p. 818; He Shutao, "Dui ershi shiji zai zhongguo zuiyou yingxing de sanda minzu dingyi de jianyao fenxi [An Analysis of Three Influential Definitions of Nation in the 20th Century China]", 04 *Heilongjiang Minzu Congkan* [*Heilongjiang National Series*] (2009), pp. 14–15; Shi Yilong, "Ethnic Group buneng zuowei Minzu de yingwen duiyi [*Minzu* Should Not Be Translated as Ethnic Group]", 04 *Shijie Minzu* [*World Ethno-National Studies*] (1999), p. 79; Jin Binghao et al., "Minzu yu zuqun: shi gainian de hubu haishi dianfu [The Differences and Similarities between Ethnic Group and Minzu]?", 02 *Heilongjiang Minzu Congkan* [*Heilongjiang National Series*] (2012), pp. 4–14; Pan Jiao, " 'Zuqun' yu minzu gainian de hubu haishi dianfu [On the Differences and Similarities between Ethnic Group and Ethnos]", 26:01 *Yunan Minzu Daxue Xuebao* [*Journal of Yunnan Nationalities University (Social Sciences)*] (2009), pp. 22–27; Hao Shiyuan, "Zhongwen 'minzu' yu 'shaoshu minzu' de yingyi wenti [The English Translation of 'Minzu' and 'Shaoshu Minzu']", *Zhonguo Minzubao* [*China Ethnic News*], 22 March 2013, p. 5; Naran Bilik, "Minzu bainian huimou [A Historical Review of 'Minzu']", 02 *Guangxi Minzu Yanjiu* [*Study of Nationalities in Guangxi*] (2000), pp. 17, 22; Chen Xinlin, "Zuqun lilun yu Zhongguo de zuqun yanjiu [Ethnic Group Theory and Ethnic Groups Research in China]", 17:01 *Qinghai Minzu Yanjiu* [*Nationalities Research in Qinghai*] (2006), pp. 5, 7. The Information Office of the State Council, the White Papers on Human Rights in China (1991), Tibet-Its Ownership and Human Rights Situation (1992), the Progress of Human Rights in China (1995), New Progress in Human Rights in the Tibet Autonomous Region (1998), National Minorities Policy and Its Practice in China (1999); and more recently, Progress in China's Human Rights in 2013 (2014) and Successful Practice of Regional Ethnic Autonomy in Tibet (2015). The English version of the White Papers is available at http://english.gov.cn/archive/whitepaper/, http://www.gov.cn/english/links/whitepapers.htm and the Chinese version can be accessed via http://www.scio.gov.cn/zfbps/index.htm, last visited on 14/05/2018.

4 The 1982 Constitution, Preamble.

5 China, the 10th, 11th, 12th, and 13th Periodic Reports Submitted by China under Article 9 of the International Convention on the Elimination of All Forms of Racial Discrimination (ICERD), UN Doc. CERD/C/CHN/10-13, p. 5, para.12; the Committee on the Elimination of All Forms of Racial Discrimination, Summary Record of the 1943rd Meeting, 75th Session, 2009, UN Doc. CERD/C/SR.1943, p. 2, para.3; China, Replies to the List of Issues, 2004, UN Doc. HR/CESCR/NONE/2004/10, pp. 5-6.

Nevertheless, this official discourse has been challenged by outbursts of regional ethnic unrest. Many commentators have also questioned the REA system and dismissed it as "paper" or "verbal" autonomy.[6] With the influx of the Han into minority areas and the uneven development of the economy, some Chinese minority groups have demanded greater autonomy or self-determination, while others have generated violent separatist movements. For example, the Tibetans attempted to claim self-determination under the General Assembly Resolution 1514 in the United Nations[7] and the monks (and nuns) launched a series of demonstrations and riots in support of Tibetan Independence in 1987–1989 and 2008.[8] In 2011, the outburst of ethnic protests in Inner Mongolia resulted in the imposition of martial law in the region. The Uyghur separatists resorted to more violent acts in seeking to establish the "Eastern Turkestan", and have plotted numerous attacks in recent years.

Indeed, the ethnic distinctions in terms of language, religion, and culture can be easily observed within the so-claimed Chinese nation. The criteria applied in the course of minority identification also have national implications.[9] If the Chinese nation had been defined differently and minority groups were once granted the right to self-determination,[10] why are the same ethnic groups now expected to exercise autonomy within the state? Who in China holds the right to self-determination? What rights, self-determination and/or autonomous rights do Chinese minorities have? How are those rights implemented in practice? This book aims to seek answers by examining the rights of Chinese minorities from the perspective of self-determination. It focuses on the definition of "peoples" and the meaning of self-determination in relation to different ethnic groups in China, with special attention paid to the REA system as an internal arrangement for the minorities to exercise the right to self-determination within the state.

Having emerged as a political principle, self-determination has been widely accepted as the right of peoples to freely determine their own future after the Second World War. In the process of decolonisation, the right of colonial and dependent peoples to self-determination has been widely considered to be a part of customary international law.[11] It has functioned as one of the major

6 Barry Sautman, "Ethnic Law and Minority Rights in China: Progress and Constraints", 21:03 *Law and Policy* (1999), p. 293.

7 See Chapter 3, Section 3.2 "The Question of Tibet".

8 Melvyn Goldstein, *The Snow Lion and the Dragon: China, Tibet and the Dalai Lama* (University of California Press, 1997), pp. 80–100.

9 See Chapter 4, Section 4.3 "the Definition of Minorities".

10 See Chapters 2 and 3.

11 The International Court of Justice held, in the Namibia case, the Western Sahara case, the Case Concerning East Timor and the Kosovo Advisory Opinion, that the principle of

legal underpinnings of decolonisation and has assisted in shaping the new international community. Beyond the colonial context, however, the application of the principle of self-determination remains unclear.[12] The meaning of the right remains ambiguous and its holders, "the peoples",[13] are famously undefined. There are divergent understandings and interpretations of the right to self-determination, and it may conversely challenge statehood and pose a threat to the international order, as it has been repeatedly contested by separatist groups. A large number of books and articles have been published on self-determination. Only a few, however, consider its influences upon China's transformation from a civilisation to a modern state and its application in the Chinese context.

Therefore, the first part of this book focuses on how self-determination as a political principle and international norm has been practised in China and in what ways it has affected the interpretation of the Chinese nation. As will be discussed in the following chapter, both nationalism and self-determination have been utilised by the political elites as the underpinning ideology for establishing an independent Chinese state. The primary concern of nationalism is to identify a nation, in China's case the Chinese nation. Different theories of nationalism have been developed and various definitions of the "nation" have been proposed.[14] This book identifies with

self-determination is one of essential principles of customary international law concerning decolonisation. Namibia, ICJ Report (1971), pp. 31–32, paras.52–53; West Sahara, ICJ Report (1975), pp. 31–33, paras.54–59; East Timor, ICJ Report (1995), p. 102, para.29; Kosovo, ICJ Report (2010), p. 37, para.79. See also Helen Quane, "The United Nations and the Evolving Right to Self-determination", 47:03 *International and Comparative Law Quarterly* (1998), p. 554.

12 In James Crawford's words, it is *lex obscura*. James Crawford, "The Right of Self-determination in International Law: its Development and Future", in Philip Alston (ed), *Peoples' Rights* (Oxford University Press, 2001), p. 38.

13 The concepts of "nations" and "peoples" are not defined in international law. Both have been considered to hold the right to self-determination. These two concepts are used synonymously in the legal context and therefore are interchangeable in most cases. In this book, the Chinese nation (*zhonghua minzu*) and the Chinese people (*zhongguo renmin*) are used interchangeably. See James Summers, *Peoples and International Law (2nd Edition)* (Martinus Nijhoff Publishers, 2014), pp. 7–8.

14 Anthony Smith, *Nationalism: Theory, Ideology, History* (Polity Press, 2001); Benedict Anderson, *Imagined Communities: Reflections on the Origin and Spread of Nationalism (Revised Edition)* (Verso, 1991); Charles Tilly, *The Formation of National States in Western Europe* (Princeton University Press, 1975); John Breuilly, *Nationalism and the State* (Manchester University Press, 1993); Ernest Gellner, *Nations and Nationalism (2nd Edition)* (Cornell University Press, 2008); Hugh Seton-Watson, *Nations and States—An Enquiry into the Origins of Nations and the Politics of Nationalism* (Methuen London, 1977); David

Anderson's definition of the nation as an imagined political community.[15] Hence, the discussion is centred on the invention of the Chinese nation by the Nationalist Party (Kuomintang/KMT) and the Communist Party of China (CPC) in accordance with political needs and the underlying reasons behind such changes. It looks at varying definitions of the Chinese nation, be it the nation of the Han, the nation of five groups, or the nation that embraces all ethnic groups, which have been proposed by different political forces in the surge of nationalist movements. On the other hand, apart from nationalism, self-determination has also been claimed by the Chinese political elites as the basis for national integrity and independence. The attempts to apply Wilson's and Lenin's ideas of self-determination in the process for establishing a modern state of China have revealed that the minorities, as the holders of the right to self-determination, might jeopardise the unified statehood, which in turn has influenced the imagination of the Chinese nation. When the PRC was established in 1949, the Chinese nation was, and still is, defined as a historically legitimated territory together with the whole population living in it. Through a close examination of the rival self-determination claims made by Tibet, Hong Kong and Macau in the decolonisation process, this book argues that the official claim that the Chinese people enjoy the right to self-determination and the minorities are entitled to autonomy as the means for exercising internal self-determination is made successful on the international level. The practice of self-determination in the Chinese context has illustrated the multifaceted nature of self-determination.

This book then continues to examine the minorities' continuous exercise of internal self-determination through the REA system. It aims to analyse the content of minority rights under both Chinese law and international law and how those rights are implemented in practice. The second part of the book intends to present a comprehensive survey of the current legal framework that is applicable to China's minorities, as a systematic appraisal of the REA system would be beneficial to all minority groups. Under the REA system, only the groups who have been officially recognised by the central government as *shaoshu minzu* (the official term for the minorities) can exercise

Miller, *On Nationality* (Clarendon Press, 1995); Eric Hobsbawm and Terence Ranger (eds), *The Invention of Tradition* (Cambridge University Press, 1983); Benjamin Schwartz, *Chinese Communism and the Rise of Mao* (Harvard University Press, 1966); Anthony Giddens, *The Nation-State and Violence, Vol. 2: A Contemporary Critique of Historical Materialism* (Polity Press, 1985).

15 According to Benedict Anderson, the nation is "an imagined political community—and imagined as both inherently limited and sovereign". Benedict Anderson, ibid, pp. 5–6.

territorial autonomy in areas where they live in concentrated communities. Therefore, the critical assessment of the rights of Chinese minorities looks into four elements as highlighted in the constitutional regime of ethnic territorial autonomy: regions, minorities, autonomous agencies and autonomous rights. It is argued that minority legislative and financial autonomy are not effectively implemented under the REA system, whilst the cultural rights of the minorities seem to be tolerated and encouraged. The REA system as a pragmatic alternative for minority protection in China needs further enforcement and implementation as it does not fully conform to China's obligations to recognise, protect and promote minority rights under international law. The book further suggests that the introduction of a comprehensive definition of discrimination in Chinese law, the adoption of an individualist approach of minority rights, the incorporation of a special consultation procedure for affected members or communities, and the appointment of more minority members to important positions in the state and party apparatus should be promoted in order to achieve the full realisation of minority rights in China.

2 Methodology

This book focuses on self-determination and minority rights in China. It is in essence a law-based study with interdisciplinary elements, combining law with theory, politics and history. First, this book is intended to examine the normative framework for China's minorities to exercise their rights and its implementation in practice. It critically examines the ethnic territorial autonomy in China and approaches the question from an international law perspective. Thus, it is essentially doctrinal: it is about the rights of Chinese minorities, including the right to self-determination, as provided by domestic law and international law. Considering the special political reality in China, this study also considers the documents of the Communist Party and relevant government policies,[16] as they have significantly influenced the interpretation and implementation of legal provisions on minority rights. For example, the identification of the minorities and the establishment of autonomous units both have a strong political and administrative nature but accordingly carry significant legal consequences. The analysis of quantitative data is necessary in the sense

16 The government here narrowly refers to the executive branch of the state institution, namely the State Council and local people's governments at different levels.

that it will help to demonstrate how the law is enforced and whether the goals have been achieved.

Second, politics are unavoidably involved in the discussion of self-determination, and there is no exception in the Chinese context. This book treats "the Chinese nation/people", which is central to the right to self-determination, as a political idea. Different interpretations of the holders of self-determination in China, varying from minorities to the Chinese nation, were proposed in accordance with political needs prior to the PRC being established. On the other hand, the historical development of the laws and policies in relation to self-determination and minority rights provides an insight into the current state of the law and the way it is implemented.[17] A political-legal

---

17 In the context of ethnic unrest in China, different theories have been proposed in regard to the appraisal of China's ethnic policy. An alternative model, focusing on the de-politicalisation of ethnic identity in China, has aroused the debate, the so-called "second-generation" ethnic policy debate, among Chinese scholars and officials in recently years. Ma Rong, Hu Angang and Hu Lianhe represent the advocates who favour a "melting-pot" model and argue for the promotion of individual rights of minority citizens which requires the elimination of ethnic status and the assimilation of the minorities into the unified Chinese nation. Other scholars criticise such an approach, arguing that the new approach of de-politicalising ethnic identity has been influenced by the Western theory of ethnicity (Hao Shiyuan, 2005) and has ignored China's ethic realities (Chen Jianyue, 2005; Chen Yuping, 2008; Jin Binghao, 2011). As the core of this book is *lex lata* and this debate has neither been adopted, as yet, nor influenced the ethnic law or its implementation, this book will not explore the "second-generation" ethnic policy debate in detail. See Mark Elliot, "The Case of the Missing Indigene: Debate Over a 'Second-Generation' Ethnic Policy", 73 *The China Journal* (2015), pp. 186–213; Jin Binghao, Sun Jun and Xiao Rui, "Minzu wenti 'qu zhengzhihua' 'wenhuahua': xin silu haishi lao taolu [The De-politicalisation and Culturalisation of the Ethnic Question: a New Approach or an Old Scheme]?", 03 *Heilongjiang Minzu Congkan* [*Heilongjiang National Series*] (2012), pp. 8–16; Barry Sautman, "Scaling Back Minority Rights? The Debate About China's Ethnic Policies", 46:01 *Stanford Journal of International Law* (2010), pp. 51–120; Matthew Erie, *China and Islam: The Prophet, the Party, and Law* (Cambridge University Press, 2016), p. 32; Ma Rong, "Lijie minzu guanxi de xin silu—shaoshu zuqun de 'qu zhengzhihua' [A New Approach to Understand Minority Group Relations: the 'De-politicisation' of the Ethnic Question]", 06 *Beijing Daxue Xuebao* [*Journal of Peking University (Philosophy and Social Science)*] (2004), pp. 122–133; and "A New Perspective in Guiding Ethnic Relations in the 21st Century: 'De-politicisation' of Ethnicity in China", 08:03 *Asian Ethnicity* (2007), pp. 199–217; Hu Angang and Hu Lianhe, "Dierdai minzu zhengce: cujin minzu jiaorong yiti he fanrong yiti [A Second-Generation Ethnic Policy: Advancing a Single Body of Ethnic Integration and Prosperity]", 35:05 *Xinjiang Shifan Daxue Xuebao* [*Journal of Xinjiang Normal University*] (2011), pp. 1–12; Hao Shiyuan, "Goujian shehui zhuyi hexie shehui yu minzu guanxi [Relations among Nationalities and the Building of a Harmonious Society of Socialism]", 03 *Minzu Yanjiu* [*Ethno-National Studies*] (2005), pp. 1–13; and "Meiguo shi zhongguo jiejue minzu wenti de bangyang ma?—ping 'dierdai minzu zhengce de 'guoji jingyan jiaoxun' shuo [Is the US a Model for Solving China's Ethnic Problems? A Critique of the Notion of

approach is thus adopted to examine the interplay of the laws and politics in the historical discourse so as to help the reader to better understand some of the most contentious issues in contemporary China.

3 An Outline of the Book

This book is divided into six chapters. The first three chapters in Part 1 deal with the application of self-determination in the Chinese context. Chapter 1 examines the definition of the Chinese nation, who are considered to be the rights holders of self-determination in China. It starts with a review of historical roots of Chinese nationalist synthesis and focuses on how theories of nationalism have been utilised by different political forces in order to mobilise the people and to build the Chinese nation. The Chinese understanding of sovereignty provides another perspective to comprehend the legitimacy of the Chinese state and the status of the minorities therein. In doing so, the chapter outlines different ways to understand the Chinese nationhood and the corresponding implications for the Han-minority relation in modern China.

Chapter 2 looks at how the political principle of self-determination has been practised in China. The first attempt to claim self-determination was the endeavour of the Beiyang Government (1912–1928), inspired by Wilsonian self-determination, to reclaim Chinese sovereignty over the Shandong peninsula at the Peace Conference of Paris, which exemplified an arbitrary application of self-determination by the Allied Powers. Lenin's theory of national self-determination has also been practised in China. Both the Nationalist Party and the Communist Party strategically interpreted the principle in different periods, with the aim of achieving national independence and appealing to the minorities. This chapter not only explains why the right of Chinese minorities

'Lessons of International Experience' in the 'Second-Generation Ethnic Policy']", 02 *Shijie Minzu* [*Journal of World Peoples Studies*] (2012), pp. 1–15; Chen Jianyue, "Duo minzu guojia hexie shehui de goujian yu minzu wenti de jiejue—ping minzu wenti de 'qu zhengzhihua' yu 'wenhuahua' [The Construction of a Harmonious Society in a Unified Multi-ethnic State: Comments on the De-politicalisation and Culturalisation of the Ethnic Question]", 05 *Shijie Minzu* [*Journal of World Peoples Studies*] (2005), pp. 1–13; Chen Yuping, "Minzu wenti nengfou 'qu zhengzhihua' zhenglun zhi wojian [Whether the Ethnic Question Could Be De-politicalised]", 07 *Xinan Minzu Daxue Xuebao* [*Journal of Southwest University for Nationalities*] (2008), pp. 1–7; Jin Binghao and Xiao Rui, "Jianchi zhongguo tese shehui zhuyi shehui minzu lilun zhengce—pingxi 'dierdai minzu zhengce' shuo [On Maintaining Socialism Ethnic Theory and Policy with Chinese Characteristics—Analysis of Second-generation Ethnic Policy]", 04 *Xibei Minzu Daxue Xuebao* [*Journal of Northwest Southwest University for Nationalities*] (2012), pp. 12–19.

to secede was eventually narrowed to territorial autonomy within the state, but also illustrates how the concept of self-determination influenced the invention of the Chinese nation.

Chapter 3 examines the application of the right to self-determination in China. It is argued that the Chinese government has made a solid claim under international law, by asserting that the Chinese people, composed of all ethnic groups, have the right to self-determination and the minorities are entitled to territorial autonomy as the means to exercise internal self-determination. Although such an assertion has been challenged by the self-determination claims made by Tibet, Hong Kong, and Macau in the decolonisation process, those rival claims were not supported by the international community. The Chinese cases reveal that the undefined term "people", the political strength of the relevant parties, and the reaction of the international community may affect the application of the right to self-determination. Furthermore, this Chapter examines the institutional arrangements specifically designed to facilitate the exercise of internal self-determination within the state, i.e. the "one country two systems" and regional autonomy for the minorities.

Part 2 of the book is mainly concerned with how Chinese minorities exercise internal self-determination through the REA system. According to Chinese law, four elements are highlighted in the REA system: regions (where), minorities (who), autonomous agencies (how) and autonomous rights (what).

Chapter 4 deals with the first three elements. It first analyses various factors that may have affected the establishment of autonomous areas. Despite the law stating that autonomous units should be established in areas where the minorities live in concentrated communities, without further explanation, standards for establishing autonomous regions or changing their administrative boundaries are not clearly provided by the law. Such a practice leads to the situation that the minorities fail to form the majority of the population in more than 70%[18]of the autonomous areas, which directly affects the exercise of autonomous rights through autonomous agencies. This Chapter then examines autonomous institutions, the local people's congress and the local people's government, through which the minorities collectively exercise autonomous rights. Some minority groups may be proportionately overrepresented in autonomous agencies. This fact, however, does not secure a majority vote for that minority since they are still numerically inferior in the local population, as demonstrated above. It should also be noted that the minorities are

18 Maria Lundberg and Yong Zhou, "Regional National Autonomy under Challenge: Law, Practice and Recommendations", 16 *International Journal on Minority and Group Rights* (2009), p. 304.

underrepresented in the political centre of the Communist Party and in important posts in the party apparatus. Who can claim the constitutional right to territorial autonomy is another crucial issue in the REA system. Compulsory minority recognition as the precondition for asserting ethnic autonomy enables the CPC to exert a macro-control of the number of minority groups, and more importantly, to divide the minority population in a way that best fits its political interests.

The following two chapters focus on the fourth element of the REA system: ethnic autonomous rights. Legislative autonomy and financial autonomy are exclusively derived from Chinese law, while the right of Chinese minorities to culture is governed by domestic law as well as international law. Chapter 5 first examines the right of the minorities to legislative autonomy, by dividing it into autonomous legislative power, adaptation power and adaptive implementation power. It reveals that the autonomous legislative right as the core of ethnic territorial autonomy has not been effectively exercised for various reasons. A special participation and consultation procedure for affected members or communities should therefore be introduced in order to guarantee the interests of the minorities in the decision-making process. This Chapter further discusses how financial autonomy is exercised through autonomous agencies in the present tax-sharing system. Compared to legislative and cultural autonomy, the exercise of financial autonomy in autonomous areas is less stable and predictive, as a result of the centre-oriented national fiscal system and the administration-led taxation reforms.

Given the scope and content of the notion of culture, Chapter 6 approaches minority cultural rights from religious and linguistic perspectives. As the cultural rights of the minorities is provided by both international law and Chinese law, this Chapter first looks at the obligations that China has undertaken under international human rights instruments in regard to minority cultural rights and compares them with the provisions of Chinese law. It, in particular, examines the religious freedom of Chinese minorities, including the practice of institutional religions and minority belief systems, and the right to language. It observes that the cultural rights of the minorities are exercised in a collective manner, which has its own constraints as it may conflict with individual human rights. To allow members of the minorities to equally take part in cultural life, regardless of their places of residence, is essential for the realisation of minority rights in China.

PART 1

Self-determination in the Chinese Context

CHAPTER 1

The Nation of China

The emergence of the principle of self-determination in international law is informed by liberalism and nationalism.[1] Liberal theory, as expressed in American and French revolutions, concerns individual freedom and places political legitimacy of a lawful government upon the consent of the governed,[2] while nationalism represents the demand of "nations" to legitimately establish their own states.[3] Both doctrines emerged in the seventeenth and eighteenth centuries,[4] and their interaction with international law "has defined the context in which self-determination has developed".[5]

Although the doctrine of nationalism was asserted to disintegrate "artificial" multinational empires in Europe,[6] it was, and still is, employed to justify that China is the state for the Chinese nation. Faced with challenges posed by foreign forces, Chinese political elites chose nationalism as the foundation for building an independent modern Chinese state since the late Qing era. Yu Ying-Shih has noted that nationalism is the driving force behind the changes

1 David Raic, *Statehood and the Law of Self-determination* (Kulwer Law International, 2002), pp. 172–177; James Summers, *Peoples and International Law (2nd Edition)* (Martinus Nijhoff Publishers, 2014), pp. 13–36.

2 John Locke (Ian Shapiro ed), *Two Treatises of Government and A Letter Concerning Toleration, Book II*, (Yale University Press, 2003), pp.101–106, 111–121, 133–157; Jack Rakove (ed), *The Annotated U.S. Constitution and Declaration of Independence* (The Belknap Press, 2009), pp. 77,79; Philip Dwyer and Peter McPhee (eds), *The French Revolution and Napoleon: the Sourcebook* (Routledge, 2002), pp. 26–28.

3 Many scholars have written on the subject and this book will not attempt to retrace their path. See, e.g. Benedict Anderson, *Imagined Communities: Reflections on the Origin and Spread of Nationalism* (Revised Edition) (Verso, 1991); John Breuilly, Nationalism and the State (Manchester University Press, 1993); Alfred Cobban, *The National State and National Self-determination* (Collins, The Fontana Library, 1969); Rupert Emerson, *From Empire to Nation: the Rise of Self-assertion of Asian and African Peoples* (Harvard University Press, 1962); Ernest Gellner, *Nations and Nationalism* (Basil Blackwell, 1983); E.J. Hobsbawm, *Nations and Nationalism Since 1780: Programme, Myth, Reality (2nd Edition)* (Cambridge University Press, 1992); Anthony Smith, *The Ethnic Origins of Nations* (Blackwell Publishing, 1986); Hugh Seton-Watson, *Nations and States: An Enquiry into the Origins of Nations and the Politics of Nationalism* (Methuen London, 1977); Rodolfo Stavenhagen, *Ethnic Conflicts and the Nation-state* (The Macmillan Press, 1996).

4 David Raic, supra note 1, pp. 175–176; James Summers, supra note 1, p. 133.

5 James Summers, ibid, p. 132.

6 David Raic, supra note 1, pp. 176, 181; Hurst Hannum, "Rethinking Self-determination", 34:1 *Virginia Journal of International Law* (1993), p. 3.

 | DOI:10.1163/9789004380578_003

of China over the last hundred years.[7] Indeed, the familial metaphor of the nation as claimed by the nationalists,[8] to a certain extent, corresponds with traditional Confucian norms and values.[9] The history of multi-ethnic Chinese empires also leaves a legacy to define the Chinese nation through historical, territorial, and racial ties.[10] Despite the fact that the Soviet ideology has been adopted by the Communist Party to build the "new" state, as Hobsbawm rightly points out, China has tended "to become national not only in form but in substance".[11] Since nationalism concerns the interests and values of a nation,[12] the understanding of the Chinese nation is central to Chinese nationalism and therefore defines the proposed Chinese state.

Self-determination as a right is defined by the features of the people who exercise it. Similarly, the minorities and their rights are commonly defined by the relation with a majority culture. China's sense of nationhood and the Han-minority relation rest on a civilisation that stretches back thousands of years. Chinese civilisation not only provides the basis for the invention of the Chinese

---

7 Yu Ying-Shih, *Qianmu yu Zhongguo Wenhua* [*Qian Mu and Chinese Culture*] (Shanghai Yuandong Chubanshe, 1994), p. 203.

8 Anthony Smith, *Myths and Memories of Modern Nations* (Oxford University Press, 1999), p. 190.

9 According to Confucianism, family has a significant role in Chinese society. Social and familial interactions are guided by the principle of Filial Piety, which tends to emphasise the role of a man not only as an individual but also as a member of family and society. Further, Confucians rely upon an analogy between family and state. A man, therefore, owes loyalty both to his family and to his country. Craig Williams, "International Human Rights and Confucianism", 7:1 *Asia-Pacific Journal on Human Rights and the Law* (2006), pp. 48–49; C.W. Chan, "Human Rights and Democracy with Chinese Characteristics?", 13:4 *Human Rights Law Review (2013), p. 649;* David Y.F. Ho, "Chapter 11 Filial Piety and its Psychological Consequences", in Michael H. Bond (ed), *The Handbook of Chinese Psychology* (Oxford University Press, 1996), pp. 155–165; Reginald F. Johnston, *Confucianism and Modern China* (Victor Gollancz Ltd, 1934), pp. 42–46; Stephen Angle, *Human Rights and Chinese Thoughts: a Cross-cultural Inquiry* (Cambridge University Press, 2002), p. 236. See also infra note 21.

10 Various definitions of nation have been proposed. Gellner defines nation by will and culture; Smith argues that nation could be understood from territorial and ethnic aspects; a nation, according to Seton-Watson, "is a community of people, whose members are bound together by a sense of solidarity, a common culture, a national consciousness"; and Anderson considers nation as "an imagined political community". Ernest Gellner, supra note 3, pp. 1–7, 53–62; Anthony Smith, supra note 3, pp. 134–138; Hugh Seton-Watson, supra note 3, p. 1; Benedict Anderson, supra note 3, pp. 6–7.

11 Eric Hobsbawm, as cited in Benedict Anderson, ibid, p. 2.

12 John Breuilly, supra note 3, p. 2; Anthony Smith, *Nationalism: Theory, Ideology, History* (Polity Press, 2001), p. 9; Robert Tombs, "Introduction", in Robert Tombs (ed), *Nationhood and Nationalism in France: From Boulangism to the Great War 1889–1918* (HarperCollins Academic, 1991), pp. 3–7 at p. 3.

nation, but also affects the interpretation of the Han-minority relation. China could be defined as a unified multiethnic state jointly founded by the people of all ethnic groups.[13] The historically legitimate territory and the whole population living in it are the key elements of this definition.[14] Alternatively, China may be understood as a Han state, which tends to emphasise the significance of the Han culture over minority cultures.[15] Different interpretations of "China" in historical terms have significantly influenced the creation of the Chinese nation and the understanding of the Han-minority relation in modern China.

Therefore, this chapter examines various interpretations of the Chinese nation and the underlying reasons behind such changes. It starts with a historical examination of the pre-modern Chinese identity. It then focuses on the theories that have been employed to create and build a modern state of China, under which the invention of the Chinese nation constitutes the central part. The Chapter also looks at the Chinese understanding of sovereignty as it may help to perceive the ethnic situation and policies in China. It aims to give the reader a detailed account of how the Chinese nationhood has been imagined and the corresponding implications for understanding the Han-minority relation in the present day.

1.1 Pre-modern Chinese Identity

The Chinese nation draws from Chinese civilisation, which survived in the same land for almost four thousand years.[16] The understanding and interpretation of Chinese civilisation profoundly affect the formation of the Chinese nation.

---

13 The Information Office of the State Council, the White Papers on National Minorities Policy and Its Practice in China (1999), Section I; China's Ethnic Policy and Common Prosperity and Development of All Ethnic Groups (2009), Preface.

14 Thomas Heberer, *China and its National Minorities: Autonomy or Assimilation* (M. E. Sharpe, Inc., 1989), pp. 22, 121.

15 Su Bingqi and Yin Weizhang, "Guangyu kaoguxue wenhua de quxi leixing wenti [The Region, System and Type of Culture in the Archaeology]", 05 *Wenwu* [*Archaeology*] (1981), p. 11; An Zhimin, "Shi lun wenming de qiyuan [A Discussion on the Origin of Civilisation]", 05 *Wenwu* [*Archaeology*] (1987), pp. 455–7; "Tantan zhongguo wenming de qiyuan [The Origin of Chinese Civilisation]", 03 *Henan Shifan Daxue Xuebal* [*Journal of Henan Normal University*] (1991), p. 69; Chen Liankai, "Lun zhonghua wenming qiyuan jiqi zaoqi fazhan de jiben tedian [On the Origin of Chinese Civilisation and the Chief Characteristics of Its Early-stage Development]", 05 *Zhongyang Minzu Daxue Xuebao* [*Journal of Central University for Nationalities (Philosophy and Social Science)*] (2000), p. 25.

16 Hugh Seton-Watson, supra note 3, p. 274.

This civilisation was based on an integral and mature set of organic institutions, led by a centralised emperor, together with the meritocratic system of official recruitment.[17] Officials, whose behaviours were bound by codified rules with pre-set standards for treatment and punishment, were selected through the national examination system and directly appointed by the emperor. Then they were sent out throughout the empire to make sure that the central decisions would be followed at regional levels. The agricultural-oriented policy was always the guiding principle of the feudal courts, although industry and business started to play important roles in economy since the 11th century.[18] This policy led to a social structure, in which the majority of the population was peasantry at the bottom of society, with a small number of landlords and a few traders. As will be discussed below, such a social structure profoundly affected the strategy of mobilising popular support against the state.

The second factor that facilitated the formation of a common sense of identity was the unity of the written language. Since the Qin Empire unified China (221 B.C.), a standard Chinese script was used as the official language across the country. This script, after orthographic simplification, with new written styles and characters coming into exist in later history, survived until the 1950s.[19] The spoken language, however, was a different situation. The ruling class and elites spoke an official language, *lingua franca* (known as Mandarin), which was mainly used in the court. For the vast majority of the population, different dialects were used according to geographical localities. Still, the communication could be done through the written language. A single written language, accompanied by diverse regional dialects, can be regarded as a reflection of Chinese civilisation from the linguistic perspective.

---

17 The Qin Empire applied a military merit system and the Han dynasty adopted the *Chaju* (Observation and recommendation) system, under which the talents were recommended by the officials of the central court and local bureaucracy and employed after the evaluation process by the emperor. The *Jiupin zhongzheng zhi* system, as an updated version of the *Chaju* system, was once implemented in the Wei state and the national examination system was developed in the Sui dynasty, which, with further modifications and elaborations, was followed for more than one thousand years until 1905.

18 Zhou Shengchun, Cao Jiangang and Hu Qian, "Zhongguo lishi shang de nongben gongshangmo sixiang yu zhengfu zhengce de shanbian [Development of Agriculture-oriented Ideology and Corresponding Government Policies in the Chinese History]", 02 *Zhejiang Daxue Xuebao* [*Journal of Zhejiang University* (*Humanities and Social Sciences*)] (2004), pp. 13, 18.

19 In the 1950s, China advocated a script reform to simplify the Chinese character. See Derk Bodde, "Chapter 1 The State and Empire of Chin", in Denis Twitchett and John Fairbank (eds), *The Cambridge History of China: Volume 1* (Cambridge University Press, 1987), pp. 20–102 at pp. 57–58.

Thirdly, ideology provided a political, ethical and religious basis for Chinese civilisation. The Mandate of Heaven,[20] together with Confucianism and elements extracted from different philosophical schools, constituted the political foundation of a legitimate government. Confucius' teaching on *Li* (rituals) and *Xiao* (filial piety) affected the attitudes of the Chinese to families and civil authority and also formed the basis of feudal hierarchy.[21] The worship of ancestors, partly arising from the religious practice and partly from the doctrine of filial piety, was a common practice of Chinese culture. Transformation from humans to immortals or gods and the worship of natural powers were the themes of Chinese type of religions, such as Daoism, Buddhism, popular religion and minority beliefs. It is worth noting that, except for the Shang dynasty, religious leaders had never been the rulers of the country. In other words, the Chinese empires had a secular nature, and religions were only utilised by the ruling strata as a means of maintaining the reign.

Furthermore, it can be argued that Chinese civilisation has a pluralistic nature, with multiple origins. The interaction and integration of the Huaxia/Han culture and diversified regional/minority cultures into a large multicultural system[22] could be traced throughout the imperial history. Such an approach was supported by archaeological evidence emerged in the studies of ancient China. More importantly, it facilitated the territorial-political construction of the nation of China. The diversified origins of Chinese civilisation, which embraces both Han and minority cultures, underpin the building of a modern state that is composed of various ethnic groups. The theory of the "pluralistic unity of the Chinese nation"[23] may find its roots in here. Meanwhile, internal

20 See Section 1.3 "Sovereignty: China's perspective"

21 In particular, filial piety as "a guiding principle governing generational Chinese patterns of socialisation, as well as specific rules of intergenerational conduct, applicable throughout the length of one's life span" determined how authority and individual rights to be conceived by the Chinese people. David Y.F. Ho, supra note 9, at p. 155; see also Hugh Seton-Watson, supra note 3, at p. 275; Dru Gladney, *Muslim Chinese: Ethnic Nationalism in the People's Republic* (*2nd Edition*) (Harvard University Press, 1996), p. 95.

22 Cho-yun Hsu, "Chapter 8 The Spring and Autumn Period", in Michael Loewe and Edward Shaughnessy (eds), *The Cambridge History of Ancient China* (Cambridge University Press, 1999), pp. 545–586, at p. 565.

23 The theory of the "pluralistic unity of the Chinese nation" argues that: (1) the Chinese nation has developed on the current territory for thousands of years; (2) the Chinese nation is composed of various ethnic groups in different regions that have actively interacted with each other and thus have formed one unified nation; and (3) the Han group plays a leading role in the process of ethnic integration. Fei Xiaotong, "Zhonghua minzu de duoyuan yiti geju [The Pluralistic Unity of the Chinese Nation]", in Fei Xiaotong (ed), *Zhonghua minzu duoyuan yiti geju* [*The Pluralistic Unity of the Chinese Nation*] (Zhongyang Minzu Xueyuan Chubanshe, 1989), pp. 1–36.

cultural boundaries were also noticeable within Chinese civilisation, as the Yi-Xia (Han-minority) distinction had been long debated.[24] A flexible standard on the determination of Xia/China and Yi (general name of barbarians) was adopted: groups that conformed to the Xia/China culture were Chinese.[25] On the other hand, when minority regimes with military strength arose to compete with the Han, the cultural difference was emphasised and the myth of the inferiority of minority cultures was preserved.[26] For example, the legitimacy

---

24 Some concepts in relation to the ethnic issues in contemporary China, for example the Xia/Huaxia, China, four barbarians (Rong, Di, Yi, Man), can be traced back to the beginning of Chinese civilisation. The Xia or Huaxia was the ancient name of the Han group. According to the Book of Rites, at first the Xia and the "barbarians" were distinguished by geographical location, customs and culture. Unlike the modern term "barbarian", the name at the time did not imply cultural superiority or inferiority. The term "outlanders" would be a more appropriate name for those peoples. The coexistence of the Xia and the Rong/Di/Yi/Man also set out the basic model of cultural interaction of the Huaxia and other peoples/cultures that went through the whole context of Chinese history. Different groups and cultures met with and influenced each other by means of military conflicts or cultural communication. Seen from this perspective, Chinese civilisation is arguably composed of various subgroups and subcultures from the very beginning. The unified Chinese empires as well as the politically divided periods promoted the development of Chinese civilisation and cultural assimilation. The significance of a politically unified empire in cultivating a common sense of identity was beyond doubt. During the disunited internals, unlike the political separation suggested, Chinese culture in fact expanded and diversified. However, due to the active participation of the minorities in the multi-state system and their military strength, a further distinction of the Han and minorities (the Hua-Yi distinction) which had cultural and political implications was emphasised. Military defeats and the loss of the geographical centre of "China" made some Han people, who were not satisfied with "alien" predominance, cultural chauvinists. The concept of Yi was thus transformed from a description of different locations and lifestyles into an expression of cultural inferiority—the barbarians. To rebut such an assertion, the Manchu emperors claimed that the Qing Empire was the great unification of all peoples under the heavenly mandate and attempted to disregard the old Han assertion of dividing inside and outside China along the Great Wall. Instead, the inside/outside concept was reinterpreted as to refer to inside/outside Beijing. This reinterpretation of "China" became the prototype of modern China. See Li Xueqin (ed), *Shisanjing zhushu: Liji Zhengyi* [*The Thirteen Classics Explanatory Notes and Commentaries: the Book of Rites*] (Beijing Daxue Chubanshe, 1999), pp. 398–400; Mark Lewis, *China Between Empires: the Northern and Southern Dynasties* (The Belknap Press of Harvard University Press, 2009), p. 2; Chen Zhi, "Yixia xinbian [The Early Concepts of Chineseness and Barbarism]", 01 *Zhongguoshi Yanjiu* [*Journal of Chinese Histocial Studies*] (2004), pp. 17–20; Cho-yun Hsu, supra note 21, at p. 550; Mark Elliot, Hua Li (Translator), "Qingdai manzhouren de minzu zhuti yishi yu manzhouren de zhongguo tongzhi [Manchu National Consciousness and Manchu Rule in China during the Qing Dynasty]", 4 *Qingshi Yanjiu* [*Studies in Qing History*] (2002), p. 92

25 Chen Zhi, ibid, at pp. 19–20.

26 Frank Dikotter, *The Discourse of Race in Modern China* (Hurst and Company, 1992), p. 29.

of the Mongol and Manchu empires had been challenged by the Han group for their "alien" origins. Nevertheless, the doctrine of the Mandate of Heaven, focusing upon the notion of "governance with virtue" regardless of ethnic origin, also served as a non-Han ideology of governance. These varying interpretations of the Xia/Han and Yi/minorities at different phases of Chinese history, to a certain degree, provide an insight into the Han-minority relation in contemporary China.

1.2 The Nation of China

The Chinese empires acted as the centre of Asia for a long time and thus generated a Sino-centric worldview in the politico-cultural sense.[27] A comparatively mature and continuous system, together with a highly self-sufficient society, made the imperial China unconcerned for the outside world.[28] As the Industrial Revolution spread throughout Western countries, China still regarded itself as the "Celestial Empire". When Western civilisation, stemming from modern science and technology, collided with the agrarian-bureaucratic based civilisation, China entered into the so-called "the century of humiliation" (1839–1949). A chain of military defeats, the conclusion of unequal treaties and aggravating foreign encroachments completely smashed the illusion of China as the centre of civilisation. The political and ideological foundations for the powerful empires in the past seemed to be questionable.

Faced with the crisis of being dismembered and colonised by foreign forces, how to transform the Chinese Empire into a modern state that inherited the territory of the Qing Empire[29] and secure the survival of such a state in a Western dominant world became the major task for the reformers and nationalists. This hundred-year period was also an era that witnessed a radical change for Chinese society: the transformation from Culturalism to nationalism. The racial theories of identity started to replace traditional ideas of civilisation and hierarchy.[30] From the reforms of the Qing court to various nationalist

27 Yu Ying-Shih, "Chapter 6 Han Foreign Relations", in Denis Twitchett and John K Fairbank (eds), *The Cambridge History of China: Volume 1* (Cambridge University Press, 1986), pp. 377–462, at p. 379.

28 Ibid.

29 Henrietta Harrison, *China* (Arnold, 2001), p. 4.

30 Pamela Crossley, cited in Dru Gladney, supra note 21, p. 95.

movements launched by different groups, the invention of the Chinese nation embodied another example that fitted the three-step process of anti-colonial nationalism.[31]

---

31 According to Rupert Emerson, in response to the conquering Western civilisation, the first reaction of the colonial peoples was generally a xenophobic defence against the colonialists. The next phase was likely to be a swing in the direction of an uncritical self-humiliation and acceptance of alien superiority, and the third phase was a nationalist synthesis while still looking in the direction of Westernisation and modernisation. Rupert Emerson, supra note 3, pp. 10–11. Chinese nationalism started with the reform movements initiated by the Qing court as the first attempt to transform the feudalist empire into a modern state. This top-down reform, however, did not achieve satisfactory results as Japan did in the Meiji Restoration which was launched during the same period. Several reasons contributed to this. First, China was under more international pressure than Japan. China was a rich and vast country and attracted more attention of the West, which left Japan in a comparatively relaxed international environment. The two decades after the 1860s were internationally "relaxed" period as the western states were temporarily satisfied with the rights in the treaty ports and did not demand further partition of China. Nonetheless, China missed a good opportunity to carry out a thorough reform from the top-down as western threats were not considered to be "imminent". China pursued a limited self-strengthening movement, while Japan took this chance to complete a thorough reform. Internally, China had a political system with a centralised emperor and a mechanism deliberately designed to prevent the concentration of local powers. The province governors were not closely attached to their administrative localities. The political structure of Japan, on the other hand, was based on the balance between the shogun and the "outer" daimyo—big aristocratic families who controlled the western, southern and northern regions. Hence, in the Chinese imperial system, the commitment to reform was dependent upon the ruling class of the central government. For those who had vested interests in the current system, the preservation of power would be the priority. On the contrary, in the power-sharing model like Japan, it was more likely for local authorities to co-ordinate an attack upon the central government. Furthermore, Chinese civilisation had a long history of regarding itself as culturally superior. The Sino-centrism made it difficult for the ruling elites to accept the superiority of another culture and adapt themselves accordingly. Japanese culture, however, arose from a combination of several influences and thus had little problem to absorb another foreign element. In addition, the size of the territory was another factor. A top-down reform in China, a country approximately 25 times larger than Japan, was more complicated and may need better preparation and longer time to complete. See Yen-p'ing Hao and Erh-Min Wang, "Chapter 3 Changing Chinese Views of Western Relations, 1840–95", in John Fairbank and Kwang-Ching Liu (eds), *The Cambridge History of China: Volume 11* (Cambridge University Press, 1980), pp. 142–201, at pp. 167–171; Hong-Ming Liang, "China", in Guntram Herb and David Kaplan (eds), *Nations and Nationalism: A Global Historical Overview, Volume 2, 1880–1945* (ABC-CLIO Inc., 2008), pp. 787–795, at p. 790; Ting-Yee Kuo, "Chapter 10 Self-strengthening: the Pursuit of Western Technology", in John Fairbank (ed), *The Cambridge History of China: Volume 10* (Cambridge University Press, 1978), pp. 491–542; John Schrecker, "The Reform Movement, Nationalism and China's

1.2.1 *Sun Yat-sen and the Nationalism of the Nationalist Party*

(1) The Republican Era

The 1911 Revolution overthrew the last imperial dynasty and established the Republic of China (ROC). The inefficient feudal system was completely destroyed in the revolution. Chinese society, however, was not ready for modern constitutionalism, which required further preparation for necessary institutions and popular consciousness of political participation. The spread of Western technology and ideology, beginning in the 1840s, had never genuinely influenced the majority of the population—the peasantry. Despite the fact that the political unity of China had collapsed and the powers were fragmentally concentrated at the hands of regional warlords shortly after the Revolution, the new national government, the Beiyang government, was generally recognised as the legitimate government of China from 1912 to 1928.

Under this background, with disappointment to the failure of the Revolution that had little popular support or Western support, Sun Yat-sen[32] and the Nationalist Party (KMT/GMD) initiated another round of revolutionary movements to rival the Beiyang government. The fragmented and chaotic situation of the warlord China left the newly founded KMT with opportunities to expand its influence in eastern cities.

During this period, Sun systematically modified and elaborated the Three Principles of the People and the Fundamentals of National Reconstruction. The Three Principles of the People were referred to as nationalism, democracy and people's livelihood. The principle of nationalism was the doctrine of the state, which defined the Chinese nation through common blood, livelihood, language, religion and customs, and habits.[33] The principle of democracy

---

Foreign Policy", 29 *The Journal of Asian Studies* (1969), pp. 48–50; Chuzo Ichiko, "Chapter 7 Political and Institutional Reform 1901–11", in John Fairbank and Kwang-Ching Liu (eds), ibid, pp. 375–415 at pp. 388–401; June Dreyer, *China's Political System: Modernisation and Tradition* (Paragon House, 1993), p. 58; Hugh Seton-Watson, supra note 3, pp. 287–290; John Breuilly, supra note 3, pp. 250–251.

32 Sun Yat-sen (also known as Sun Zhongshan), the son of a farmer, was born in Guangdong (Canton). He received traditional Confucian education in his early life, Western education in Hawaii, and medical training in Hong Kong at the College of Medicine for Chinese. He also spent time living in Japan, Britain and the US for political reasons. The experience of living abroad gave him access to Western political and ideological thoughts and values. Sun's political thoughts synthesised ideas from both Chinese and Western values. See also Audrey Wells, *The Political Thought of Sun Yat-sen: Development and Impact* (Palgrave, 2001), p. 47.

33 In Lecture One of the Principle of Nationalism, Sun divided mankind into five main races—white, black, red, yellow and brown. He further stated that, if divided further, there were many sub-races, such as the Asiatic races which included Mongolian, Malay, Japanese, Manchurian and Chinese. He argued that the forces that developed these races

concerned the power of government and linked sovereignty with the people. The ultimate goal of both principles was to give full happiness to the people (rather than the freedom to pursue it): the livelihood, which, according to his observation, was unlikely to be achieved by Western states.[34]

It was difficult to assess the achievements of the nationalist regime since they successfully seized the power and nominally unified China in 1928. Admittedly, the KMT reversed the trend of territorial disintegration, preserved the nation's borders, and expanded effective control of the government.[35] They also, to some extent, though temporarily, improved regional economy. However, the emphasis on territorial expansion and the consolidation of political power made the KMT ignore social reform. The Party leaders, which represented the interests of the upper class and the military leadership of the government, failed "to identify with the people, but rather stood above them".[36] The nationalists were not concerned with the livelihood of the people. Externally, the KMT adopted a peaceful approach towards imperialism, preferring negotiations in foreign relations. The military nature, the indifference of the livelihood and little progress in democratic training of the people suggested that the KMT had departed from Sun's Three Principles of the People after his death in 1925. Put differently, the nationalists failed to establish a truly or ideologically nationalist government.[37]

---

were, in general, natural forces. According to Sun, "the greatest force is common blood—Chinese belong to the yellow race because they come from the blood stock of the yellow race and the blood of ancestors is transmitted by heredity down through the race, making blood kinship a powerful force". The second great force is livelihood and the third great force in forming races is language. The fourth force is religion and the fifth force is customs and habits. Sun Yat-sen, *The Three Principles of the People: San Min Chu I* (China Publishing Co.), pp. 3–4.

34 This is the revised version of the Three Principles of the People. Sun first stated his governmental theories in 1906. At the time, he believed that the Principle of Nationalism equated to the government of the great Han people and the political revolution was unavoidable in order to realise freedom and equality. And the Principle of Livelihood involved a peaceful social revolution. Sun Yat-sen, ibid; Audrey Wells, supra note 32, at pp. 34–36, 61–101.

35 Lloyd Eastman, "Chapter 3 Nationalist China during the Nanking Decade 1927–1937", in John Fairbank and Albert Feuerwerker (eds), *The Cambridge History of China: Volume 13* (Cambridge University Press, 1986), pp. 116–167 at p. 148; William Kirby, "The Internationalisation of China: Foreign Relations at Home and Abroad in the Republican Era", 150 *The China Quarterly* (1997), pp. 437–439, 441.

36 Lloyd Eastman, ibid, at p. 165.

37 Lucien Bianco, translated by Muriel Bell, *Origins of the Chinese Revolution 1915–1949* (Stanford University Press, 1971), p. 138.

(2) The Nationalist Definition of the Chinese Nation

In the process of establishing a modern Chinese state, another essential question in relation to nation-building was: if there existed a Chinese nation, how to accommodate the traditional minority "nations" within it? The term "nation" was first introduced into China in 1903[38] and was translated into two characters "*min zu*" in Chinese. In regard to ethnicity, *min* literally meant "people" and *zu* equated to lineage/clan. As early as the Zhou dynasty (ca. 1046 BC—256 BC), these two terms were used interchangeably, as both defined a group of people living in certain localities who shared common features—blood, history, way of living, customs, and so forth. This was reflected in the words "Miao *min*" and the phrase "feiwo *zu*lei, qixin biyi" (if he is not of our lineage, he is sure to have a different heart).[39] But it was rare to put *min zu* together to refer to ethnicities in classic literature. After the introduction of the nation concept, people began to name those traditional groups as the Han *minzu*/*zu* or Tibetan *minzu*/*zu*, alongside the "new" Chinese nation (*zhonghua minzu*).[40] The use of the terminology in this sense was very confusing, as it represented the Chinese nation on the one hand and referred to its constituent parts on the other. What differentiated minority ethnic groups (*minzu*) from the Chinese *minzu* (nation)? Was *zu* an abbreviation of *minzu*?

The last decades of the Qing Empire were regarded as the beginning of "the century of national humiliation". The inability of the Manchu court to defend the country from foreign threats and scrambles of concessions aroused a number of uprisings, which blamed the Manchu rule for the defeats and decline. Sun once held a similar opinion. The purposes of his Chinese Revolutionary Alliance were "to expel the *Tatar barbarians*, to revive *Zhonghua*, to establish

38 Frank Dikotter, supra note 26, pp. 97, 107–109; He Shutao, "Dui ershi shiji zai zhongguo zuiyou yingxing de sanda minzu dingyi de jianyao fenxi [An Analysis of Three Influential Definitions of Nation in the 20th century China]", 04 *Heilongjiang Minzu Congkan* [*Heilongjiang National Series*] (2009), p. 15.

39 Liu E, "Chapter 1 Minzu yici de hanyi jiqi fazhan guilv [The Definition of Minzu and Its Development]", in Huang Guangxue and Shi Lianzhu (eds), *Zhongguo de minzu shibie* [*The Ethnic Identification in China*] (Minzu chubanshe, 2005), pp. 1–25 at pp. 1–2; Li Min and Wang Jian, *Shangshu yizhu* [*Commentaries to the Book of Documents*] (Shanghai guji chubanshe, 2004), pp. 399–400. On the other hand, Yang Bojun interpreted *zu* as race. *Chunqiu zuozhuan zhu* [*Commentaries to Spring and Autumn (annals) and Zuo' Tradition*] *Volume II* (Zhonghua shuju, 1995), p. 818.

40 The term "Chinese nation (*zhonghua minzu*)" first appeared in the late Qing period. See Wang Zhonghan (ed), *Zhongguo minzu shi* [*The National History of China*] (Zhongguo shehui kexue chubanshe, 1994), p. 22.

Republic and to distribute the land equitably".[41] In his 1906 speech,[42] Sun interpreted the principle of nationalism into a single Han nation: "the Han people should have their own government".[43] He explained that they had no intention to take revenge or kill the Manchus, but "to recover their own government (of the Han)".[44] The initial concept of the Chinese nation, according to Sun, equated to a mono-ethnic Han state, as he considered the Manchus as "inferior nomadic barbarians".[45]

As the revolutionary situation developed, the establishment of a single Han state would inevitably lead to a situation that a vast territory, largely inhabited by the minorities, would be excluded from the Chinese state. This precisely fitted the foreign ambition of dismembering China. Hence, when the Manchu rule was overturned, the imminent concern of the revolutionaries was to build a new state, which would inherit the whole feudal territory.

After the 1911 Revolution, the republicans invented a concept of the "five-nations" republic (*wuzu gonghe*). It was difficult to evaluate to what extent Sun concurred with this concept, considering the repeated criticism in his later works.[46] In the Declaration of Provisional President, Sun stated that:

> [trans. L. W.] "[t]he state roots in the people. The uniting of the Han, Manchu, Mongolian, Moslem and Tibetan lands as one state, to wit, the

41 Zhongguo Tongmenghui Zongzhang [The Charter of the Chinese Revolutionary Alliance] (20/08/1905), Article 2, in Sun Yat-sen, *Sun Zhongshan quanji* [*Collected Works of Sun Yat-sen*] *Volume 1* (Zhonghua shuju, 1981), p. 284.

42 The Speech on the First Anniversary of Min Bao, the official newspaper of the Chinese Revolutionary Alliance.

43 Audrey Wells, supra note 32, at p. 35.

44 Ibid.

45 Jinggao tongxiang shu [A Communication to the Follow Men] (12/1903), in Sun Yat-sen, supra note 41, at p. 232.

46 Dru Gladney argued that Sun advocated this concept and the "five nations" republic theory served as the main platform for his nationalist revolutions. Dru Gladney, supra note 21, p. 83; *Dislocating China: Reflections on Muslims, Minorities, and Other Subaltern Subjects* (Hurst and Company, 2004), p. 15. However, apart from repeated criticism of the "five nations" republic theory in his later writings, Sun disagreed with the proposal of adopting the five-colour flag as the national flag from the very beginning. He believed that the "Blue Sky, White Sun, and a Wholly Red Earth" flag, which was made the official flag of the ROC in 1928, would better reflect the political ideal of the revolutionists and the party-state concept. See Li Xuezhi, "Minyuan guoqi zhizheng [The Debate Over the National Flag of the Republic of China in 1912]", 01 *Shixue Yuekan* [*Journal of Historical Science*] (1998), pp. 46–50; Yu Lingyun, "Guoqi de xianfa yiyi [The Constitutional Significance of the National Flag]", 03 *Faxue Pinglun* [*Law Review*] (2015), pp. 21–22.

FIGURE 1 Red stands for the Han, yellow for the Manchu, blue for the Mongol, white for the Hui (Muslim) and black for the Tibetan.[a]
[a] Murata Yujiro, "Sun Zhongshan yu xinhai geming shiqi de 'wuzu gonghe' lun [Sun Yat-sen and the Theory of 'Five Nations' Republic During the Period of the 1911 Revolution]", 05 *Guangdong Shehui Kexue* [*Social Sciences in Guangdong*] (2004), p. 123; Zhang Yong, "Cong 'shiba xingqi' dao 'wuse qi' [From the Eighteen–star Flag to Five-colour Flag]", 39:02 *Beijing Daxue Xuebao* [*Journal of Peking University (Humanities and Social Sciences)*] (2002), p. 110. Another interpretation of the meaning of five colours argues that "the colours refer to areas: red stands for China, yellow for Manchuria, blue for Mongolia, white for the north-west and back for Siberia". See Henrietta Harrison, supra note 29, at p. 171.

> unification of the Han, Manchu, Mongol, Moslem and Tibetan ethnicities as one nation, is [our] national unification".[47]

The Provisional Constitution defined China as the state of the Chinese people, consisting of 22 provinces, Inner and Outer Mongolia, Tibet and Qinghai.[48] It further recognised the equality of Chinese citizens "without racial, class or religious distinction".[49] Accordingly, the five-colour flag became the national flag, representing the unification of five nations (*zu*). (Figure 1.)

Nevertheless, the party platform of the KMT incorporated a "racial assimilation" provision.[50] When interpreting the principle of nationalism in 1917, Sun

47 "Linshi Dazongtong Xuanyanshu [Declaration of Provisional President] (01/01/1912)", in Sun Yat-sen, *Sun Zhongshan quanji* [*Collected Works of Sun Yat-sen*] *Volume* 2, (Zhonghua shuju, 1982), p. 2.

48 The Provisional Constitution of the Republic of China, Articles 1, 3. See Zhang Jinfan, *Zhongguo xianfa shi* [*Chinese Constitution History*] (Jilin Renmin Chubanshe, 2004), Appendix Two, p. 404; Supplement: Official Documents (07/1912), 06:03 *American Journal of International Law*, pp. 149–154 at p. 149.

49 The Provisional Constitution of the Republic of China, Article 5.

50 "Assimilation" is used in this book to translate the Chinese term "*tonghua*" and "integration" to refer to the Chinese term "*ronghe*". See "Zhi tongmenghui ge zhibu dian [The

criticised the notion of the "five-nations (*zu*)" republic and the adoption of the five-colour flag.[51] He argued that the overthrow of the Manchu Empire was merely the realisation of the negative nationalism.[52] The positive nationalism would only be achieved when:

> [trans. L. W.] "the Han, sacrificing their bloodline, history and identity that they have been proud of, sincerely treat the Manchu, Mongol, Moslem and Tibetan, and integrate all the ethnicities into one melting pot to create a new Chinese nationalism".[53]

He referred to the United States and Switzerland as illustrations of successful national integration.[54] In his speech at the 1920 Headquarters' Meeting of the KMT, Sun reiterated his opinion on the issue.[55] Again, he stressed that the KMT should endeavour to assimilate the Manchu, Mongol, Moslem and Tibetan into the Han nation, and then transform the Han into the Chinese nation, modelling after the pattern of the American nation.[56]

After the Soviet-KMT collaboration, Sun revised and reiterated the principle of nationalism into *guozu* (literally meant "state nation" in Chinese) in 1924 so as to avoid unnecessary confusion and political implication stemming from the use of "*minzu*" for national minorities.[57] In the post-Sun era, Jiang Jieshi (also known as Chiang Kai-shek) claimed that "the Chinese nation was formed

---

Telegraph to the Branches of the Chinese Revolutionary Alliance and the Declaration of the KMT (13/08/1912)]", in Sun Yat-sen, supra note 47, at pp. 395, 399; Binh Phan, How Autonomous Are the National Autonomous Areas of the PRC? An Analysis of Documents and Cases, 32 *Issues and Studies* (1996), p. 86.

51 As the five-colour flag had been used as the symbol flag of the senior military attaché in the Qing court, Sun criticised such an ideology and blamed the flag for the disintegration of the ROC. "Sanmin zhuyi [The Three Principles of the People 1919]", in Sun Yat-sen, *Sun Zhongshan quanji* [*Collected Works of Sun Yat-sen*] *Volume 5* (Zhonghua shuju, 1985), p. 187.

52 Ibid.

53 Ibid.

54 Ibid; Binh Phan, supra note 50, at p. 87.

55 He again argued that the five-nations republic was inappropriate in the sense that there were more than five nations (*minzu*) in China. Sun stated that "we should mold all nations into one Chinese nation". Sun Yat-sen, supra note 51, pp. 392–394.

56 "Zai zhongguo guomindang benbu teshe zhuyue banshichu de yanshuo [The Speech at the Headquarter of the KMT upon the Establishment of the Canton Branch (06/03/1921)]", in Sun Yat-sen, ibid, pp. 473–474.

57 "Sanmin zhuyi [The Three Principles of the People 1924]", in Sun Yat-sen, *Sun Zhongshan quanji* [*Collected Works of Sun Yat-sen*] *Volume 9* (Zhonghua shuju, 1986), p. 185.

by the blending of numerous clans", such as the Han, Mongol and Manchu.[58] Hence, there were no five-nations or small nations, only different clans in China. This assertion might be Jiang's response to the foreign offers of self-determination to Chinese minorities at the time.

Without any doubts, in the nationalist postulation of the ROC, the ultimate goal of the principle of nationalism was to build a state of the Chinese nation. To accomplish this goal, Sun seemed to suggest that the Han should be the basis of the invented Chinese nation, as a nation could not exist without national ties, such as ancestry, religion, history and/or language.[59] It might be inappropriate to analogise Sun's principle of nationalism (during the period 1912–21) to the Han chauvinism. However, there was indeed a distinction between building a unified nation that integrated all ethnicities and assimilating of other nations into the Han and then transforming the Han nation into the Chinese nation.

1.2.2 *The Communist Nationalism*

(1) The Peasant Nationalism

Unlike the nationalists, the Communist Party of China focused upon social reform, with the purpose of mobilising workers and peasants. After being compelled underground by the KMT, the communists sought to control rural areas and to appeal to the peasants. In Breuilly's terms, it was about "a single, concentrated and socially homogeneous elite [to] mobilise peasant support on the basis of social reform and the provision of security against outside forces, be they nationalists, warlords or, later on, Japan".[60]

Although the communist elites attempted to utilise all possible methods to reform the political order in rural areas, they failed in most instances in the pre-war period. The reason was rooted deeply in the extraordinary continuity of the Chinese way of life, which came down undisrupted from the Neolithic times: family groups in settled villages, who lived an agricultural-led life with continuity, seemed unbreakable and they had a special concern with the maintenance of peace and order among village communities.[61] The pre-national peasants had little idea of the concept of state, as their life had not undergone fundamental changes. In this regard, imperialism or warlordism was merely

58 Chiang Kai-shek, *China's Destiny and Chinese Economic Theory* (Dennis Dobson Ltd., 1947), pp. 30–39.

59 "Sanmin zhuyi [The Three Principles of the People 1919]", in Sun Yat-sen, supra note 51, at pp. 186–187; Luo Gang, *Zhonghua minguo guofu shilu [The Factual Account of Dr. Sun Yat-sen]: Volume 5* (Zhengzhong Shuju, 1988), p. 3770.

60 John Breuilly, supra note 3, p. 235.

61 John Fairbank, "Introduction: the Old Order", in John Fairbank (ed), *The Cambridge History of China: Volume 10* (Cambridge University Press, 1978), pp. 1–34 at p. 9.

another form of the old feudal court. The sole communist policy of social reform was not so radical as to shock the peasants' individual or communal life. Furthermore, the main concern of the CPC before 1937 was to establish local bases in order to compete with the nationalists, in which nationalism played a small part.[62]

Japanese aggressions in the 1930s saw the watershed of the history.[63] Prior to this event, the spread of nationalist sentiments were mainly confined to political elites, intellectuals and students, whereas the full scale of the Japanese invasion in 1937 was the force for the peasants to join the national resistance against the Japanese invaders as it genuinely threatened the basic survival of village communities. Under the slogan of "Defend the Motherland", communal resistance forces emerged. Compared with the passive attitude of the KMT to resist the Japanese, the communists' assertion of establishing the united front and national resistance fulfilled the need of the illiterate masses for military and political leadership.[64] With patriotic propaganda and educational efforts from the CPC,[65] the peasants, for the first time, actively participated in the local *ad hoc* governments and experienced political life therein. This formed the very basis for the invention of the Chinese nation in future, as nation-ness was "virtually inseparable from political consciousness".[66]

The communists, utilising guerrilla bases and the mobilised peasants, led an efficient military resistance against Japan. This efficient resistance strengthened the faith of the peasants in the CPC and attracted support from intellectuals, including some nationalists. The war destroyed traditional social order in rural areas, and gave the communists a golden opportunity to mobilise the masses with a new national identity and patriotism.[67] This new Chinese nationalism, with obvious communist marks, was created as the political consciousness of the masses gradually awoke. In this process, communism and nationalism were fused.[68] Japan, in a way, "assisted" the CPC in accomplishing its final goal. The CPC won the popular support after successfully defeated the Japanese, whereas the KMT still held to its elitist ideology and continued

62 John Breuilly, supra note 3, p. 235.

63 Robert Weatherley, *Making China Strong: the Role of Nationalism in Chinese Thinking on Democracy and Human Rights* (Palgrave Macmillan, 2014), p. 23.

64 Chalmers Johnson, *Peasant Nationalism and Communist Power* (Stanford University Press, 1963), p. 3.

65 Ibid, p. 4.

66 Benedict Anderson, supra note 3, p. 135.

67 Chalmers Johnson, supra note 64, at p. 5.

68 Ibid, p. 8.

to ignore the people.[69] Seen from this perspective, the Chinese communists could consider themselves to be more nationalist than the KMT who kept close ties with the Western powers during and after the war.[70]

The CPC persisted in the mass movements, a strategy that they had been carried out since the 1920s, and continued to advocate land reform in base areas. The communist land policy particularly appealed to the masses, as it tackled the long-time contradiction between the landlord stratum and the peasants—"the corrupt and arbitrary use of political power and social position in the village community".[71] In doing so, the CPC successfully transformed the military-political movement, which they had used to mobilise the masses in resisting the Japanese, into the one that could build a new indigenous political structure with popular participation.[72] The equal distribution of the land taken from landlords and productive resources among the peasants facilitated their following call for military recruitment, a crucial factor in defeating the KMT during the Civil War. It also assisted to spread the idea of "class struggle", which later became the instrument of state-building after 1949.

(2) The Communist Nation Building: 1949–1978

After the establishment of the PRC, the Soviet ideology was adopted by the CPC to build the "new"state. Nonetheless, the Chinese road of socialism was not a rigid copy of the Soviet model. On the contrary, it associated with Chinese history and culture and thus headed in a different direction from the Soviet style of socialism. As early as 1936, Mao Zedong (also known as Mao Tse-tung) proposed the idea of establishing a unique and independent socialist China. In his answer to Edgar Snow's question as to whether, in event of a Communist victory, there would be "some kind of actual merger of governments" between China and the Soviet Russia, he said:

> the Chinese Communist Party is only one party in China, and in its victory it will have to speak for the whole nation. It cannot speak for the Russian people, or rule for the Third International, but only in the interests of the Chinese masses.[73]

---

69 In his speech to the National Assembly in 1946, Jiang expressed the adherence to the elitist politics. See Audrey Wells, supra note 32, p. 129.

70 Lucien Bianco, supra note 37, at p. 165.

71 Suzanne Pepper, "Chapter 13 The KMD-CPC Conflict 1945–1949", in John Fairbank and Albert Feuerwerker (eds), supra note 35, pp. 723–788, at p. 753.

72 Ibid.

73 Stuart Schram, "Chapter 14 Mao Tse-tung's Thought to 1949", in John Fairbank and Albert Feuerwerker (eds), ibid, pp. 789–870, at p. 844.

Mao's personal desire for political power, as well as the feeling of national dignity, might be the possible reasons for such a statement. However, it also suggested that a nationalist nature was concealed in the communist ideological foundation of the state from the very beginning.

Although Mao considered China as a different nation from all other communist nations, he relied on the Soviet ideology to build the nation. Nationality was mentioned in nation-building. The emphasis was laid from the Marx-Leninist perspective: the national identity was depicted as a false consciousness, which in essence was the reflection of economic classification.[74] Mao wrote that "in a struggle that is national in character, the class struggle takes the form of national struggle, which demonstrates the identity between the two".[75] Hence, the CPC, to a certain extent, avoided the problem of defining the relationship between the Chinese nation (*zhonghua minzu*) and its component ethnic groups (e.g. the Tibetan *minzu*). Apart from the Han, all other ethnic groups were generally referred to as minority nationalities (*shaoshu minzu*), without clarifying its substance as a nation, nationality or ethnicity.[76] From 1949 to 1978, the Mao-led CPC experimented with various forms of "class struggle" in the Chinese territory, which reached its climax in the Cultural Revolution. The Soviet ideology operated effectively as the basis for the legitimacy of the CPC, even though the collective farming policy, the Great Leap Forward, and the Cultural Revolution severely impeded the development of the newly formed state. Such an ideology

74 The classical Marxism believes that: (1) the most fundamental human divisions are horizontal class distinctions which cut across national grouping; (2) national differences between the peoples are vanishing; and (3) the supremacy of the proletariat will cause them to vanish faster. The strategic Marxism revolves about formal support for the right to national self-determination in the abstract, coupling with very selective support for national movement in practice, whereas the national Marxism involves the reference to national characteristics that transcend epochs and the role of nations as the principal instrumentality of historical forces. Walker Connor, *The National Question in Marxist-Leninist Theory and Strategy* (Princeton University Press, 1984), pp. 5–20.

75 "Tongyi zhanxian zhong de duli zizhu wenti [the Question of Independence and Initiative within the United Front (05/11/1938)]", in Mao Zedong, *Mao Zedong xuanji* [*the Selected Works of Mao Zedong*] *Volume* 2, http://cpc.people.com.cn/GB/64184/64185/66616/4488931.html; English translation is available at: http://www.marxists.org/reference/archive/mao/selected-works/volume-2/mswv2_11.htm, last accessed on 05/01/2017.

76 Mao argued that "we must unite with all various nationalities, no matter whether it is a large or small nationality... As long as they are Chinese people, regardless of national distinction, we must be united with all those who are opposed to imperialism and who stand for patriotism and advocate unity". Mao Zedong, "Jiejian Xizang guoqing guanlituan, canguantuan daibiao de jianghua [Speech at Reception for Tibetan Delegation (18/10/1953)]", in Michael Y. M. Kau and John K. Leung (eds), *The Writing of Mao Zedong 1949–1976, Volume 1* (M.E. Sharpe Inc, 1986), p. 420.

also prevented regional separatism of ethnic groups, since the class orientation was the barrier that differentiated the people, rather than the nationality. In other words, the CPC first defined China as an independent nation-state that was not subordinate to any other countries, and then divided the Chinese people into different classes from the inside. The five stars on the national flag of the PRC corresponded with such classifications.[77]

Legally, the Common Program of the Chinese People's Political Consultative Conference 1949 (the Common Program), the first constitutional document of the PRC, was deeply influenced by Lenin's theory of democratic centralism. It defined China as:

> [trans. L. W.] "a New Democratic or a People's Democratic state under the people's democratic dictatorship which is led by the proletariat, based on the alliance of workers and peasants, and unites all democratic classes and all nationalities".[78]

"All democratic classes" embraced the proletariat, the peasantry, the urban petit bourgeoisie, national bourgeoisie and other patriotic democratic elements.[79] Nonetheless, "the people" and "the nationals" were distinguished under the Common Program. "The people" were the holders of the state power who came from the "democratic classes", whilst the latter referred to those who pursued counter-revolutionary activities. "The nationals" were the targets of the "dictatorship", until they reformed themselves through labour and became "new men".[80] Article 50 addressed the unity of all nationalities in "one big family" of China and called on all nationalities to oppose imperialism and their own public enemies.[81] The Common Program further provided that all nationalities were equal and were entitled to regional ethnic autonomy.[82] The cultural rights of all nationalities were also constitutionally recognised.[83]

---

77 The large star represents the CPC and four small stars that orbit the greater star symbolise four revolutionary social classes—the proletariat, the peasantry, the urban petit bourgeoisie, and national bourgeoisie. See also John Fitzgerald, "The Nationless State: the Search for a Nation in Modern Chinese Nationalism", 33 *Australian Journal of Chinese Affairs* (1995), p. 103.

78 The Common Program, Article 1.

79 The Common Program, the Preamble.

80 Xu Chongde, *Zhonghua renmin gongheguo xianfa shi* [*The Constitutional History of the People's Republic of China*] (Fujian Renmin Chubanshe, 2003), p. 90; the Common Program, Article 7.

81 The Common Program, Article 50.

82 The Common Program, Articles 9, 51.

83 The Common Program, Article 53.

(3) The Communist Nation Building: 1978 Onwards

The change came along with the Economic Reform in 1978. The Reform intended to establish a free-market economic mechanism in the socialist China. Despite the fact that many reform measures are of a non-communist nature, the official propaganda insists that "China is a communist state" and that "only socialism could save and develop China". The Reform, however, provokes both ideological and political crisis. Conflicts arise as the reform proceeds.

Firstly, the contrast between the public pursuit of wealth and the official gloss of portraying "a united people striving together for China's modernisation" undermines the socialist ideological foundation.[84] In particular, during the first stage of the reform, a large sum of foreign investment met the planned economy, which was controlled by the only party of the state. The inability of the people to supervise and to prevent corruption, combined with improper acts of certain party officials, triggered massive student protest movements in 1989. After seeing the strength of the masses displayed in the June 4th Incident, the CPC has attempted to limit political involvement of the populace in terms of state affairs. With controversy, local democracy at grassroots level was legally formalised in the 1980s.[85] Some commentators argue that this village election as the local self-government system has an empowering effect[86] and contributes to the rise of political citizenship in rural China.[87] Nonetheless, village election does not amount to real village democracy.[88] According to the Organic Law of the Villagers Committees, local party branches remain the "leading nucleus" (*lingdao hexin*) in the villages[89] and the party cadres in many cases hold more than half chairs in the villagers committees.[90] Moreover, since the villagers committee is

84 James Townsend, Chinese Nationalism, 27 *Australian Journal of Chinese Affairs* (1992), pp. 121–122.

85 The Election Law of the People's Republic of China for the National People's Congress and Local People's Congresses at All Levels (adopted in 1979 and recently amended in 2015), Article 2; the Organic Law of the Villagers Committees of the People's Republic of China (adopted in 1998 and recently amended in 2010), Articles 1, 2, 3, 11. Kevin J. O'Brien and Lianjiang Li, Accommodating "Democracy" in a One-Party State: Introducing Village Elections in China, 162 *The China Quarterly* (2000), pp. 465–489; Audrey Wells, supra note 32, at p. 151.

86 Lianjiang Li, The Empowering Effect of Village Elections in China, 43 *Asian Survey* (2003), pp. 649–651; Phil C.W. Chan, supra note 9, pp. 683–684.

87 Kevin J. O'Brien, Villagers, Elections, and Citizenship in Contemporary China, 27 *Modern China* (2001), pp. 423–426.

88 Kevin J. O'Brien and Lianjiang Li, supra note 85, p. 488.

89 The Organic Law of the Villagers Committees, Article 4. See also Kevin J. O'Brien and Lianjiang Li, ibid; Phil C.W. Chan, supra note 9, p. 687.

90 Robert A. Pastor and Qingshan Tan, The Meaning of China's Village Elections, 162 *The China Quarterly* (2000), p. 491.

not a national administrative division, its responsibilities are confined to neighbourhood affairs.[91] Direct election of deputies to the people's congresses at county and township levels as provided by the Constitution, however, has not been properly implemented.[92] Despite Deng's argument that "the success of all reforms depends on the reform of the political system",[93] the political institutional reform seems not to be on the agenda of the CPC in the near future.

The dramatic contrast between the ideology and social reality also forces the Party and the people to rethink the ideological foundation of the state. The class struggle theory clearly no longer fits into the new situation, as "the exploiting classes as such have been eliminated" in the country.[94] On the premise that the PRC adheres to socialism, Deng Xiaoping developed a theory of "socialism with Chinese characteristics".[95] He encouraged a greater openness to the outside and reduced socialism to the liberation of productive forces.[96] Such a decision was made on the basis that the CPC would not have survived 1989, "if the population had not experienced a rising standard of living throughout the 1980s".[97] Economic development became the top priority in communist nation-building thereafter. The Deng-centred CPC also adopted patriotism as the ideological orthodoxy. Deng stated that "we deem it the highest honour to love our socialist motherland and contribute our all to her socialist construction. We deem it the deepest disgrace to impair her interests, dignity or honour".[98] National rejuvenation, together with socialism, became the goals of

91 Kevin J. O'Brien and Lianjiang Li, supra note 85, p. 487.

92 The 1982 Constitution (recently amended in 2018), Article 97.

93 Deng Xiaoping stated that "the reform of the political system and the reform of the economic system should depend on and complement each other? In the final analysis, the success of all reforms depends on the reform of the political system" and that "without political institutional reform, the achievements of economic institutional reform cannot be secured. Also, economic reform will not be able to continue further". Deng Xiaoping, as cited in Robert A. Pastor and Qingshan Tan, supra note 90, p. 490; Phil C.W. Chan, supra note 9, p. 646.

94 The 1982 Constitution, the Preamble.

95 Christopher Hughes, *Chinese Nationalism in the Global Era* (Routledge, 2006), pp. 68–69.

96 Ibid, p. 64.

97 Ibid. Deng stated that "why do people support us? Because over the last ten years our economy has been developing… If the economy stagnated for five years or developed at only a slow rate…what effects would be produced? This would be not only an economic problem but also a political one". Deng Xiaoping, as cited in Yonghong Yang, *Sovereignty in China's Perspective* (Peter Lang Academic Research, 2017), p. 199.

98 Opening Speech at the 12th National Congress of the Communist Party of China, in Deng Xiaoping, *Selected Works Volume 3*, http://english.peopledaily.com.cn/dengxp/vol3/text/c1010.html, last accessed on 05/01/2017.

the state by the 1990s. On the other hand, it has been suggested that the CPC also consciously use nationalism to maintain political stability and to unify the nation, alongside the socialist ideology.[99]

The repudiation of the class struggle theory may again raise the problem of defining one unified Chinese nation that embraces all minorities with diverse ethnic and cultural characteristics. Based on cultural pluralism of Chinese civilisation, the communists advocate "the pluralistic unity of the Chinese nation". The Chinese nation has been invented on the basis of imperial history and territory. For example, Xi Jinping's approach to the Chinese nation is reflected in his initiative of the China dream, which refers to national prosperity and glory, socialism, happiness of the people and collective effort.[100] Xi declares:

> [trans. L. W.] "the Chinese nation has a long history of more than five thousand years and has created the glorious Chinese civilisation ... 56 ethnic groups and 1.3 billion people are unified by the collective effort we have made, the beautiful homeland we have created, and the national spirit we have cultivated ... Now it is our obligation to make continued efforts to achieve the great revival of the Chinese nation".[101]

He traces the Chinese nation back to the glorious civilisation of the Chinese empires. Nonetheless, Chinese civilisation with past glories may have different meanings to minority groups, as some groups are not considered themselves as a part of that glory. The official propaganda of the multi-ethnic China has been challenged by outbursts of regional ethnic unrest.[102] The communists' solution to the problem is straightforward: economic development and improved

---

99 Leong Liew and Doug Smith, "Chapter 1 The Nexus between Nationalism, Democracy and National Integration", in Leong H. Liew and Shaoguang Wang (eds), *Nationalism, Democracy and National Integration in China* (Routledge Curzon, 2004), pp. 3–20 at pp. 5–6, 13; Joseph Cheng and Kinglun Ngok, "Chapter 5 Chinese Nationalism and Sino-US Relations: the NATO Bombing of the Chinese Embassy in Belgrade", in Liew and Shaoguang Wang (eds), ibid, pp. 85–104 at p. 101.

100 "Zai dishier jie quanguo renmin daibiao dahui diyici huiyi shang de jianghua [Speech at the First Session of the 12th National People's Congress (17/03/2013)]", in Xi Jinping, *Xi Jinping tan zhiguo lizheng* [*The Governance of China*], (Foreign Languages Press, 2014), pp. 38–43.

101 Ibid; Xi Jinping, "Zai xinren zhengzhiju changwei yu jizhe jianmianhui shang de jianghua [Speech at the Politburo Standing Committee Members' Meeting with the Press]", in Xi Jinping, ibid, pp. 3–4.

102 For example, the Tibetans, the Uyghurs, and the Mongolians have sought to secede from China.

livelihood. For instance, the Party Committee and the People's Government of Tibet Autonomous Region have declared that development as the unyielding principle is the key to solve all problems in Tibet.[103] New economic development programs associated with the Western Development Strategy have also been launched in Xinjiang.[104] The CPC is of the opinion that economic development and modernisation are crucial in solving ethnic unrest. The question is, however, whether improved livelihood would be sufficient in integrating ethnic minorities as it did in mobilising and appealing to the peasants in rural China.

1.2.3 *The Nation of China*

After approximately one hundred years of experiments, one of the key issues of the Chinese revolution centred on the invention of the Chinese nation. Various theories have been employed and developed.

Both the KMT and the CPC attempted to build a Chinese nation that could embrace all ethnicities residing the territory, regardless of their different ethnic features. Sun and the KMT sought to link the Chinese nation with its past. The interpretations of the Chinese nation varied in the nationalist propositions. Sun's nationalism placed its emphasis upon the cultural and national unity.[105] In order to secure the territory of the Qing Empire, Sun finalised his definition of the Chinese nation as "*zhonghua minzu*" that comprised various ethnic groups with common blood and ancestry.[106] He argued:

> the greatest force is common blood. Chinese belong to the yellow race because they come from the blood stock of the yellow race. The blood of ancestors is transmitted by heredity down through the race, making blood kinship a powerful force.[107]

Dikotter has noted that a racial element was also concealed in Mao's sense of nationalism.[108] History is another essential part in the communist definition of the Chinese nation. Mao once stated:

---

103 The Party Committee and the People's Government of TAR, "Puxie hao zhonghua minzu weida fuxing zhongguomeng de Xizang pianzhang [the Tibetan Chapter of the China Dream to the Great Revival of the Chinese Nation: the 50th anniversary of Tibet Autonomous Region]", 17 *Qiushi* (2015), p. 22.

104 The Information Office of the State Council, the White Paper on History and Development of Xinjiang (2004), Section X.

105 Dru Gladney, supra note 21, at p. 84.

106 Audrey Wells, supra note 32, at p. 71.

107 Sun Yat-sen, supra note 33, at p. 3.

108 Frank Dikotter, supra note 26, at p. 192.

> [f]rom ancient times our forefathers have laboured, lived and multiplied on this vast territory ... All the nationalities of China have resisted foreign oppression and have invariably resorted to rebellion to shake it off. They favour a union on the basis of equality but are against the oppression of one nationality by another. During the thousands of years of recorded history, the Chinese nation has given birth to many national heroes and revolutionary leaders. Thus the Chinese nation has a glorious revolutionary tradition and a splendid historical heritage.[109]

A similar message was delivered in the Preamble of the 1982 Constitution.[110] From this aspect, both the nationalists and communists defined the Chinese nation as a historically legitimate territory together with the whole population living in it, differing from the European concept of nation which was defined as "the sum of the government plus its people".[111]

Another feature of Chinese nationalism is its correlation with international threats. Chinese nationalism was born to strive against imperialism, and it succeeded in sweeping the Western powers away. International incidents continued to stimulate nationalist movements and sentiments after 1949.[112] The Korean War in the 1950s was one example. It unified the nation to resist another round of "imperialist attacks" of the US and mobilised the masses to support the war. Thousands of volunteers joined or were involved in the war against the "aggressors". Soviet threats after the Sino-Soviet split and a series of border conflicts between China and the neighbours constantly aroused popular sentiments of defending the Chinese nation. In the post-Mao era, with the decline of the faith in Marxism, the attacks from the West again are emphasised so as to sharpen the boundaries between "us" and "them". The NATO bombing of the Chinese Embassy in Belgrade was perceived as another grievance of the nation and provoked a large scale protests in China. The frequent occurrence of anti-Japan campaigns also illustrated the unity of the Chinese nation in confronting external "enemies".

The nationalists' efforts of nation-building, did not achieve, and indeed, might not be able to achieve, expected outcomes. Two reasons may have attributed to it. First, after Sun's death, the KMT had little genuine nationalist enthusiasm. More importantly, the nationalists never exercised effective

109 Mao Zedong, "The Chinese Revolution and the Chinese Communist Party (12/1939)", *Selected Works of Mao Zedong Volume II* (Foreign Language Press, 1965), pp. 305, 307.

110 The 1982 Constitution, the Preamble.

111 Thomas Heberer, supra note 14.

112 James Townsend, supra note 84, at p. 119.

control of the whole territory as they claimed. Thus, it was difficult for them to systematically inculcate nationalist ideology nationwide "through the mass media, the educational system, administrative regulations, and so forth".[113] On the contrary, the Mao-centred CPC, using national terms in the beginning, successfully mobilised the peasantry, defeated Japan and won the Civil War. This provided the communists with every condition or privilege to build a new nation. State controlled media and mass education enabled the CPC to redefine the nation according to its own ideology. The socialist theory of class struggle dominated the nation-building during the period 1949–1978, upon which the Party was able to unite the majority of the people, since class enemies only accounted for a small portion. After 1978, the theory of class struggle has been replaced by the construction of socialist spiritual civilisation and patriotism.[114] The new ideology is said to evolve from Marxism-Leninism and Mao Zedong's thoughts, but also absorb the essence of the traditional Chinese culture. Apart from the socialist ideology, critical elements for inventing the Chinese nation have already existed. The communist elites can draw on previous abundant experiences and three earlier models of nationalism.[115] Whether nationalism could serve to create a unified Chinese nationhood which comprises all ethnic groups depends upon its relationship with the communist ideology: how it could fill the ideological gap left open in the post-opening up era,[116] and how strong its rival claims would be, e.g. the Tibetan, Taiwanese, and the rising Uyghur nationalism.[117] *Minzu*, therefore, has two meanings in the Chinese context: *minzu* means "nation" as in *zhonghua*

113 Benedict Anderson, supra note 3, pp. 113–114, 163.

114 The concept was first proposed by Deng Xiaoping in 1980. The socialist spiritual civilisation programme involves two key issues: the ideological and moral construction, which advocates civic virtues of love for the motherland, for the people, for labour, for science and for socialism, and the scientific and cultural construction, which provides intellectual support for modernisation. See also the 1982 Constitution, Article 24.

115 According to Anderson, there are three models of nationalism: civil and military educational systems modelled on official nationalism; election, party organisations, and cultural celebrations modelled on the popular nationalisms of the 19th century Europe; and the citizen-republican idea brought into the world by the Americas. Benedict Anderson, supra note 3, at p. 135.

116 Zheng Yongnian argued that "the Chinese leadership certainly welcomes this resurgence of nationalism because a new ideology is necessary as faith in Marxism or Maoism declines, and nationalism, if handled properly, can justify the political legitimacy of the leadership. In other words, nationalism can become the ideological basis of a transitional regime that turns away from totalitarianism but is not yet democratised". Zheng Yongnian, *Discovering Chinese Nationalism in China: Modernisation, Identity, and International Relations* (Cambridge University Press, 1999), p. 2.

117 Dru Gladney, supra note 21, p. xiv.

minzu, or it refers to ethnic groups "forming part of one or more political nation",[118] i.e. *shaoshu minzu*. The latter may stay in harmony with the former; it, however, could also challenge the concept of the Chinese nation and transform itself into a nation. This, to a great extent, depends on how successful the CPC could integrate the ethnic groups into the unified Chinese nation as they claim.

1.3 Sovereignty: China's Perspective

In the West, the sovereignty concept has been discussed and defined by different scholars. Jean Bodin interpreted sovereignty as the absolute and perpetual power which was divine and indivisible,[119] whereas Carl Schmitt considered that the essence of sovereignty was "to decide what is an exception and to make the decisions appropriate to that exception".[120] Sovereignty, as Grotius argued, also meant a power "whose actions are not subject to the legal control of another".[121] Contemporary international law, in general, defines sovereignty as the supreme power over a defined territory.[122]

As Anghie has commented that "the structure of sovereignty, the identity of sovereignty, no less than the identity of an individual or people, is formed by its history, its origins in and engagement with colonial encounter",[123] China's perception of sovereignty is informed by its own history and western influence. The traditional Chinese concept of sovereignty was interrelated with the political principle—the Mandate of Heaven. This traditional principle gradually merged with the Western sovereignty concept in the transformation process. Affected by the arrival of foreign forces in the 1800s, the accommodation of the modern concept of sovereignty in China had its special emphasis: to free from foreign intervention and to achieve national reunification.

118 C. Mackerras, *China's Minority Cultures: Identities and Integration since 1912* (Longman, 1995,) p. 45.

119 Jean Bodin, *On Sovereignty: Four Chapters from the Six Books of the Commonwealth* (Cambridge University Press, 1992), pp. 1, 46, xiii, xxii.

120 Carl Schmitt, *Political Theology: Four Chapters on the Concept of Sovereignty* (University of Chicago Press, 2005), p. 5; and in the Forward by Tracy Strong, p. xii.

121 Quoted in Benjamin Straumann, "Early Modern Sovereignty and Its Limits", 16 *Theoretical Inquiries in Law* (2015), p. 424.

122 The Montevideo Convention on Rights and Duties of States, Article 1.

123 Antony Anghie, *Imperialism, Sovereignty and the Making of International Law* (Cambridge University Press, 2005), p. 312.

(1) The Imperial Understanding of Sovereignty

The legitimacy of imperial reign was justified by the Mandate of Heaven, one of the fundamental doctrines of the Chinese empires. According to this doctrine, the supremacy of the emperor derived from the Heaven.[124] Once a virtuous man, regardless of his ethnic origin and background, could represent and match the Heaven's Mandate, he would be vested with the power to rule the empire. As the agent of the Heaven, a virtuous emperor can make genuine decisions on state affairs.[125] In turn, he was morally obliged to rule with virtue in order to preserve the Mandate. The virtue was interpreted as the common feeling of the people, or in modern terms the "popular support".[126] This traditional view placed its emphasis upon the collective aspect of the people, the people as a whole.[127] Therefore, the primary purpose of the reign was to respect and cherish the people so as to preserve the virtue and match the Mandate, as the Heaven would repudiate its Mandate and bestow it to a man with good personal quality and achievement. Put differently, sovereignty in imperial China was theoretically conditioned on the possession of the virtue. Otherwise, in Angle's terms, the people may have the right to rebel.[128]

Nonetheless, the traditional Sino-centric worldview of Chinese civilisation has caused problems in defining sovereignty. The scope of the reign—the imperial territory—was not clearly defined. As Gladney has argued, Chinese civilisation "had less to do with territory than with civilisation and hierarchy".[129] The emperor considered himself as the ruler of "*tianxia*" (under the Heaven), with China at the centre of the civilised world.[130] This "*tianxia*",[131] the imperial territory, usually contained two layers: the heartland and the outlying areas.

124 The Heaven literally means the sky. Differing from the Western notions of "the divine right comes from God" and "the king is the agent of God in the world", the Heaven is an abstract notion, which is used to describe the invisible power that determines everything on earth.

125 Carl Schmitt, supra note 120.

126 See Taishi, Jiugao and Shaogao, in Li Min and Wang Jian (eds), supra note 39, at pp. 119, 270–274, 285–293.

127 Stephen Angle, supra note 9, p. 126.

128 Ibid, p.124.

129 Dru Gladney, supra note 21, p. 95.

130 Ibid; see also Yonghong Yang, supra note 97, pp. 35–41.

131 According to Yang, *Tianxia* had different meanings: *Tianxia* in a narrow sense was a synonym of *Zhongguo* (China), referring to the post-Qin empires directly controlled by the central dynasties; it can also be understood from a geographical and security sense which included *Zhongguo* and its peripheral areas, such as its tributary states; and the third one was the broadest sense of *Tianxia* which meant "all under heaven", including *Zhongguo*, peripheral countries, and the outside world. Yonghong Yang, ibid, p. 40.

The heartland referred to areas firmly controlled by the emperor through the centralised administrative system. It also included newly incorporated territories, which were jointly administered by local leaders and the court officials sent out by the emperor. In contrast, the outlying areas, usually through cultural influence and/or military clashes, could either be incorporated into the Chinese empire or become its tributary states. Those areas varied from time to time, as the strength and tension between the Chinese empire and its neighbours kept changing. Correspondingly, "the Chinese people" who lived under the Heaven was an ambiguous term as well.

(2) The Modern Concept of Chinese Sovereignty

The traditional notion of sovereignty was forced to update in the late 1800s, as Western civilisation gave a critical strike on the Chinese Empire. Territory, as the geographical foundation for exercising sovereignty, was first affected by the Western forces. By 1899, nearly half of the Chinese land was ceded or leased to foreign powers and became their spheres of interests. Therefore, the modernisation reform in relation to sovereignty was launched after losing control of the imperial heartland.

The Qing court relied on the Western principle of sovereignty and initiated reforms in order to preserve the reign. The Manchu court, however, had vested interests in preserving the feudal rule. The maximum preservation of such privileges outweighed other considerations. In the early stages, the reforms mainly concerned the external aspect of sovereignty—free from foreign intervention. The Qing court still intended to maintain the principle of the Mandate of Heaven to justify their reign internally. During the same period, the concept of "a defined territory" attracted the attention of the elites. It paved the way for the further claim of inheriting the territory of the Qing Empire. Furthermore, some reformers proposed to recognise the people's authority (*minquan*).[132] Instead of establishing a Western democratic model of popular sovereignty, the Chinese concept of the people's authority preferred a shared model of joint governance between the ruler and the people.[133] Nonetheless, those proposals were not adopted by the Manchu rulers. The Constitutional reforms initiated by the Manchu elites from the top-down had no genuine intent to reform the system so as to give the people the right to sovereignty.[134]

---

132 Stephen Angle, supra note 9, at pp. 128–130.

133 Ibid.

134 Under the Principles of the Constitution (1908), the Qing Emperor still held great power. The 19 Articles of the Expected Constitution divided the state power among the sovereign, the National Assembly and the Parliament. It also provided that popular elections

The 1911 Revolution overthrew the feudal system and its ideological underpinnings. The principle of the Mandate of Heaven was abandoned. After the Revolution, China slowly slipped into the warlord regime, under which the sovereignty was fragmentally controlled by regional warlords. The primary goal of Sun and the KMT, therefore, was to reunify the territory. In the blueprint depicted by the nationalists, the Chinese nation replaced the Heaven and the emperors and became the sovereign. Consequently, the old imperial territory should be the territory of the ROC. The 1912 Provisional Constitution specifically stipulated that "the territory of the Chinese Republic consists of 22 provinces, Inner and Outer Mongolia, Tibet and Qinghai".[135] The republican constitutions, for the first time, laid down the claim for a defined territory, with the purposes of guaranteeing the historical territory inherited from the old Empire, preventing separation and enhancing popular consciousness of the territorial and multinational nature of the state.[136] However, the nationalist government, as the representative of the Chinese people, was not sovereign in reality as they claimed to be. The privileges of the Western powers in coastal regions limited its "absoluteness" and supremacy. Nor did the nationalist government have effective control over the frontier areas in the western China.

National independence was achieved in the newly founded PRC. Most of the territory claimed by the ROC was "liberated" and subject to effective control of the new regime. Allegedly, the Chinese people become the master of the state, since "all power in the PRC belongs to the people".[137] In communist propaganda, it is the Chinese people who have made the historical choice. They have selected the CPC, out of all political forces, to lead the state. Except for the Communist Party, "no other political party (bourgeois or petty-bourgeois) is equal to the task of leading China's two great revolutions, the democratic and the socialist revolutions, to the complete fulfilment".[138] "Serve the People" is one of the fundamental principles of the CPC. Otherwise, the people would choose to remove them. To participate in the Party system is the easiest way for individuals to realise their ambitions in political arena. The people's interests,

---

would be promoted at national, provincial and local levels. But the sources of the representatives and the advisory nature of the institutions substantially limited the scope of the so-called "popular election". See Chuzo Ichiko, supra note 31, at pp. 397, 398–401.

135 The 1912 Provisional Constitution of the ROC, Article 3.

136 Kirby argued that the amazing fact of the Republican era was that this space was not only redefined as "Chinese" and as the sacred soil of China, but also defended diplomatically to such a degree that the borders of the PRC today were essentially those of the Qing, minus only Outer Mongolia. William Kirby, supra note 35, p. 437.

137 The 1982 Constitution, Article 2.

138 Mao Zedong, supra note 109, at p. 331.

historical choice and the uniqueness of the CPC, those terms appear to be quite similar with those used under the doctrine of the Mandate of Heaven. As Zheng Yongnian observes, the CPC is in a way presented as a modern organisational form of traditional emperors.[139]

The communist concept of sovereignty has, in part, shared similar features with the Western concepts, while retaining its focuses on national reunification and non-intervention. It is noteworthy that national independence and territorial integrity are prioritised in the CPC's understanding of sovereignty. Non-intervention (by foreign forces) and national reunification play important roles in the communist governance of China. Any form of foreign interference would be interpreted by the communists as "China is still not independent".[140] During the meeting with Margaret Thatcher, Deng clearly indicated that "on the question of sovereignty, China has no room for manoeuvre. To be frank, the question is not open to discussion".[141] On the other hand, any attempts to secede from China would also be perceived as the incompetence of the CPC to maintain the territorial integrity of the "motherland". The 1982 Constitution provides that "[T]aiwan is part of the sacred territory of the People's Republic of China. It is the inviolable duty of all Chinese people, including our compatriots in Taiwan, to accomplish the great task of reunifying the motherland".[142] Therefore, the communists' unease with self-determination, which now might challenge the statehood and lead to dismemberment, affects China's view over the relationship between self-determination and territorial integrity. China repeatedly claims that "the exercise of the right of self-determination shall not undermine the sovereignty and territorial integrity of the State concerned".[143] Mackerras has noted that the fewer the separatist threats are, the more autonomous rights of Chinese minorities would be tolerated and encouraged.[144] As will be discussed in Part II, this emphasis on territorial integrity has significant influences upon China's ethnic policy.

---

139 Zheng Yongnian, *The Chinese Communist Party as Organisational Emperor: Culture, Reproduction and Transformation* (Routledge, 2010).

140 "An Idea for the Peaceful Reunification of the Mainland and Taiwan (26/06/1983)", in Deng Xiaoping, *Selected Works Volume 3*, http://english.peopledaily.com.cn/dengxp/vol3/text/c1120.html, last accessed on 05/01/2017.

141 "Our Basic Position on the Question of Hong Kong (24/09/1982)", in Deng Xiaoping, *Selected Works Volume 3*, http://english.peopledaily.com.cn/dengxp/vol3/text/c1040.html, last accessed on 05/01/2017.

142 The 1982 Constitution, the Preamble.

143 The Written Statement of the PRC to the International Court of Justice on the Issue of Kosovo, p. 4.

144 C. Mackerras, *China's Minorities: Integration and Modernisation in the 20th Century* (Oxford University Press, 1994), pp. 164, 265.

1.4 Concluding Remarks

The significance of Chinese civilisation in producing a common sense of identity is beyond argument. Its inclusive nature provides the possibility of defining a Chinese nation, which comprises diversified cultures and sub-groups, by political, historical, and territorial ties. The political principle of the Mandate of Heaven generates a traditional concept of sovereignty with Chinese marks. The Chinese people have undergone a difficult struggle in their endeavour to establish a modern state. Different theories, from nationalist movements to communist ideology, have been applied, compared and selected. In general, China's transformation from a civilisation to a modern state focuses upon the invention of a unified national identity.

In the Chinese context, the understandings of the Chinese nationhood varied in the transformation process. The proposition of establishing a single Han state considered the Han as a different nation from the minorities and thus precluded the minorities from the proposed state. The concept of the five-nations republic, which recognised the Han, Manchu, Mongol, Hui, and Tibetan, attempted to unify five major groups as well as their lands. However, other ethnic groups were disregarded according to this concept. The theory of the five-nations republic had a clear emphasis over territory as the basis of the Chinese nation. Apart from geographical bond, Sun further claimed that the Chinese people were united by common blood and ancestry. The communist notion of nationhood also showed a strong desire to maintain national unity, which defined the Chinese nation as a historically legitimated territory together with the whole population living in it. The Chinese nation, in essence, is defined by territorial and historical ties, which results in maintaining minority status for the non-Han groups within the state.

Meanwhile, Chinese nationalism was born to resist foreign oppression. The Chinese nation was, and still is, defined against foreign occupation and intervention. Started with foreign cession and occupation of the imperial heartland, territorial factor plays an important role in the Chinese understanding of sovereignty. National reunification and non-intervention have been repeatedly emphasised in China's national policy. Such a focus on national integrity has profound influences upon the rights of the minorities in China, as the implementation of minority autonomous rights, to a certain extent, depends on whether it would jeopardise the territorial integrity of the state. Internally, the Mandate of Heaven doctrine was renounced and the semi-divine nature of the emperors' authority was replaced by the idea of popular sovereignty. The consent of the people has become the ultimate source of all power in China. The will of the Chinese people, however, is allegedly expressed through the CPC who is argued to be the historical choice of the Chinese people. Seen from this perspective, the Communist Party represents a modern organisational form of traditional emperors.

To "identify a nation, identify with it and make demands in its name" is the central argument in nationalism.[145] The Yi/Xia distinction had varying interpretations throughout the imperial history and the Han-minority relation accordingly had a dynamic nature in the multi-ethnic Chinese empires. On the one hand, a unified Chinese nation has been claimed by the political elites, while on the other hand counter-arguments are made by the minorities within the Chinese borders. Indeed, the ethnic distinctions can be easily observed within the Chinese nation. Minority groups are distinguishable from the majority Han and from each other in terms of culture, religious belief and language. How to appeal to the minorities and integrate them into the unified Chinese nation is the key of nation-building.

145 James Summers, supra note 1, p. 17.

CHAPTER 2

China and the Political Principle of Self-determination

China has long been involved in the evolving process of self-determination from a political principle into a legal right. Apart from the doctrine of nationalism, self-determination was asserted by the Chinese political elites as the basis for national integrity and independence. When the idea that national aspirations should be respected in terms of territorial transfers was put forward by Wilson after the First World War,[1] the Chinese government saw the opportunity to restore sovereignty over the occupied territories by foreign countries at the Peace Conference of Paris. After the Western principle of national self-determination proved not to work, the Chinese political elites were forced to turn to the Soviet Union for assistance and Lenin's theory of national self-determination was followed. Both the KMT and the CPC strategically advocated self-determination to achieve national independence and to appeal to minority support under the Soviet influence. However, the Chinese political regimes were not genuinely in favour of minority self-determination, since the application of the political principle of self-determination in China exhibited its effects as a double-edged sword. It could serve as the legitimising basis for national independence of the Chinese people on the one hand, while it may become the foundation for the minorities to claim for statehood on the other.

This Chapter looks at how the political principle of self-determination has been practised prior to the PRC was established in 1949. Taking a historical perspective, it examines the attempt to rely on Wilson's idea of self-determination as the basis for reclaiming sovereignty over the occupied Shandong peninsula at the Peace Conference of Paris. It then focuses on the flexible and strategic application of Lenin's theory of national self-determination by the KMT and the CPC in order to achieve national independence and to appeal to the minorities. The Chapter provides insight into the involvement of the politics in the rhetoric of self-determination and explains why the right of Chinese minorities to secede was eventually tailored into territorial autonomy within the

1 Woodrow Wilson, as cited in James Summers, *Peoples and International Law (2nd Edition)* (Martinus Nijhoff Publishers, 2014), p. 177.

 DOI:10.1163/9789004380578_004

state. It will direct the reader to understand the imagination of the Chinese nation and ethnic grouping in China from the perspective of self-determination.

2.1 National Self-determination at the Peace Conference of Paris and the Shandong (Shantung) Issue

National self-determination was repeatedly asserted by victorious states in the process of establishing a new international order after the First World War. It was considered to be the leading principle, or so the world thought, of the Peace Conference.[2] Among the Big Four Powers, Great Britain and the United States were the two states that favoured the principle, especially the latter. As early as 1916, Great Britain claimed that "the principle of nationality should ... be one of the governing factors in the consideration of territorial arrangements after the war".[3] British Prime Minister Lloyd George wrote in a Memorandum:

> ... I would therefore take as a guiding principle of the peace that as far as is humanly possible the different races should be allocated to their motherlands, and that this human criterion should have preference over considerations of strategy or economics or communications, which can usually be adjusted by other means.[4]

Whereas the British approach was maybe concerned more with the realisation of nation-states, Woodrow Wilson, on the other hand, proposed an approach to self-determination that blended various elements.[5] His initial perception of self-determination equated to the concept of self-government (e.g. free selection of the form of government and democracy). Then he brought "national desires for states" into the concept and advocated applying the principle of self-determination in territorial settlements. He further argued that self-determination should be one of the considerations in settling colonial claims.[6] Wilson stated:

2 Alfred Cobban, *The National State and National Self-determination* (Collins, The Fontana Library, 1969), p. 57.

3 Cited in James Summers, supra note 1, p. 174.

4 Quoted in Alfred Cobban, supra note 2, at p. 71.

5 Antonio Cassese, *Self-Determination of Peoples: A Legal Reappraisal* (Cambridge University Press, 1995), pp. 19–21; Michla Pomerance, "The United States and Self-determination: Perspectives on the Wilsonian Conception", 70 *American Journal of International Law* (1976), pp. 18–21, 26.

6 Ibid.

> ...[p]eoples are not to be handed about from one sovereignty to another by an international conference or an understanding between rivals and antagonists. National aspirations must be respected; peoples may now be dominated and governed only by their own consent. "Self-determination" is not a mere phrase, which statesmen will henceforth ignore at their peril.[7]

His idea of self-determination appeared to promote the realisation of "right and justice" in the new international order. The inherent ambiguity and contradiction in the principle itself, however, made its application rather problematic at the Conference and thereafter.[8] Wilson's idea of self-determination, together with his assertion of "right and justice", raised for the newly-founded ROC the hope of reclaiming Chinese sovereignty over the Shandong peninsula and of abrogating the unequal treaties.

2.1.1 *The Origin of the Shandong Issue*

Germany occupied the Shangdong province (Jiaozhou/Kiaochow Bay) in 1897 and later "legitimised" its rights to remain in the region by signing the Sino-German Kiaochow Convention. According to the Convention, an area of about 193 square miles surrounding Kiaochow Bay, together with the bay and outlying islands, was transferred to Germany on a lease of 99 years. Germany also attained comprehensive economic rights and privileges in the area, including railway, mining and other commercial affairs.[9] The Convention further provided that "in order to avoid the possibility of conflicts, the Imperial Chinese Government will abstain from exercising rights of sovereignty in the ceded territory during the term of the lease, and leaves the exercise of the same to Germany ..."[10] This translation seemed to suggest that "there was a theoretical and legal as well as actual transfer of sovereignty to Germany".[11]

---

7 Woodrow Wilson, supra note 1.

8 Antonio Cassese, supra note 5, at pp. 22–23; James Summers, supra note 1, at pp. 180–184; Michla Pomerance, supra note 5, at pp. 16, 20–24; Alfred Cobban, supra note 2, at pp. 64–66.

9 The 1898 Kiaochow Convention between China and Germany (The Kiaochow Convention), Sections 2 and 3, in the Research Centre of the General Office of the National People's Congress Standing Committee (ed), *Zhongguo jindai bupingdeng tiaoyue huiyao* [*The Collection of the Unequal Treaties in Modern History of China*] (Zhongguo Minzhu Fazhi Chubanshe, 1996), p. 184; S. Hornbeck, "Chapter IV Part II Shantung at the Peace Conference", in H. W. V. Temperley (ed), *A History of the Peace Conference of Paris: Volume VI* (Henry Frowde and Hodder & Stoughton, 1924), pp. 368–390 at p. 369; Amos Hershey, The Shantung Cession, 13 *American Journal of International Law* (1919), pp. 533–534.

10 The Kiaochow Convention, Article 3; Amos Hershey, ibid, p. 532.

11 Ibid.

However, the Chinese version of the treaty stipulated that the Chinese government was prohibited from exercising the right to administer the territory, as such a right was delegated to Germany.[12] Section 1 Article 5 of the Convention explicitly stated that Germany had to pledge that they would never sublet the leased territory to other states.

After Japan declared war against Germany in 1914, Japanese and British forces seized German "territory" in China. Japan took the occasion to deploy their troops and navy in the Shandong and Liaodong peninsulas, a much greater area of land than the territory leased by Germany.[13] In order to secure their status and privileges, Japan entered in to a series of treaties and exchanged a number of notes with China so as to maintain Japanese influence in the area in 1915. Those treaties and notes were generally known as the Twenty-One Demands, the conclusion of which were claimed to be the result of Japan's increasing number of troops and war vessels in Shandong and Liaodong. Article 1 of The Treaty Respecting Shandong read:

> [t]he Chinese Government agrees to give full assent to all matters upon which the Japanese Government may hereafter agree with the German Government relating to the disposition of all rights, interests and concessions which Germany, by virtue of treaties or otherwise, possesses in relation to the Province of Shantung.[14]

Japan agreed, in an Exchange of Notes, to restore the leased territory in Kiaochow Bay to China when commercial requirements were satisfied.[15] In view

12 "中国不得治理，均归德国管辖". The Chinese version of the sentence did not refer to sovereignty. The Kiaochow Convention, Article 3, in the Research Centre of the General Office of the NPC Standing Committee (ed), supra note 9, at p. 184; S. Hornbeck, supra note 9.

13 S. Hornbeck, supra note 9, at p. 372.

14 Huang Jilian (ed), *Zhongri "ershiyi tiao" jiaoshe shiliao quanbian* [*The Collection of Historical Records of Chinese-Japanese Negotiation on Twenty-one Demands 1915–23*] (Anhui Daxue Chubanshe, 2001), p. 172; cited in Amos Hershey, supra note 9, at p. 534.

15 The conditions are: (1) the whole of Kiaochow Bay to be opened as a Commercial Port; (2) a concession under the exclusive jurisdiction of Japan to be established at a place designated by the Japanese Government; (3) if the foreign powers desire it, an international concession may be established; (4) as regards the disposal to be made of the buildings and properties of Germany and the conditions and procedure relating thereto, the Japanese Government and the Chinese Government shall arrange the matter by mutual agreement before the restoration. Cited in Amos Hershey, supra note 9, at p. 535; see also the Research Centre of the General Office of the NPC Standing Committee (ed), supra note 9, at pp. 263–264.

of the geographical significance of Shandong—its connective function in North-South communication and close position to Beijing,[16] the possession of ports and railways in Shandong as well as its influence in Liaodong peninsula, would give Japan strategic privileges in controlling Northern China. In the following years, Japan secretly received formal support from Russia, Great Britain, France, and Italy "in regard to the disposal of Germany's rights in Shandong" at the Peace Conference, without the notice of the Chinese government.[17]

On the other hand, the United States held a different position from the other Allies. The 1917 Exchange of Notes between America and Japan acknowledged the Japanese interests in China, but it rejected any activities that would "infringe in any way the independence or territorial integrity of China" and insisted on the "Open Door" policy in commerce and industry.[18] The Open Door policy, regardless of its real purpose of maintaining American commercial advantages in China,[19] did, to some extent, help China in terms of reducing the risk of being partitioned by the West. Therefore, when the Chinese people were unable to save China from Japanese ambitions, Wilson—with his ideals of "a new international order based upon universal principles of right and justice"[20] and self-determination—became "the embodiment of … [the] best hopes and aspirations"[21] of the Chinese people at the Peace Conference.

2.1.2 *Japanese and Chinese Positions*

In the Conference, the Japanese delegation made their claim first: a transfer of all German rights in regard to Shandong, which was justified on *de facto* territorial occupation during the war and the Japanese contribution to the victory.[22] Then V. K. Wellington Koo, on behalf of the Chinese government, stated the claim of China: the restoration of the leased territory, of the railway and of

16 Roy Curry, *Woodrow Wilson and Far East Policy 1913-21* (Bookman Associates, 1957), p. 261.

17 S. Hornbeck, supra note 9, at pp. 376, 634–637.

18 Ibid, pp. 638, 377.

19 The Open Door Policy was first proposed by the US Secretary of State, John Hay, in 1899. Wilson disagreed with Hay's Open Door Policy, stating: "they did not make the least effort to save the rights of China; they only tried to save the commercial advantages of the United States". Cited in Michla Pomerance, supra note 5, at p. 15.

20 James Summers, supra note 1, at p. 177.

21 Roy Curry, supra note 16, at p. 252.

22 Later, in response to Koo's claim, the Japanese delegates referenced to the friendly understanding between China and Japan under the Twenty-one Demands and 1918 agreements. Roy Curry, supra note 16, at pp. 262–263; S. Hornbeck, supra note 9, at pp. 375–376.

all other rights which Germany had possessed in the area.[23] The Chinese claim was based on the following reasons:

- the territory in question was an integral part of China;
- it was the cradle of Chinese civilisation, the birthplace of Confucius, a Chinese Holy Land;
- Germany took it from China by force, therefore all Sino-German treaties were abrogated after the war broke between the two, and restoration was one of the conditions of "a just peace";
- 1915 Chinese-Japanese treaties with respect to Shandong and the subsequent agreements of 1918 thereafter were not justifiable, since the conclusion of the treaties resulted from Japan's ultimatum; and
- it was consistent with the principle of nationality and the preservation of territorial integrity.[24]

Weighing up the validity of the treaties, the US was initially favourably disposed towards China. The US once insisted: "with respect to Shantung, the German rights there were lapsed with all Sino-German treaties upon the declaration of war. A succession of treaty rights from Germany to Japan is therefore not possible".[25] The American government refused to recognise the binding force of the agreements growing out of the Twenty-One Demands and the subsequent 1918 treaties.[26] As the Conference proceeded, France and Great Britain expressed that they would respect their respective pledges made to Japan previously and support Japanese claims in the Shandong peninsula. After refusing the Japanese demand to incorporate a racial equality clause into the proposed peace treaty and the early withdrawal of the Italian delegation, Wilson dropped the American position on the matter in exchange for Japanese support for the Conference. Hence, the decision made by the Council of Three was no surprise: Germany transferred all rights in Shandong that it obtained from China to Japan.

It was assumed that Japan's title was to rest not on a bilateral agreement, but on a broad, international act. The Conference made no reference to the 1898 Sino-German Convention or to the 1915 and 1918 Sino-Japan treaties, as Wilson insisted at the time, and repeatedly thereafter, that the settlement should not

---

23 Yue Qianhou, *Gu Weijun yu kangri waijiao [V. K. Wellington Koo and Anti-Japanese Diplomacy]* (Hebei Remin Chubanshe, 1998), p. 30; S. Hornbeck, supra note 9, at p. 377; Roy Curry, supra note 16, at pp. 262–263.

24 Yue Qianhou, ibid, pp. 30–31; S. Hornbeck, ibid, pp. 377–378; Roy Curry, ibid.

25 The State Department, Wilson's advices, the Naval Advisory Staff and the Intelligence Section were of this opinion. See Roy Curry, supra note 16, at p. 262.

26 Ibid.

be construed as dependent upon the Chinese-Japanese agreements of 1915 and 1918.[27] Nevertheless, the terms of the Treaty of Versailles seemed to recognise the validity of those treaties.[28] Despite China's repeated denial of the validity of those "unequal" treaties, the use of force was not prohibited under international law at the time. "Unequal" treaties as a result of conquest or duress were not assumed to be invalid. Even if the use of force was outlawed at the Conference later, the retrospectivity would continue to be the obstacle. The general opinion at the Conference believed that both countries had strong arguments, the Japanese from a legal point of view and the Chinese in terms of political and moral principles.[29]

On the other hand, while Japan reckoned on the "express convention" with China to assert rights over Shandong, China realised that it might be able to justify the restoration claim upon the "newly" proposed principle of self-determination. According to the principle, the will of the peoples concerned should be respected in regard to territorial transfers. In the case of Shandong, the "people" could be interpreted as the Shandong people or the population of China as a whole. Koo's statement seemed to prefer the interpretation that it referred to the Chinese people.[30] E. Williams expressed a similar opinion.[31] Lansing, however, gave a different view. In a meeting with the Japanese delegates, Lansing said: "we looked upon the people of Shantung as a people wronged and oppressed [by Germany] and now that the enemy was removed we could not bear to see the evil continue through placing one foreign nation by another".[32] He insisted that the US stood for the rights of nationalities and self-determination of the peoples.[33]

---

27 S. Hornbeck, supra note 9, at pp. 382, 387.

28 The London Times stated: "...Japan receives the free disposition of Kioachau, to which she is entitled under the treaty with China of 1915, and which was all she asked from the Conference. In the Treaty Germany will surrender the Kiaochau territory to Japan, who will, in accordance with her Treaty with China, transfer it to the latter in due course". See S. Hornbeck, supra note 9, at pp. 383, 386.

29 Mr. Langsing and Mr. White also sent President Wilson a letter, cogently discussing the conflicting claims from the perspective of the "moral right or wrong involved" on 29th April. See S.Hornbeck, supra note 9, at pp. 379, 381.

30 Yue Qianhou, supra note 23; S. Hornbeck, supra note 9, at pp. 377–378.

31 In the consultation with Ronald Macleay on the matter as to whether China would best benefit from direct cession of German rights to Japan or under the Sino-Japanese agreements, Williams believed that the Chinese opinion was determined in its resistance to the Japanese claims. He stated that "nowhere have the people of a district spoken more plainly". Cited in Roy Curry, supra note 16, at pp. 271–272.

32 The Japanese delegate replied: "we have express conventions with China dealing with the question and we mean to insist upon their exact fulfilment". See ibid, p. 274.

33 Ibid.

In either case, it was understood that the people's free will would amount to be the restoration of Shandong sovereignty. In other words, the application of self-determination may nullify existing treaties on the Shandong issue. If this was plausible, it would, in turn, imply that all other "unequal" treaties upon which the political and economic rights and privileges of the West in China had built were also void. Seen in this perspective, the free will of the people might not only decide territorial settlement but also economic sovereignty. Economic self-determination was apparently quite avant-garde at the time, even for Wilson. He by no means had the intention to embrace economic self-determination as part and parcel of self-determination.[34] Were the principle of self-determination applied to Shandong, the result might have turned out differently.

Yet Japan had successfully transformed into a powerful modern state after the Meiji Restoration and appeared as a new imperial power in the Conference, whereas China was still weak and struggling in the process of modernisation. Considering the strategic balance and pragmatic purpose, the principle of self-determination, as in most other cases, yielded to political calculations and the needs of the Great Powers.[35] The will of the people, be it Chinese people or Shandong people, was ignored in the Shandong settlement. The theoretical application of self-determination in the Shandong case in a way reflected inherent problems of the principle itself: the long-argued definition of "people", and how to accommodate self-determination in the existing international order.

2.1.3 *Consequences of the Conference*

The diplomatic failure of China in the Conference was widely considered to be another "national humiliation". Nevertheless, it did affect China positively in the sense that it further awakened the national consciousness of the people. Also, the confidence in the benevolent professions of the Western powers was smashed as the result of the Conference.[36] The long-term negative responses from the European powers towards Chinese nationalist movements, the ambitious Japanese and the profound disappointment with the US, who had initially shown great sympathy for China and seemed to have the power to see justice done,[37] rendered China no choice but to resort to the USSR for support.

---

34 Michla Pomerance, supra note 5, at pp. 14–15.

35 Hurst Hannum, *Autonomy, Sovereignty, and Self-determination: the Accommodation of Conflicting Rights* (*Revised Edition*) (University of Pennsylvania Press, 1990), p. 28.

36 S. Hornbeck, supra note 9, at p. 389.

37 Roy Curry, supra note 16, at pp. 252–253, 262, 280; Yue Qianhou, supra note 23, at p. 41; V. K. Wellington Koo, The Institute of Modern History of the Chinese Academy of Science

Although anti-Bolshevism was taken into consideration in delimiting European frontiers, China was too weak to be recalled at the Conference. The Soviet Union later gained one of the most important fellow socialist states by assisting different political forces in China.

2.2 Lenin's Theory of Self-determination and Its Influence upon China

The principle of self-determination served as an integral part of Lenin's theory of socialism. It was considered to be "the political extension of Lenin's primarily economic analysis of imperialism".[38] His reference to the right to self-determination appeared to be interchangeable with the right to secession.[39] Other soviet leaders, Stalin for instance, further developed a more comprehensive definition of self-determination which in essence concerned the free will of a nation to determine its own future.[40] Besides political independence, regional autonomy and minority regime would be the alternatives in the communist concept of self-determination.[41] The Soviet principle of self-determination also incorporated an anti-colonial postulate which aimed at the liberation of all colonial countries.[42]

(Translator), *Gu Weijun huiyi lu* [*Memoir of V. K. Wellington Koo: Volume I*] (Zhonghua Shuju 1983), pp. 166, 169–170, 173.

38 Cited in Antonio Cassese, supra note 5, at p. 15.

39 V. Lenin, "<Shehui zhuyi geming he minzu zijuequan>tigang de duanji [Note to the Thesis on the Socialist Revolution and the Right of Nations to Self-determination]", in the Compilation Bureau of the CPC Central Committee on the Works of Marx, Engels, Lenin and Stalin (Translator), *Liening quanji* [*Collected Works of Lenin: Volume 27*] (Renmin Chubanshe, 1990), p. 269; "the Revolutionary Proletariat and the Right of Nations to Self-determination", *Collected Works of Lenin: Volume 21* (Lawrence & Wishart London), p. 409; "Theses on the Socialist Revolution and the Right of Nations to self-determination", *Collected Works of Lenin: Volume 22* (Lawrence & Wishart London), pp. 146–147.

40 He argued that "the right of self-determination means that a nation can arrange its life according to its own will. It has the right to arrange its life on the basis of autonomy. It has the right to enter into federal relations with other nations. It has the right to complete secession. Nations are sovereign and all nations are equal". Quoted in Walker Connor, *The National Question in Marxist-Leninist Theory and Strategy* (Princeton University Press, 1984), p. 33.

41 Cited in ibid, p. 33. According to Stalin, the Bolshevik national programme has four propositions: (a) the recognition of the right of peoples to secession; (b) regional autonomy for the peoples which remain within the given state; (c) specific laws guaranteeing freedom of development for the national minorities; (d) a single, indivisible proletarian collective body, a single party, for the proletarians of all the nationalities in a given state. See Alfred Cobban, supra note 2, at pp. 194–195.

42 Antonio Cassese, supra note 5, at p. 16.

However, Lenin had no intention to advocate ethnic separation when granting national groups the right to self-determination. He believed that "… because we want large states and the closer unity and even fusion of nations, only on a truly democratic, truly internationalist basis, which is inconceivable without the freedom to secede".[43] According to Lenin, political independence of nations was merely one stage in the process of realising socialism. The exercise of the right to self-determination had to be "consistently democratic, revolutionary, and in accord with the general task of the immediate struggle for socialism".[44] Bearing this in mind, it would be easy to understand situations in which the application of the principle could be tailored to military and economic considerations.[45] The communist advocacy of national self-determination was "a tactical rather than a philosophical decision".[46]

In the early 1920s, Lenin's proposition of self-determination as an anti-colonial device gave China an opportunity to get rid of foreign exploitation and to achieve national independence. From 1923 onwards, two major political forces, the KMT and the CPC, commenced with the application of various adaptions of self-determination in China.

2.2.1 *The Nationalist Self-determination*

Sun and the KMT were not placed first on the list of possible Soviet allies in China.[47] The Soviet Union first showed an interest in developing China as an alliance in Asia after the October Revolution. Before the Nationalist Party, the Soviet Union had contacted the Beiyang Government[48] and different warlords. Sun did not become a possible ally of the Soviet Union until 1922. The 1923 Sun-Joffe Manifesto was signed after further contact and negotiations. Sun

---

43 This logic came from Marx who endorsed the separation of Ireland from Great Britain, as he assumed that "the separation of an oppressed nation to be a step towards federation, and consequently, not towards a split, but towards concentration, both political and economic, but concentration on the basis of democracy". See V. Lenin, "The Revolutionary Proletariat and The Right of Nations to Self-determination", supra note 39, at pp. 410, 413–414.

44 Ibid, p. 409.

45 Alfred Cobban, supra note 2, at p. 198.

46 Hurst Hannum, supra note 35, at p. 33.

47 Dan Jacobs, Yin Gang (Translator), *Bao Luoting: Sidalin paidao zhongguo de ren* [*Borodin: Stalin's Man in China*] (Shijie Zhishi Chubanshe, 1989), pp. 106–109; Yang Yuqing, "Guojia liyi: su'e dui zaihua hezuozhe de xuanze [State Interests: the Choice of the Soviet Union on Its Alliance in China]", 4 *Lishi Yanjiu* [*Historical Research*] (1999), pp. 142–152.

48 The Beiyang Government was the internationally recognised authority of the ROC from 1912 to 1928, although its legitimacy was challenged by Sun and the KMT. It was replaced by the Nationalist Government in 1928.

acknowledged the "desirability of friendships" with the Soviet Union[49] and clarified that soviet help would be limited to financial and military aid, as well as other relevant support. The alliance by no means implied the adoption of the communist ideology in China.[50]

Being influenced by the Soviet ideology, Sun revised the Three Principles of the People to embrace the right of the oppressed nations to self-determination. The Declaration of the First National Congress of the KMT in 1924 defined nationalism as the liberation of the Chinese nation and the equality of racial groups within China. It recognised "the right of all racial groups of China to self-determination and as soon as militarism and imperialism have been expelled from the land ... we will do our best to organise (upon the voluntary agreement of all racial groups) a free and united Republic of China".[51] According to the Outline of the National Government's Plans for National Reconstruction, it was one of the responsibilities of the National Government to assist small and weak nationalities of China to develop the capacity to self-determination and self-government.[52]

The principle of self-determination in Sun's context, however, did not in any way equate to the right to secession,[53] particularly with his awareness of Soviet policy in Outer Mongolia. As a nationalist, he simply meant the right of China—a race-nation that comprised of the Han, Mongol, Manchu, Tibetan and Moslem—to self-determination against imperial powers.[54] Sun's assertion of

---

49 June Dreyer, *China's Political System: Modernisation and Tradition* (Paragon House, 1993), p. 73.

50 Sun stressed that "the Communist order or even the Soviet system cannot actually be introduced into China because there do not exist here the conditions for the successful establishment of either communism and sovietism". Consensus was reached on the chief immediate objective of China, which was to achieve national unity and independence. Cited in the United States Department of State, *The China White Paper: August 1949, Volume 1* (Stanford University Press, 1967), p. 42

51 Sun Yat-sen, "Zhongguo guomin dang diyici quanguo daibiao dahui xuanyan [the Declaration of the First National Congress of the KMT] (01/23/1924)", in *Sun Zhongshan quanji* [*Collected Works of Sun Yat-sen: Volume 9*] (Zhonghua Shuju, 1986), p. 119; the English translation is cited in Walker Connor, supra note 40, at p. 67.

52 Sun Yat-sen, "Guomin zhengfu jianguo dagang [Outline of the National Government's Plans for National Reconstruction] (01/23/1924)", in *Sun Zhongshan quanji* [*Collected Works of Sun Yat-sen: Volume 9*] (Zhonghua Shuju, 1986), at p. 127.

53 Despite the acknowledgment of self-determination for the minorities, Sun never gave up his idea of unifying all races in China to form a great *zhonghua* nation on the basis of ancient Chinese culture. See Shao Chuan Leng and Norman D. Palmer, *Sun Yat-Sen and Communism* (Thames and Hudson, 1961), p. 93.

54 Sun Yat-sen, supra note 51, at p. 188.

self-determination mainly served as the basis for national independence. Internally, it appeared to imply the right of racial groups to autonomy.[55]

After Sun's passing, Jiang Jieshi (also known as Chiang Kai-shek,) was reluctant to endorse the principle of self-determination, not to mention the right of secession. He argued that there could be no national questions within China since the Chinese nation was of one stock with the blend of numerous clans.[56] In his words, "... the territory of the Chinese state is determined by the requirements for national survival and by the limits of Chinese cultural bonds ... The breaking up of this territory meant the undermining of the nation's security as well as the decline of the nation's culture".[57] The 1931 Provisional Constitution of the Political Tutelage Period did not refer to the right to self-determination. Instead, Article 3 provided that the ROC shall be a unified Republic forever.[58] Furthermore, the equality of all ethnic groups and the state's obligation to provide legal protection for the status of ethnic groups in frontier areas and special assistance to develop regional self-government were guaranteed in the 1946 Constitution.[59]

The right to self-determination contemplated by the KMT apparently had different implications. It may have operated as a synonym for nationalism or the right of the minorities to self-government. But it seemed not to entail a right of secession. The freedom to secede, which may work as "the best and the only political method"[60] to realise socialism, was unavailable to the KMT. Also, Soviet policy towards Outer Mongolia, the Middle-East Railway and Xinjiang embodied the ambitions of the Soviet Union. The leaders of the KMT, even before the Soviet-KMT collaboration, had noticed its neighbour's interests in breaking territories away from China. It consequently affected the way that the Nationalist Party interpreted the principle of self-determination and its resistance to secession. The considerations of facilitating China's revolution against imperialism and in the meantime maintaining Soviet interests in

55 Binh Phan, How Autonomous are the National Autonomous Areas of the PRC? An Analysis of Documents and Cases, 32:7 *Issues and Studies* (1996), p. 87.

56 Jiang stated that the fusion of various clans had continued "dynasty after dynasty, but the motive power was cultural rather than military, and it was accompanied by assimilation rather than by conquest". Chiang Kai-shek, *China's Destiny and Chinese Economic Theory*, (Dennis Dobson Ltd., 1947), p. 30; Walker Connor, supra note 40, at p. 68.

57 Chiang Kai-shek, ibid, p. 34.

58 Zhang Jinfan, *Zhongguo Xianfa shi* [*Chinese Constitution History*] (Jilin Renmin Chubanshe, 2004), Appendix Two, p. 430; Walker Connor, supra note 40, at p. 68.

59 The 1946 Constitution of the ROC, Articles 5, 168. See Zhang Jinfan, ibid, pp. 436, 452.

60 V. Lenin, "<Shehui zhuyi geming he minzu zijuequan>tigang de duanji [Note to the Thesis on the Socialist Revolution and the Right of Nations to Self-determination]", supra note 39, at p. 269.

China, therefore, caused compromise and inconsistency of the Soviet exporting of the principle of self-determination and other socialist ideologies.

Despite the nationalist assertion of self-determination or self-government of racial groups, in practice the republican government was not concerned much with the minorities. Apart from five frequently involved groups, namely the Han, Manchu, Mongol, Moslem and Tibetan, other minorities of a considerably smaller number[61] were not treated with equal importance. Special arrangements for Mongolia and Tibet were necessary in order to compete with western offers of self-determination. The constitutional reassurance of "regional governmental variants for Mongolia and Tibet in accordance with local conditions"[62] may be considered as a right of regional autonomy. However, in regard to other minority groups, the republican government was reluctant to approve the internal aspect of self-determination—the right to self-government within the ROC.[63]

Unlike the big minority groups mentioned above, the minorities in the southwest and northwest were normally mingled together, living in separate compact communities among each other. Most of them lived a tribal way of life which, according to the civilised groups, was a synonym for barbarianism.[64] Traditionally, the Qing court exerted effective control over those areas by reforming the local hereditary native chiefs system in accordance with the imperial civil administration. It thus left those groups with a lower degree of autonomy. During the ROC period, the south-western region was in general controlled by warlords. Except for sporadic missionary activities, foreign influence and intervention could hardly be traced in the area, compared with the British ambition in Tibet, the Russian intervention in Mongolia and Xinjiang, and the Japanese influence in Manchuria. The nationalist ignorance of the minorities in the southwest could possibly be understood for these reasons.

In addition, local governments and leaders considered "civilising the savages" a responsibility of the Han and therefore launched a series of "civilisation programmes", aimed at the minorities in the south-west.[65] For example, the

61 The ROC approximately had a population of 450 million in 1926. The population of the minorities in the south-west was a few million altogether. For more statistics, see Gee-Yuen Chang, *A Study on the Chinese Ethnology* (The Commercial Press, 1929), pp. 58–62, 121.

62 The 1931 Provisional Constitution of the Political Tutelage Period, Article 80.

63 C. Mackerras, *China's Minority Cultures: Edentities and Integration since 1912* (Longman, 1995), p. 9.

64 Gee-Yuen Chang, supra note 61, pp. 121–125.

65 Ibid, pp. 122, 124; Zhao Xuexian, Peng Qian and Yang Wenshun (eds), *Zhongguo guomin dang minzu lilun yu minzu zhengce yanjiu* [*The Study on the National Theory and Policy of the KMT*] (Zhongyang Minzu Daxue Chubanshe, 2010), p. 127.

Guangdong government, in compliance with Sun's appeal "to assist the small and weak nationalities of China to develop the capacity to self-determination and self-government", set up the Bureau of Civilising the Li and Bureau of Civilising the Yao in 1937.[66] A number of Custom Reform Committees were established in Guangxi counties to replace the traditional "barbaric" customs of the minorities with the Han culture.[67] Administrative reforms and education policy were carried out accordingly. In Guizhou, the provincial governor called for forcefully eradicating ethnic differences among the minorities.[68] Seen in this manner, the KMT implemented a policy of national assimilation.[69]

2.2.2 *The CPC and Soviet Self-determination*

Considering the close relationship between the CPC and the Communist International (the Comintern), the adoption of the principle of self-determination was comparatively easier for the communists. Yet the distinctive social background and revolutionary situation of China resulted in a different understanding and application of the principle in practice. The CPC's application of self-determination went through four stages: the pre-Long March period, the Long March, the Anti-Japanese War, and the Civil War onwards.

(1) The Pre-Long March Period (1921–1934)

In the first stage, the embryonic CPC, with obvious Soviet influence, passed a number of documents concerning self-determination. The first record was the Manifesto of the Second National Congress of the CPC (July 1922). It made no direct reference to the principle of self-determination, but came up with the concept of self-government and the establishment of a federal republic in the fully independent China. It envisaged the objectives of the Party as:

> …
>
> (2) the removal of oppression by international imperialism and the complete independence of the Chinese nation;

---

66 The Guangdong Government, "Resolution on the Civilisation of the Li and Yao *minzu* (1937)", cited in Gee-Yuen Chang, supra note 61, at pp. 122–125.

67 Tan Zhaoyi, "Minguo shiqi xingguixi de minzu zhengce pingshu [A Comment on the Policy concerning the Ethnic Nationalities by Neo-Guangxi Regime during 1911–1949 Period in China]", 41:2 *Guangxi Shifan Daxue Xuebao* [*Journal of Guangxi Normal University*] (2005), p. 135.

68 C. Mackerras, *China's Minorities: Integration and Modernisation in the Twentieth Century* (Oxford University Press, 1994), p. 60.

69 Ibid, p. 77; Binh Phan, supra note 55, at p. 88.

(3) the unification of China proper (including Manchuria) into a genuine democratic republic;
(4) the achievement of the self-government and the establishment of democratic republic of Mongolia, Tibet and Xinjiang;[70]
(5) the establishment of a Chinese Federated Republic by the unification of China proper, Mongolia, Tibet and Xinjiang into a free federation ...[71]

The principle of self-determination was expressly termed in the 1923 instruments. It was conceived as the underpinning of the national struggle against imperialism as well as a fundamental principle for the minorities.[72] It stated that the relationship between Tibet, Mongolia, Xinjiang, Qinghai and other provinces, and China proper, should be decided by each group on the basis of self-determination.[73] A similar policy continued to be valid during the period of the first KMT-CPC cooperation.[74] The Sixth National Congress of the CPC (held in Moscow 1928) addressed the importance of the minorities in the Chinese revolution and proposed a programme of "unifying China and recognising the principle of national self-determination".[75] Then, the 1931 Constitution of the Chinese Soviet Republic adopted a complete Soviet article and pledged an explicit recognition of the right of the national minorities to secede. Article 14, which was further reaffirmed in the 1934 Constitution, stated:

70 This is my understanding of the Chinese expression "蒙古、西藏、回疆三部实行自治，成为民主自治邦", which is different from the English translation provided in "A Documentary History of Chinese Communism". See infra note; "Zhongguo gongchandang dierci quanguo daibiao dahui xuanyan [the Declaration of the Second National Congress of the CPC] (07/1922)", in Jin Binghao (ed), *Minzu gangling zhengce wenxian xuanbian* [*The Collected Works of the Documents on the National Program and Policy*] (Zhongyang Minzu Daxue Chubanshe, 2006), p. 19.

71 Conrad Brandt, Benjamin Schwartz and John Fairbank (eds), *A Documentary History of Chinese Communism* (George Allen & Unwin Ltd, 1952), p. 64.

72 "The Manifesto of the Third National Congress of the CPC", in Conrad Brandt, Benjamin Schwartz and John Fairbank (eds), ibid, p. 71; "Zhongguo gongchandang danggang cao'an [the Draft Program of the CPC (06/1923)]", in Jin Binghao (ed), supra note 70, at p. 31

73 Ibid.

74 The Declaration of the First National Congress of the KMT 1924, supra note 51; Outline of the National Government's Plans for National Reconstruction, supra note 52.

75 "Zhongguo gongchandang diliuci quanguo daibiao dahui tongguo de zhengzhi jueyi an he guanyu minzu wenti de juyi an [the Political Resolution and National Resolution of the Sixth National Congress of the CPC] (09/07/1928)", in Jin Binghao (ed), supra note 70, at pp. 65, 66; and in Conrad Brandt, Benjamin Schwartz and John Fairbank (eds), supra note 71, at p. 132.

> [t]he Soviet government of China recognises the right of self-determination of the national minorities in China, their right to complete separation from China, and to the formation of an independent state for each national minority. All Mongolians, Tibetans, Miao, Yao, Koreans, and others living on the territory of China shall enjoy the *full* right to self-determination, i.e. they may either join the Union of Chinese Soviets or secede from it and form their own state as they may prefer. The Soviet regime of China will do its utmost to assist the national minorities in liberating themselves from the yoke of imperialists, the KMT (GMD) militarists, t'u-ssu [tribal headmen], the princes, lamas, and others, and in achieving complete freedom and autonomy. The Soviet regime must encourage the development of the national cultures and of the respective national languages of these peoples.[76]

Despite the recognition of a general right to secede, the CPC alternatively interpreted it as a right exclusively enjoyed by the toiling masses of the national minorities.[77] The 1931 Resolution of the First All-China Congress of Soviets on the Question of the National Minorities in China aimed to establish a fully liberated state without oppression or national barriers.[78] It called for the co-operation of the toiling masses of the Han and the minorities as both were suffering from common exploiters and oppressing classes, i.e. imperialists, warlords, landlords and the bourgeoisie.[79] Therefore, a full and unconditional recognition of the right of the national minorities to self-determination meant "the toiling masses of all nationalities"[80] would have the right to determine for themselves whether to withdraw from the Chinese Soviet Republic and create an independent state of their own, or whether to join the Chinese Soviet Republic and form autonomous regions therein.[81] This suggested that the right of secession, from the CPC's point of view, was of a "class-based" nature. Thus, the

76 Conrad Brandt, Benjamin Schwartz and John Fairbank (eds), ibid, pp. 223–224.

77 Stephen Angle, *Human Rights and Chinese Thoughts: a Cross-cultural Inquiry* (Cambridge University Press, 2002), p. 203.

78 "Guanyu zhongguo jingnei shaoshu minzu wenti de juyi an [the 1931 Resolution of the First All-China Congress of Soviets on the Question of the National Minorities in China] (11/1931)" in Jin Binghao (ed), supra note 70, at p. 93.

79 Ibid.

80 The nationalities here referred to those who resided in Mongolia, Tibet, Xinjiang, Yunnan, Guizhou, and other places, where the non-Han people constituted the majority population.

81 "Guanyu zhongguo jingnei shaoshu minzu wenti de juyi an [the 1931 Resolution of the First All-China Congress of Soviets on the Question of the National Minorities in China] (11/1931)", supra note 78, at pp. 94–96.

CPC not only laid the foundations for unifying various nationalities in order to resist foreign powers,[82] but it also left itself enough space to deal with possible future secession claims from the minorities. In the context of the early 1930s, "a *full* right to self-determination",[83] was phrased so as to emphasise the right to secede. Such terminology rarely showed up in later instruments.

The CPC, as a communist party, in principal, followed the Marxist-Leninist theories and principles from the moment of its establishment, including the principle of self-determination. Many revolutionary tactics, during the period 1928–1934, were formulated under direct Soviet instruction. Unlike Lenin's advocacy of secession, the CPC, in most cases, equated self-determination to self-government within the unified state of Chinese federation, which was notable, especially in view of the exclusive Soviet influence in its establishing process. This might be explained partially by the Soviet expansion policy as taken into account by Sun and the KMT, and partially by the scepticism deriving from "the record of secessionist movements that had afflicted the Soviet Union during its revolutionary and immediate post revolutionary periods".[84]

(2) The Long March Period (1934–1936)

Although the recognition of secession might have been a result of Soviet pressure, the CPC anticipated no harm to revolutionary movements at the time, as the communists mainly focused upon the urban proletariat in eastern coastal cities and then shifted to the peasant mobilisation in the Han dominated hinterland. The non-involvement of ethnic minorities made self-determination and secession a theoretical stipulation.[85] The failure of the fifth counter-campaign

---

82 The CPC accused the KMT of conceding territories to the imperialists and called for the alliance of all national toiling workers and peasants to fight against the common enemies, i.e. the bourgeoisie and imperialists, and to achieve national independence and liberation. See e.g. "zhongguo gongchandang wei fandui guomindang wuchi chumai minzu liyi xuanyan [the 1931 CPC Declaration on the Objection to the KMT's Betrayal to the Interests of the People]" and "zhonghua suweiai gongheguo linshi zhongyang zhengfu xuanbu duiri zhanzheng xuanyan [the 1932 Declaration of Anti-Japanese War by the Provisional Government of the Chinese Soviet Republic]", in Jin Binghao (ed), supra note 70, at pp. 97–103.

83 See "zhongguo gongchandang dui muqian shiju de xuanyan [the CPC Declaration on Current Situation] (14/08/1930)", "zhonggong zhongyang wei diyici quanguo suweiai dabiao dahui gao quangguo gongnong laoku minzhong shu [A letter to the National Toiling Workers and Peasants by the First All-China Congress of Soviets] (20/10/1931)"; "zhonghua suweiai gongheguo xianfa dagang [the 1931 and 1934 Constitutions of the Chinese Soviet Republic]", in Jin Binghao (ed), supra note 70, at pp. 79, 86, 89, 110.

84 Walker Connor, supra note 40, at p. 73.

85 For example, in a letter addressed to the Sichuan Provincial Committee in 1933, the Central Committee criticised the local branch for not proposing any concrete plans to

against "encirclement and annihilation" left the communists no space in the midland. It forced the Red Army to launch a strategic retreat to remote areas by and large inhabited by the minorities. The Party leaders then had to think about applying the principle of self-determination into practice. The Long March also witnessed the ascent of Mao's influence in the Party, during which he received the support of party members and eventually took over the leadership of the CPC. Mao's thoughts on nationalities, which focused upon national unification,[86] dominated the party ever since.

In the early stage of the Long March, the Red Army and the CPC employed various tactics so as to appeal to minority support or at least to adopt a neutral attitude towards them. One stream of thought advocated the right of secession and the union of the toiling masses of the minorities and the Han people.[87] Another practice aimed to create a federal soviet government for the Chinese Soviet Republic. The proposed federal soviet government pledged the right of self-determination for the Hui (Moslems), Fan and Yi nationalities, and the right to establish revolutionary governments of their own nationality,[88] which should then join the federal soviet government and ally with the USSR.[89] Other approaches relied on the general principle of self-determination and national equality.[90]

---

mobilise and unite the minorities so as to launch a joint struggle against the KMT and the British Imperialism. The 1934 Political Resolution of the Fifth Plenary Session of the Sixth Central Committee admitted the Party's unbearable weakness in the work of the national minorities and readdressed the significance of the CPC leadership in the minority liberation. "Zhonggong zhongyang gei Sichuan shengwei de xin [A Letter Addressed to the Sichuan Provincial Committee] (20/05/1933)"; "zhonggong zhongyang liujie wuzhong quanhui zhengzhi jueyi an [Political Resolution of the Fifth Plenary Session of the Sixth Central Committee] (18/01/1934)", in Jin Binghao (ed), supra note 70, pp. 104–106.

86 Mao's long term view consistently emphasised, from 1917 to the end of his life, the importance of national unification and a strong state. See Stuart Schram, "Chapter 14 Mao Tse-tung's Thought to 1949", in John Fairbank and Albert Feuerwerker (eds), *The Cambridge History of China: Volume 13* (Cambridge University Press, 1986), pp. 789–870, at p. 801.

87 "Zhongguo gongnong hongjun zhengzhibu guanyu miaoyao minzu zhong gongzuo yuanze de zhishi [the Directive of the First Red Army on the Working Principles in Regard to the Miao and Yao] (29/11/1934)", in Jin Binghao (ed), supra note 70, at pp. 127–130.

88 "Zhonghua suweiai xibei lianbang linshi zhengfu huifanyi shaoshu minzu weiyuanhui bugao [the Announcement of the Minority Committee of the Provisional Western Federal Government of the Chinese Soviet Republic] (20/05/1935)", in the United Front Work Department of the CPCCC (ed), *Minzu wenti wenxian huibian* [*the Collection of Documents on the National Question* (*July 1921– September 1949*)] (Zhonggong Zhongyang Dagnxiao Chubanshe, 1991), pp. 263–264.

89 Ibid.

90 "Zhongguo gongnong hongjun zong zhengzhibu guanyu zhengqu shaoshu minzu de zhishi [the Directive of the General Political Department of the Red Army on Appealing to

By the end of 1935, as foreign forces such as Japan and Great Britain stretched out to minority regions, the CPC then offered the Mongols and Hui people the right to build a system of their own choice, either to establish their own governments or to separate from the Chinese Soviet Republic.[91] Such a policy was sustained until the second KMT-CPC coopcration in 1937. Thc cxplanation for doing so was likely to be found in Liu Shaoqi's writings. He considered the practical granting of the right of secession to be a tactical instrument for winning minority support when competing with rival offers, arguing:

> [t]he independence and self-government of the minority nationalities is nothing to be afraid of, for after they are given independence and self-government, they can still join China in the common struggle against the Japanese. What is to be feared is their opposition to China and the Han, initiated at the deception of and for utilisation by the Japanese.[92]

(3) The Anti-Japanese War (1937–1945)

The breakout of the Second Sino-Japanese War in 1937 represented another strategic change for the CPC. In order to ensure national survival and combat Japanese invaders, the CPC needed to form a united front of all forces against Japan. The communists temporally adjusted their strategy from building a soviet federation to the establishment of a people's republic. The CPC rarely referred to the principle of self-determination after 1938.[93] First, the united front depended upon the mobilisation of all possible strengths of the nation without distinctions of nationality or class. Second, the principle of self-determination had proved not to work well in mobilising the minorities. On the contrary, the Japanese advocacy of self-determination, which derived from the "divide

---

the Minorities] (1935)"; "zhognguo gongchandang zhongyang weiyuanhui he zhonghua suweiai zhongyang zhengfu wei kangri jiuguo gao quanti tongbao shu [An Open Letter to the Whole People for Resisting the Japanese and Savaging the Nation] (01/08/1935)", in Jin Binghao (ed), supra note 70, at pp. 138, 144–145.

91 "Zhonghua suweiai zhongyang zhengfu dui neimenggu remin xuanyan [the 1935 Declaration of the Chinese Soviet Central Government to the Inner Mongolian People] (20/12/1935)" and "zhongguo gongnong hongjun disi fangmian jun zong zhengzhibu guanyu jinru huimin quyu gongzuo de zhishi [the 1936 Directive of the General Political Department of the Fourth Red Army on the Entrance into the Hui Region] (13/06/1936)", in Jin Binghao (ed), supra note 70, at pp. 157–159, 176–179.

92 As cited in Walker Connor, supra note 40, at p. 86. In Connor's book, the Chinese term "自治(*zizhi*)" is translated into "autonomy".

93 Suisheng Zhao, *A Nation-State by Construction: Dynamics of Modern Chinese Nationalism* (Stanford University Press, 2004), p. 175.

and conquer" tactic, was more successful in appealing to the minorities,[94] as demonstrated in the creation of the "State of Manchuria" in 1932 and the United Autonomous Government of Mongolia in 1937.

Hence, with an aim to win non-communist elements, Sun's Three Principles of the People were reasserted by Mao and the CPC on many occasions as "the paramount need of China".[95] On the nationality policy, by the same token, Mao recognised the equality of all racial groups and, under the same Anti-Japanese policy, the right of the minorities to govern their own affairs within the unified state.[96] Further, in The Chinese Revolution and the Chinese Communist Party (1939), Mao envisaged China as "a country with a very large population composed of many nationalities".[97] Equality and self-government within the unified state thus became the basic ethnic principle of the CPC during the Anti-Japanese War. In the early 1940s, the concept of establishing autonomous districts for the Mongols and Hui on the basis of ethnic equality was proposed and promoted by the Shensi-Kansu-Ningsia Border Region (one of the Bases of the CPC) and by other "liberated" areas in northern China.[98] Ethnic equality, autonomous rights in relation to political, economic and cultural affairs, minority representation in local governments and congresses, respect for minority customs, traditions, religion and language, improvement of livelihood were highlighted in the autonomous districts' policies.[99] Although

94 Liu Shaoqi, "Kangri youji zhanzheng zhong de ruogan jiben wenti [Some Questions in Relation to the Fundamental Policies in Anti-Japan Guerrilla Warfare] (16/10/1937)", in Jin Binghao (ed), supra note 70, at pp. 207–208.

95 "The CPC's Public Statement on the KMT-CPC Co-operation (22/09/1937)"; Mao Zedong, "Urgent Tasks of the Chinese Revolution since the Formation of the KMT-CPC United Front (29/09/1937)". Full English text is available in Conrad Brandt, Benjamin Schwartz and John Fairbank (eds), supra note 71, at pp. 245–257.

96 Mao Zedong, "Lun xin jieduan [On the New Stage] (10/1938)", in Jin Binghao (ed), supra note 70, at p. 223.

97 Mao Zedong, *Selected Works of Mao Tse-Tung: Volume II* (Pergamon Press, 1965), p. 306; "zhongguo geming he zhongguo gongchandang [the Chinese Revolution and the Chinese Communist Party] (12/1939)", in the United Front Work Department of the CPCCC (ed), supra note 88, p. 626.

98 "Shanganning bianqu shizheng gangling [the Administrative Programme of the Shensi-Kansu-Ningsia Border Region] (01/05/1941)", in Jin Binghao (ed), supra note 70, p. 285; the North-western Working Committee of the CPCCC, "zhonggong zhongyang xibei gognzuo weiyuanhui guanyu huihui minzu wenti de tigang [An Outline of the Nationality Question of the Hui] (1940)" and "zhonggong zhongyang xibei gognzuo weiyuanhui guanyu kangzhan zhong menggu minzu wenti tigang [An Outline of the Nationality Question of the Mongols] (1940)", in the United Front Work Department of the CPCCC (ed), supra note 88, pp. 652–655, 664–667.

99 Ibid.

self-determination was referenced to by Mao in On Coalition Government (1945), the emphasis was placed on assisting the minorities to realise self-government in autonomous republics within the Chinese federation.[100]

100 The 1965 English edition of "On Coalition Government (1945)" reads: "[g]ive the minority nationalities in China better treatment and grant them autonomous rights... In 1924 Dr. Sun Yat-sen wrote in the Manifesto of the First National Congress of the Kuomintang that 'the Kuomintang's Principle of Nationalism has a twofold meaning, first, the liberation of the Chinese nation, and second, the equality of all the nationalities in China' and that 'the Kuomintang solemnly declares that it recognises the right to self-determination of all the nationalities in China and that a free and united republic of China (a free union of all the nationalities) will be established when the anti-imperialist and anti-warlord revolution is victorious'. The Communist Party of China is in full agreement with Dr. Sun's policy on nationalities as stated here. Communists must actively help the people of all the minority nationalities to fight for it, and help them, including all their leaders who have ties with the masses, to fight for their political, economic and cultural emancipation and development and to establish their own armies which will safeguard the people's interests. Their spoken and written languages, their manners and customs and their religious beliefs must be respected. The attitude which the Shensi-Kansu-Ningsia Border Region and the Liberated Areas in northern China have for years adopted towards the Mongolian and Hui nationalities is correct, and the work they have done has been fruitful". This English translation is cited from Mao Zedong, *Selected Works of Mao Tse-Tung: Volume III* (Pergamon Press, 1965), pp. 255–256. Some commentators have suggested that there has been a change of wording in the later edition of "On Coalition Government (1945)", where the original terms of "granting of the right to national self-determination to all national minorities" were replaced by the phrase "granting of the right to national autonomy to all national minorities". The original version stated that "[g]ive minority nationalities in China better treatment and grant them the right to self-determination and the right to establish a federal state with the Han on the basis of their free will". As cited in Huang Zhu, "Zhongguo gongchandang minzu zhengce de zhongda zhuanbian [A Great Transformation of the CPC's Policy towards Nationalities—from Federalism to Regional Autonomy of Ethnic Groups]", 04:23 *Zhongnan Minzu Daxue Xuebao* [*Journal of the South-Central University for Nationalities* (*Humanities and Social Sciences*)] (2003), p. 5; see also He Baogang, "China's National Identity: a Source of Conflict Between Democracy and State Nationalism", in Leong H. Liew and Shaoguang Wang (eds), *Nationalism, Democracy and National Integration in China* (Routledge Curzon, 2004), pp. 170–195 at pp. 177–178. Although self-determination was used in the document, it did not imply that Mao genuinely supported the right of minorities to self-determination, especially the right to secede, in 1945. The reasons were as follows: first, prior to and after this specific period, self-determination was rarely mentioned in Mao's writings. In contrast, autonomy was the term often used by him in regard to the treatment of the minorities. Second, "On Coalition Government" was written in 1945 to advocate a coalition government with the KMT. By referencing to the principle of nationalism proposed by Sun in 1924, which recognised the right to self-determination, Mao was offering the KMT a gesture of good will. Third, self-determination and federalism were often used together. Considering the fact that federalism was indeed mentioned and discussed a number of times in the preparatory stage of establishing the PRC, self-determination should be understood as minority

(4) The Civil War (1946–1949)

After the breakdown of the post-war negotiation, the communists put its concept of regional autonomy into practice as a new form of self-determination and ethnic equality.[101] The Autonomous Government of Inner Mongolia, a regional democratic government with a high degree of autonomy for all nationalities settling in Inner Mongolia, was first established as an example.[102] With the "liberation" of more territories, the CPC indicated its attitude towards the national minorities by advocating "national equality and unification", "self-government" and "regional autonomy". The 1949 editorial of the Xinhua News Agency on Tibet could be considered as a sign of the repudiation of the right to secede. It stated that "Tibet is a part of Chinese territory and has a long history of being a member of the Chinese nation and maintaining the brotherhood with Han and other nationalities".[103] The Chinese People's Liberation Army (PLA), therefore, "must liberate all Chinese territories, including Tibet, Xinjiang, Hainan Islands and Taiwan; not even one inch of land could be left outside of the reign of the PRC".[104] In the discussion of the Chinese People's Political Consultative Conference on the form of the new Chinese state, the establishment of a unitary multiethnic people's republic replaced the CPC's long-term alleged goal of federalism, with the aim of preventing the imperialists from taking advantage of the right to self-determination.[105] The minority right to self-determination was thus tailored into a regime of regional autonomy, which later became constitutionalised in the PRC.[106]

---

self-government in autonomous republics within the Chinese federation. See also Chapter 3, Section 4 "China's Approach to the Right to Self-determination".

101 Mengyuan (Yolanda) Yu, *Instrumental Autonomy, Political Socialisation, and Citizenship Identity: A Case Study of Korean Minority Citizenship Identity, Bilingual Education and Modern Media Life in the Post-Communism Transitioning China* (Springer, 2017), p. 43; Qianfan Zhang, *The Constitution of China: A Contextual Analysis* (Hart Publishing, 2012), p. 109.

102 "Neimenggu zizhi zhengfu shizheng gangling [the Administrative Programme of the Inner Mongolia Autonomous Government] (27/04/1947)", in Jin Binghao (ed), supra note 70, at p. 345.

103 The Editorial of Xinhua News Agency, "Juebu rongxu waiguo qinluezhe tunbing zhongguo de lingtu—Xizang [Never Allow the Foreign Aggressors to Annex Chinese Territory—Tibet] (02/09/1949)", in Jin Binghao (ed), ibid, at pp. 404–405.

104 Ibid, p. 406.

105 Zhou Enlai, "Guanyu renmin zhengxie de jige wenti [On A Few Questions of the Chinese People's Political Consultative Conference] (07/09/1949)", in Jin Binghao (ed), ibid, at pp. 408–409.

106 The Common Program of the Chinese People's Political Consultative Conference, Article 51; the 1954 Constitution, Article 3; the 1975, 1978 and 1982 Constitutions, Article 4.

The CPC's understanding of self-determination underwent a few jumps, swinging back and forth between Soviet influence and Mao's thoughts. The utilisation of soviet assertion of self-determination and the secession of nationalities, to some extent, benefited the survival of the CPC from Jiang's Encirclement Campaigns. In the struggle for socialism, however, the principle was ignored by the CPC after 1938 and totally disregarded in the post-revolutionary era. The fact that the Han people populated about 90 percent of the country left the minorities in a comparatively insignificant position. Furthermore, although the Long March may have "seeded (the principle of self-determination) in eleven provinces", before it sprouted, the imperialists' advocacy of self-determination had appealed to minority groups more successfully than the CPC's proposals. Mao's seizure of Party power also contributed to the policy changes. As mentioned above, national unification was one of Mao's lifetime ventures. As early as 1919, he wrote: "… the great union of the Chinese people will be achieved earlier than that of any other place or people …"[107] In a private interview in 1936, he stated:

> when the People's revolution has been victorious in China the Outer Mongolian Republic will automatically become a part of the Chinese federation, at their own will. The Mohanmmedan and Tibetan peoples likewise will form autonomous republics attached to the China federation.[108]

Seen in that light, it is not difficult to understand the gradually decreased emphasis on self-determination in the communist context.

2.3 Concluding Remarks

In China's struggle for statehood, the political principle of self-determination was applied in different contexts. On the one hand, it had been claimed by different forces as the basis for national independence. The first attempt of China to rely upon the principle to restore territorial sovereignty at the Peace Conference of Paris did not achieve a satisfactory result. The voice of the Chinese people was ignored and yielded to the political needs of the Great Powers. Sun and the KMT advocated self-determination to justify Chinese nationalism after the Soviet-KMT collaboration. The communists also adopted the Soviet approach,

107 Quoted in Stuart Schram, supra note 86, at p. 799.
108 As quoted in Walker Connor, supra note 40, at p. 80.

pledging the principle of national self-determination in the proposed Soviet Republic of China in the early phase of the CPC. On the other hand, the Soviet model of self-determination connotated a right of the minorities to secede. Minority groups, therefore, were accorded opportunities to determine their own destiny and indeed successfully established regional regimes with foreign assistance. The application of self-determination would inevitably lead to a result that the modern state of China would lose much of the Qing's imperial territory that both the KMT and CPC had attempted to claim. This was unacceptable to both parties. Hence, the nationalists emphasised the racial tie of all ethnic groups and reinterpreted the right of the minorities to self-determination as the right to regional self-government, while the communists gradually abandoned self-determination in the official discourse, starting from limiting self-determination to "the tolling masses" of all nationalities to ethnic equality and autonomy within the unified Chinese state.

The adoption and application of self-determination in the Chinese context reinforced the invention of a Chinese nation that embraced all ethnic groups living in the territory. Minority claims of self-determination supported by foreign forces during this period, e.g. independence movements in Manchuria, Mongolia, Xinjiang and Tibet in the 1930s, revealed the actual threats that the concept of self-determination may exert upon the proposed nationhood and territorial integrity. Therefore, different political forces in China assumed a very cautious attitude towards the principle of self-determination, insisting that the Chinese nation had the right to self-determination and the minorities as the constituent groups were guaranteed the right to self-government and autonomy. Such an approach was followed since then by the governments of China.

CHAPTER 3

The Right to Self-determination in the Chinese Context

This Chapter examines the application of the right to self-determination in the Chinese context. It is divided into three sections. It first looks at international legal understanding of the right to self-determination and explains key concepts in international law that are related to self-determination, i.e. remedial secession, autonomy, and minority rights. The second section focuses on three rival self-determination claims made by Tibet, Hong Kong and Macau in the decolonisation process, which have challenged the official assertion that self-determination is exercised by the whole Chinese people. It is argued that the Chinese government has made a solid claim under international law, by asserting that the Chinese people, composed of all ethnic groups, have the right to self-determination and the minorities are entitled to territorial autonomy as a means of exercising internal self-determination. The last section of the chapter examines two constitutional arrangements specifically designed to facilitate the exercise of internal self-determination within the state, i.e. the "one country two systems" and regional autonomy for the minorities.

3.1 An Overview of the Right to Self-determination in International Law

Self-determination as a fundamental principle[1] of international law became well established after the Second World War.[2] A number of international

1 Self-determination has been referred to as a principle and/or a right by different international documents and by international and domestic judicial bodies. Unless otherwise stated, the term in this book is loosely used. The principle of self-determination is interchangeable with the right to self-determination. See James Crawford, *The Creation of States in International Law (2nd Edition)* (Clarendon Press, 2006), pp. 114–115; Karen Knop, *Diversity and Self-determination in International Law* (Cambridge University Press, 2002), pp. 33–34; James Summers, *Peoples and International Law (2nd Edition)* (Martinus Nijhoff Publishers, 2014), pp. 70–78; Alexandra Xanthaki, *Indigenous Rights and United Nations Standards: Self-determination, Culture and Land* (Cambridge University Press, 2007), pp. 155–157.

2 Antonio Cassese, *Self-determination of Peoples: A Legal Reappraisal* (Cambridge University Press, 1995); James Crawford, ibid, p. 122; "The Right of Self-determination in International Law: Its Development and Future", in Philip Alston (ed), *Peoples' Rights* (Oxford University

 | DOI:10.1163/9789004380578_005

instruments have incorporated this principle, such as the UN Charter, the 1966 twin Covenants on human rights, and the GA Resolution 1514.[3] In the process of decolonisation, the right of colonial and dependent peoples to self-determination is widely considered to be a part of customary international law.[4] Beyond the colonial context, however, the application of the principle of self-determination remains unclear.[5] The uncertainty stems from the contradictory nature of the concept itself: self-determination could be the basis of statehood, or it may challenge it.[6] The application of self-determination is also contentious in the light of diverse interpretations of the undefined concept "peoples", or "nations". The term "peoples" has been interpreted to refer to the population of a state, the population of a colony, or the inhabitants of a particular territory within a national unit.[7]

Press, 2001), pp. 7–67 at p. 38; Thomas Musgrave, *Self-determination and National Minorities* (Oxford University Press, 1997), p. 62.

3 The Charter of the United Nation, Articles 1, 55; the GA Resolution 1514, Clause 2; the GA Resolution 2625; the UN Declaration on the Rights of Indigenous Peoples (UNDRIP), Articles 3, 4; the International Covenant on Civil and Political Rights (ICCPR), Article 1; the International Covenant on Economic, Social and Cultural Rights (ICESCR), Article 1.

4 The International Court of Justice held in the Namibia case, the Western Sahara case, the Case Concerning East Timor, and the Kosovo Advisory Opinion that the principle of self-determination is one of essential principles of customary international law concerning decolonisation. Namibia, ICJ Report (1971), pp. 31–32, paras.52–53; West Sahara, ICJ Report (1975), pp. 31–33, paras.54–59; East Timor, ICJ Report (1995), p. 102, para.29; Kosovo, ICJ Report (2010), p. 37, para.79. See also Helen Quane, "The United Nations and the Evolving Right to Self-determination", 47:03 *International and Comparative Law Quarterly* (1998), pp. 554.

5 In James Crawford's words, it is *lex obscura*. James Crawford, supra note 2, 2001, p. 38.

6 Martti Koskenniemi, "National Self-determination Today: Problems of Legal Theory and Practice", 43 *International and Comparative Law Quarterly* (1994), p. 249; Jan Klabbers, "The Right To Be Taken Seriously: Self-determination in International Law", 28 *Human Rights Quarterly* (2006), pp. 187–188; Marc Weller, *Escaping the Self-determination Trap* (Martinus Nijhoff Publishers, 2008), pp. 30–31; Joshua Castellino, *International Law and Self-determination: the Interplay of the Politics of Territorial Possession with Formulations of Post-colonial "National" Identity Developments in International Law* (Martinus Nijhoff Publishers, 2000), p. 9.

7 Indigenous peoples have recently been considered to have the right to self-determination under Article 3 of the United Nations Declaration on the Rights of Indigenous Peoples. Cassese argues that the inhabitants of a particular territory within a territorial state may also have the right if they are so recognised in the state constitution. A. Cassese, "Chapter 4 The Self-determination of Peoples", in L. Henkin (ed), *The International Bill of Rights: the Covenant on Civil and Political Rights* (Columbia University Press, 1981), pp. 92–113 at pp. 94–95. Pomerance holds the view that the peoples who are dependent or subject to alien subjugation, domination and exploitation could invoke the right as well. M. Pomerance, *Self-determination in Law and Practice: the New Doctrine in the United Nations* (Martinus Nijhoff Publishers, 1982), pp. 14–15. Raic contends that, apart from the entire population of states as a people, subdivisions and subgroups within a state who have "collective individuality" could

3.1.1 *Colonial Self-determination*

Two important resolutions on colonial self-determination were adopted by the General Assembly in 1960. The first one—Declaration on the Granting of Independence to Colonial Countries and Peoples (Resolution 1514), as the name suggested, vested colonial peoples with the right to freely determine their own future. Paragraph 1 provided that the subjection of the peoples to alien subjugation, domination and exploitation constituted a denial of fundamental human rights and was thus contrary to the Charter. Immediate steps shall be taken to transfer all powers to the peoples in "trust and non-self-governing territories or all other territories which have not yet attained independence" to enable them to express their free will and desire.[8] The International Court of Justice (ICJ) further reaffirmed in the Advisory Opinion on *Namibia*:

> the subsequent development of international law in regard to non-self-governing territories, as enshrined in the Charter of the United Nations, made the principle of self-determination applicable to all of them.[9]

The Resolution 1541 with its Annex then set out criteria for testing the achievement of "a full measure of self-government" and non-self-governing status. It stated that the realisation of self-determination could be achieved by establishing an independent state, or associating with or integrating into an existing state.[10] Hence, Cassese has argued that the application of self-determination in the colonial context focuses upon the external dimension of self-determination and such a right expires once it has been exercised.[11] The internal self-determination of colonial peoples, however, was not emphasised in the process.[12] To identify a non-self-governing status, Principle IV required geographical separateness and ethnical and/or cultural distinction to establish a *prima facie* case.[13] It appeared to preclude geographically contiguous

also be considered as peoples. David Raic, *Statehood and the Law of Self-determination* (Kulwer Law International, 2002), pp. 242–171. See also Helen Quane, supra note 4, pp. 537–558.

8 The GA Resolution 1514, para.5.

9 Namibia, ICJ Report (1971), p. 31, para.52.

10 The GA Resolution 1541, Principle VI.

11 Weller also held a similar opinion. See Antonio Cassese, supra note 2, pp. 72–73; Marc Weller, supra note 6, pp. 39–40; see also Simone Van Den Driest, *Remedial Secession: A Right to External Self-determination As a Remedy to Serious Injustices?* (Intersentia, 2013), p. 37; Christopher Fromherz, "Indigenous Peoples' Courts: Egalitarian Juridical Pluralism, Self-determination, and the UN Declaration on the Rights of Indigenous Peoples", 156 *University of Pennsylvania Law Review* (2008), p. 1359.

12 Antonio Cassese, ibid, p.74.

13 The GA Resolution 1541 (XV), 15 GAOR(1960) Supplement No.16, (A/4684).

territories from the definition,[14] as the colonial situation may only be found in the territory which was separate by ocean or sea from the dominating powers, i.e. the overseas territories.[15]

Although the Resolution 1514 aimed to grant colonial peoples independence, "colonialism" itself was not explicitly defined by the Resolution.[16] The application of self-determination to the peoples of trust and non-self-governing territories, the old forms of colonialism, seemed to be beyond doubt.[17] The Annex contained 12 principles on the determinacy of whether or not an obligation of member states existed to transmit the information called for under Article 73(e) of the Charter. While the main stream approach seemed to agree that the principle applied to colonial/dependent peoples,[18] a different argument was made, with an attempt to establish that "alien domination" may also exist within sovereign states.[19] Tibet had been specifically referred to by some delegates as an illustration of this kind during the GA discussions.[20]

Colonial self-determination aimed to grant dependent peoples a right to freely determine their own future, be it independence, or association with or integration into other states. The application of such a right was limited in the sense that the right was exercised by the population of the colony as a whole and the territorial integrity of the colony as well as the existing states

14 James Crawford, "The Creation of States in International Law (1979)", cited in Steven Wheatley, *Democracy, Minorities and International Law* (Cambridge University Press, 2005), p. 74.

15 Rhiannon Morgan, *Transforming Law and Institution: Indigenous Peoples, the UN and Human Rights* (Ashgate Publishing, 2011), pp. 94–95.

16 James Summers, supra note 1, at pp. 207–209.

17 Namibia, ICJ Report (1971), p. 31, para.52; Simone Van Den Driest, supra note 11, p. 31.

18 Helen Quane, supra note 4, p. 555; Joshua Castellino and Jeremie Gilbert, "Self-determination, Indigenous Peoples and Minorities", 3 *Macquarie Law Journal* (2003), p. 162.

19 H. Gros Espiell, "The Right to Self-Determination: Implementation of United Nations Resolutions", UN Doc E/CN.4/Sub.2/405/Rev.1, 1980, p. 10, para.60; p. 14, para.90; M. Pomerance, supra note 7, p. 14. Koskenniemi notes that self-determination was used in the GA resolutions on the apartheid regime in South Africa. Martti Koskenniemi, supra note 6, pp. 247–248. The so-called Belgian Thesis also argues that "a number of States were administering within their own frontiers which were not governed by the ordinary law; territories with well-defined limits, inhabited by homogeneous peoples differing from the rest of the population in race, language and culture. Those populations were disenfranchised; they took no part in the national life; they did not enjoy self-government in any sense of the word". Belgium, 9 GAOR (1954) 4th Committee, 419th Meeting, (UN Doc. A/C.4/SR. 419) para.20, cited in James Summers, supra note 1, at p. 218.

20 For instance, Ireland, Thailand and Italy. See Ireland, 15 GAOR, 935th Meeting, (A/PV 935), para.93; Thailand, 15 GAOR, 938th Meeting, (A/PV 938), para.111; Italy, 15 GAOR, 937th Meeting, (A/PV 937), para.85.

should be respected.[21] This territorial emphasis in the decolonisation process, however, was not without exceptions. Pomerance noted that the partition of a colony, usually on ethnic grounds, could also be found in practice, e.g. Ruanda-Urundi, British Cameroons, British India, and the Gilbert and Ellice Islands.[22] Furthermore, the right of dependent peoples to self-determination had been disregarded in certain cases, including East Timor, West Irian, Damao and Din, and Goa. The ICJ stated in the *West Sahara* Advisory Opinion:

> the validity of the principle of self-determination ... is not affected by the fact that in certain cases the General Assembly has dispensed with the requirement of consulting the inhabitants of a given territory ... [which] were based either on the consideration that a certain population did not constitute a "people" entitled to self-determination or on the conviction that a consultation was totally unnecessary, in view of special circumstances.[23]

The political strength of the parties involved or the consideration of regional security and stability might be possible reasons that contributed to this inconsistent application.[24] As will be discussed in the next sections, Hong Kong and Macau constituted such exceptions to colonial self-determination, as the will of the population concerned was disregarded in the territorial transfers.[25]

3.1.2 *Self-determination in the Post-colonial Era*

The principle of self-determination continues to evolve beyond the decolonisation process. Outside of the colonial context, self-determination is still expected to be exercised consistently with the principle of territorial integrity. In international documents, self-determination is usually balanced with territorial integrity. The GA Resolution 2625, the UN Declaration on the Rights of Indigenous Peoples (UNDRIP), and the 1975 Helsinki Final Act provide that the right to self-determination should not be interpreted as "authorising or encouraging

21 The GA Resolution 1514, Para. 6; Antonio Cassese, supra note 2, at pp.72–73; M. Pomerance, supra note 7, at pp. 18–19; David Raic, supra note 7, at pp. 208–209; Helen Quane, supra note 4, at pp. 555–556; Joshua Castellino, supra note 6, at pp. 109–115.

22 M. Pomerance, supra note 7, pp. 19–20; Hurst Hannum, *Autonomy, Sovereignty, and Self-determination: the Accommodation of Conflicting Rights* (*Revised Edition*) (University of Pennsylvania Press, 1990), p. 36.

23 West Sahara, ICJ Report (1975), p. 25, para.59.

24 J. Engers, "From Sacred Trust to Self-determination", 24:1–2 *Netherlands International Law Review* (1977), p. 91

25 See Sections 3.3 and 3.4.

any action that would dismember or impair ... the territorial integrity or political unity of sovereign and independent States ..."[26] Judicial bodies are also in support of such an opinion. In *Reference re Secession of Quebec,* the Canadian Supreme Court states that the principle of self-determination "has evolved within a framework of respect for the territorial integrity of existing states" and the exercise of such a right "must be sufficiently limited to prevent threats to an existing state's territorial integrity".[27] This idea could be found in *Tatarstan,*[28] *Chechnya,*[29] *Katangese Peoples' Congress,*[30] and *Kevin Mgwanga Gunme.*[31] More importantly, sovereignty and territorial integrity of states are inclined to be respected and preserved in practice.[32] Self-determination does not necessarily challenge the principle of territorial integrity, as self-determination can be fulfilled internally through a domestic framework. The conflict, however, may arise in exceptional cases when self-determination is claimed by segment(s) of a state's population.[33]

(1) Remedial Secession

Many authors tend to emphasise self-determination as the continuous "entitlement" of the peoples within sovereign states in the post-colonial era, the effective exercise of which would secure territorial sovereignty.[34] This, in turn, involves the situation that the continuous exercise of self-determination of a specific group is denied. This approach then argues that the aggrieved group may claim secession as a self-help remedy, or in Buchheit's words, the remedial

26 The GA Resolution 2625, Principle 5 Paragraph 7; the UNDRIP, Article 46 (1); the 1975 Helsinki Final Act, Principle VIII (1). The 1993 Vienna Declaration and Programme of Action, Principle I (2), adopts a similar clause.

27 Reference re: Secession of Quebec, [1998] 2 S.C.R. 217, paras.112, 127.

28 The Constitutional Court of the Russian Federation, the Tatarstan Case, 1992, in 30:3 *Statutes and Decisions—the Laws of the USSR and Its Successor States* (1994), pp. 32–48 at p. 40.

29 The Constitutional Court of the Russian Federation, the Chechnya Case, 1995, in 31:5 *Statutes and Decisions—the Laws of the USSR and Its Successor States* (1995), pp. 48–94 at p. 52.

30 The African Commission on Human and Peoples' Right (ACHPR), 75/92 Katangese Peoples' Congress *v.* Zaire. para.26–28

31 The ACHPR, 266/03 Kevin Mgwanga Gunme et al *v.* Cameroon, paras.188–191,199.

32 See infra note 50.

33 Reference re: Secession of Quebec, [1998] 2 S.C.R. 217, para.126.

34 Antonio Cassese, supra note 2, pp. 101–140; James Crawford, supra note 1, p. 117; David Raic, supra note 7, pp. 226–307; Simone Van Den Driest, supra note 11, p. 4; Michael Scharf, "Earned Sovereignty: Juridical Underpinnings", 31:3 *Denver Journal of International Law and Policy* (2004), pp. 381–383.

secession.[35] The rationale of this argument can be found in Principle 5 Paragraph 7 of the GA Resolution 2625.[36] Paragraph 7 states that the protection of the territorial integrity of a state is conditioned upon the existence of a government that represents the whole people of the territory without distinction as to "race, creed or colour". It suggests that secession could be justified under the Resolution if the government is discriminatory and unrepresentative. A literal reading of Paragraph 7 may reach a conclusion that a representative government would exist as long as it is not a racist regime.[37] However, Paragraph 7 has been broadly interpreted to encompass racial and religious groups[38] as well as ethnic or national groups[39] living in the states, who are denied access to government. The conditions that may trigger secession are also extended to include oppression[40] and gross violation of human rights and freedoms.[41] Therefore, some scholars assert that when internal self-determination is exhausted, for example if no effective and realistic remedy is available or can be reasonably expected, secession should be seen as a remedy of last resort under these circumstances.[42] In the meantime, Buchanan finds the underpinning of secession in the democratic theory.[43] Unlike some writers who, relying on the plebiscitary theory,[44] support a general right to secede on the basis of democracy, he instead argues that the right to secede would only arise "in response to serious and persisting grievances".[45] Buchanan points out that allowing a majority of persons in a particular territory within the state to secede when they so decide does not fit democratic values, as the plebiscitary right to secede

35 Lee Buchheit, *Secession: the Legitimacy of Self-determination* (Yale University Press, 1978), p. 222.

36 The 1993 Vienna Declaration and Programme of Action, Principle I (2).

37 M. Pomerance, supra note 7, p. 39; Thomas Musgrave, supra note 2, p. 188.

38 Antonio Cassese, supra note 2, pp. 114, 120.

39 James Summers, supra note 1, p. 230; David Raic, supra note 7, pp. 251–258.

40 Lee Buchheit, supra note 35, p. 222.

41 Antonio Cassese, supra note 2, pp. 119–120; James Summers, supra note 1, p. 236; Christian Tomuschat, "Chapter 1 Secession and Self-determination", in Marcelo Kohen (ed), *Secession: International Law Perspective* (Cambridge University Press, 2006), pp. 23–45 at p. 39; Jose Woehrling, as cited in Karen Knop, supra note 1, p. 77. See also the African Commission on Human and Peoples' Right, 75/92 Katangese Peoples' Congress *v.* Zaire. para.27; Communication 266/03 Kevin Mgwanga Gunme et al *v.* Cameroon, para.199.

42 David Raic, supra note 7, p. 326; Simone Van Den Driest, supra note 11, p. 113; James Summers, supra note 1, p. 236.

43 Allen Buchanan, "Chapter 2 Democracy and Secession", in Margaret Moore (ed), *National Self-determination and Secession* (Oxford University Press, 1998), pp. 14–33.

44 Steven Wheatley, supra note 14, p. 89.

45 Allen Buchanan, supra note 43; *Justice, Legitimacy and Self-determination: Moral Foundations for International Law* (Oxford University Press, 2004), pp. 350–354.

might be used as a strategic bargaining tool which would in essence jeopardise democracy.[46]

Although there are scholarly arguments favouring secession, the right to secede is not widely accepted as a part of positive international law outside of the colonial context.[47] International documents, i.e. the GA Resolution 2625 and the 1993 Vienna Declaration and Programme of Action, as the touchstone for the right of secession, are considered to be soft law,[48] and the democracy theory may only serve as the moral underpinning for secession.[49] More importantly, state practice and *opinio juris* suggest that there is no general support for a right to secede in international law.[50] The cases of *Quebec*,[51] *Kosovo*,[52] *Tatarstan*,[53] and *Chechnya*[54] deliver a similar opinion. Furthermore, it could be difficult to find a case in international practice that has been unanimously referred to as the example of this kind.[55] Bangladesh is considered to be a good illustration of unilateral secession, but arguments have been made that Bangladesh was not accepted by the international community as a secessionist movement,[56] or that Bangladesh was recognised on the basis of

46 Allen Buchanan, supra note 43, pp. 21–25.

47 Christian Tomuschat, supra note 41; Daniel Philpott, "Chapter 5 Self-determination in Practice", in Margaret Moore (ed), supra note 43, pp. 79–102; P. Hilpold, "Self-determination in the 21st Century—Modern Perspectives for an Old Concept", 36 *Israel Yearbook on Human Rights* (2005), pp. 247, 269; Jan Klabbers, supra note 6, p. 198; Karen Knop, supra note 1, p. 73; Hurst Hannum, supra note 22, p. 49; Simone Van Den Driest, supra note 11, pp. 297–319; Steven Wheatley, supra note 14, p. 91; Mauro Barelli, "Shaping Indigenous Self-determination: Promising or Unsatisfactory Solutions?", 13 *International Community Law Review* (2011), pp. 415, 423.

48 Christian Tomuschat, ibid, pp. 35–36

49 Thomas Franck argues that international law has gone some distance toward the recognition of a right to democratic governance. Put differently, the right to democracy is still *de lege ferenda*. See Thomas Franck, "The Emerging Right to Democratic Governance", 86 *American Journal of International Law* (1992), pp. 46–91; Allen Buchanan, supra note 43, p. 14; Donald Horowtiz, "Chapter 9 Self-determination: Politics, Philosophy and Law", in Margaret Moore (ed), supra note 43, pp. 181–214 at p. 204; David Raic, supra note 7, p. 278.

50 Simone Van Den Driest, supra note 11, at pp. 189–311; Christian Tomuschat, supra note 41, at pp. 26–37; James Summers, supra note 1, at pp. 230–239; Thomas Musgrave, supra note 2, at p. 104; Caroline Foster, "Articulating Self-determination in the Draft Declaration on the Rights of Indigenous Peoples", 21 *European Journal of International Law* (2001), p. 153.

51 Reference re: Secession of Quebec, [1998] 2 S.C.R. 217, paras.111, 112.

52 Kosovo, ICJ Report (2010), para.82.

53 The Constitutional Court of the Russian Federation, the Tatarstan Case, 1992, supra note 29, at p. 41.

54 The Constitutional Court of the Russian Federation, the Chechnya Case, 1995, supra note 30.

55 Simone Van Den Driest, supra note 11, at p. 309.

56 Hurst Hannum, supra note 22, at p. 46.

"effectiveness".[57] On the contrary, the principle of sovereignty and territorial integrity is usually upheld in international practice, which again has been confirmed in the Kosovo case,[58] Crimea Annexation,[59] and Catalan crisis.[60] Hence, it is arguable that contemporary international law does not entail a right to secede.

(2) The Right to Self-determination in the Human Rights Context

Self-determination has also been developed from human rights perspective. A number of international human rights documents embrace the right to self-determination, including the 1966 twin Covenants on human rights, the UNDRIP, as well as certain regional instruments.[61] The twin Covenants on human rights recognise the right of all peoples to self-determination, which entails the right to "freely determine their political status and freely pursue their economic, social and cultural development".[62] In Cassese's view, Article 1 of the Covenants provides all members of a population an ongoing right to express the popular will through internal decision-making process.[63] Higgins links the

57 Christian Tomuschat, supra note 41, at p. 30.

58 Ibid, pp. 27–29; Daniel Philpott, supra note 47, at p. 86. In the dissenting opinion of Judge Koroma, he asserts that the principle of sovereignty and territorial integrity of states should prevail over the principle of self-determination. Dissenting Opinion of Judge Koroma, paras.22, 23. Statements submitted by many states also emphasise the importance of the principle of territorial integrity. See James Summers, supra note 1, pp. 233–237.

59 General Assembly Resolution 68/262: Territorial integrity of Ukraine, UN Doc. A/RES/68/262. Russia, however, has retreated from its previous position, claiming the right to self-determination includes a right to independence. See Simone Van Den Driest, "Crimea's Separation from Ukraine: An Analysis of the Right to Self-determination and (Remedial) Secession in International Law", 62 *Netherlands International Law Review* (2015), pp. 330–331.

60 The spokeswoman for the Ministry of Foreign Affairs reaffirms China's position, stating that "China's position on this issue has been consistent and unequivocal. We think it falls within Spain's internal affairs. We understand and support the Spanish government's effort to uphold national unity, ethnic solidarity and territorial integrity, oppose the act of splitting the country and undermining the rule of law, and believe Spain is capable of upholding the social order and safeguarding the rights and interests of its citizens". Foreign Ministry Spokesperson Hua Chunying's Regular Press Conference on 30/10/2017, http://www.fmprc.gov.cn/mfa_eng/xwfw_665399/s2510_665401/2511_665403/t1505871.shtml, last accessed on 11/12/2017. France, Russia, the UK, the US, and EU have expressed a similar opinion.

61 For instance, the African Charter on Human and Peoples Rights, Article 20; the Arab Charter on Human Rights, Article 1.

62 The twin Covenant on human rights, Article 1 (1).

63 Antonio Cassese, supra note 2, pp. 53–54;

right to self-determination with "representative and participatory democracy" under Article 25 of the International Covenant on Civil and Political Rights (ICCPR).[64] She argues that "if Article 1 is the 'what', Article 25 is 'how' ".[65] This, however, does not preclude other forms of representative government if it is the result of the free expression of the popular will.[66]

The peoples are the rights holders under the Covenants. However, the Covenants fail to clarify who the peoples are under Article 1, as the states are so divided on the issue during the *travaux preparatoires* and in subsequent practice.[67] Various definitions of the term "peoples" had been submitted by the states in their draft proposals.[68] But no elaborate definition of "peoples" was finally included under Article 1. It was only agreed that the term "peoples" should be understood "in its most general sense and that no definition was necessary".[69] Interpretations on the scope of application of Article 1 include "peoples under foreign domination",[70] populations of sovereign states,[71] and constituent peoples within sovereign states.[72] The UNDRIP further extends the right to self-determination to embrace indigenous peoples.[73] The indigenous right to self-determination, however, places its emphasis upon the right to autonomy or self-government and political participation within sovereign states.[74]

Nonetheless, it seems that the majority of states do not intend to apply the notion of peoples to embrace minorities.[75] Instead, a minority clause is

64 Rosalyn Higgins, "Self-determination and Secession", in Julie Dahlitz (ed), *Secession and International Law* (The United Nations, 2003), pp. 21–38 at p. 30; also cited in David Raic, supra note 7, p. 274.

65 Rosalyn Higgins, ibid, p. 30.

66 David Raic, supra note 7, pp. 278–279.

67 Helen Quane, supra note 4, pp. 559–560; James Summers, supra note 1, pp. 310–315.

68 Helen Quane, ibid, p. 559.

69 Cited in Helen Quane, ibid, p. 560.

70 The Declaration of India, as cited in Thomas Musgrave, supra note 2, p. 93.

71 Steven Wheatley, supra note 14, p. 80; Antonio Cassese, supra note 2, p.59; James Summers, supra note 1, p. 305; Joshua Castellino and Jeremie Gilbert, supra note 18, p. 165.

72 Finland, the 5th Periodic Report Submitted under Article 40 of the ICCPR (2003), CCPR/C/FIN/2003/5, paras.86–92. Many states from the former soviet bloc constitutionally recognise the existence of the "peoples" within their states.

73 The UNDRIP, Article 3. See also Chapter 4, Section 4.4 "The Definition of Indigenous Peoples and Indigenous Situation in China".

74 The UNDRIP, Articles 4, 46. See also Alexandra Xanthaki, supra note 1, at pp. 110–112; Caroline Foster, supra note 50; James Summers, supra note 1, at p. 271–272; Mauro Barelli, supra note 47, at pp. 419–423, 426–434.

75 Joshua Castellino and Jeremie Gilbert, supra note 18, p. 165; Antonio Cassese, supra note 2, pp. 61–62; Helen Quane, supra note 4, p. 561;

formulated separately. Article 27 of the ICCPR lays down special rights for persons belonging to ethnic, religious or linguistic minorities. In general, the right of the peoples, as a collective, to self-determination is distinguishable from individual rights[76] protected under Article 27.[77] Minority rights are considered to be different from the peoples' rights. In practice, the Human Rights Committee (HRC) has been reluctant to link the right of self-determination to minorities.[78] The rights of minorities can be divided into two categories: the right of minorities as a part of the population to participate in public life on the basis of equality under Article 1, and other rights that have been granted by the Covenants.

Participation in public life on the basis of equality may not be enough to secure minorities' interests in the society,[79] due to its feature of being numerically inferior to the rest of the population. In this case, the will of the majority does not necessarily equate the will of the whole population. Thus, power-sharing schemes to balance power and different interests are recommended to resolve the issue.[80] Autonomy, as the middle way between independence and territorial integrity, has been viewed as an alternative to guarantee participatory democracy, to avoid ethnic conflicts, and to implement minority rights.[81] According to geographic distribution of ethnic groups and the scope

76 The HRC admits that Article 27 has a collective nature. See also Chapter 6, Section 6.1.2 "State Obligations under the ICCPR".

77 The HRC, General Comment 23, para.3.1.

78 Joshua Castellino, "The Protection of Minorities and Indigenous Peoples in International Law: a Comparative Temporal Analysis", 17 *International Journal on Minority and Group Rights* (2010), pp. 412–413.

79 Yash Ghai, "Autonomy as a Participatory Right in the Modern Democratic State: Public participation, Autonomy and Minorities", in Zelim Skurbaty (ed), *Beyond a One-dimensional State: an Emerging Right to Autonomy?* (Martinus Nijhoff Publishers, 2005), pp. 3–45 at p. 5.

80 Asbjorn Eide, "In Search of Constructive Alternatives to Secession", in Christian Tomuschat (ed), *Modern Law of Self-determination* (Martinus Nijhoff Publishers, 1993), pp. 139–176 at pp. 165–166; Marc Weller, "Settling Self-determination Conflicts: An Introduction", in Marc Weller and Barbara Metzger (eds), *Settling Self-determination Disputes: Complex Power-sharing in Theory and Practice* (Martinus Nijhoff Publishers, 2008), pp. xii-xvii.

81 Hans-Joachim Heintze, "Territorial Autonomy and International Stability: Pros and Cons from the Viewpoint of International Law", in Zelim Skurbaty (ed), supra note 79, pp. 47–62, at pp. 50–54; Hurst Hannum, "Territorial Autonomy: Permanent Solution or Step Towards Secession?", in Zelim Skurbaty (ed), ibid, pp.153–159 at p.153; Markku Suksi, "Autonomy, Minorities and Self-determination—the Protection of the Rights of Minorities by Means of Autonomy: the Cases of the Aland and Kosovo", in Zelim Skurbaty (ed), ibid, pp. 379–399 at p. 380; Yash Ghai, supra note 79, at pp. 38–41.

and content of autonomy, there are two basic models: territorial autonomy and personal/cultural/group autonomy.[82]

Whether autonomy has been widely accepted as a right in international law is still a question in doubt. The incorporation of an autonomy clause in international and regional instruments indicates an increasing acceptance. For example, the 1990 CSCE/OSCE Copenhagen Document, which recommends a wide range of rights for national minorities, considers autonomy as "one of possible means" to secure such rights; and the UNDRIP also provides indigenous peoples the right to autonomy or self-government in internal and local affairs.[83] States, however, are reluctant to recognise a collective right of minorities to autonomy as a part of positive international law, particularly in regard to political autonomy which is closely related to territorial integrity.[84] It has been argued that internal arrangements, such as autonomous regimes, usually fall within the sphere of domestic law, rather than being the concern of international law, unless the sovereign states are obligated to do so.[85] Put differently, autonomy is seen as an arrangement, not a right in international law.[86] Despite the fact that a number of autonomous units can be easily found in state practice, autonomy is an indefinite and general legal term which has to be given a concrete content in individual cases.[87]

To sum up, there are four sets of rights in international law: the general individual human rights, the additional rights specific to persons belonging to national or ethnic, religious or linguistic minorities, the special rights of indigenous peoples and of indigenous individuals, and the rights of peoples under

82 Gnanapala Welhengama, *Minorities' Claims: From Autonomy To Secession—International Law and State Practice* (Ashgate, 2000), p. 102; Yash Ghai, ibid, at p. 38. Hans-Joachim Heintze divides autonomy into two basic models: territorial autonomy and non-territorial autonomy. The latter further includes cultural autonomy, personal autonomy and functional autonomy. For a further discussion on the non-territorial autonomy, see Hans-Joachim Heintze, "On the Legal Understanding of Autonomy", in Markku Suksi (ed), *Autonomy: Applications and Implications* (Kluwer Law International, 1998), pp. 7–32 at pp. 18–24.

83 The CSCE/OSCE Copenhagen Documents 1990, paras.30–35; the UNDRIP, Article 4.

84 Hans-Joachim Heintze, supra note 82, at p. 13; Gnanapala Welhengama, supra note 82, at p. 133; James Summers, supra note 1, at p. 498; James Summers, *Peoples and International Law (1st Edition)* (Martinus Nijhoff Publishers, 2007), p. 342.

85 Lauri Hannikainen, "Self-determination and Autonomy in International Law", in Markku Suksi (ed), supra note 82, pp. 79–95 at p. 87; Gnanapala Welhengama, supra note 82, at p. 133.

86 Thornberry describes it as "a grant, not a right". Patrick Thornberry, "Images of Autonomy and Individual and Collective Rights in International Instruments on the Rights of Minorities", in Markku Suksi (ed), supra note 82, pp. 97–124 at p. 123; Zelim Skurbaty, "Introduction", in Zelim Skurbaty (ed), supra note 79, p. xxxvii; David Raic, supra note 7, p. 283.

87 Hans-Joachim Heintze, supra note 81, at p. 47; supra note 82, at p. 13.

Article 1 of two Covenants of 1966.[88] Minorities, therefore, are not generally accepted as the peoples who are entitled to the right to self-determination. Some commentators suggest that there is a right to secede, as the last resort, in extreme cases when minorities suffer oppression,[89] and that remedial secession might be justified as a remedy for persistent and serious injustices from moral perspective. Its development as a right in international law, however, is still *de lege ferenda*.[90] Furthermore, international law does not explicitly recognise a right to autonomy, though autonomy within the domestic framework may effectively promote minority rights in the plural society.

3.2 The Question of Tibet

The right of peoples, who were subject to alien subjugation, domination and exploitation, to freely determine their own future was recognised by the GA Resolutions. Scholarly opinions were divided on whether alien subjugation, domination and exploitation could exist within a sovereign state.[91] Even though Tibet was not geographically separate from China, it was considered as an example of internal alien subjugation and domination in the decolonisation process.

3.2.1 *The Background*

Before entering into discussion about Tibet, a few concepts first need to be clarified. According to Sir Charles Bell, political Tibet refers to "the lands controlled by the Tibetan government and the Tibetan tribal authorities where had been asserted to enjoy *de facto* independence during the period from 1911 to 1950".[92] Ethnographic Tibet, on the other hand, includes "the lands inhabited by the people of Tibetan race" who are, by and large, settled on/around the

88 Asbjorn Eide, "Working Paper on the Relationship and Distinction between the Rights of Persons Belonging to Minorities and Those of Indigenous Peoples", UN Doc. E/CN.4/Sub.2/2000/10, p. 2, para. 2.

89 Buchheit argues that minorities could be potential peoples and, according to the reversion theory, minorities may attain the status of peoples and thus exercise a right to self-determination if they suffer oppression. Lee Buchheit, supra note 35, pp. 51–58, 72. Franck likewise asserts that there may be a right to secede if minority rights have been grossly violated. Thomas Franck, cited in Rosalyn Higgins, supra note 64, p. 36. See also Thomas Musgrave, supra note 2, pp. 170–171.

90 Joshua Castellino and Jeremie Gilbert, supra note 18, p. 167.

91 Supra notes 19, 20.

92 Sir Charles Bell, *Tibet Past and Present* (Oxford At The Clarendon Press, 1968), p. 5; H. Richardson, *Tibet and Its History* (Oxford University Press, 1962), p. 2.

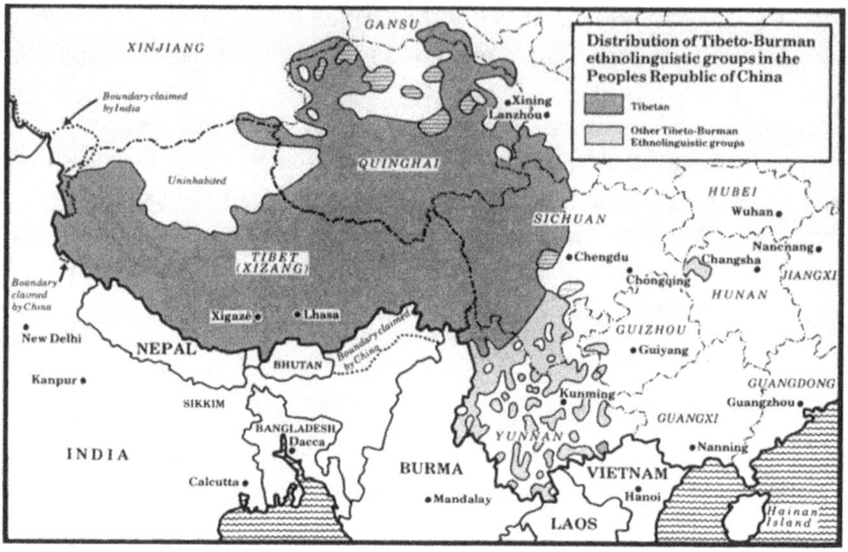

MAP 1 The Map of Tibet
A. GRUNFELD, THE MAKING OF MODERN TIBET, M. E. SHARPE, INC, 1996, P. XVI.

Tibetan Plateau, mainly in China but also in neighbouring states.[93] Greater Tibet is an assertion articulated by the Dalai Lama and the Tibetan government in exile. It incorporates "the entire community, comprising all the areas currently designated by the PRC as Tibetan autonomous areas, (which) should be under one single administrative entity".[94] Unless specified otherwise, in the following context "Tibet" is used to refer to political Tibet, whilst the Tibetan inhabited areas within the PRC are referred to as Greater Tibet. (See Map.1).

The first UN discussion on Tibet began with the Appeal to the Secretary General in 1950. In the Appeal, the Tibetan government admitted China's historical suzerainty over Tibet, but denied any diplomatic relations with China. It further proclaimed their independence to be "*de jure* status", and accused the Beijing Government of aggression and a threat to Asian stability.[95] The Appeal was at the time a reaction to the Changdu (Chamdo) Campaign of the PLA in

93 Ibid.

94 Memorandum on Genuine Autonomy for the Tibetan People, http://tibet.net/important-issues/sino-tibetan-dialogue/memorandum-on-geniune-autonomy-for-the-tibetan-people/, last accessed on 17/10/2013.

95 The Tibet Appeal to the Secretary General of the UN in November 1950. See Melvyn Goldstein, *A History of Modern Tibet Volume 2: the Calm Before the Storm, 1951–1955* (University of California Press, 2007), pp. 59–62.

October 1950. The PLA won a quick victory in "liberating" Changdu, the centre of the eastern Tibet, thus it strategically controlled the road to Lhasa.

However, the Tibet Appeal was listed in communications from nongovernmental organisations for the reason that it was not transmitted by the Tibetan government, but instead by a delegation outside of Tibet. It was not passed to the Security Council since the Secretary General did not consider this matter to fall within "the consideration of the Security Council in accordance with the provisions of the Charter".[96] Tibet was therefore forced to turn to UN members for support, particularly those who had provided the territory with long-term assistance, namely the US and the UK.[97] The subsequent development exceeded expectations. El Salvador responded to the Appeal and proposed the inclusion of the item—Invasion of Tibet by foreign forces—into the GA's agenda under Article 1 (1) of the Charter.[98] The UK and India, who had more interests in the area and had retained close relations with Tibet since the 20th century,[99] assumed a rather negative attitude. The UK argued that the proposed agenda should be adjourned *sine die,* due to the uncertainty of the legal position of Tibet.[100] The Indian delegate opposed the discussion in the GA, suggesting instead that a possible peaceful settlement of the question could "safeguard the autonomy which Tibet had enjoyed for several decades while maintaining its

96 Rule 6 of the Provisional Rules of Procedure of the Security Council (S/96/Rev.3, 1948) provides that "the Secretary-General shall immediately bring to the attention of all representatives on the Security Council all communications from States, organs of the United Nations, or the Secretary-General concerning any matter for the consideration of the Security Council in accordance with the provisions of the Charter". See also Melvyn Goldstein, ibid, p. 62.

97 The Letters Sent by the Tibetan Government to the UK and US. Full text is available in Melvyn Goldstein, ibid, pp. 62–63.

98 GAOR, 5th Session, Annexes, Agenda Item 8, UN Doc. A/1534; see also GAOR, 14th Session, 833rd Plenary Meeting, para. 2.

99 Thomas Heberer, *China and Its National Minorities: Autonomy or Assimilation* (M. E. Sharpe, Inc., 1989), pp. 22, 122.

100 The UK delegate stated that "... The Committee did not know exactly what was happening in Tibet nor was the legal position of the country very clear. Moreover, it could still be hoped that the existing difficulties in Tibet could be settled amicably by agreement between the parties concerned. In those circumstances, before taking a decision the members of the General Committee would be wiser to wait until a better idea could be formed of the possibilities of a peaceful settlement. He proposed, therefore, that the Committee should defer decision on the request made by the delegation of El Salvador". Quoted in Melvyn Goldstein, supra note 95, at p. 79; see also *A Report to the International Commission of Jurists by its Legal Inquiry Committee on Tibet: Tibet and the Chinese People's Republic* (International Commission of Jurists Geneva, 1960), p. 161.

historical association with China".[101] Many other states agreed with the UK and India's proposal to postpone the inclusion of the item. The USSR delegate, on the other hand, emphasised the fact that Tibet was an inalienable part of China, thus based their argument on the non-intervention in the internal affairs of the Chinese people.[102] The unanimous decision to defer the consideration of the Tibet Appeal signified the first failure of Tibet's attempt to seek international support in the UN context.[103] The second attempt to appeal to the UN and to seek foreign assistance and aid, particularly from the UK, India and the US, was made right after the GA's adjournment in December 1950. Once again, little assistance was offered by those "friendly" states. Tibetan leaders were left with no choice but to consider the alternative of peaceful negotiation.

Meanwhile, though Mao had not precluded the possibility of military "liberation" as the last resort, in Goldstein's view, he preferred a peaceful resolution to one won through force. The communists had to consider "international consequences for the legitimacy of the PRC's assertion of sovereignty over Tibet, as well as for the attitudes and loyalty of the Tibetans, who would become part of the new Chinese state".[104] To deal with the resistance and uncooperative attitude from the Tibetan, Mao adopted a "carrot and stick" approach.[105] After the seizure of Changdu, instead of marching further to Lhasa, the CPC ceased military action and urged the Tibetan government to start dialogue with Beijing. With twenty thousand troops deployed in the eastern area,[106] Kashag (the Cabinet) sent five representatives to Beijing to negotiate the settlement. On 23 May 1951, representatives from both sides signed "The Agreement of the Central People's Government and the Local Government of Tibet on Measures for the Peaceful Liberation of Tibet" (the 17 Points Agreement), the terms of which accorded to contemporary international law. Sovereignty, instead of the old terminology of suzerainty, was expressly used in the document. The 17 Points Agreement started with the reaffirmation of the arguable historical position of Tibet in China—one of the nationalities that had contributed to the long history and

101 He expressed that "he had no desire to express an opinion on the difficulties which had arisen between China and Tibet, but would point out that, in the latest note received by his Government, the Peking Government had declared that it had not abandoned its intention to settle those difficulties by peaceful means". Cited in Melvyn Goldstein, supra note 95, at pp. 79–80.

102 Melvyn Goldstein, supra note 95, at p. 80.

103 Ibid, p. 81.

104 Ibid, p. 22.

105 Ibid, p. 25.

106 John Powers, *History as Propaganda: Tibetans Exiles Versus the People's Republic of China* (Oxford University Press, 2004), p. 113.

glory of the "Motherland".[107] Then it pointed out the regrettable fact that the local government of Tibet once held an "unpatriotic attitude" towards China due to imperialist deception and provocation.[108] Tibet should now unify with other nationalities so as to oppose the imperialism and to accomplish national unity and safeguard the territory and sovereignty of the PRC.[109]

After the initial shock,[110] the Dalai Lama and ruling elites soon found themselves in a dilemma. On the one hand, the Dalai Lama's establishment in Yadong gave him the opportunity to denounce the Agreement on the grounds of lack of authority for the representatives to sign it and to flee into exile with help offered by the US.[111] On the other hand, the Tibetan leaders worried about losing the best offer they would possibly have received from the CPC.[112] After a heated debate in the Tibetan Assembly (now the Tibetan Parliament), the final decision—the return of the Dalai Lama to Lhasa and ratification of the Agreement—was reached. The majority opinion of ruling elites for the Agreement was neatly reflected in a telegram from the Dalai Lama to the Beijing Government:

> [To the Central People's Government] Chairman Mao:
>
> At the end of April 1951 there arrived in Peking a special delegate, Kashag (the Cabinet) Minister Ngabö and four other plenipotentiary representatives sent by the local Tibet government. They held *peaceful negotiations* with the plenipotentiary delegates appointed by the Central People's Government. The representatives of both sides, on May 23, 1951, signed on *a friendly basis* an agreement relating to the measures for the peaceful liberation of Tibet. *The local government of Tibet, the monks, and the entire Tibetan people express their unanimous support for this agreement.* Under the leadership of Chairman Mao Zedung and the Central People's

107 "Zhongyang renmin zhengfu he Xizang defang zhengfu guanyu heping jiefang Xizang banfa de xieyi [the Agreement of the Central People's Government and the Local Government of Tibet on Measures for the Peaceful Liberation of Tibet]", in Jin Binghao (ed), *Minzu gangling zhengce wenxian xuanbian* [*The Collected Works of the Documents on the National Program and Policy*] (Zhongyang Minzu Daxue Chubanshe, 2006), p. 450. The English translation is available in H. Richardson, supra note 92, at p. 275.

108 Ibid.

109 The Agreement of the Central People's Government and the Local Government of Tibet on Measures for the Peaceful Liberation of Tibet, supra note 107, at p. 451; H. Richardson, supra note 92, at p. 276.

110 Tenzin Gyatso, *The Fourteenth Dalai Lama of Tibet, Freedom in Exile: the Autobiography of HH the Dalai Lama of Tibet* (A John Curtis Book, Hodder & Stoughton, 1990), p. 68.

111 Melvyn Goldstein, supra note 95, at pp. 130–137.

112 Ibid, pp. 108, 140.

> Government they are actively helping units of the People's Liberation Army which entered Tibet for strengthening the national defences, driving out of imperialist forces from Tibet and guaranteeing of *sovereignty* of the entire territory of the motherland. [emphasis added][113]

According to the Chinese government, the 17 Points Agreement clarified the legal position of Tibet: it confirmed China's sovereignty over Tibet. The Tibetan attitude, however, varied greatly in different periods. After his return to Lhasa in 1951, the Dalai Lama and the Beijing Government experienced a short period of nominal cooperation. Incidents, which were followed by organised protests of the Tibetans, had never stopped in the area.[114] Although the Beijing Government had, through the Agreement, pledged not to impose reforms, including land reform and social reform, the irreconcilable conflict between the Tibetan Lamaism and Aristocracy and the soviet regime implied that the Tibetan elites would lose the privileges they had traditionally enjoyed sooner or later. The storm broke on 10 March 1959, resulting in the asylum of the Dalai Lama in India and the Tibetan government in exile.[115] As the PLA put the "armed rebellion" down, the Beijing Government launched a series of "democratic reform" measures and alleged that they had "liberated" a million of serfs and slaves. Two contradictory sets of stories on the event and the subsequent development were insisted upon by the opposing sides.

3.2.2 *Resolution 1353 (1959)*

In the first statement issued in Tezpur, 18 April 1959, the Dalai Lama appeared to hold a comparatively moderate opinion on the Agreement. He merely alleged that the 17 Points Agreement was made under "the pressure of the Chinese government" and that Tibet was left with no alternative.[116] In the

---

113 Wang Junhua and Zhou Zhenfan, "Dalai yonghu 'guanyu heping jiefang xizang banfa de xieyi' de dianbao [the Telegram from the Dalai Lama to Validate the 17 Points Agreement]", 3 *Zhongguo Dang'an* [*China Archives*] (2009), p. 77; the English translation, see Melvyn Goldstein, supra note 95, at p. 226.

114 A. Grunfeld, *The Making of Modern Tibet* (M. E. Sharpe, Inc, 1996), p. 131.

115 The situation was tensed since the early February and aggravated on 9th March and thereafter. Later the Dalai Lama announced the 10th of March to be the Tibetan National Uprising Day. See "HH the Dalai Lama's Press Statements on the 'Agreement'—Statement Issued at Tezpur (18/04/1959)", in A. Shiromany (ed), *The Spirit of Tibet, Universal Heritage: Selected Speeches and Writings of HH the Dalai Lama XIV* (Allied Publishers, 1995), pp. 5–8; see also H. Richardson, supra note 92, at pp. 208–209.

116 HH the Dalai Lama's Press Statements on the "Agreement"—statement issued in Tezpur, ibid.

well-known Mussoorie statement, however, the Dalai Lama announced the repudiation of the 17 Points Agreement for the first time.[117] He claimed that the threat of arms and the use of coercion were the only reasons that led to the conclusion of the 17 Points Agreement. But according to Grunfeld and Goldstein, military threat and coercion could hardly be found in the negotiation.[118] In the 1959 Appeal to the UN Secretary General, the Tibet leader did not bother to mention the 17 Points Agreement, only explaining the sovereignty that Tibet had enjoyed since 1912.[119] The non-appearance of the Agreement might not be difficult to understand, as it could be conceived as the obstacle to the assertion of an independent Tibet. Nevertheless, such a political claim failed to win the support of UN members. The joint proposal made by Malaya and Ireland focused on violations of fundamental human rights that were alleged to have occurred in Tibet—the second concern in the 1959 Appeal—and deliberately used the vague description of "traditionally enjoyed autonomy" in the draft resolution.[120]

Despite the fact that many states repeatedly expressed their intention not to debate Chinese sovereignty or suzerainty over Tibet, the discussion, to a great extent, centred on the competence of the GA to discuss the Question of Tibet under Article 2, paragraph 7 of the Charter. Paragraph 7 stipulated:

> [*n*]*othing* contained in the present Charter shall authorise the United Nations to intervene in matters which are essentially within the domestic jurisdiction of any state or shall require the Members to submit such matters to settlement under the present Charter; but this principle shall not prejudice the application of enforcement measures under Chapter VII.

As far as the non-intervention of domestic jurisdiction was concerned, it was mainly the Soviet bloc that strongly opposed the inclusion of the question of Tibet in the agenda for the reason that Tibet was an integral part of China.[121] Some other states had to abstain from the draft resolution because of the

117 "Statement Issued at the Press Conference Held at Mussoorie (20/06/1959)", in A. Shiromany (ed), supra note 115, at pp. 10–14.

118 John Powers, supra note 106, at p. 117.

119 "The Dalai Lama's Appeal to the Secretary General of the UN (09/09/1959)", in A. Shiromany (ed), supra note 115, at pp. 26–28.

120 GAOR (1959), 14th Session, Agenda Item 73, A/L. 264.

121 USSR, 14 GAOR (1959), 831st Meeting, para.70; Bulgaria, 14 GAOR (1959), 832nd Meeting, para. 64; Albania, 14 GAOR (1959), 833rd Meeting, para. 40; Poland, 14 GAOR (1959), 833rd Meeting, para.104; Spain, 14 GAOR (1959), 833rd Meeting, paras.91, 94; Ethiopia, 14 GAOR (1959), 834th Meeting, para.152.

uncertainty of the application of Article 2, para.7 in the current situation.[122] In the words of the British delegate, "the question [of Tibet] is far from clear and that some of the more important facts are in doubt".[123] Another tangential direction taken in the interpretation of the article was the question of how to balance the protection of human rights and domestic jurisdiction. This actually referred to an extensive debate on the hierarchy of the fundamental principles of international law. The two sponsors of the draft, the US and the ROC, advocated a liberal approach of interpretation. They argued that the GA was competent enough to concern itself with gross violations of human rights,[124] considering the value and principle of human rights as enshrined in the Charter and the Universal Declaration of Human Rights, and particularly with precedents passed by the GA on the race issue in South Africa.[125] Another approach concentrated on the imperative nature of Article 2, para.7, which deemed to concern the international community as whole, denying the priority of the principle of human rights over all others.[126] The abstaining states of Belgium and France attached to this restrictive approach. The political status of Tibet seemed to be of no relevance here.

The discussion on Article 2, para.7 itself, to certain degree, implied the attitude of the majority of the international community on the status of Tibet. Had Tibet enjoyed the full sovereignty, as the Dalai Lama had claimed in his 1959 Appeal, it should be Article 2, para.4 that was relevant, rather than para.7. Only the Cuban delegate recognised *de facto* independence of Tibet before 1951.[127] El Salvador once again treated Tibet as a "semi-sovereign state" that had been enjoying political independence, accusing the PRC of aggression.[128]

---

122 Finland, 14 GAOR (1959), 831st Meeting, para. 63; Belgium, 14 GAOR (1959), 832nd Meeting, paras. 44-47; France, 14 GAOR (1959), 832nd Meeting, paras.116-117; Union of South Africa, 14 GAOR (1959), 834th Meeting, paras.168–170.

123 UK, 14 GAOR (1959), 834th Meeting, paras.21-22.

124 In the opinion of the International Commission of Jurists, "almost all the rights which together allow the full and legitimate expression of human personality appear to be denied to the Tibetans at the present time and, in most cases, for some time past. On the basis of the available evidence it would seem difficult to recall a case in which ruthless suppression of man's essential dignity has been more systematically and efficiently carried out". See International Commission of Jurists, *The Question of Tibet and the Rule of Law—A Preliminary Report* (Geneva, 1959), p. 59.

125 Malaya, 14 GAOR (1959), 831st Meeting, para.7; Ireland, 14 GAOR (1959), 831st Meeting, para.31; US, 14 GAOR (1959), 832nd Meeting, para.84.

126 Belgium, 14 GAOR (1959), 832nd Meeting, paras.40–41; France, 14 GAOR (1959), 832nd Meeting, paras.119–120; Spain, 14 GAOR (1959), 833rd Meeting, paras.93–94.

127 Cuba, 14 GAOR (1959), 831st Meeting, paras.117–118.

128 El Salvador, 14 GAOR (1959), 832nd Meeting, paras.3-16.

However, the UK, India and Nepal, who had treaty relations with Tibet and were therefore considered to have special qualifications to give an authoritative clarification of Tibet's status,[129] held a different opinion. The British opinion of the uncertainty of Tibet's status remained the same as they had argued in 1950. India claimed to inherit the British position on Tibet in 1947: Tibet was under Chinese suzerainty and India maintained its desire "to maintain friendly relations with China", despite its deep sympathy for the people of Tibet.[130] The Indian Government continued to acknowledge the validity of the 17 Points Agreement.[131] The draft resolution's statement of "the distinctive cultural and religious heritage of the people of Tibet and of the autonomy which they have traditionally enjoyed", to the Nepali delegate, indicated "clearly that even the sponsors of the item recognise China's suzerainty over Tibet".[132] There were also Sino-Nepali agreements clearly defining the relationship between Nepal and China, including matters concerning Tibet.[133] In addition, some member states argued that Tibet had "some sort of dependent relationship"[134] and it was "an integral part of China". The numbers, 45 votes to 9 with 26 abstentions, may have not implied international support for Tibetan independence, but rather a concern for human rights.

In this session, the principle of self-determination hardly drew the attention of delegates. It was the delegate of the ROC that initially mentioned the principle of self-determination.[135] It would be questionable to interpret Jiang's advocacy of self-determination as an intent to support Tibetan independence, considering his previous stand on the principle (see Chapter 2). The subsequent speech of the Chinese delegate reaffirmed it: the question of Tibet was "the question of the rights of a minority nationality in a multinational state"[136] and "Tibet has been a part of China, in one fashion or another, for many centuries".[137] The French reference to self-determination was of little importance since it merely constituted a general appeal to the principle without specifying the holder or the content as regards the Tibetan situation.

129 H. Richardson, supra note 92, at p. 221.
130 India, 14 GAOR (1959), 834th Meeting, paras.74, 85.
131 Ibid, para.87.
132 Nepal, 14 GAOR (1959), 831st Meeting, para.59.
133 Ibid, para.58.
134 France, 14 GAOR (1959), 832nd Meeting, para.117.
135 ROC, 14 GAOR (1959), 833rd Meeting, para.65.
136 ROC, 14 GAOR (1959), 833rd Meeting, para.66
137 Ibid, para.84.

3.2.3 *Resolution 1723 (1961)*

The transformation of the principle of self-determination into a right during the process of decolonisation provided a new perspective to discuss the Tibet situation. GA Resolution 1514 vested colonial peoples with the right to determine their own future.[138] However, according to the Charter, Tibet fell out of the scope of trust territories.[139] To identify a non-self-governing status, Principle IV of Resolution 1541 required geographical separation and ethnical and/or cultural distinction to establish a *prima facie* case.[140] Tibet was not a non-self-governing territory under such a definition. However, it is necessary to consider whether the Tibet situation corresponded to other types of colonialism. In the GA debate on the draft of Resolution 1514, apart from classical imperialism, many states interpreted "alien subjugation, domination and exploitation" in a broader sense so as to embrace all types of domination, no matter whether it was of old form or new type, physical exploitation or ideological subjugation.[141] Tibet had been specifically referred to by some delegates as an illustration that some peoples in the present day were still suffering from oppression and suppression and had been deprived of traditional freedoms.[142]

The assertion on the distinction between internal and external self-determination suggested another possibility. Syria, in 1952, defined domestic self-determination as the "people's right to adopt representative institutions and freely choose the form of government" and equated international self-determination with independence.[143] The Netherlands also argued that the principle of self-determination had internal and external aspects. It reminded that due to the complexity and uncertainty around the concept, it should be

---

138 Resolution 1514, Articles 1, 2, 5.

139 Article 77 Clause 1 of the UN Charter states that "the trusteeship system shall apply to such territories in the following categories as may be placed thereunder by means of trusteeship agreements: a. territories now held under mandate; b. territories which may be detached from enemy states as a result of the Second World War; and c. territories voluntarily placed under the system by states responsible for their administration". Tibet was not a territory under mandate nor a territory detached from enemy states of Second World War. Further, neither the Republican Government of China nor the Tibetan Government voluntarily offered to place the territory under the system according to subsection (c).

140 GA Resolution 1541 (XV), 15 GAOR(1960) Supplement No.16, (A/4684).

141 Malaya, 15 GAOR, 935th Meeting, (A/PV 935), para.128; ROC, 15 GAOR, 935th Meeting, (A/PV 935), paras.138–144, 146–147. See also James Summers, supra note 1, at p. 207.

142 Ireland, Thailand and Italy. See Ireland, 15 GAOR, 935th Meeting, (A/PV 935), para.93; Thailand, 15 GAOR, 938th Meeting, (A/PV 938), para.111; Italy, 15 GAOR, 937th Meeting, (A/PV 937), para.85.

143 James Summers, supra note 1, at p. 341.

applied cautiously.[144] Beaufort, the Dutch delegate, repeatedly asserted that self-determination was a universal value and "not a merely anti-colonial device".[145] He argued:

> the idea of self-determination was a complex of ideas rather than a single concept. Thus the principle of internal self-determination, or self-determination on the national level, should be distinguished from that of external self-determination, or self-determination on the international level. The former was the right of a nation, already constituted as a State, to choose its form of government and to determine the policy it meant to pursue. The latter was the right of a group which considered itself a nation to form a State of its own.[146]

From this point of view, whether Tibet constituted a nation that enjoyed the right to external self-determination was in question. The uncertainty remained, as there was no international consensus on, in the words of Beaufort, "the concept of a nation or upon the moment when a nation arises as such".[147]

Against this political backdrop, the Dalai Lama, in the 1961 statement, reasserted Tibet independence on the grounds of self-determination. He claimed that Tibet had been "reduced to the status of a colonial possession" and complained of the suffering of the Tibetan people under "foreign domination".[148] His statement relied on the reports of the International Commission of Jurists.[149] A special reference was made to the second report, Tibet and the PRC, which had subsequently been referred to by many member states during the GA debate. This Report first accused the PRC of committing genocide in Tibet, with "an attempt to destroy the Tibetans as a religious group" and then of other violations of fundamental freedoms.[150]

---

144 P. Kuyper and P. Kapteyn, "Chapter 22 A Colonial Power as Champion of Self-Determination: Netherlands State Practice in the period 1945–1975", in H. F. van Panhys et al (ed), *International Law in the Netherlands* (Sijthoff&Noordhoff Oceana, 1980), pp. 149–218, at p. 185.

145 Ibid, p. 198.

146 Cited in James Summers, supra note 1, at p. 341.

147 P. Kuyper and P. Kapteyn, supra note 144, at pp. 184-185.

148 The Statement of HH the Dalai Lama on the Second Anniversary of the Tibetan National Uprising Day (10/03/1961). Full text is available at http://www.dalailama.com/messages/tibet/10th-march-archive/1961, last accessed on 02/01/2014.

149 These two reports were: the Question of Tibet and The Rule of Law 1959 and Tibet and the People's Republic of China 1960.

150 International Commission of Jurists, *A Report to the International Commission of Jurists by its Legal Inquiry Committee on Tibet: Tibet and the Chinese People's Republic* (Geneva, 1960), pp. 3–5, 117.

It stressed that Tibet was "at the very least a *de facto* independent state" when the 17 Points Agreement was signed in 1951.[151] The Legal Inquiry Committee believed that throughout the period of 1912–1950 the Government of Tibet had exercised exclusive control in domestic affairs and engaged in foreign relations with Great Britain, Nepal and India.[152] The Report further approved the repudiation by the Tibetan Government in 1959, which "was found to be fully justified" since the representatives signed the 17 Points Agreement under the threat of "violent conquest of their country" by the Beijing regime.[153] The Legal Inquiry Committee concluded that the organs of the UN had the power to discuss and decide on the matter as Tibet had enjoyed *de facto* independence from 1912–1950 and had discharged itself of the obligations arising from the 17 Points Agreement.[154]

In 1961, Ireland and Thailand, together with El Salvador and the Federation of Malaya, sponsored a new draft resolution on the question of Tibet on the basis of the suppression that the Tibetan people had suffered and the denial of their rights to fundamental freedoms.[155] During the debate on the draft of Resolution 1723, apart from the continuous support of the Soviet bloc,[156] the discussion generally focused on two aspects: (1) calling for the respect of principles on fundamental human rights and (2) the right of the Tibetan people to self-determination.

As one of co-sponsors of the draft, the Thai delegate concentrated on the denial of fundamental freedoms of the Tibetans and called again for the restoration of the autonomy that the Tibetans had traditionally enjoyed—a term that had been used in the 1959 resolution.[157] France held a similar opinion: the French people hoped that the human rights guaranteed by international instruments would be respected.[158]

Unlike those member states who principally concerned themselves with the human rights situation, the US suggested that the "national right" to self-determination should apply to the people of Tibet since Tibet was an

151 Ibid, p. 5.

152 The Committee invoked the 1914 Simla Anglo-Tibetan Convention, which was only initialled by the Chinese representative and had never been officially ratified by the Chinese government, as the main proof to illustrate the Tibet's ability to engage in international relations. Ibid, pp. 148–160.

153 Ibid, pp. 5, 164–165.

154 Ibid, p. 165.

155 GAOR (1961), 16th Session, Agenda Item 83, A/L. 376.

156 USSR, 16 GAOR, 1085th Meeting, (A/PV 1085), para.58, Czechoslovakia, 16 GAOR, 1085th Meeting, (A/PV 1085), para.26; Albania, 16 GAOR, 1085th Meeting, (A/PV 1085), paras.83, 87, 88; Poland, 16 GAOR, 1085th Meeting, (A/PV 1085), paras.112–3.

157 Thailand, 16 GAOR, 1085th Meeting, (A/PV 1085), paras.40–50.

158 France, 16 GAOR, 1085th Meeting, (A/PV 1085), para.99.

autonomous country under the suzerainty of China.[159] The American delegate seemed to view Tibet as a nation that was different from the Chinese nation. The Malay delegate believed that traditional colonialism needed to be abolished, and also that the GA was obligated to adopt a consistent attitude as long as the domination and suppression of man by man was involved.[160] Hence, in the case of Tibet, to restore the right of the Tibetans to determine "their own life and destiny consistent with their desires and traditions" was the objective.[161] The US and Malayan delegates may somehow describe Tibet as a nation or people, whereas Ireland explicitly identified Tibet as experiencing the "worst kind of colonialism" and upheld the application of Resolution 1514 in the Tibetan case.[162]

When some states eagerly attempted to link Tibet with the right to self-determination, the ROC had no attention to refer to such a right at this time. The Republican speech addressed the repressive policies of the CPC on Tibet and attributed unfortunate events to the genuine hostility of the communist regime towards religion.[163] The delegate then claimed the CPC to be "un-Chinese" and unrepresentative of the Chinese nation, thereby deliberately distinguishing the CPC from the Chinese nation of which the Tibetans formed a part.[164]

The UK, in this session, changed its standing on the status of Tibet from "the matter of doubt" into "Chinese suzerainty over Tibet".[165] Yet the British government specified that its recognition of the suzerainty was conditioned on Tibet retaining its autonomy.[166] Since the Chinese government had attempted to suppress Tibetan autonomy permanently, as showed in the report of the International Commission of Jurists, the UK voted in favour of the draft resolution.[167] India and Nepal, did not speak in the GA and for the second time they abstained in the vote. The draft resolution was eventually adopted by 56 votes to 10, with 29 abstentions. But the implication of the right to self-determination in the language of the resolution was ambiguous. It may be interpreted as the right to independence of the Tibetan people under Resolution 1514. Or it could possibly refer to an appeal to general principles of fundamental human rights enshrined in the Charter and other instruments.

159 US, 16 GAOR, 1084th Meeting, (A/PV 1084), paras.195-6.
160 Federation of Malaya, 16 GAOR, 1084th Meeting, (A/PV 1084), para.127.
161 Federation of Malaya, 16 GAOR, 1084th Meeting, (A/PV 1084), paras.129, 147.
162 Ireland, 16 GAOR, 1084th Meeting, (A/PV 1084), paras.239, 241-2.
163 ROC, 16 GAOR, 1084th Meeting, (A/PV 1084), paras.209–212, 215–222, 226–234.
164 Ibid, paras.213-4.
165 UK, 16 GAOR, 1085th Meeting, (A/PV 1085), para.97.
166 Ibid.
167 Ibid, paras.96–97.

3.2.4 *Resolution 2079 (1965)*

Although the UN resolutions were ignored by the Beijing regime, some states raised the Tibet question in the GA again, since the human rights situation in Tibet had not changed since 1960.[168] Another round of discussions on Tibet started in 1965, based on a draft resolution presented by El Salvador, Ireland, Malaysia, Malta, Nicaragua, Philippine and Thailand. This draft resolution was distinguishable from previous ones as no reference was made to the right of self-determination.

However, the focuses of the debate remained unchanged. Some states regarded Tibet as a colonial territory[169] or as a territory under foreign domination.[170] Such a situation called for the application of Resolution 1514 in the view of Ireland, or the free determination of Tibet's own political future, according to the delegates of Costa Rica.[171] American advocacy of the "basic right of self-determination", once again, was termed in a rather vague manner.[172] Whether the American argument equated to colonial self-determination or the principle of self-determination of peoples in the human rights context was unclear. The ROC reinstated its position in 1959.[173]

Among the sponsors, Malta and Malaysia in particular reasserted that the political relation between China and Tibet should not be the issue of the debate.[174] In the words of the Malay delegate, the draft resolution intended to call upon "the PRC to observe ordinary standards that any humane government owes to its own peoples".[175] The human rights situation within a state should be the exclusive concern of the draft.[176] Malaysia amended the initial draft resolution, omitting "take all measures" from the beginning of its speech, as calling upon/appealing to states to "take any measures" was considered to be inappropriate.[177] The new draft resolution appeared to be another general concern and sympathy of the GA over the Tibet situation, similar to the Resolution 1353.

---

168 Bulletin of the International Commission of Jurists, No. 21, December 1964, quoted in Philippines, 20 GAOR, 1394th Meeting, (A/PV. 1394), para.15.

169 Ireland, 20 GAOR, 1394th Meeting, (A/PV. 1394), para.72; New Zealand, 20 GAOR, 1401st Meeting, (A/PV. 1401), para.4; Costa Rica, 20 GAOR, 1403rd Meeting, (A/PV. 1403), para.62.

170 Philippines, 20 GAOR, 1394th Meeting, (A/PV. 1394), paras.1, 22; Costa Rica, 20 GAOR, 1403rd Meeting, (A/PV. 1403), paras.61, 64.

171 Ireland, 20 GAOR, 1394th Meeting, (A/PV. 1394), para.72; Costa Rica, 20 GAOR, 1403rd Meeting, (A/PV. 1403), para.64.

172 US, 20 GAOR, 1401st Meeting, (A/PV. 1401), paras.109, 123.

173 ROC, 20 GAOR, 1394th Meeting, (A/PV. 1394), paras.81, 99.

174 Malta 20 GAOR, 1401st Meeting, (A/PV. 1401), para.65; Malaysia, 20 GAOR, 1403rd Meeting, (A/PV. 1403), paras.69–70.

175 Ibid.

176 Ibid.

177 Malaysia, 20 GAOR, 1403rd Meeting, (A/PV. 1403), paras.66-7.

The resolution was passed by a vote of 43 to 26, with 22 abstentions. India voted in favour of the resolution, which was not against expectations, as Sino-Indian border conflicts had broken out in 1962. Despite the fact that Sino-Indian relations had deteriorated at the time, India had not endeavoured to argue for Tibetan independence in the GA discussion. The non-inclusion of the right to self-determination in Resolution 2079 was not accidental. After heated discussions of the international community on self-determination in the early 1960s, the application of the principle entered a cooling-off period. The generally unsupportive attitude of states towards Tibetan independence may provide another possible explanation for the non-inclusion of self-determination.

Since the 1959 Event, intense efforts were made by the Dalai Lama and the Tibetan government in exile to seek international support for Tibetan independence. In the UN context, the adoption of three resolutions in a way signified some sort of "victory". But those resolutions served little practical purpose for the following reasons.[178] First, the GA resolutions were not legally binding upon member states. Second, the resolutions in principle expressed the GA's general concern regarding the human rights situation in Tibet. Third, all three resolutions were completely ignored by the Beijing regime, since the PRC received no representation in the UN and the resolutions had not even addressed it by name.

The exiles' efforts, indeed, had no impact on the situation in Tibet and did nothing to create an international consensus on its right to self-determination or independence.[179] The traditionally relevant and qualified states, namely the UK, India and Nepal, were reluctant to get involved in the issue and the US, the major sponsor for Tibet in the post 1959 era, refused to formally recognise Tibetan independence and confined its support to financial aid. The PRC's restoration of lawful rights in the UN in 1971,[180] together with the emergence of the PRC on the international level, implied an end to further resolutions on the question of Tibet.[181] Both the PRC and the US adjusted their strategies in foreign relations, as influenced by the deterioration of Sino-Soviet relations and the hardship of the US that had been caused by its domestic economy and the Vietnam War. With the development of unofficial relations between the two states, the Tibet question no long fitted US national interests.[182] As Goldstein

178 A. Grunfeld, supra note 114, at p. 180.

179 Tibet began to seek for international recognition in the 1940s. However, no state acknowledged its independence at the time. Thomas Heberer, supra note 99, at p. 120; see also Melvyn Goldstein, *The Snow Lion and the Dragon: China, Tibet and the Dalai Lama* (University of California Press, 1997), p. 59.

180 GA Resolution 2758.

181 A. Grunfeld, supra note 114, at p. 187.

182 Melvyn Goldstein, supra note 179, at p. 58.

observed, "by the 1970s … shifting world alignments placed the Tibetan exiles in a much weakened position".[183] Therefore, the exiles' efforts on the international level entered a comparatively silent period until the next shift of world orders occurred in the mid-1980s.

3.3 Self-determination in the Situation of Hong Kong and Macau

After being admitted to the UN, the PRC on many occasions condemned colonialism and neo-colonialism.[184] It expressed deep sympathy and support for colonial peoples and their struggles for national independence on the basis of the right to self-determination.[185] However, Hong Kong and Macau, two territories that were once placed on the list of non-self-governing territories, returned to China in 1997 and 1999, according to the treaties concluded between the metropolitan states and China. In this process, the right to self-determination as enshrined in the GA resolutions on decolonisation was set aside and the will of the peoples in relevant territories was never consulted. The question of whether the cases of Hong Kong and Macau breached international law on self-determination or whether they symbolised another exceptional application of the principle in the process of decolonisation will be analysed next.

183 Ibid.

184 China, 27 GAOR (1972) 4th Committee., 1978th Meeting, (A/C.4/SR.1978) para.3; China, 27 GAOR (1972) 4th Committee., 1991st Meeting, (A/C.4/SR.1991) para.24; China, 27 GAOR (1972) 4th Committee., 2018th Meeting, (A/C.4/SR.2018) para.59; China, 28 GAOR (1973) 4th Committee., 2030th Meeting, (A/C.4/SR.2030) para.35; China, 28 GAOR (1973) 4th Committee., 2042nd Meeting, (A/C.4/SR.2042) para.27; China, 28 GAOR (1973) 4th Committee., 2059th Meeting, (A/C.4/SR.2059) para.50; China, 29 GAOR (1974) 4th Committee., 2084th Meeting, (A/C.4/SR.2084) paras.33–34,36; China, 29 GAOR (1974) 4th Committee., 2095th Meeting, (A/C.4/SR.2095) paras.36-7; China, 29 GAOR (1974) 4th Committee., 2103rd Meeting, (A/C.4/SR.2203) paras.40-1; China, 29 GAOR (1974) 4th Committee., 2111st Meeting, (A/C.4/SR.2111) paras.13-9.

185 China, 27 GAOR (1972) 4th Committee., 1978th Meeting, (A/C.4/SR.1978) paras.5–6; China, 27 GAOR (1972) 4th Committee., 1991st Meeting, (A/C.4/SR.1991) paras.26–28; China, 27 GAOR (1972) 4th Committee., 2015th Meeting, (A/C.4/SR.2015) para.2; China, 27 GAOR (1972) 4th Committee., 2018th Meeting, (A/C.4/SR.2018) para.65; China, 28 GAOR (1973) 4th Committee., 2042nd Meeting, (A/C.4/SR.2042) paras.34-5; China, 29 GAOR (1974) 4th Committee., 2084th Meeting, (A/C.4/SR.2084) paras.32,38; China, 29 GAOR (1974) 4th Committee., 2095th Meeting, (A/C.4/SR.2095) paras.41-2; China, 29 GAOR (1974) 4th Committee., 2103rd Meeting, (A/C.4/SR.2103) para.43; China, 29 GAOR (1974) 4th Committee., 2122nd Meeting, (A/C.4/SR.2122) para.75.

3.3.1 *Hong Kong*

(1) The Origin of the Issue

The colonial history of Hong Kong began in 1842 under the Treaty of Nanjing, which ceded the island of Hong Kong (an area of 75.6 square kilometres) to Great Britain after China's defeat in the first Opium War.[186] The island soon became the importing base of Britain. Later, the territorial cession enlarged to include the Kowloon Peninsula (11.1 square kilometres) in the 1860 Treaty of Beijing.[187] The New Territories, a region of 965.1 square kilometres, was later transferred to Great Britain under a 99-year lease through the 1898 Convention.[188] Without the New Territories, the rest of Hong Kong would not be viable alone, as the former provided water and electricity to the whole territory.[189] An effective administration of the colony, as well as food, water and other resources, to a certain extent depended on the good will of the mainland.[190] More than 95 percent of the population were Chinese by race and culture.[191] Being a Crown Colony for almost a century, Hong Kong had in many ways detached from the mainland, yet geographically, ethnically and culturally, Hong Kong was a segment of China.[192]

186 "Nanjing tiaoyue (1842) [the 1842 Treaty of Nanjing]", in the Research Centre of the General Office of the National People's Congress Standing Committee (ed), *Zhongguo jindai bupingdeng tiaoyue huiyao [The Collection of the Unequal Treaties in Modern History of China]* (Zhongguo Minzhu Fazhi Chubanshe, 1996), p. 3; Hurst Hannum, supra note 22, p. 129.

187 "Zhongying Beijing tiaoyue (1860) [the 1860 Treaty of Beijing Between China and the United Kingdom]", in the Research Centre of the General Office of the NPC Standing Committee (ed), ibid, at pp. 96–97, 192–193; Hurst Hannum, supra note 22, at pp. 129–130.

188 "Zhantuo xianggang jiezhi zhuantiao (1898) [the 1898 Convention Between China and the United Kingdom Respecting an Extension of Hong Kong Territory (the Second Convention of Beijing)", in the Research Centre of the General Office of the NPC Standing Committee (ed), supra note 186, at pp. 192–193.

189 A Draft Agreement between the Government of the United Kingdom of Great Britain and Northern Ireland and the Government of the People's Republic of China on the Future of Hong Kong (26/09/1984), p. 8; Hurst Hannum, supra note 22, at p. 130.

190 Evan Luard, *Britain and China* (Chatto &Windus, 1962), pp. 195, 223.

191 In the 1960s, the estimated figure was 99 percent. In the 1980s, the figure decreased 1 percent. According to the 2001 census, 94.9 percent of the population in Hong Kong were ethnically Chinese. See Evan Luard, ibid, p. 236; Hurst Hannum, supra note 22, at p. 129; the Census and Statistics Department of the Government of Hong Kong Special Administrative Region, 2001, Population Census: Summary Results, p. 36. Full text is available at http://www.censtatd.gov.hk/products_and_services/products/publications/statistical_report/population_and_vital_events/index_cd_B1120018_dt_latest.jsp, last accessed on 21/12/2013.

192 Evan Luard, supra note 190, p. 198.

As early as the Peace Conference of Paris, apart from demands for the restoration of Shandong, the Chinese delegation proposed a program which included the return of all the leased territories.[193] But the program was excluded from the agenda as it fell "beyond the scope of the Conference". In 1930, after eight years' of negotiation, China restored its sovereignty over Weihaiwei, another Crown Colony under a 25-year lease.[194] This restoration was not complete in the sense that the Royal Navy retained the control of Liugong (Liukung) Island and other privileges in the area under a ten-year lease that was renewable if both parties agreed.[195] The nominal return of sovereignty to China did not seem to affect British interests in the area very much. The political and military weakness of the Republican Government at the time was the main reason for the compromise on territorial claims. Although the British managed to acquire China's consent to renew the lease, the Royal Navy was forced to withdraw from the island in 1940 due to Japanese pressure.[196]

As the Second Sino-Japanese War escalated, the Japanese army seized Hong Kong in 1941 as well as other Crown colonies in southeast Asia[197] that Britain was no longer in a position to protect.[198] The outbreak of the Pacific War urged the US and Britain to adjust their policy in the Far East. In the negotiation to abrogate extraterritorial rights and other privileges that Britain used to enjoy in China, the Chinese delegation demanded the return of the New Territories as leased territory.[199] This demand became the obstacle to an agreement. Both

---

193 Wang Jianlang, "Zhongguo feichu bupingdeng tiaoyue de lishi kaocha [A Historical Investigation of the Abolition of Unequal Treaties in China]", 05 *Lishi Yanjiu* [*Historical Research*] (1997), p. 7.

194 The 1898 Convention on the Lease of Weihaiwei provided that the port was leased to Great Britain "as long as the Port Arthur shall remain in the occupation of Russia". According to the 1898 Convention between Russia and China on the Lease of Lvshun and Dalian, the Port Arthur was under a 25-year lease. "Dingzu Weihaiwei zhuantiao [the 1898 Convention on the Lease of Weihaiwei]" and "Zhong'e lvda zudi tiaoyue [the 1898 Convention between Russia and China on the Lease of Lvshun and Dalian]", in the Research Centre of the General Office of the NPC Standing Committee (ed), supra note 186, at pp. 195–196, 189.

195 "Zhongying shoujiao Weihaiwei zhuanyue ji xieding [the Convention between China and Great Britain for the Rendition of Weihaiwei and Agreement regarding Certain Facilities for British Navy after Rendition (1930)]", in the Compilation Committee on the Local History of Weihai City (ed), *The History of Weihai* (Shandong Renmin Chubanshe, 1986), pp. 56–59; Clarence Davis and Robert Gowen, "The British at Weihaiwei: A Case Study in the Irrationality of Empire", 63:1 *Historian* (2000), p. 101.

196 Clarence Davis and Robert Gowen, ibid, pp. 101–103.

197 The fall of Malaysia and the surrender of Singapore in 1942.

198 Steve Tsang, *A Modern History of Hong Kong* (I.B. Tauris & Co Ltd, 2007), p. 115.

199 Evan Luard, supra note 190, at p. 50.

sides eventually managed to compromise on the issue by agreeing that "the Chinese government reserves its right to raise the issue of the New Territories lease again for discussion at a later date".[200]

As the war drew an end, with the support of the US, the Republican Government announced that China would accept the surrender of Hong Kong as "Hong Kong had been regarded as within the Chinese theatre" throughout the war.[201] London, on the other hand, demanded that Hong Kong should be accepted by British commander. The British Government argued, regardless of operational theatres, that "wherever the sovereign power has sufficient forces available it should resume its authority and accept Japanese surrender in its own territory".[202] Then it ordered the fleet towards Hong Kong. In response to the provocative action of Britain, Jiang Jieshi merely expressed the hope of the Chinese government to settle the Hong Kong issue through legal procedure, rather than sending troops to remedy the situation.[203] His position might be explained as a desire to avoid confronting Britain and to preserve forces in the mainland in order to fight against the communist regime. In other words, the nationalists gave up the opportunity to restore the sovereignty over Hong Kong, due to considerations for civil war. The Chinese government afterwards made a gesture to claim the restoration of Hong Kong, as Jiang declared "now that other leased territories had, one after the other, been returned to China, Kowloon [apparently he meant the New Territories] should not remain the exception".[204] Nonetheless, it was Britain that accepted Japanese surrender and brought Hong Kong back into the Crown territory.

Unlike Tibet and Taiwan, the CPC never made any claims for the return of the colonies in public statements when the communist regime was first established.[205] The Communists assumed that the conditions for territorial resumption were not ripe. They preferred to maintain the *status quo* till the right time for flexible and/or peaceful resolutions came up.[206] On the one hand, Hong

200 Steve Tsang, supra note 198, at p. 125.

201 It was generally known that President Roosevelt wished to see the territory returned. See Evan Luard, supra note 190, at p. 181.

202 FO371/46252, Foreign Office to Chungking 916, 18/08/1945, cited in Steve Tsang, supra note 198, at p. 134.

203 Evan Luard, supra note 190, at p. 182.

204 Quoted in Evan Luard, ibid.

205 Ibid, p.186.

206 According to the Directive on Diplomatic Affairs, the CPC must abolish imperialist prerogative in China and achieve national independence. This principle cannot be changed. However, in practice, each case should be solved individually according to its nature and circumstance. In the conversation with Anastas Mikoyan, Mao explained that the situation in the mainland could be easily resolved by sending the troops over, whereas with respect to the islands, due to its complexity, flexible or peaceful methods might be

Kong was a small territory, compared to other territories that were waiting for "liberation" in the mainland.[207] On the other hand, the new born regime urgently needed a channel to break through the blocks of the Western states in the early stages of the Cold War, especially after the outbreak of the Korean War.[208]

(2) Hong Kong as a Non-self-governing Territory

The status of Hong Kong as a non-self-governing territory was established in Resolution 66(I), through which Britain declared its intention to transmit economic, social and educational information in Hong Kong under Article 73e of the Charter.[209] Macau was placed on the list of non-self-governing territories by the GA, although Portugal did not express such an intention. The ROC delegates on occasion opposed the inclusion of Macau on the non-self-governing territory list, claiming "the status of Macau and dependencies was a matter concerning the Chinese and Portuguese government, as parties to a treaty agreement".[210] The same status for Hong Kong, however, was rarely challenged.

The political climate changed shortly after the PRC resumed rights in the UN. In a letter to the Special Committee, China reiterated that "Hong Kong and Macau are part of Chinese territory occupied by the British and Portuguese authority" and the settlement of the status of both territories was "entirely within

more appropriate, which may take a longer time. Therefore, it was in no hurry to solve the questions of Hong Kong and Macau under such circumstances. See the CPC Central Committee (CPCCC), "Zhongyang guanyu waijiao gongzuo de zhishi [Directive on Diplomatic Affairs] (19/01/1949)", http://cpc.people.com.cn/GB/64184/64186/66650/4491619.html, last accessed on 21/12/2016; Shi Zhe, *Zai lishi juren shenbian—Shizhe huiyi lu* [*At the Side of the Giant in History: Shi Zhe's Memoirs*] (Zhongyang Wenxian Chubanshe, 1991), p. 380.

207 In answering Hamer's question on the CPC's attitude towards Hong Kong, Mao said: "[trans. L. W.] we will not demand an immediate restoration. China is a huge country and many places are not under the proper administration. Why do we rush the restoration of such a small land? It would be settled through negotiation in the future". Mao Zedong, "Tong sanwei xifang jizhe de tanhua [A Talk to Three Western Journalists]" (09/12/1946), in *Mao Zedong wenji* [*the Writings of Mao Zedong: Volume 4*] (Renmin Chubanshe, 1996), p. 207; also available at http://cpc.people.com.cn/GB/64184/64185/189964/11567791.html, last accessed on 21/12/2016.

208 Ye Zhangyu, "Zhonggong diyidai zhongyang lingdao jiti jiejue xianggang wenti zhanjue juece de lishi kaocha [A Historical Investigation of the Strategic Decision on the Settlement of the Question of Hong Kong by the First Generation of Collective Leadership of the CPC Central Committee]", 03 *Dangdai Zhongguoshi Yanjiu* [*Contemporary China History Studies*] (2007), pp. 47–50.

209 GA Resolution 66(I).

210 China, 15 GAOR (1960) 4th Committee., 1049th Meeting, (A/C.4/SR.1049) para.16; China, 18 GAOR (1963) 4th Committee., 1489th Meeting, (A/C.4/SR.1489) para.37.

China's sovereign right".[211] It requested the removal of these territories from the list of colonial territories under Resolution 1514 since "the UN has no right to discuss those questions".[212] At the 873rd meeting of the Special Committee, in regard to the recommendation of the Working Group on the exclusion of Hong Kong and Macau from the list of colonial territories, the delegates from Mali, Afghanistan and the USSR voted in favour.[213] Fiji reserved on the recommendation, as it believed that Hong Kong and Macau were "in fact non-self-governing"; Venezuela also reserved, suggesting referral to the General Assembly for a "substantive decision"; Sweden made the reservation without further statement.[214] Hence, the recommendation for the exclusion of Hong Kong and Macau was adopted as a part of the Special Committee Annual Report without objection, which later received the approval of the GA.[215] Great Britain, as the administering state, did not raise any formal protests against the removal. This was probably because it had no intention of affecting newly upgraded diplomatic relations at ambassadorial level with the PRC.[216] However, Britain did state that "the action of the GA in no way affects the legal status of Hong Kong" in its letter to the GA.[217]

Before the formal negotiation, the Chinese plan for Hong Kong was to safeguard the PRC's sovereignty and in the meantime to maintain Hong Kong's prosperity and stability.[218] British concern, on the other hand, focused on obtaining the most favourable terms for Britain and for the people of Hong Kong, considering the fact that Hong Kong was militarily indefensible and that the

---

211 Letter Dated 08/03/1972 from the Permanent Representative of China to the UN Addressed to the Chairman of the Special Committee, 27 GAOR, Supplement No.23, A/8723/Rev.1, p. 70.

212 Ibid.

213 Mr. Dao (Mali) stated that China had an absolute right to ask the UN to remove the questions which "concern a part of its territory" and further pointed out that the request of China indirectly reflected the intention of the administering powers themselves, especially Great Britain; Afghanistan supported the recommendation and the PRC's position; the USSR reaffirmed the Soviet position on the unequal treaties. The Special Committee, 873rd Meeting, 1972, A/AC.109/PV.873, pp. 17–19.

214 Ibid.

215 GA Resolution 2908.

216 Robert Mccorquodale, "Negotiating Sovereignty: the Practice of the United Kingdom in Regard to the Right of Self-determination", 66 *British Yearbook of International law* (1995), at p. 291.

217 Letter from the Permanent Representative of the United Kingdom of Great Britain to the UN Secretary General, quoted in Patricia Dagati, "Hong Kong's Lost Right to Self-Determination: A Denial of Due Process in the United Nations", 13 *New York Law School Journal of International and Comparative Law* (1992), p. 172.

218 Steve Tsang, supra note 198, at pp. 217–218.

permanently ceded parts were unviable without the New Territories.[219] During a meeting with Deng Xiaoping in 1982, however, Margaret Thatcher insisted that British sovereignty over Hong Kong was based on valid treaties and thus proposed a continued British administration of Hong Kong after 1997.[220] In reply, Deng made a clear stand that " the question [of sovereignty] is not open to discussion" and "China will recover Hong Kong in 1997".[221] Deng further clarified that a unilateral solution would be announced if no agreement was reached after a two-year negotiation.[222] He then assured, in case the declaration of resuming the exercise of sovereignty over Hong Kong in 1997 caused severe disturbances, that "the Chinese government would then be compelled to reconsider the timing and manner of the recovery".[223]

The disagreement on the PRC's sovereignty over Hong Kong as expressed by Thatcher and Deng necessarily led to an impasse at the very beginning of the negotiation.[224] For a few months thereafter, the negotiation moved slowly and no matters of substance were ever touched upon until Thatcher sent a letter to the Chinese Premier. In the letter, she indicated that she "would be prepared to recommend to Parliament that sovereignty over the whole of Hong Kong should *revert* to China".[225] Even though the Chinese government still felt unsatisfied with the British stance, the negotiation entered into its second phase in 1983. In this phase, the British proposed the relinquishment of their sovereignty over Hong Kong in exchange for administration, which unsurprisingly became a major obstacle to the progression of negotiations. China strongly opposed this since the continued British administration would be interpreted as another national concession to the imperialists, which could not distinguish the CPC from the Nationalist Party or the old Qing Court. Indeed, an essential part of the communist national rejuvenation was the full recovery of the feudal territory. The colonial existence of Hong Kong and Macau constantly reminded them of past "humiliation". With China's rigid position on sovereignty and

219 Ibid, p.218.

220 Ibid, p.218,223.

221 Deng Xiaoping, "Women dui xianggang wenti de jiben lichang" [Our Basic Position on the Question of Hong Kong], in *Selected Works of Deng Xiaoping: Volume 3* (Renmin Chubanshe, 1993), p. 12; the English version is available at http://english.peopledaily.com.cn/dengxp/vol3/text/c1040.html, last accessed on 21/12/2016.

222 Steve Tsang, supra note 198, at p. 219.

223 Deng Xiaoping, supra note 221, at p. 14.

224 Steve Tsang, supra note 198, at p. 219.

225 Zong Daoyi, "Deng Xiaoping yu zhongying xianggang wenti de tanpan [Deng Xiaoping and the Talks on the Question of Hong Kong between China and the United Kingdom]", 13:3 *Dangdai Zhongguoshi Yanjiu* [*Contemporary China History Studies*] (2007), p. 56; Steve Tsang, supra note 198, at p. 221.

the approaching of the two-year deadline, the British eventually compromised on the matter in order to secure its economic interests in China.

(3) An Exception to the Colonial Self-determination

The conclusion of the 1984 Joint Declaration, which stipulated a transfer of sovereignty of the whole territory in 1997 when the lease of the New Territories expired,[226] meant that the question of Hong Kong was settled through peaceful measures without resorting to another "Falklands War". To the Hong Kong people, however, the right to self-determination, if there ever was one, was totally ignored in the process. The people's will in Hong Kong was not formally consulted. Nor did the Joint Declaration refer to self-determination.[227]

Nonetheless, as Engers rightly pointed out, the right to self-determination may be denied or restricted if "the parties concerned are sufficiently powerful, or on a cogent claim for its subordination to the requirements of the security of the region".[228] The practice of the right to self-determination in the decolonisation process suggested a selective application of the principle. There were a number of instances where the people's right to self-determination had been limited or ignored for various reasons during the decolonisation process, including East Timor, Gibraltar, and Goa. The ICJ also stated in the *West Sahara* Advisory Opinion that the consultation of the inhabitants of a given territory was not necessary in some cases if "a certain population did not constitute a 'people' entitled to self-determination or on the conviction that a consultation was totally unnecessary, in view of special circumstances".[229]

One mystery surrounding the concept of self-determination was the undefined term "peoples". Even in the colonial context where the right to self-determination was widely accepted as a customary international law, the disagreements on the definition of "peoples" had greatly influenced its implementation. In the case of Hong Kong, according to the PRC, Hong Kong was "Chinese territory occupied by the British ... authorities".[230] The Chinese government viewed the people of Hong Kong as part of the Chinese nation. Therefore, they were not a "people" who were entitled to colonial self-determination. The Legal Adviser to the UK Foreign and Commonwealth Office suggested that

---

226 The 1984 Joint Declaration between the Government of the United Kingdom of Great Britain and Northern Ireland and the Government of the PRC on the Future of Hong Kong.

227 Ibid.

228 J. Engers, supra note 24, at p. 91.

229 West Sahara, ICJ Report (1975), p. 25, para.59.

230 Letter Dated 08/03/1972 from the Permanent Representative of China to the UN Addressed to the Chairman of the Special Committee, 27 GAOR, Supplement No.23, A/8723/Rev.1, p. 70.

"what one needs to consider are the circumstances of each particular case in which the [right to self-determination] may be invoked".[231] Britain disregarded the will of the people in Hong Kong on the grounds that Hong Kong's unique situation made it fall within the category of "special circumstance", existing British obligations arising from treaties with China.[232]

Those Sino-British treaties, according to the Chinese government, were not valid due to the unequal bargaining power of the parties. The invalidity argument was not justifiable under international law at the time as the threat/ use of force was not yet outlawed. Nor had contemporary international law allowed for voiding a treaty on the basis of the inequality of the contracting parties.[233] In theory, the New Territories should be restored to China when the 1898 lease expired in 1997, unless the parties agreed otherwise. The parties then reached an agreement to return the territory in the 1984 Joint Declaration without consulting the residents. However, were old treaties and the subsequent Joint Declaration still valid under the newly emerging principle of self-determination? Article 64 of the Vienna Convention on the Law of Treaties provided that "if a new peremptory norm of general international law emerges, any existing treaty which is in conflict with that norm becomes void and terminates". Some commentators argued that the right to self-determination was of a nature *jus cogens*, a peremptory norm of international law.[234] The peremptory status of the principle would terminate any treaties that contravened it. This, nonetheless, was arguably not the case. The right to self-determination appeared to fail the test of establishing a peremptory norm: 1) there was a lack of the evidence of international consensus on the peremptory nature of self-determination; 2) the existence of a number of treaties illustrated the opposite; 3) self-determination was not superior in relation to other legal principles.[235] In practice, no other states challenged the validity of the 1984 Joint Declaration.

Although the principle of self-determination may not be *jus cogens*, the conclusion of the 1984 Joint Declaration may have breached international law, considering the status of self-determination as a customary international law (in the colonial context).[236] Neither the Vienna Convention on the Law of

---

231 Quoted in Robert Mccorquodale, supra note 216, at p. 288.

232 Robert Mccorquodale, ibid, at p. 320.

233 Robert Mccorquodale, ibid, p. 327.

234 See James Summers, supra note 1, at pp. 78–79; Hurst Hannum, supra note 22, at pp. 44–45, 48.

235 James Summers, ibid, pp. 79–84.

236 Marcel Hooijmaijers, "Hong Kong and the Right of Self-determination", 6:197 *Tilburg Foreign Law Review* (1997), p. 222.

Treaties nor the general practice of states, however, explicitly stated the hierarchy between the treaty and customary international law. Customary norms could exist alongside treaty law,[237] but a new international custom might not necessarily terminate existing conflicting treaties. Otherwise, the Chinese denouncement of an "unequal" treaty would have had a plausible stand.

On the other hand, even if it were possible that the population of Hong Kong could be considered a colonial "people", according to Resolution 1514, such a "people" was not automatically accorded the right to self-determination since "any attempt aimed at the partial or total disruption of the national unity and the territorial integrity of a country is incompatible with the purposes and principles of the Charter of the United Nations".[238] The open concept of "country" could be construed to mean a nation.[239] So the national unity and the territorial integrity of the Chinese nation should be protected. The question then went back to the definition of "nation" and its relation to that of "people".

All in all, Hong Kong appeared to be another example that illustrated a selective application of the right to self-determination during the decolonisation process. The transfer of sovereignty of the whole territory in 1997 could possibly have been justified on the grounds that the status of self-determination was not *jus cogens,* or that Hong Kong residents did not represent a "people". The settlement of the Hong Kong question may also be explained in another way: as Mccorquodale argued, the GA's unclear guideline on "whether the people of a 'colonial enclave' cannot exercise their right of self-determination when there is a competing territorial claim" may be explainable as it had "less to do with [the territory's] factual characteristics and more to do with the political reactions to the particular situation of member states of the UN".[240]

3.3.2 *Macau*

The process of resuming sovereignty over Macau went fairly smoothly, without raising too many debates as did the case of Hong Kong. The Portuguese presence in the small enclave of 17.5 square kilometres with few resources could be dated back to the 1540s.[241] The Portuguese were formally allowed by the local authority to settle down in the territory by 1557. Upon regular payments

237 Nicaragua *v.* United States of America (Merits), ICJ Reports, 1986, paras.176–177.

238 GA Resolution 1514 (XV), Principle 6.

239 It may also be interpreted as a colony or a state. The Resolution 1514 itself failed to clarify the concept and all three different interpretations could be found in state practice. See James Summers, supra note 1, at pp. 206–207.

240 Robert Mccorquodale, supra note 216, at p. 324.

241 Herbert S. Yee and Sonny S. H. Lo, "Macau in Transition: the Political Decolonisation", 31:10 *Asian Survey* (1991), p. 907.

of the ground rent, the settlement was legitimised with the consent of the imperial Chinese authority in Canton.[242] This formal approval led to contentions that the early occupation was based on the lease. The legal status of Macau, however, remained undetermined, despite the *de facto* occupation of the Portuguese. In the 1887 Treaty of Friendship and Commerce, China acknowledged the perpetual occupation and administration of Macao by Portugal, while Portugal in return agreed not to alienate the territory to other states without China's prior consent.[243]

During the ROC period, the Nationalist Party initiated a modification program of "unequal" treaties, which aimed to abolish foreign privileges within China.[244] The Revised Treaty of Friendship and Commerce restored the control over the tariff administration and abolished the extraterritoriality.[245] But the sovereignty of Macau was excluded from the negotiation agenda, due to political considerations.[246] On the Portuguese side, the 1933 Colonial Act integrated Macau into the Portuguese empire and the 1951 constitutional revision specified it as an "overseas province".[247]

The removal of Macau from the colonial territories list, together with domestic regime change in Portugal, provided a proper basis for settling the "historic" question of Macau. After the 1974 coup, Portuguese delegates assured China that Portugal had no intention to seize the territory and then classified Macau as a "special case".[248] A secret agreement, which introduced an obligation of future negotiation on the return of the territory, was said to have been reached in 1979 during the negotiation on the establishment of the diplomatic

242 Stewart Lloyd-Jones and Antonio Costa Pinto (eds), *The Last Empire: Thirty Years of Portuguese Decolonisation* (Intellect, 2003), p. 57; Geoffrey Gunn, Qin Chuanan (Translator), *Aomen shi 1557–1999* [*Encountering Macau: A Portuguese City-state on the Periphery of China 1557–1999*] (Zhongyang Bianyi Chubanshe, 2009), p. 23; Yash Ghai, "The Basic Law of the Special Administrative Region of Macau: Some Reflections", 49-1 *International and Comparative Law Quarterly* (2000), p. 185.

243 "Zhongpu youhao tongshang tiaoyue [the 1887 Treaty of Friendship and Commerce between China and Portugal]", in Huang Hongzhao, *Aomen shi* [*the History of Macau*] (Fujian Renmin Chubanshe, 1999), Appendix, p. 667; Stewart Lloyd-Jones and Antonio Costa Pinto (eds), ibid, p. 58; Yash Ghai, ibid, p. 186.

244 Huang Hongzhao, ibid, pp. 355–356.

245 Ibid, pp. 358–359.

246 Ibid. The Republican Government's hesitation to incorporate sovereignty issue into negotiation arose from the consideration that it may deadlock the whole modification program, through which the nationalists eagerly wanted to improve the image of its power.

247 Stewart Lloyd-Jones and Antonio Costa Pinto (eds), supra note 242, at p. 58.

248 Ibid.

relation between two states.[249] The involved states concluded the Joint Declaration of the Government of the People's Republic of China and the Government of the Republic of Portugal on the question of Macau after formal negotiation in 1986. The Sino-Portuguese Declaration stated that the exercise of sovereignty over Macau would be resumed by China in 1999. China made the same argument as it did on the question of Hong Kong: Macau was an "occupied territory", so the population did not constitute a "people" for the purpose of colonial self-determination. It was a matter that only concerned the Chinese and Portuguese governments, especially after Portugal relinquished its sovereignty over the territory through a constitutional amendment in 1974.[250]

Compared with Hong Kong, dissenting opinions were rarely raised in the process of Macau's return. There were a few reasons for this. First, the local society had a three-layer structure: the Portuguese, the Macanese (Macau-born people with mixed blood of Chinese and Portuguese, less than 3% of the population) and the Chinese (approximately 97% of the population).[251] The Macanese formed the majority in the middle service rank.[252] The legitimacy of the Portuguese governor was challenged by them from time to time. The Chinese were mainly voiced through the Chinese Chamber of Commerce.[253] When the situation changed in the mid-1970s the Macanese, as the leading force in politics, inclined to maintain Macau's political autonomy from China's interference rather than to seek independence, in view of its dependent relationship with China.[254] The Chinese continued their pro-China policy. More importantly, despite the fact that the Portuguese government had yielded to Chinese pressure many times,[255] the Portuguese actually lost control of the enclave after the 12-3 Incident in 1966.[256] It was the Chinese who exercised *de*

249 Ibid, pp. 58–59; Huang Hongzhao, supra note 243, at p. 374; Yash Ghai, supra note 242, at p. 186.

250 Stewart Lloyd-Jones and Antonio Costa Pinto (eds), supra note 242, at p.58; Yash Ghai, supra note 242, at p. 186.

251 Herbert S. Yee and Sonny S. H. Lo, supra note 241, at p. 906.

252 Ibid, pp. 906, 908.

253 Ibid.

254 Ibid, p. 908.

255 Ibid, p. 907.

256 The origin of the Incident was the tolerant attitude of the Portuguese government to the KMT's activities and its use of Macau as a base camp for "reactionary" propaganda against the Beijing regime. Riots broke out on the 3rd December, targeting the Portuguese officials and the Portuguese and Chinese supporters of the KMT. As the situation degenerated and the tension aggravated with the presence of Chinese warships in the waters, the Portuguese government issued a statement of apology by the end of January and in fact handed over the power to the Chinese Chamber of Commerce. Geoffrey Gunn, Qin

facto control of the territory thereafter. Communist historians even labelled Macau as a "half liberated area", which again illustrated the inability of Portugal to rule the enclave without the consent of China.[257] Furthermore, there was no controversy over sovereignty between China and Portugal when the negotiation started. Also, the economic significance upon world trade distinguished Macau from Hong Kong.

3.4 China's Approach to the Right to Self-determination

The establishment of the PRC in 1949 has been considered to be the realisation of a unified and independent Chinese state for the Chinese people. Even though the "class theory" dominated the nation-building for decades in the aftermath, the official discourse of "the pluralistic unity of the Chinese nation" has remained unchanged. The taking of state power enabled the CPC to promote such an ideology internally through the state controlled media, educational system, legal framework, and so on. Externally, China insists that the Chinese people, composed of all ethnic groups, have determined to establish an independent state, within which they exercise the right to freely determine their political status and pursue economic, social and cultural development.[258]

However, the official claim, "self-determination exercised by the whole Chinese people", was challenged by the Tibetans in the 1960s when they successfully managed to include the question of Tibet in the GA agenda. The international hesitation to support Tibetan self-determination, however, seems to suggest that the Chinese assertion of nationhood has prevailed over the rival claim of the Tibet nation. In the cases of Hong Kong and Macau, China eventually resumed the exercise of sovereignty in those territories. But the will of the peoples in the territories concerned was not consulted in the process, as they were not considered to be the peoples for the purpose of colonial self-determination, according to the Chinese government. The Chinese practice of self-determination has revealed the importance of political strength and international support in relation to the success of a self-determination claim, which is further illustrated by the cases of Kosovo, Crimea, and Catalonia. The

---

Chuanan (Translator), supra note 242, at pp. 230–232; Huang Hongzhao, supra note 243, at pp. 372–373.

257 Huang Hongzhao, supra note 243, at p. 373; Herbert S. Yee and Sonny S. H. Lo, supra note 241, at p. 908.

258 The Common Program of the Chinese People's Political Consultative Conference, Preamble; the 1954 Constitution of the People's Republic of China, Preamble, Articles 2, 3, 6, 7.

undefined term "peoples" leads to another possibility in regard to excluding the application of the principle.

China's approach to self-determination is probably best reflected in the Written Statement on the Question of the Unilateral Declaration of Independence by Kosovo, which states:

> [a]lthough the principle of self-determination has become a basic principle of international law, it applies within specific limits, primarily restricted to situations of colonial rule or foreign occupation. The right to self-determination is different in nature from the so-called right of secession. The exercise of the right of self-determination shall not undermine the sovereignty and territorial integrity of the State concerned ... Secession is not recognised by international law and has always been opposed by the international community of States.

As discussed in previous chapters, territory is the key element in China's perception of nationalism and sovereignty. The ultimate goal of the CPC was, and still is, to regain the lost territories of the Qing Empire via any possible measures. Therefore, any claims that may jeopardise territorial integrity would be construed as a challenge to the Beijing regime. Hence, according to the Chinese government, the right to self-determination should be exercised consistently with the principle of territorial integrity.

In the human rights context, in its periodic reports to the Committee on Economic, Social and Cultural Rights (CESCR) concerning the obligations set out in Article 1 of the ICESCR, China emphasises that the right to self-determination is fully exercised by the people of China as a whole.[259] With respect to the issue addressed by the CESCR, which asked, "to what extent is non-violent advocacy of self-determination by the officially recognised ethnic minorities considered lawful" under Chinese law, China replied that minority self-determination is exercised through the right to regional self-rule (autonomy) within the state.[260] No further issues on the subject have been raised by the CESCR since. Hence, the "peoples" in the context of the twin human rights

259 The Initial Report Submitted by China under Articles 16 and 17 of the International Covenant on Economic, Social and Cultural Rights (ICESCR), 2004, UN Doc. E/1990/5/Add.59, pp. 5–6, para.6; the 2nd Periodic Report Submitted by China under Articles 16 and 17 of the ICESCR, 2010, UN Doc. E/C.12/CHN/2, p. 5; Replies of China to the List of Issues, 2005, CESCR/NONE/2004/10 pp. 5–6.

260 Replies of China to the List of Issues , 2005, ibid, pp. 5–6.

covenants refer to the whole Chinese people and the minorities are expected to exercise internal self-determination through territorial autonomy within the state.[261] As autonomy is seen as an arrangement, not a right in international law,[262] and China undertakes no international obligations to recognise such a right, the content of territorial autonomy in China should be examined under Chinese law.

3.4.1 *Autonomy as a Means of Exercising Internal Self-determination*

Territorial autonomy has been deployed by the CPC on occasion to facilitate the accommodation of the minorities, or to serve as political arrangements for a few unsolved territorial problems left over from the past. The constitutional regime of regional autonomy for the minorities theoretically grants minority groups comprehensive powers to govern their regional affairs. In the cases of unsolved territories, a varying higher degree of autonomy is tolerated and allowed so as to achieve the national unification, regardless of the differences in the political systems in particular territories.

(1) One Country Two Systems

The "one country two systems" model is officially viewed as a "creative development" of the Marxist-Leninist theory by the Chinese communists and as the "best solution" to peacefully reunify the Chinese state without resorting to any sort of conflict.[263] The full expression of the principle is "peaceful reunification and one country two systems". This regime in essence would be summarised as "allowing the existence of different political systems in certain territories within the unified socialist China" in the form of regional autonomy.[264]

The concept of "one country two systems" is traceable to the first generation of Chinese leaders, which was proposed so as to achieve peaceful reunification with Taiwan.[265] In regard to Taiwan's "liberation", the Beijing government

261 Periodic Reports of China under the ICESCR, supra note 259.

262 Patrick Thornberry, supra note 86, at p. 123; Zelim Skurbaty, supra note 86, at p. xxxvii; David Raic, supra note 7, at p. 283.

263 Xu Chongde, "Lun 'yiguo liangzhi' dui shixian guojia tongyi de yiyi [the Strategic Importance of 'One Country Two Systems' " to the Realisation of National Unity]", 02 *Zhongguo Faxue* [*China Legal Science*] (1990), p. 13.

264 Ibid.

265 Ibid, pp. 14–15; Di Chengguang, "Deng Xiaoping 'yiguo liangzhi" gouxiang de xingcheng yu fazhan [Formation and Development of Deng Xiaoping's 'One Country Two Systems' Conception]", 03 *Anhui Shixue* [*Historical Research in Auhui*] (2007), pp. 69–71; Sean Cooney, "Why Taiwan is not Hong Kong: A Review of the PRC's 'One Country Two Systems' Model for Reunification with Taiwan", 06:03 *Pacific Rim Law & Policy Journal* (1997), p. 501.

shifted its strategy from "liberation" by force to possible negotiations in the mid-1950s, due to the changing atmosphere of international relations. The Beijing regime repeatedly referred to "equal footing negotiation" and "the third KMT-CPC cooperation" to appeal to the Taiwanese authority.[266] Although this endeavour turned out to be fruitless for Taiwanese reunification at the time, the establishment of formal diplomatic relations between China and the US brought a new opportunity to solve the Taiwan problem. The Party leaders elaborated this general idea into the principle of "one country two systems", which was later written into the 1982 Constitution.[267] Under the new doctrine, the CPC offered Taiwan a high degree of autonomy as a special administrative region of the PRC, and pledged to respect the *status quo* of Taiwan and the views of its people.[268]

However, the "one country two systems" model was first implemented in Hong Kong and Macau as the conditions became ripe. The Hong Kong Special Administrative Region and the Macau Special Administrative Region (SAR) were established in accordance with Article 31 of the 1982 Constitution. Except for foreign and defence affairs, which are the responsibilities of the Central People's Government, the two SARs kept their socio-political systems unchanged and enjoy a high degree of autonomy.[269]

---

266 Zhou Enlai, "Taiwan de jiefang yiding nenggou shixian [Taiwan Will Be Liberated]", in *Zhou Enlai xuanji (xiajuan)* [*Selected Works of Zhou Enlai: Volume 2*] (Renmin Chubanshe, 1984), pp. 200–203; Di Chengguang, supra note 265, at pp. 70–71.

267 Article 31 of the 1982 Constitution provides that "[t]he state may establish special administrative regions when necessary. The systems to be instituted in special administrative regions shall be prescribed by law enacted by the National People's Congress in the light of the specific conditions".

268 "Zhonghua renmin gonghe guo quanguo renmin daibiao dahui changwu weiyuan hui gao Taiwan tongbao shu [the NPC Standing Committee's Message to the Taiwan Compatriots (01/01/1979)]", http://cpc.people.com.cn/GB/64184/64186/66677/4493866.html, last accessed on 21/10/ 2013; Ye Jianying, "Guanyu Taiwan huigui zuguo shixian heping tongyi de fangzhen zhengce de jianghua [Elaborations on Policy concerning the Return of Taiwan to the Motherland and Peaceful Reunification] (30/09/1981)", 22 *Gazette of the State Council* (1981), pp. 687–688; Deng Xiaoping, "Zhongguo dalu he taiwan heping tongyi de shexiang [An Idea for the Peaceful Reunification of the Chinese Mainland and Taiwan]", in *Selected Works of Deng Xiaoping: Volume 3*, supra note 221, pp. 30–31; the English translation is available at http://english.peopledaily.com.cn/dengxp/vol3/text/c1120.html, last accessed on 21/10/2015.

269 The 1984 Joint Declaration of the Government of the United Kingdom of Great Britain and Northern Ireland and the Government of the People's Republic of China on the Question of Hong Kong and the 1987 Joint Declaration of the Government of the People's Republic of China and the Government of the Republic of Portugal on the Question of Macao; the Basic Laws of the Hong Kong SAR and the Macau SAR, the Preamble, Articles 2, 5, 11–14.

The scope of autonomous powers of the SARs varies from case to case. In Hong Kong and Macau, autonomy extends to executive, legislative and judicial affairs, including final adjudication.[270] Nevertheless, the Taiwan proposal is a looser form of the "one country two systems" model, as the Beijing government "acknowledges the differences between Taiwan one the one hand and Hong Kong and Macau on the other".[271] This would enable Taiwan to keep its own military forces, provided that it did not threaten the mainland, and to "enjoy certain rights in foreign affairs", for example, "to conclude commercial and cultural agreements with foreign countries".[272] These variations, according to Chinese scholars, derive from the nature of the question.[273] Taiwan is a question left over from the civil war, and therefore it constitutes an internal affair of the Chinese people, whereas the questions of Hong Kong and Macau have a colonial feature as they involve China and other sovereign states. This may help us to understand that the base line in the Taiwan situation is that any matters can be discussed on the premise of "one-China", including the consideration of the will of the Taiwanese people.[274] Hence, the degree of autonomy of a special administrative region depends, to a certain extent, on the bargaining power of the parties concerned, in particular its military, economic and factual independence from the control of the CPC.

"One country two systems" is essentially a political tactic formulated by the communists to expand their sovereignty to territories that they did not formerly control. It also helps to make the solution more acceptable to the residents in the relevant territories, when compared to involuntary settlement, which follows reunification by force. This may explain the unique autonomous status that the Tibetans obtained after the defeat against the communist army in 1951. Tibet autonomy at the time was somewhere in-between regional ethnic autonomy and the "one country two systems" model. Under the 17 Points Agreement, the Tibetans were vested with a greater extent of autonomous powers than other minority groups enjoying regional autonomy under the Common Program of the Chinese People's Political Consultative

270 The Basic Laws of the Hong Kong SAR and Macau SAR, Article 2.

271 The Information Office of the State Council, the White Papers on the Taiwan Question and Reunification of China (1993); the One-China Principle and the Taiwan Issue (2000). See also Deng Xiaoping, supra note 268.

272 Ibid.

273 Zhang Dinghuai and Li Yanchao, "Shijian lixing: 'yiguo liangzhi' zhengce de lilun jichu [the Theoretical Basis for the 'One Country Two Systems' Policy]", 00 *Dangdai Zhongguo Zhengzhi Yanjiu Baogao* [*Research Reports on the Politics of Contemporary China*] (2011), p. 315.

274 The Information Office of the State Council, the White Papers, supra note 271.

Conference.[275] For example, the Tibetans had the right to maintain their social-political system unchanged, unless the people requested otherwise,[276] which only left national defence and foreign affairs to the central government.[277] Arguably the 1951 Tibetan arrangement could be viewed as an antecedent attempt of the "one country two systems" theory, with the purpose of rendering the transfer of sovereignty and the "liberation" more acceptable to the Tibetans. However, the proposed "two systems" experiment in Tibet failed shortly after the 1959 rebellion, and ended up with an imposed "democratic reform" and the consequent establishment of the Tibet Autonomous Region, as well as the ongoing disputes between the CPC and the Dalai Lama.

The "one country two systems" proposal might be feasible in solving the Taiwan problem and achieving a peaceful reunification. The subsequent knock-on effects it might initiate, however, are also noteworthy. Unlike Hong Kong and Macau, Taiwan is a province-sized territory with self-sustaining capacity. The Taiwanese autonomy may set a precedent that a higher degree of autonomy at the provincial level is achievable. The CPC might be able to argue the "uniqueness" of the Taiwan case, but if the precedent were to be established, the implications would not diminish as it expects. For instance, the Dalai Lama's claim of "the Middle-Way Approach"[278] embodies a similar logic. He argues for the "genuine" autonomy for Tibet, which leaves only Beijing with responsibility for foreign affairs.[279] Furthermore, if Taiwan constitutes a "special case", why is Tibet not special? If Tibet is entitled to "genuine autonomy", what about other minority groups? If the minorities were eligible for a higher degree of autonomy, the Han dominated provinces may, as a result, ask for the same treatment. Perhaps strong and powerful local governments are unlikely to exist, as long as China remains a super power and the CPC continues its firm control of the country. The implementation of the "one country two systems" principle in large territories may operate as a double-edged sword. The questions of Taiwanese and Tibetan autonomy need to be handled delicately.[280]

275 Until the first constitution was adopted in 1954, the Common Program functioned as the provisional constitution of the PRC.

276 The Agreement of the Central People's Government and the Local Government of Tibet on Measures for the Peaceful Liberation of Tibet (the 17 Points Agreement), Articles 4, 5, 11.

277 The 17 Points Agreement, Articles 2, 8, 14.

278 The Dalai Lama, Memorandum on Genuine Autonomy for the Tibetan People. The full text is available at http://tibet.net/important-issues/sino-tibetan-dialogue/memorandum-on-geniune-autonomy-for-the-tibetan-people/, last accessed on 22/10/2013.

279 Ibid; see also Thomas Heberer, supra note 99, at p. 126.

280 The Beijing authority is unwilling to offer the Tibetans a similar autonomous status under Article 31 of the 1982 Constitution. As illustrated by rounds of fruitless talks with the

(2) Ethnic Territorial Autonomy

As discussed in Chapter 2, the ethnic autonomy of China's minorities originated from Lenin's theory of self-determination. However, the right of the minorities to secession has been gradually narrowed to the right to self-government. The establishment of the Autonomous Government of Inner Mongolia in 1947 has been considered by some commentators as the first practice of the CPC's theory of ethnic territorial autonomy.[281] However, other scholars disagree, arguing that the alteration of the terminology alone does not necessarily imply that the CPC has relinquished the long-term advocated theory of minority self-determination.[282] They assert that minority autonomy may only be a temporary strategic adjustment when the situation changes and emphasise that this autonomy is a territorially based self-government in the federal state, not regional autonomy within a unitary state.[283] Such an argument might possibly be correct in the sense that Mao continued to refer to "self-determination" and the "federal republic of China" until the mid-1940s.[284]

Tibetan Exiles, the Chinese government emphasises in the 2004 White Paper on Regional Ethnic Autonomy in Tibet that "the situation in Tibet is entirely different from that in Hong Kong and Macao. The Hong Kong and Macao issue was a product of imperialist aggression against China; it was an issue of China's resumption of exercise of its sovereignty. Since ancient times Tibet has been an inseparable part of Chinese territory, where the Central Government has always exercised effective sovereign jurisdiction over the region". The Information Office of the State Council, the White Paper on Regional Ethnic Autonomy in Tibet (2004).

281 Chen Yangyong, "Gongtong gangling yu xinzhongguo sanda zhengzhi zhidu de queli [the Common Programme and the Establishment of Three Fundamental Policies in the New China]", 04 *Dangde Wenxian* [*Literature of Chinese Communist Party*] (2009), p. 24.

282 Ibid.

283 Ibid.

284 In the 1948 version of "On Coalition Government (1945)", Mao stated that: "[trans. L. W.] ... the questions of the new democratic state and political regime embrace the question of federalism. All nationalities within the territory of China, in conformity with the principle of 'voluntary and democracy', should establish a Democratic Republic of Chinese Federation and organise a Federal Government on that basis. ... [we demand] to improve minority treatment and grant minorities the rights to self-determination and to establish a federal state with the Han on the basis of their free will". Cited in Huang Zhu, "Zhongguo gongchandang minzu zhengce de zhongda zhuanbian [A Great Transformation of the CPC's Policy towards Nationalities—from Federalism to Regional Autonomy of Ethnic Groups]", 04:23 *Zhongnan Minzu Daxue Xuebao* [*Journal of the South-Central University for Nationalities* (*Humanities and Social Sciences*)] (2003), p. 5. In the 1947 Declaration of the People's Liberation Army (the 1948 version), Mao again argued that "minority nationalities shall enjoy the rights of equality and autonomy and shall have the freedom to join the Chinese federation at their own will". Cited in Suisheng Zhao, *A Nation-State by Construction: Dynamics of Modern Chinese Nationalism*

Federalism was indeed mentioned and discussed a number of times in the preparatory stage of the establishment process. Nevertheless, the communists eventually adopted a unitary system of government, rather than the Soviet federal-republic model. They claimed that China's historical development and revolutionary circumstances were different from those of the USSR.[285] Zhu Suli argued that China's political leaders did not seriously consider federalism as an alternative, as a strong centralised government was required to maintain national unity and encourage economic development and to extend the power of the state into society.[286] Although many provinces had not yet been "liberated" by the time Mao declared the establishment of the PRC in 1949, the Beijing Regime progressively took effective control over most of the territories on the mainland, including traditional minority regions. This left the minorities with less bargaining power when finalising the terms of their ethnic territorial autonomy. The following chapters will focus on the current legal framework that is applicable to the minorities and examine how internal self-determination is practised through the institutional arrangement of Regional Ethnic Autonomy (REA).

(Stanford University Press, 2004), p. 175. See also Chapter 2, Section 2.2.2 "The CPC and Soviet Self-determination".

285 Zhou Enlai, "Guanyu woguo minzu zhengce de jige wenti [Some Questions of the Ethnic Policy in Our Country] (04/08/1957)", in Jin Binghao (ed), supra note 107, at pp. 578, 581–585.

286 Zhu Suli, "Federalism in Contemporary China: A Reflection on the Allocation of Power Between Central and Local Government", 7 *Singapore Journal of International & Comparative Law* (2003), p. 2.

PART 2

Minority Rights in China

CHAPTER 4

The Regional Ethnic Autonomy System

The 1949 Common Program of the Chinese People's Political Consultative Conference (the Common Program) laid down a rough idea of regional autonomy for the minorities.[1] Article 51 provided that "regional autonomy shall be exercised in areas where the national minorities are concentrated and various kinds of autonomy organisations shall be set up according to the size of population and the regions".[2] The General Programme for the Implementation of Regional Ethnic Autonomy (the General Programme) was adopted in 1952, which made the constitutional regime of REA implementable. The constitutions, together with the laws and regulations on autonomy, have formed the legal framework of REA. At present, the 1982 Constitution and the Law on REA are the two basic legal documents on the matter. The status of the REA is stated as the "basic political system" of the state[3] and "the basic policy adopted by the Communist Party of China for resolving the ethnic issue in China through its application of Marxism-Leninism".[4] Considering the close relationship between the CPC and the state, apart from the legal framework, internal regulations (e.g. notice, decision, and instruction) of the CPC in regard to China's minorities are influential as well.

According to the Law on REA, REA is defined as:

> ethnic minorities, under the unified state leadership, practice regional autonomy in areas where they live in concentrated communities and set up autonomous agencies for the exercise of the power of autonomy.[5]

---

1 This Chapter contains materials previously published. The details are as follows: Linzhu Wang, "The Definition of Indigenous Peoples and Its Applicability in China", 22:2 *International Journal on Minority and Group Rights* (2015), pp. 232–258, © International Journal on Minority and Group Rights, published by Brill, Reprinted with permission; Linzhu Wang, "The Identification of Minorities in China", 16:2 *Asian-Pacific Law and Policy Journal* (2015), pp. 1–21, blog.hawaii.edu/aplpj/files/2015/09/APLPJ_16_2_Wang.pdf, published by Asian-Pacific Law and Policy Journal, © Linzhu Wang.

2 The Common Program, Article 51.

3 According to the 1984 Law on REA, ethnic territorial autonomy was "an important political system", whereas in the amended 2001 Law on REA, it has become the "basic political system" of the state. Therefore, there are three basic political systems in China: the People's Congress, the People's Political Consultative Conference, and the REA.

4 The Law on REA, Preface.

5 Ibid.

 DOI:10.1163/9789004380578_006

Four elements are highlighted in this definition: regions, minorities, autonomous agencies and autonomous rights.[6] The non-Han groups, who have been officially recognised by the central government as *shaoshu minzu*, are entitled to territorial autonomy. Therefore, the self-identified/reported and unidentified groups cannot claim such rights. Compared with the political-oriented minority identification, the other three factors—regions (*quyu*), autonomous agencies and autonomous powers—are mainly covered and defined in legal terms.

This Chapter is the first of three examining the current legal framework that is applicable to China's minorities. It deals with the first three elements of the REA system: regions, minorities, and autonomous agencies. The Chapter examines various factors that may have affected the establishment of autonomous areas and looks at how the division of autonomous areas would significantly affect the exercise of autonomous rights. By comparing the legal provisions of minority representation to the political reality of minority representation in autonomous agencies, it demonstrates the importance of the size of the minority population in an autonomous area, arguing for an urgent need to include more minority members in positions of leadership. Finally, this Chapter assesses how the minorities are identified and recognised in the Ethnic Identification Project and considers the applicability of the concept of indigenous peoples in the Chinese context.

4.1 Regions in the REA System

REA, according to the Constitution and the Law on REA, is implemented at the provincial (autonomous regions), prefectural and county levels where the minorities live in concentrated communities.[7] Those autonomous areas could be further divided into "appropriate autonomous areas or nationality

6 Maria Lundberg and Yong Zhou, "Regional National Autonomy under Challenge: Law, Practice and Recommendations", 16 *International Journal on Minority and Group Rights* (2009), p. 272. Ao Junde identified five elements in the REA system: *minzu* that exercises regional autonomy, autonomous areas, organs of self-government, autonomous power and self-governing regulations. See Ao Junde, "Guanyu minzu quyu zizhi fa de liangge jiben wenti [Two Fundamental Questions About Autonomy of Ethnic Regions—in Commemoration of the 20th Anniversary of the Promulgation of the Law of Ethnic Regions Autonomy]", 06 *Guizhou Minzu Xueyuan Xuebao* [*Journal of Guizhou University for Ethnic Minorities(Philosophy and Social Sciences)*] (2004), p. 40.

7 Article 30 of the 1982 Constitution states: "…[a]ll autonomous regions, autonomous prefectures and autonomous counties are national autonomous areas"; the Law on REA, Article 2.

townships",[8] if other minorities also live in concentrated communities within the administrative boundaries of the established autonomous areas.[9] Concentration, as the prerequisite of REA, is an undefined term, as the law does not specify the number or the ratio of the minorities in the local population in order to claim autonomous status. Geographic boundaries of autonomous areas are delimited, according to the law, "in the light of local conditions, such as the relationship among various nationalities and the level of economic development, and with due consideration for historical background".[10]

4.1.1 *Historical Factors*

Article 9 of the 1952 General Programme provided:

> [trans. L. W.] "the delineation and alteration of administrative boundaries, the status, and the name of autonomous areas shall be determined after the consultation between the people's government at the direct higher level and the representatives of the minorities. Then it should be submitted to the people's government at the next higher level for approval; all autonomous areas at and above the county level should be approved by the Central People's Government Council".[11]

In the pre-PRC era, communist powers stretched out in the form of revolutionary bases. Upon the "liberation", most administrative units were set up

8 However, nationality townships within the established autonomous areas are not autonomous areas *per se*. Chinese law only recognises autonomous regions, prefectures and counties as national autonomous areas. Only national autonomous areas can exercise the right to autonomy through the people's congresses and people's governments. The 1982 Constitution, Article 30; the Law on REA, Article 15; see also TABLE 2 Administrative Structure of the PRC.

9 The Law on REA, Article 12.

10 The Law on REA, Article 12.

11 Article 14 of the 1984 Law on REA had a similar provision, which stated: "[t]he establishment of an ethnic autonomous area, the delineation of its boundaries and the elements of its name are proposed by the state organ at the next higher level jointly with the state organ in the relevant locality, after full consultation with representatives of the relevant nationalities, before they are submitted for approval according to the procedures prescribed by law. Once established, an autonomous area may not be revoked or merged without proper legal procedures. Once defined, the boundaries of an ethnic autonomous area may not be altered without proper legal procedures. If it is truly necessary to revoke autonomy, or merge or change areas, the ethnic autonomous organs and the concerned department of the next higher level state organs must thoroughly consult and formulate an agreement to submit for approval according to the procedures prescribed by law".

according to historical divisions in the Qing Empire and the ROC.[12] At the provincial level, many traditional minority regions restored their historical boundaries. Tibet recovered the Changdu area and reinstated its territory as it was during the Qing period.[13] In the 1950s, Inner Mongolia substantially expanded its jurisdiction to an area that was comparable to traditional Mongolian region during the Qing dynasty as well. Geographic boundaries of Xinjiang, Guangxi and other minority provinces almost remained unchanged. The Ningxia Hui Autonomous Region (NHAR) was still a sub-division of Gansu province up to this time. As to the establishment of sub-provincial autonomous areas, the setting-up was, in principle, based on historical layouts and existing local conditions, as well as the will of the minorities concerned.[14]

4.1.2 *The Size of Population*

Article 51 of the Common Program stipulated that autonomy agencies should be established according to the minority population and the size of the region. Article 4 of the General Programme, however, omitted the population requirement from the condition list. Furthermore, it provided that "[trans. L. W.] according to local economic and political needs and with due consideration for historical background, all autonomous areas shall incorporate certain Han communities, towns and cities".[15] This made it very flexible, as incorporating or excluding specific Han communities might be justified on those grounds. Although the physical concentration of the minorities was the precondition to establish an autonomous area, the minority population ratio was not the decisive element. Among all provincial-level autonomous

12 Chen Chao, *Zhongguo xingzheng quhua yange shouce* [*The History of Administrative Divisions in China*] (Zhongguo Ditu Chubanshe, 2000), pp. 206–207.

13 Changdu area was taken from Tibet and incorporated into the defunct Chuanbian Special Administrative District in 1914, which later became Sikang province in 1939, so as to stabilise the local situation and to strengthen the central control in Tibetan areas. See Tan Qixiang (ed), *Zhongguo lishi ditu ji* [*The Historical Atlas of China Volume VIII: The Qing Dynasty Period*] (Zhongguo Ditu Chubanshe,1996), pp. 61–62; Chen Chao, ibid, at pp. 209–210; Zhang Minggeng and Zhang Mingju (eds), *Zhongguo lidai xingzheng quhua* [*The History of Administrative DivisionS in China: 221 BC to 1991*] (Zhongguo Huaqiao Chubanshe, 1996), pp. 548–550.

14 Deng Xiaoping, "Guanyu xinan shaoshu minzu wenti [the Minority Question in the Southwest] (21/07/1950)", in the Policy Research Office of the State Ethnic Affairs Commission (ed), *Zhongguo gongchandang zhuyao lingdaoren lun minzu wenti* [*The Comments of the Main Leaders of the CPC on the Ethnic Questions*] (Minzu Chubanshe, 1994), p. 56; the English translation is available at: http://english.peopledaily.com.cn/dengxp/vol1/text/a1200.html, last accessed on 22/10/2013.

15 The 1952 General Programme, Article 5.

TABLE 1

Name of the Autonomous Region	Establishment Year	Population Composition (By Establishing Year)	
Inner Mongolia Autonomous Region	1947	Han	84.7%
		Mongol	13.7%
Xinjiang Uyghur Autonomous Region	1955	Han	10.8%
		Uyghur	72.8%
Guangxi Zhuang Autonomous Region	1958	Han	58.4%
		Zhuang	36.9%
Ningxia Hui Autonomous Region	1958	Han	67.3%
		Hui	32.5%
Tibet Autonomous Region	1965	Han	2.93%
		Tibetan	96.6%

SOURCES: IMAR STATISTICAL YEARBOOK 1997, 2009; XUAR FIFTY YEARS 1955–2005 (STATISTICAL BOOK); REPORT ON THE ESTABLISHMENT OF GUANGXI ZHUANG AND NINGXIA HUI AUTONOMOUS REGION (05/07/1957) AT THE FOURTH SESSION OF THE FIRST NPC; NHAR STATISTICAL YEARBOOK 2012; HE JINGXI, "WOGUO ZANGZU RENKOU DE BIANDONG [THE CHANGE OF THE TIBETAN POPULATION IN CHINA: A RESEARCH ON THE ETHNIC COMPOSITION OF THE POPULATION IN TIBETAN AUTONOMOUS AREAS]", 04 *ZHONGGUO SHEHUI KEXUE* [*SOCIAL SCIENCES IN CHINA*] (1995), PP. 107, 109.

units, only Tibet and Xinjiang were minority dominant provinces in the early PRC era. (See Table 1)

The ethnic structure of the population, however, became a flexible instrument to achieve the political purpose of the CPC. The incorporation of Changdu into the Tibet Autonomous Region (TAR) in 1955 would in no way affect the majority status of Tibetans in the region. But, on the contrary, it showed great sincerity of the communists for peaceful reunification under the 17 Points Agreement. Likewise, a similar strategy could also be traced in the Mongolian situation. The "return" of vast historical land to the Inner Mongolia Autonomous Region (IMAR) approximately trippled its territory. This expansion of the administrative division, however, did not change the Han dominance in the local population.

On the other hand, as the Mongols, Uyghurs and Tibetans founded their own autonomous areas, territorial arrangements for the Zhuang and Hui at the provincial level became politically urgent. Despite the fact that these two groups had already acquired autonomous status at the prefecture and/or county level, the size of the population, the Zhuang as the largest minority group and the Hui as the third largest, required the establishment of autonomous units at the provincial level.[16] In the process of establishing the Guangxi Zhuang Autonomous Region (GZAR), one of the two plans suggested to divide the former Guangxi province into a Han province in the east and a Zhuang autonomous region in the west.[17] Thus, the Zhuang would form a majority in the proposed Zhuang autonomous area. However, this proposal was rejected after consulting with the local government and the people. It had been argued that the Han-Zhuang cooperation would better fit the long-term interests of all groups in Guangxi, whereas a small Zhuang autonomous area would isolate the two parts and impair the local economy and development.[18] In the case of the Ningxia Hui Autonomous Region, the Han domination would be established in the area, no matter how geographic boundaries were delineated. Hence, a smaller Hui autonomous region was established, after taking into account the local ethnic relation and history.[19]

When it came to Xinjiang, a Uyghur dominant area with clear administrative boundary and long separatist history, to increase the Han presence in the area became the strategy. Zhou Enlai repeatedly referred to the richness of resources in "brother" minority areas. He pointed out that those resources would be important backup for socialist construction, emphasising the urgent need of involving other ethnic groups who had technologies and labour forces, the Han in particular, in resource exploitation and economic development.[20] Since "Xinjiang's development depends on the cooperation of different minorities", apart from regular garrisons that were deployed in border areas for national defence, the CPC mobilised thousands of the Han into Xinjiang, under the

---

16 Ulanfu, "Guanyu jianli Guangxi Zhuangzu zizhiqu he Ningxia Huizu zizhiqu de baogao [Report at the Fourth Session of the First National People's Congress on the Establishment of the Guangxi Zhuang Autonomous Region and Ningxia Hui Autonomous Region] (07/07/1957)", http://www.npc.gov.cn/wxzl/gongbao/2000-12/23/content_5328393.htm, last visited on 22/10/2013.

17 Ibid; George Moseley, *The Consolidation of the South China Frontier* (University of California Press, 1973), p. 82.

18 Ibid; Zhou Enlai, "Guanyu woguo minzu zhengce de jige wenti [Some Questions of the Ethnic Policy in Our Country] (04/08/1957)", in Jin Binghao (ed), *Minzu gangling zhengce wenxian xuanbian* [*The Collected Works of the Documents on the National Program and Policy*] (Zhongyang Minzu Daxue Chubanshe, 2006), p. 581.

19 Ulanfu, supra note 16.

20 Zhou Enlai, supra note 18, at pp. 576–577, 584–585.

name of developing local economy, constructing socialism and defending the frontiers of "motherland" against reactionary forces.[21] Besides these communist mandated population flows, a large number of Han migrants flooded into Xinjiang at their own initiatives.[22] For example, thousands of them were driven by the disastrous famine of 1959–1960.[23] By the mid-1960s, more than one million[24] cadres, female soldiers, youth intellectuals, Production and Construction Corps,[25] and ordinary people migrated into Xinjiang for various reasons.

4.1.3 *Other Factors*

The will of the minorities was another element to be considered in the process of establishing autonomous areas, as the General Programme required the consultation with representatives of relevant minorities on the matter.[26] Deng Xiaoping also stressed that administrative divisions shall not be set up without the consent of the minorities concerned.[27] But it was difficult to evaluate to what extent the will of the minorities would affect the final decision.

Taking Guangxi as an example, the Zhuang did not demand to establish an autonomous area at the provincial level, as the Guixi Zhuang Autonomous Prefecture already existed, where they made up 70% of the population.[28] The suggestion to decide the establishment of a Zhuang autonomous region on the basis of a referendum was rejected, "since the referendum together with the principle of self-determination, though as the name suggested, might be easily manipulated by the imperialists, and thus would jeopardise national

21 Ibid, p. 584; Jing Binhao (ed), *Zhongguo gongchandang minzu gongzuo fazhan yanjiu dier bian: xinjiang xizang* [*Research on the Developments of the CPC's Ethnic Work Volume 2: Xinjiang and Tibet*] (Zhongyang Minzu Daxue Chubanshe, 2007), pp. 80–82, 84–85.

22 Gardner Bovingdon, "Chapter 4 Heteronomy and Its Discontents—'Minzu Regional Autonomy' in Xinjiang", in Morris Rossabi, *Governing China's Multiethnic Frontiers* (University of Washington Press, 2004), pp. 117–154 at p. 123; Thomas Heberer, *China and Its National Minorities: Autonomy or Assimilation?* (M. E. Sharpe, Inc., 1989), p. 94; Robyn Iredale and Fei Guo, "Chapter 1 Overview of Minority Migration", in Robyn Iredale, Naran Bilik, and Fei Guo (eds), *China's Minorities On the Move: Selected Case Studies* (M. E. Sharpe, 2003), pp. 3–31 at pp. 4–6, 28–29; Ren Qiang and Yuan Xin, "Chapter 5 Impacts of Migration to Xinjiang since the 1950s", in ibid, pp. 89–104, at p. 100.

23 Gardner Bovingdon, ibid, p. 123.

24 Thomas Heberer, supra note 22, at p. 94.

25 Initially, the Production and Construction Corps were stationary soldiers who were ordered to participate in communist construction. They were then discharged from the Army and became members of the Production and Construction Corps, which gradually evolved into special social units.

26 The 1952 General Programme, Article 9.

27 Deng Xiaoping, supra note 14.

28 George Moseley, supra note 17, at pp. 81–85.

unity and socialist construction".[29] The communists argued that the scheme of establishing a Zhuang autonomous region should be under the good guidance (of the CPC), which ought to serve the interests of the majority people and, in the meantime, take the dissenting opinions into consideration.[30] Kaup instead pointed out that, through the identification of the Zhuang and the establishment of a Zhuang autonomous region, the CPC was intended to weaken localist ties of minority groups in the southwest and integrate them into the unified Chinese state.[31]

In practice, the schemes of establishing autonomous areas were generally formulated by internal discussions of the CPC or its regional committees. For example, the Dali Bai Autonomous Prefecture in Yunnan Province was founded upon the decision of the CPC Dali Regional Committee.[32] The proposals of establishing the Yili Kazakh Autonomous Prefecture in Xinjiang resulted from the discussions between the CPC Xinjiang Regional Committee and the Xinjiang People's Council, which were finalised by the CPC Xinjiang Regional Committee.[33] Next, those proposed schemes were intensively propagated, and consultations with cadres and the masses would be followed. If the local people disagreed with preliminary proposals, "persuasion" would be used in the consultation process. It is also worth noting that no new autonomous regions or prefectures have been established after the dissolution of the USSR and Former Yugoslavia in the 1990s. Only one autonomous county, the Beichuan Qiang Autonomous County,[34] has been established after this time.

---

29 Zhou Enlai, "Minzu quyu zizhi youliyu minzu tuanjie he gongtong jinbu [Regional Ethnic Autonomy Contributes to National Unity and Common Progress] (25/03/1957)", in the Policy Research Centre of the State Ethnic Affairs Commission (ed), supra note 14, at pp. 156–157.

30 Ibid.

31 Katherine Kaup, *Creating the Zhuang: Ethnic Politics in China* (Lynne Rienner Publishers, 2000), pp. 8, 25, 171.

32 Dali Baizu zizhizhou gaikuang bianxie zu [the Writing Group of the Overview of the Dali Bai Autonomous Prefecture], *Dali Baizu zizhizhou gaikuang* [*Overview of the Dali Bai Autonomous Prefecture*] (Yunnan Minzu Chubanshe, 1986), pp. 64–65.

33 Kuerbanali Wusipanuofu, "Recalling the Founding Process of the Yili Kazakh Autonomous Prefecture", http://www.xjyl.gov.cn/Article/ShowArticle.aspx?ArticleID=8333, last accessed on 22/10/2013.

34 According to the statement of the Beichuan County Government, it was treated as a quasi-minority county by the Sichuan People's Government since 1988 and formally established in 2003 after received the approval of the State Council. See http://www.beichuan.gov.cn/content.jsp?id=8a868a3458d73386015900b4ec6206b99&classid=bda5dfcb093d42b-8bad85db45ffd82d2, last accessed on 31/03/2018.

MAP 2 The Administrative Division of the Xinjiang Uyghur Autonomous Region. Bortola (Mongol), Ili (Kazakh), Bayinguoleng (Mongol), Changji (Hui) and Kizilsu (Kyrgyz) are autonomous prefectures.
Cited in Gardner Bovingdon, supra note 22, at p. 119.

Measures of internal balance within autonomous areas were also utilised by the CPC so as to strengthen its control in minority areas. Further administrative divisions within multiethnic autonomous areas were precisely designed to maintain internal Han-minority and minority-minority balance.[35] Xinjiang, for example, was subdivided into two Mongol Autonomous Prefectures, one Kazakh Autonomous Prefecture, one Kirghiz Autonomous Prefecture, one Hui Autonomous Prefecture and other administrative districts (see Map 2).

35 The 1952 Programme did not specify the structure of the autonomous organs. Zhou Enlai suggested that "[trans. L. W.] ...a proper arrangement to the personnel of the organs of self-government should be made accordingly in a Han dominant autonomous area. Therefore, in the GZAR, the chairman of the Region shall be a citizen of the nationality exercising regional autonomy in the area concerned. As the Han constituted a majority in the GZAR, the Han shall have a proportional representation in the overall number of the representatives and the chairman of the standing committee of the people's congress may also be a Han". See Zhou Enlai, supra note 29, at p. 155.

4.2 Autonomous Agencies

When the PRC was founded, there was no established governmental structure and institution, upon which the communists could rely.[36] The CPC had to create and build its own governmental machinery. The Common Program, therefore, enclosed no explicit provisions on the tiers of local governments. Accordingly, the status of autonomous areas in national administrative layout was not regulated in the 1952 General Programme. The General Programme then accorded the minorities exercising regional autonomy the power to decide the forms of autonomous agencies, based on the majority will of the people and their leaders.[37] The 1954 Constitution laid down a four-level division system to organise local governments—provincial, prefectural, county and township, which was reinstated in the 1982 Constitution.[38] At each level, there existed appropriate administrative units for the minorities to exercise autonomy (see Table 2). The 1954 Constitution retained a flexible attitude towards the forms of autonomous agencies, which could be determined in accordance with the majority will of the minority group(s) exercising regional autonomy.[39] The change came in the 1982 Constitution. It provided that autonomous powers can only be exercised through the Local People's Congress (LPC), its Standing Committee (LPCSC) and the Local People's Government (LPG).[40] The right to freely choose the forms of autonomous agencies was deleted from the law, since the "people's congress—people's government" model of the governmental structure became constitutionalised. So far, 44 out of 55 officially recognised minorities have already established 5 autonomous regions, 30 autonomous prefectures and 120 autonomous counties/banners.[41]

---

36 Peter Ferdinand, *Communist Regimes in Comparative Perspective: the Evolution of the Soviet, Chinese and Yugoslav Systems* (Harvester Wheatsheaf, Barnes & Noble Books, 1991), p. 232; Sybille Van Der Sprenkel, "Chapter 7: The Role of Law in the Changing Society", in Jack Gray (ed), *Modern China's Search for a Political Form* (Oxford University Press, 1969), pp. 225–267 at p. 232.

37 The 1952 General Programme, Articles 10, 14, 18.

38 The 1954 Constitution, Article 53; the 1982 Constitution, Article 30.

39 The 1954 Constitution, Article 67.

40 The 1982 Constitution, Articles 4, 95, 112; the Law on REA, Articles 3, 15.

41 The State Ethnic Affairs Commission (SEAC): http://www.seac.gov.cn/col/col108/index.html, last accessed on 31/03/2018. 9 out of 11 minorities who fail to establish autonomous areas have established their own ethnic townships. See Maria Lundberg and Yong Zhou, supra note 6, at p. 299.

TABLE 2 Administrative Structure of the PRC[a]

Provincial Level (*sheng ji*)	– Provinces (22+1*) Municipalities directly under the Central Government (4) Special Administrative Regions (2) *Autonomous Regions* (5)
Prefectural Level (*di ji*)	– Prefecture Prefectural-level cities Leagues (*meng*)** *Autonomous Prefectures*
County Level (*xian ji*)	– Counties/ Banners Districts (city-governed districts) County-level cities *Autonomous counties/banners***
Township Level (*xiang ji*)	– Town (*zhen*) Township (*xiang*) Ethnic township (*minzu xiang*)[b]

NOTE: THE DIVISIONS IN ITALICS ARE CONSTITUTIONALLY ETHNIC AUTONOMOUS AREAS; * IS TAIWAN; ** REFERS TO TRADITIONAL TERMS SPECIFICALLY USED IN THE IMAR.

a See the 1982 Constitution; the Law on REA; the 1983 State Council Notice on Questions of Establishing Ethnic Township; the 1993 Administrative Regulation on Ethnic Township.

b According to the 1982 Constitution and the Law on REA, autonomous areas are defined as autonomous regions, autonomous prefectures and autonomous counties. Ethnic regional autonomy is exercised through the LPCs and LPGs of autonomous areas. Ethnic townships are not considered as autonomous areas. Although the Chinese government has argued in its report to the Committee on the Elimination of Racial Discrimination that "ethnic townships plays an important role in safeguarding the right of dispersed ethnic minorities to manage their own internal affairs and has become an important complement to regional ethnic autonomy", ethnic townships *per se* are not considered to be autonomous and do not enjoy autonomous rights guaranteed by the Constitution and the law. Ethnic townships, therefore, are not covered by this study. The 1982 Constitution, Articles 30, 112; the Law on REA, Articles 2, 15; the 14th-17th Periodic Reports of China under Article 9 of the International Convention on the Elimination of All Forms of Racial Discrimination (ICERD), CERD/C/CHN/14-17, 2017, p. 14, para.62.

4.2.1 *The Local People's Congress and Local People's Government*

LPCs and LPGs as autonomous agencies legally assume a dual character. On the one hand, they function as the local branches of state institution. On the other hand, they are self-government bodies, through which the minorities exercise autonomy as prescribed by the Constitution and the law.[42] Apart from repeated emphasis on the leadership of the CPC and on the status of autonomous areas as being integral parts of the PRC,[43] 5 out of 11 articles in Chapter 1 "General Principles" of the Law on REA focus on the nature of autonomous agencies as components of state institution to achieve overall interests. Article 7 specifically stated that "autonomous agencies shall place the interests of the state as a whole above all else and actively fulfil all tasks assigned by state institutions at higher levels".[44]

Under the principle of "by the people, for the people", the LPC at various levels is the institution, in which the local people can exercise state power within administrative units.[45] The Deputies of LPCs, according to their administrative level, are elected by the people's congresses at the next lower level or directly by constituencies.[46] Hence, LPCs are not responsible to the NPC on a superior-subordinate basis. Under Chinese law, the relation between LPCs and the NPC is confined to legal supervision and functional linkage and guidance. In the unitary state of China, LPCs undertake the responsibility to ensure the observance and implementation of the laws and regulations of higher people's congresses in their administrative divisions.[47] They shall elect the governor and deputy governors of the LPG, the president of the people's court and the chief procurator of the people's procuratorate at the corresponding level.[48] LPCs also possess the power to adopt local regulation, and to examine and decide on plans for economic, cultural and social development, as well as on other crucial matters.[49] LPCs meet frequently, at least once a year (normally once a year).[50] LPCs at and above the county level establish standing committees

42 The 1982 Constitution, Article 115.

43 The 1982 Constitution, Preamble, Article 4; the Law on REA, Preamble.

44 The Law on REA, Article 7.

45 The 1982 Constitution, Article 96.

46 The 1982 Constitution, Article 97; the Organic Law for Local People's Congresses and Local Governments at All Levels (recently amended in 2015, the Organic Law), Article 5; the Election Law of the National People's Congress and the Various Levels of Local People's Congresses (the Election Law), Article 2.

47 The 1982 Constitution, Article 99; the Organic Law, Articles 8, 9.

48 The 1982 Constitution, Article 101; the Organic Law, Articles 8, 9.

49 Ibid.

50 The Organic Law, Article 11.

as their permanent agencies, which in turn are responsible and answer to the local people's congresses.[51]

Meanwhile, the LPG is the executive agency of the LPC at the corresponding level, as well as the local branch of the state administration.[52] Unlike LPCs, all LPGs are "state administrative organs under the unified leadership of the State Council and are subordinate to it".[53] A LPG is obligated to report to the LPC at the same level and to state administrative agencies at higher levels.[54] The tension may arise from this parallel accountability of the LPG to different state institutions. However, neither the Constitution nor the Organic Law for Local People's Congresses and Local Governments at All Levels (the Organic Law) further clarifies the hierarchy of these parallel accountabilities.[55]

4.2.2 *Minority Representation in Autonomous Agencies*

(1) Minorities in the Local People's Congress and Its Standing Committee

Article 12 of the 1952 General Programme provided that officials of autonomous agencies should be mainly drawn from citizens of the minority exercising regional autonomy. Inhabitants of the Han and other minorities in the autonomous area were entitled to appropriate representation as well.[56] This, in fact, echoed with the CPC's ethnicisation policy in order to win the trust of the minorities and to ensure social stability. Minority areas enjoyed a significant degree of autonomy for the time being. Ethnicisation, in the words of Zhou Enlai, involved matters of minority language, cadre trainings, religion and customs.[57] As a result, during the 1950s, minority languages and scripts were created and systemised. Great efforts were made to provide access for the minorities to education. Ethnic customs and religions were respected and left unaffected. Most importantly, the training and inclusion of minority cadres into the regime became one of the Party's focuses.[58] It was estimated that the Han-minority membership figure in the party apparatus in Xinjiang reached up to half-and-half between 1949 and 1965.[59] In Inner Mongolia, approximately

---

51 Ibid, Article 40; the 1982 Constitution, Article 96.

52 The 1982 Constitution, Article 105.

53 Ibid.

54 Ibid, Article 110.

55 Yash Ghai, Sophia Woodman and Kelley Loper, "Is There Space for 'Genuine Autonomy' for Tibetan areas in the PRC's System of Nationalities Regional Autonomy?", 17 *International journal on minority and group rights* (2010), p. 150.

56 The 1952 General Programme, Article 12.

57 Zhou Enlai, supra note 18, at pp. 592–594.

58 Ibid; Peter Ferdinand, supra note 36, at p. 241.

59 Peter Ferdinand, supra note 36, at p. 240

50% of cadre posts were reserved for the Mongols. They also dominated the provincial party secretariat until the Cultural Revolution.[60] Unfortunately, this comparatively moderate minority policy was replaced by an extreme assimilation policy, as the Great Leap Forward and the Cultural Revolution approached.

Later, the Law on REA modified the minority dominance clause. As the local institution of state power, the number and proportion of deputies to the LPC in autonomous areas are decided by the standing committee of the people's congress at a higher level.[61] The Election Law of the National People's Congress and the Various Levels of Local People's Congresses (the Election Law) introduces a model of "base number + additional number = a total number with limitations" for the LPC deputy election.[62] For example, the base number of deputies for an autonomous region is 350. One more deputy may be added for every one hundred and fifty thousand people. The total number of deputies shall not exceed 1,000.[63] When the minorities inhabit concentrated communities, whether in an autonomous area or not, the total deputy numbers may be raised by 5%.[64] On the allocation of deputy quotas, where the minority population makes up more than 30 % of the local population, no preferential treatment would be applied to this minority; where the minority population is less than 15 %, more minority deputies may be elected than the average representation ratio, but cannot exceed the double of that ratio; where the minority population exceeds 15% but less than 30%, the election of more deputies from that minority is also allowed, as long as it would not surpass 30% of the total deputy number.[65]

This model, in essence, is a proportionate quota based on the size of the population. In order to guarantee a decisive vote in the LPC, a minority needs to make up to 50% of the population in an autonomous area. Since the size of the minority population was not a critical factor in the establishment of autonomous areas, the minorities fail to form a population majority in more than 70%[66]of the autonomous areas. The TAR is the only autonomous region that the minority easily constitutes a majority in the LPC. In the XUAR, the Uyghur and Han account for 46% and 40% of the total population respectively.[67] None

---

60 Ibid, p. 241.

61 The Law on REA, Article 16; the Election Law, Article 12.

62 The Election Law, Article 11.

63 Ibid.

64 Ibid.

65 Ibid, Article 18.

66 Maria Lundberg and Yong Zhou, supra note 6, at p. 304.

67 By 2010, the population in the XUAR is 21,815,815, among which the Han population is 8,829,994 and the population of the Uyghur is 10,001,302. See Zhongguo 2010 nian renkou

of them may be able to secure a 1/2 majority vote and prevail the LPC, unless they could win support from the remaining 14% minority population.

The deputies of the standing committee are elected by the LPC at the corresponding level, from the pool of the LPC deputies.[68] Considering the meeting frequency and the number of the LPC deputies, the standing committees with a more compact size of members, which meet at least once every two months, to some extent, outweigh the importance of the LPCs at each level, particularly after the 1982 Constitution has granted them a similar legislative power.[69] The member quotas of the standing committee at the provincial level are to be determined by the provincial LPC, in accordance with the size of the population.[70] The standing committee of the LPC at the provincial level then decides the allocation of the deputy quotas of the LPC Standing Committees at lower levels.[71] Thus, the proportion of minority deputies in the standing committee is subject to the size of the minority population as well. In case a minority group is unable to secure a majority in the LPC, it is very unlikely for this group to prevail in the standing committee. Although the law provides that the chairman or vice-chairman of the LPC standing committee in an autonomous area should be a citizen of the minority that is exercising autonomy, it may not substantially affect the decision of the standing committee under the principle of majority rule.[72] This in fact means that in most autonomous areas the minority representatives can be outvoted. (See Table 3)

(2) Minority Representation in the LPG

Article 17 of the Law on REA deals with the minority representation ratio in LPG s. It reserves the most important position, the governor of the LPG, to a citizen from the minority exercising regional autonomy. Also, a reasonable number of posts should be allocated to this minority group and to other minorities inhabiting the area. But the law remains silent on the ethnic structure of LPG s.

---

pucha ziliao [the Statistics of the 6th National Census in 2010], Table 1–6, http://www.stats.gov.cn/tjsj/pcsj/rkpc/6rp/indexch.htm, last accessed on 16/06/2018.

68 The 1982 Constitution, Article 103; the Organic Law, Articles 8, 21.

69 Article 41 of the Organic Law states: "the number of members of standing committees at provincial level is normally from 35 to 65; provinces with populations over 80 million may have up to 85; prefectural level is from 19 to 41; prefectural-level cities with populations over 8 million could have 51 members at most; and county level is 15 to 27; and the total number of 35 for the divisions have over 1 million population". See also the Organic Law, Articles 11, 43, 45; the 1982 Constitution, Article 100.

70 The Organic Law, Article 41.

71 Ibid.

72 Ibid, Article 20; the Law on REA, Article 16.

TABLE 3 The Ethnic Composition of the LPC Standing Committees in Autonomous Regions[a]

The Number of Deputies of Standing Committees (2013)	The Figures of Overall Minority Deputies and the Deputies of the Minorities Exercising Autonomy	
Inner Mongolia Autonomous	Minorities: 22	40%
Region: 55	Mongol: 19	35%
Xinjiang Uyghur Autonomous	Minorities: 39	67%
Region: 58	Uyghur: 22	38%
Guangxi Zhuang Autonomous	Minorities: 27	43%
Region: 63	Zhuang: 17	27%
Ningxia Hui Autonomous	Minorities: 22	36%
Region: 61	Hui: 22	36%
Tibet Autonomous	Minorities: 25	57%
Region: 44	Tibetan: 21	48%

a SOURCES: IMAR: HTTP://WWW.NMGRD.GOV.CN/XJRM/XJ/INDEX.HTML; XUAR: HTTP://WWW.XJPCSC.GOV.CN/RDYW/201302/T4028E48A3C90225B013C942A66A800A8.HTML; GZAR: HTTP://WWW.GXRD.GOV.CN/DBDH2013/NEWS/YAOWEN/2013-01-29/1260.HTML; NHAR: HTTP://WWW.NX.XINHUANET.COM/2013-01/30/C_114551309.HTM; TAR: HTTP://WWW.XIZANG.GOV.CN/BGJY/63725.JHTML, LAST ACCESSED ON 24/10/2013.

Both the chief executive and deputy executives of the LPG at each level are to be elected by the LPC correspondingly.[73] The accountability of the chief executive in the LPG seems to grant the head of the LPG the power to nominate his/her own office and personnel, except for the deputy leaders, to the LPC Standing Committee at the same level.[74] In other words, the minority government leader can freely nominate officials for relatively less important posts as prescribed by the law, but has no influence on the appointment of his/her deputies.

Nevertheless, these are merely provisions of the law. In reality, because of the *nomenklatura* system (party management of cadres/*dangguan ganbu*), it may be difficult to evaluate to what extent an elected minority leader of the

73 The 1982 Constitution, Article 101; the Organic Law, Article 8.

74 The 1982 Constitution, Articles 86,105; the Organic Law, Article 57. But the premier of the State Council is empowered to nominate vice premiers and other chief officials of the central government. See the 1982 Constitution, Article 62.

government could actually nominate an office according to his/her own will.[75] Based on the Soviet model, the Chinese *nomenklatura* system also contains two lists: the first list is about "leading positions, over which Party units exercise the power to make appointments and dismissals"; and the second list specifies "reserves or candidates for these positions".[76] Government officials, the nominally elected chief executives and all leading posts in the LPCs are in a way selected through the *nomenklatura* system. The *nomenklatura* system, as Zheng Yongnian puts it, is "the most important organisational pillar" for the CPC to dominate the personnel decision of all important positions in the country, and thus to put the state apparatus and armed forces more effectively under its control.[77]

(3) Political Reality of Minority Representation

The Soviet theory of the party-state relation stated that the party undertook the responsibility of formulating the general direction and framework for policy, whilst the role of the state was to elaborate and implement such policy.[78] Unlike the USSR and Yugoslavia that relied upon institutional mechanism, legal framework and the codification of the power of different institutions to regulate the central-local relationship, the CPC mainly depended on the Party and its ideology to integrate the nation.[79] The imperial tradition and thoughts may have contributed to the situation that the Party dominates the state: "the CPC is the owner of the country since the party established the PRC …; and the government can be regarded as the manager of the state".[80] The 1956 Party Constitution laid down the role of the CPC as "the leader and core in every

---

75 The *nomenklatura* system was introduced by the Bolshevik party of the Soviet Union in 1922. Initially, it referred to two lists: "the first contained all leading posts in various institutions which lay within the power of that party organisation to fill; and the secondary, or reserve *nomenklatura* contained the names of all party members judged capable of being appointed to one of these posts". Peter Ferdinand, supra note 36, at p. 66. The CPC adopts a similar system to emphasise the Party's control over the state. See Huang Xianhong, "Lun wanshan xingzheng shouzhang fuzezhi [the Perfection of the Chief Executive Responsibility System]", 03 *Zhongguo Faxue* [*China Legal Science*] (1999), pp. 100–101; Xiao Ping and Li Xiaowu, "Xingzheng shouzhang fuze zhi de gengxin yu fazhan [Renewal and Development of Chief Executive Responsibility System]", 02 *Nanchang Daxue Xuebao* [*Journal of Nanchang University* (*Humanities and Social Sciences*)], 2002, p. 49.

76 Quoted in Zheng Yongnian, *The Chinese Communist Party as Organisational Emperor: Culture, Reproduction, and Transformation* (Routledge, 2010), p. 103.

77 Zheng Yongnian, ibid; Peter Ferdinand, supra note 36, at p. 317.

78 Peter Ferdinand, supra note 36, at p. 118.

79 Ibid, pp. 231, 239.

80 Zheng Yongnian, supra note 76, at pp. 98–99.

aspect of the state's life".[81] The 2007 Party Constitution specifically designated the CPC as the leader of economic, political, cultural and societal development as well as of the PLA and all other armed forces.[82] Apart from the excessive control over personnel decisions for leading posts in the state apparatus through the *nomenklatura* system, the CPC has also achieved its dominance over the state by the institutional design and the interlocking membership between the state agencies and party apparatus.

Local Party Congress and its Party Committee are set up at each administrative level accordingly.[83] The CPC Central Committee (CPCCC) manages the appointment of the First Secretary of the party committee (*dangwei shuji*) at the provincial level, who in most cases concurrently acts as the head of the LPC. For example, in 2018 the First Secretaries of the local party committees in 29 provincial units are the Han and 19 of them serve as the chairman of the LPC standing committee, including in the IMAR and NHAR.[84] It is difficult to calculate the exact ratio of party membership of the state officials, since no such statistics are made publicly available. The CPC, however, is said to be successful in infiltrating party members into the state apparatus.[85]

Furthermore, the communists also establish agencies within the party apparatus, which are parallel to the state institutions.[86] The party group (*dangzu*) represents another form of party extension in state agencies, people's organisations, economic organisations, cultural organisations and all other non-CPC organisations.[87] A party group is usually made up of the party members who hold senior positions in state agencies. Its functions include: guaranteeing the implementation of party policy, deciding on important issues, and more importantly overseeing the state agency on behalf of the CPC.[88]

Seen in this manner, the legal provisions on the ethnic requirement of "the chief executive of the LPG and the chairman or vice-chairmen of the LPC standing committees of autonomous areas" may not be able to accomplish their underlying purposes. The Han First Secretary of the local party committee at the

81 The 1956 Party Constitution, the Preamble.
82 The 2007 Party Constitution, the Preamble.
83 The 2017 Party Constitution, Articles 10, 25.
84 The Database of Local Leaders, http://ldzl.people.com.cn/dfzlk/front/personProvince2089.htm, last visited on 15/06/2018.
85 Peter Ferdinand, supra note 36, at p. 120.
86 Zheng Yongnian, supra note 76, at p. 101.
87 The 2017 Party Constitution, Article 48. For a further discussion on the relationship between the local party committee and the party group, see Zheng Yongnian, supra note 76, at pp. 111–112.
88 Ibid.

corresponding level is the one who holds the real power. Up to March 2018, only 2 First Secretaries are minority party members in all 31 provincial units: one is ethnic Miao and the other is of Mongolian origin. Likewise, even though the minority governor of the LPG manages to organise an administration based on his/her choices, e.g. appointing a considerable number of minority officials (cadres), he/she might not be governing in his/her way, due to the existence of the parallel party committees and party groups inside the government. In many situations, minority officials are also party members, who are subject to party discipline. Conflicts could arise from different identities: as a minority, as an official and as a party member.

In the Centre, the highest party institution is the National Party Congress.[89] The National Party Congress meets every five years. There were 2287 delegates attending the 19th National Party Congress in 2017, among which minority representatives made up to 11.5%.[90] The National Party Congress could hardly exercise the power efficiently, due to its meeting frequency and size. It then elects the Central Committee,[91] which usually has 175–210 delegates since the 12th Party Congress in 1982. The CPCCC meets on a yearly basis and comprises the heads of the NPC, the State Council, the Supreme Court and the Supreme Procuratorate, the Ministers, the First Secretaries of regional party committees who also serve as the heads of local state apparatus, and the leaders of the party groups in important organisations.[92] The representation ratio of the minorities in the CPCCC is reduced to 7%–9% of the total number of delegates.

Theoretically, the CPCCC represents the Party and leads the party work when the National Party Congress is not in session.[93] But the real power is exercised by the Central Politburo (of 13 to 25 members), more accurately by the Central Politburo Standing Committee in reality. Both agencies are, in theory, elected by and responsible to the CPCCC to act on its behalf when it is not in session.[94] But the Party Constitution fails to provide a clear division of

89 The 2017 Party Constitution, Article 10.

90 The number of minority delegates of the 17th Party Congress was 242, accounting for 10.9% of the total 2200 delegates, and 249 minority representatives attended the 18th National Party Congress in 2012, making up to 11% of the total 2270 delegates. Source: http://dangjian.people.com.cn/n1/2017/0930/c117092-29570771.html, http://cpc.people.com.cn/n/2012/0814/c241220-18743004.html, last accessed on 25/11/2017.

91 The 2017 Party Constitution, Article 10.

92 The data is collected on the basis of the delegate list of the CPCCC of the 17th Party Congress. The list is available at http://cpc.people.com.cn/GB/64162/64168/106155/106156/6426830.html, last visited on 28/12/2013.

93 The 2017 Party Constitution, Article 22.

94 Ibid, Article 23.

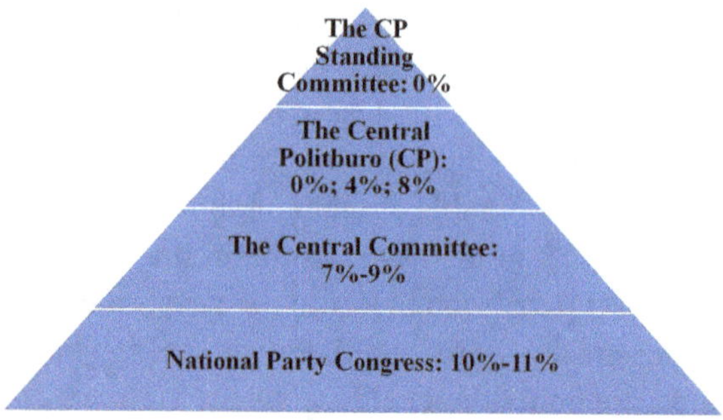

CHART 1 The Ethnic Composition of the CPC Core Leadership From 1949 to Present.
Note: % is the minority representation ratio.

the power. The Central Politburo Standing Committee plays a more important role than the Central Politburo does: it is the *de facto* highest and most powerful institution in China. The minorities have successfully reached the Central Politburo, and the best record is 2 minority delegates, out of 23, in the Central Politburo of the 11th Party Congress.[95] In most cases, there is none or one minority representative in the core leadership. However, no minority delegate has ever been elected a member of the Central Politburo Standing Committee.

It is arguable that the lack of minority presence in the Central Politburo Standing Committee, which is usually composed of 7 to 9 members, is not entirely unexpected since the minority population only makes up 8.5%[96] of the total population. But the minority delegates in fact account for more than 10% in the National Party Congress. In terms of the population proportion, the minorities are underrepresented in the CPCCC and the Central Politburo. Proportionately the minorities should be reserved at least 1 or 2 seats in the Central Politburo. Therefore, regardless of the numbers of minority delegates in the National Party Congress, the minorities fail to secure a proper representation among the top ruling elites in the political centre. Even though minority delegates have been elected in the Central Politburo, this again provides no proportionate representation of the overall minority population in terms of diversity. (See Chart 1 & Table 4)

---

95 Sources: the database of the CPC National Congress: http://cpc.people.com.cn/GB/64162/64168/106155/index.html, last visited on 28/12/2013.

96 The 2010 Census, http://data.stats.gov.cn/workspace/index?a=q&type=global&dbcode=hgnd&m=hgnd&dimension=zb&code=A03060E&region=000000&time=2010,2010, last visited on 25/10/2013.

TABLE 4 Membership of the Central Politburo and the Central Politburo Standing Committee[a]

	The Central Politburo (Total/Minority)	The CP Standing Committee (Total/Minority)
7th (1945–56)	13/0	N/A
8th (1956–69)	17/0	6/0
9th (1969–73)	21/0	5/0
10th (1973–77)	21/1 (Zhuang)	9/0
11th (1977–82)	23/2 (Mongol and Zhuang)	5/0
12th (1982–87)	25/2 (Mongol and Zhuang)	6/0
13th (1987–92)	17/0	5/0
14th (1992–97)	20/0	7/0
15th (1997–2002)	22/0	7/0
16th (2002–07)	24/1 (Hui)	9/0
17th (2007–12)	25/1 (Hui)	9/0
18th (2012–17)	25/0	7/0
19th (2017–Present)	25/0	7/0

a The 2010 Census, http://data.stats.gov.cn/workspace/index?a=q&type=global&dbcode=hgnd&m=hgnd&dimension=zb&code=A03060E&region=000000&time=2010,2010, last visited on 25/10/2013.

SOURCES: THE DATABASE OF THE CPC NATIONAL CONGRESS HTTP://CPC.PEOPLE.COM.CN/GB/64162/64168/INDEX.HTML, LAST VISITED ON 25/11/2017.

4.3 The Definition of Minorities

Since the Han constitute an absolute majority of the total population, all other groups are generally referred to as minorities (*shaoshu minzu*). Following the Soviet tradition, *minzu* was used as the synonym of nationality within the PRC until 1990s. According to Chinese law, the minorities have the collective right to territorial autonomy under the REA system.[97] Members of the minorities can also claim favourable treatment in many areas, including civil service

97 The Law on REA, Preface, Articles 2, 55–66, 69–71; Provisions on Implementing the Regional Ethnic Autonomy Law, Articles 5, 7–12, 14–19.

recruitments, university admissions, family planning etc.[98] However, not all non-Han ethnic groups in China are the "minorities". Only those who have been officially recognised by the central government as *shaoshu minzu* could claim minority rights. The minority status of ethnic groups was confirmed through the Ethnic Identification Project (the Project). This identification project took about 30 years to complete, in a period spanning the 1950s and 1980s. As a result, groups who identified themselves as a separate ethnicity but failed to acquire the official recognition cannot claim minority status and thus were effectively denied minority rights.[99] Generally, *shaoshu minzu* is seen as a legal-political concept in relation to Chinese minorities, which may also have cultural implications.

4.3.1 *The Ethnic Identification Project*

The 1949 Common Program recognised the equal status of all ethnicities in China and provided for regional autonomy where the national minorities were concentrated.[100] The 1952 General Programme further elaborated the ethnic territorial autonomy system. It provided autonomous agencies a wide range of rights within the autonomous area on the matters of local economy, finance and culture.[101] With the ethnic territorial autonomy system first confirmed, the holders of such rights, the minorities, were still undetermined since there were no accurate records on the minority ethnic situation at the time.

Hence, a number of Minority Visitation Teams were sent to minority areas from 1950 to 1953, including Southwest, Northwest, Northeast, and Middle South. The major tasks of the teams were to convey the Party's greetings and solicitude, to provide a medical and inoculation service, to propagate the Party's ethnonational policy,[102] and to investigate and collect relevant information on the minorities. In the 1953 national census, over 400 self-reported groups were recorded. This number, however, was apparently too many to be a suitable figure for implementing regional autonomy or a manageable figure for the CPC. Furthermore, the forthcoming NPC (scheduled in September

98 The Law on REA, Articles 23, 71; Core Document Forming Part of the Reports of China, UN Doc. HRI/CORE/CHN/2010, part 2, p. 30; the Committee on the Elimination of Racial Discrimination (CERD), UN Doc. A/51/18(SUPP), para.396; C. Mackerras, *China's Ethnic Minorities and Globalisation* (Routledge Curzon, 2003), pp. 233–237.

99 Barry Sautman, "Ethnic Law and Minority Rights in China: Progress and Constraints", 21:03 *Law and Policy*, (1999), p. 288.

100 The Common Program, Articles 9, 50, 51.

101 1952 General Programme, Articles 15–21.

102 Huang Guangxue and Shi Lianzhu (eds), *Zhongguo de minzu shibie* [*The Ethnic Identification in China*] (Minzu chubanshe, 2005), p. 105.

1954) only reserved 150 seats for minority representatives, "more than twice the number to which they would be entitled on a proportional basis".[103] With these issues in mind, an official project of ethnic identification with distinctive Chinese characteristics commenced nationwide after the self-reported census.

Hundreds of ethnologists, linguists, historians, sociologists and archaeologists were divided into various teams to investigate the claims of self-reported groups. It has been pointed out that a group of soviet linguists were involved in the process as well.[104] The Ethnic Identification Project (*minzu shibie*), as Thomas Mullaney put it, was:

> ... a collective term for a series of Communist-era expeditions wherein ethnologists and linguists set out to determine once and for all the precise ethnonational composition of the country, so that these different groups might be integrated into a centralized, territorially stable polity.[105]

As in many other aspects, the Chinese ethnic practice had also been influenced by the Marxist doctrines.[106] Marxists had developed many theories on nationalities, but the widely cited definition on nationality could be found in Stalin's writing.[107] According to Stalin, nation could be defined as "a historically constituted, stable community of people, formed on the basis of a common language, territory, economic life, and psychological make-up manifested in

---

103 The 1953 Election Law, Articles 21, 24; see also George Moseley, supra note 17, p. 7.

104 A group of Soviet linguists were sent to China as a part of the Soviet Advisors Program (1949–1960), with the purpose of assisting China's socialist construction. See Zhou Minglang, *Multilingualism in China: the Politics of Writing Reforms for Minority Languages 1949–2002* (Mouton de Gruyter, 2003), pp. 170, 171, 177–179, 187–190, 199–201; Fu Maoji, "Bang zhu shaoshu minzu chuangli gaijin he gaige wenzi gongzuo de qingkuang he wenti [the Work of Assisting Minorities to Create, Improve and Reform Their Writing Systems and the Questions Therein]", 02 *Kexue Tongbao* [*Chinese Science Bulletin*] (1956), pp. 22–24.

105 Thomas Mullaney, *Coming to Terms with the Nation—Ethnic Classification in Modern China* (University of California Press, 2011), p. 3.

106 Huang Guangxue and Shi Lianzhu (eds), supra note 102, at pp. 76–103; Fei Xiaotong, "Guanyu woguo minzu de shibie wenti [Ethnic Identification in China]", 01 *Zhongguo Shehui Kexue* [*Social Science in China*] (1980), pp. 154–155; Lin Yaohua, "Zhongguo xinan diqu de minzu shibie [Ethnic Identification in Southwest China]", 02 *Yunnan Shehui Kexue* [*Social Science in Yunan*] (1984), pp. 2–3.

107 Huang Guangxue and Shi Lianzhu (eds), ibid, pp. 11–25; Qin Naichang, "Makesi zhuyi minzu lilun zhongguohua de zhongda shijian [Ethnic Edentification: Great Practice of the Localisation of Marxist Ethnic Theory in China]", 02 *Guangxi Minzu Yanjiu* [*Study of Ethnics in Guangxi*] (2009), p. 21.

a common culture".[108] He observed that the presence of each of the four elements constituted a nation in the epoch of rising capitalism.[109]

In terms of the definition and criteria employed in the Chinese identification project, the official statement was that the minorities were identified with flexibilities, in accordance with Stalin's four-element concept of nation and the reality of Chinese ethnonational situation.[110] In addition, the will of the categorised was also considered in the identification process. However, minority groups in China experienced uneven socio-economic development. At the time of identification, many of them were still in the pre-capitalist stage, living in a primitive, subservient or feudal system,[111] and a multitude of the minorities were spread over and coexisted on the vast land. The strict application of Stalin's definition may have ruled out many minority groups from being classified as *shaoshu minzu*. Mao Zedong then instructed that politically all minority ethnic groups should be treated as *minzu*, regardless of the Soviet orthodox classification of "clan/tribe/tribal alliance/nation", since all ethnic groups were equal in the PRC.[112]

As a result, the minorities were classified pursuant to various criteria with contingency.[113] Some identification was based on language. For example, the ethnic classification in Yunnan province was essentially based on linguistic categorisation.[114] Some categorisation was made in accordance with history and ancestry origin, such as different Muslim groups in Xinjiang. Groups were also identified on the basis of religious beliefs. The Hui group was simply considered to be the Muslim Han.[115] Others were recognised on the basis of

---

108 Joseph Stalin, "Marxism and the National Question", in Bruce Franklin (ed), *The Essential Stalin: Major Theoretical Writings 1905-52* (Croom Helm London, 1973), pp. 54–84 at p. 60.

109 Ibid, p. 65.

110 Huang Guangxue and Shi Lianzhu (eds), supra note 102, at p. 87; Fei Xiaotong, supra note 106, at p.150; Lin Yaohua, supra note 106, at pp. 2–3.

111 Fei Xiaotong and Lin Yaohua, *Zhongguo minzu xue dangqian de renweu* [*the Current Task of the Ethnology in China*] (Minzu Chubanshe, 1957), pp. 14–21.

112 Huang Guangxue and Shi Lianzhu (eds), supra note 102, at pp. 80–81.

113 Chen Xinlin, "Zuqun lilun yu Zhongguo de zuqun yanjiu [Ethnic Group's Theory and Nationalities Research in Chin]", 06 *Guizhou Minzu Yanjiu* [*Guizhou Ethnic Studies*] (2005), p. 2.

114 Thomas Mullaney argued that the ethnic classification in Yunan province was actually decided on the basis of linguistic categorisation. See Thomas Mullaney, supra note 105, at p. 65.

115 Judith Banister, cited in Dru Gladney, *Muslim Chinese: Ethnic Nationalism in the People's Republic (2nd Edition)* (Harvard University Press, 1996), p. 25. Matthew Erie, however, argued that the Hui are the descents of the Persian and Arab businessmen, migrants and envoys who entered China during the Tang Dynasty and thus have had a long history. Matthew Erie, *China and Islam: The Prophet, the Party, and Law* (Cambridge University Press, 2016), p. 10.

national consciousness and ancestral heritage. The Manchu, for instance, were typically classified using this perspective. In practice, large groups, geographically or numerically, were very likely to be approved as minorities whereas small-numbered groups might often be ruled out or incorporated into other minorities.[116] The selective application of a set of standards left enough space for the communists to control the identification process for political and/or economic considerations.

According to Chinese scholars, the basic identification procedure usually followed five steps. First, the proposed minorities identified themselves. Then the provincial government or the central government sent out researchers to investigate and analyse the case. The researchers, normally ethnologists, had to consider two questions during the investigation: was the proposed group a part of the Han or was it a minority; if the group belonged to minority, was it a separate minority by itself or was it a part of the already recognised minorities.[117] After the completion of the investigation, the researchers then gave "scientific" recommendations, based on their findings. Next, they would present the findings to the proposed group, demonstrating whether their request of being identified as minority was plausible or not. Finally, the claimants would make the final decision of being a Han, a separate minority, or a part or branch of an existing minority.[118]

Mullaney, however, revealed a different approach, using Yunnan province as the paradigm. According to him, scholars and researchers first developed preliminary recommendations on classifying the minorities in Yunnan into two dozen groups by linguistic commonality, based on the taxonomic theories of the Republican period.[119] Then they analysed and located plausible communities with "ethnic potentials" from self-reported groups and persuaded them to accept "scientific recommendations".[120] Eventually, over 260 self-identified groups in Yunnan were reduced to 26 recognised minorities.

By 1954, before the first National People's Congress, 38 groups received official recognition. 11 of them, the Mongol, Hui, Tibetan, Uyghur, Miao, Yao, Yi, Korean, Manchu, Li and Gaoshan (in Taiwan), were the so-called "generally accepted minorities", and thus had no need to be assessed in the Ethnic

116 David Y. H. Wu, "Chinese Minority Policy and the Meaning of Minority Culture: the Example of Bai in Yunnan, China", 49:01 *Human Organisation* (1990), p. 3.

117 Fei Xiaotong, supra note 106.

118 Huang Guangxue and Shi Lianzhu (eds), supra note 102, Chapters 3, 5; Thomas Mullaney, supra note 105, Chapters 2, 3, 4; Lin Yaohua, supra note 106, at pp. 1–5; Fei Xiaotong and Lin Yaohua, supra note 111, at pp. 12–13.

119 Thomas Mullaney, supra note 105, at pp. 42–106.

120 Ibid.

Identification Project.[121] Later, 183 self-reported groups in the 1964 census became another 15 minorities in the so-called "family of nationalities".[122]

Alongside the ethnic identification, a nationwide linguistic research expedition also started in order to further assist the minorities to create and reform their scripts.[123] Meanwhile, an intensive investigation of minority social history was carried out to make sure that each newly identified minority would have its own concise history (*jianshi/jianzhi*) from the official narrative.[124] Hundreds of books on minority history and language were published following the investigation. Those linguistic and historical materials aimed to enhance the state recognised ethnic structure.

The Cultural Revolution nearly suspended all ethnological activities. It was not until the late 1970s that the ethnonational work was resumed. Minority individuals who had not expressed their identities (*minzu chengfen*) accurately for whatever reasons in the past acquired a second chance to change ethnic identity.[125] Approximately five million people were involved in the wave of recovering or changing minority status from 1981 to 1989.[126] As the ethnic identification work was primarily completed in the 1950s and the purpose of the new ethnic campaign was to "recover or change" minority identity, the practice in the 1980s seemed to avoid identifying new minorities. The ethnic identification during this period attempted to absorb and incorporate the proposed groups into already identified minorities through linguistic, territorial and/or historical ties as much as possible.[127] Guizhou province, for example, classified 23 self-reported ethnic groups (numbering 900,000) into the Han and other minorities.[128] Since the Jino group received the official recognition in 1979, no new minority has been identified thereafter.

121 Huang Guangxue and Shi Lianzhu, (eds), supra note 102, at p. 106.

122 Ibid, p.109; Joshua Castellino and Elvira Redondo (eds), *Minority Rights in Asia: A Comparative Legal Analysis* (Oxford University Press, 2006), p. 115.

123 Wang Jun, "Minzu yuwen kexue taolunhui [the Scientific Symposium on National Languages]", 01 *Kexue Tongbao* [*Chinese Science Bulletin*] (1956), pp. 96–97.

124 Thomas Mullaney, supra note 105, at p. 124; see also http://cpc.people.com.cn/GB/69112/99985/100001/9809365.html, last accessed on 15/06/2015.

125 "Guanyu huifu huo gaizheng minzu chengfen de chuli yuanze de tongzhi [the 1981 Circular Concerning the Principles of Recovering or Changing Ethnic Identity]", cited in Huang Guangxue and Shi Lianzhu (eds), supra note 102, at pp. 111, 116.

126 Ibid, p.116.

127 The Ethnic Affair Commission of Guizhou Province, *Guizhou minzu gongzuo wushi nian* [*Fifty Years of the Ethnic Work in Guizhou*] (Guizhou Minzu Chuanshe, 1999), p. 232.

128 Ibid; Huang Guangxue and Shi Lianzhu (eds), supra note 102, at p. 116; Yan Qiyan, "Guizhou weishibie minzu renkou de fenbu tedian he lishi chengyin [the Historical Causes and Distribution Characteristics of the Unidentified Ethnic Groups in Guizhou]", 02 *Minban Jiaoyu Yanjiu* [*Private Education Research*] (2009), p. 27.

The dissolution of the USSR and Former Yugoslavia sounded a warning to the communist China. The CPC announced the completion of the ethnic identification to avoid further demands for ethnic identification or alteration, which might cause unrest, though assured that the remaining problems would be handled properly.[129] The remaining issues could be categorised into two main categories: the unidentified groups, and the groups that have been controversially classified into other minorities.

Upon the completion of the ethnic identification in the late 1980s, Huang Guangxue, the Vice Director of the SEAC, concluded that the criteria used in the Project to identify a *minzu* included 1) whether the proposed group fit the characteristics of the Stalinist definition; 2) the majority will of the group, the advantages and disadvantages of future development, and its influence over other groups in similar situation, and 3) the unity of the [Chinese] nation.[130] In 2005, the CPC rephrased these criteria and suggested a more flexible definition of minority/*shaoshu minzu*, namely:

> [trans. L. W.] "a historically constituted, stable community of people who, in general, shared common characteristics of historical origins, mode of production, language, culture, customs, and a sense of solidarity; for some minorities, religion also plays an important role in their formation and development process".[131]

Hence, the ethnic "family" of the Chinese nation officially comprises 56 members. The majority Han and 55 minorities, together with a few unidentified groups and some contentious groups, form the Chinese ethnic structure. This 56-ethnic-group structure and the fixed ethnic identity model were finally stabilised in the 1990s and founded the basis for the future development of national "knowledge, policies, sentiments and actions".[132]

---

129 "Minzu shibie he genggai minzu chengfen gongzuo yi jiben wancheng [Ethnic Identification and the Alteration of Ethnic Identity Have Completed—An Interview with Huang Guangxue, the Vice Director of the SEAC]", 02 *Zhongguo Minzu* [*China's Ethnic Groups*] (1987), p. 16.

130 Ibid.

131 "[The Decision of the CPCCC and the State Council on Further Strengthening Ethnic Work and Accelerating Economic and Social Development of the Minorities (*shaoshu minzu*) and Minority Regions (2005)]", http://www.seac.gov.cn/art/2012/8/31/art_6081_164887.html, last visited on 10/06/2018; see also He shutao, "Dui ershi shiji zai zhongguo zuiyou yingxing de sanda minzu dingyi de jianyao fenxi [An Analysis of Three Influential Definitions of Nation in the 20th Century China]", 04 *Heilongjiang Minzu Congkan* [*Heilongjiang National Series*] (2009), p. 14.

132 Thomas Mullaney, supra note 105, at p. 134.

4.3.2 *Problems of the Ethnic Identification Project*

The Ethnic Identification Project is officially described as a scientific work with academic features.[133] However, it also has a strong political and administrative nature.[134] This government-led project has significant legal consequences, as only officially recognised minorities can claim autonomous rights under Chinese law. As the only means by which such rights can be attained, the Project and resultant policies necessitate closer scrutiny.

Firstly, the identification criteria were not unequivocally and consistently applied in the process. The application of the Stalinist definition was very selective in practice. The Project took a wide range of factors into consideration, including language, culture, customs, mode of production, religion, history, origins, consciousness, and so forth. However, the recognition of a group might result from the emphasis of one or two of these features, whereas the denial could be justified by the lack of any.[135] Many minorities were identified as "existing" simply because the government determined it should. By doing so, the communists could exert a macro-control of the number of minority groups, and more importantly, they could divide the minority population in a way that best fitted their political interests.

After a short training program, scholars and researchers were divided into several teams and sent to various areas to work with local governments. The provincial government retained the jurisdiction to report to the central government with regard to the ethnic situation within its administrative division. Without any accurate identification standards, the ethnic categorisation in reality illustrated a distinctive regional feature.[136] For example, the self-reported "Nari" group that inhabited the shores of the Lugu Lake was identified as the Naxi in Yunnan province, while those in Sichuan province were considered to be the Mongols.[137] The only difference between the Zhuang in northern

---

133 Huang Guangxue and Shi Lianzhu (eds), supra note 102, at p. 113; Wang Wenguang and You Weiqiong, "Xin zhongguo chengli yilai Yunnan minzu shibie de renshi yu fansi [the Identification of Yunnan's Ethnic Groups since the Founding of the PRC and Its Enlightenment]", 02 *Yunnan Minzu Daxue Xuebao* [*Journal of Yunnan Nationalities University* (*Social Sciences*)] (2010), p. 10.

134 Ibid; Dru Gladney, supra note 115, at p. 309.

135 Chen Xinlin, supra note 113, at p.2; Joshua Castellino and Elvira Redondo (eds), supra note 122, at p. 139.

136 Han Zhongtai, "Yizhong zicheng, sange minzu: dui Huangnihe youan buyi zuqun minzu shibie de zaidiacha [A Restudy of the Ethnic Identification of the Buyi Ethnic Group on the Right Bank of the Huangni River]", 03 *Yunnan Minzu Daxue Xuebao* [*Journal of Yunnan Nationalities University* (*Social Sciences*)] (2012), p. 9.

137 Stevan Harrell (Bamo Ayi and Qumo Tiexi, Translators), *Tianye zhong de zuqun guanxi yu minzu renting* [*Field Studies of Ethnic Identity: Yi communities of Southwest China*]

Guangxi province and the Buyi in southern Guizhou was the provincial boundary.[138] Even within one provincial unit, the recognition varied, because of the different application of identification criteria in various localities. One ethnic group in Yunnan, who named themselves as the "Buyi" and shared similar modes of production, language, culture, customs, and religion, was classified into three minorities: the Shui, Buyi, and Zhuang.[139] A number of cases in the recovery and alteration project of ethnic identity in the 1980s may have revealed such issues.

On the other hand, it has been argued that "minority groups in contemporary China do in fact identify themselves more or less in accordance with the *minzu* designations", after years of the practice.[140] The 56-ethnic-group model and its supporting measures indeed appear to be effective in regard to incorporating the minorities in borderlands into the multiethnic state as the CPC had expected. Nevertheless, the categorisation of 56 groups also consciously creates group divisions inside the nation in the sense that a minority identity is decided at birth, which is not optional.[141] Once registered and confirmed by the Family Book or citizen ID card, minority identity becomes the evidence for the entitlement to all minority privileges. The status of being a member of minority might foster a sense of difference among the population, since minority division motivates an ethnic distinction. This imbues a sense of belonging, which seems to be in existence relative to other groups rather than to the specific group itself.[142] As Cohen argues, "contemporary

---

(Guangxi Renmin Chubanshe, 2008), p. 268; Huang Ze, "Yunnan weishibie qunti yuanjiu de zuqun lilun yiyi [the Significance of the Research about the Unidentified Ethnic Groups in Yunnan]", 02 *Guangxi Minzu Xueyuan Xuebao* [*Journal of Guangxi University for Nationalities* (*Philosophy and Social Science*)] (2001), p. 28.

138 Stevan Harrell, ibid, p. 268; Thomas Mullaney, supra note 105, at p. 88.

139 Han Zhongtai, supra note 136, at pp. 5–8.

140 Thomas Mullaney, supra note 105, at p. 135; Dru Gladney, supra note 115, at pp. 299, 304.

141 Generally, children inherit ethnic status from their parents and children of the marriage of mixed *minzu* are entitled to change their ethnic identity at the age of eighteen. See the SEAC, Guanyu zhongguo gongmin queding minzu chengfen de guiding [Regulation on the Determination of Ethnic Identity of Chinese Citizen] (1990) (the SEAC-1990-No.217), Articles 2, 3. See also Dru Gladney, *Dislocating China: Reflections on Muslims, Minorities, and Other Subaltern Subjects* (Hurst and Company, 2004), p. 170.

142 Naran Bilik argued that in the situation of the coexistence of ethnic groups, a sense of belonging to one group would be persisted as long as other groups maintain their distinctive identities. See Naran Bilik, "Minzu yu minzu gainian zai bianzheng [Another Dialectic of Minzu and Minzu Concept]", 03 *Minzu Yanjiu* [*Ethno-National Studies*] (1995), pp. 13, 15–16.

ethnicity is the result of intensive interaction between ethnic groupings".[143] Gladney also notes that dialogical interactions between groups might lead to the invention of some identities.[144] The current ethnic divisions potentially create and harden differences among the minorities[145] and in some cases within one minority group. Apart from the Han, the remaining fifty-five groups are distinguishable from each other. An internal ethnic balance would then be achieved.

Without the right to freely identify with one or more groups, the current practice of fixed ethnic identity at birth in a way emphasises individual connection to a particular group. The consciousness as a group, thus, is enhanced. For those who had little knowledge of *minzu* or group identity in the 1950s, they now identify themselves with minority communities after years of practice. For instance, some communities initially did not classify themselves as belonging to minority groups. The reasons that they demanded to be identified as minorities were simply political: to establish an autonomous regime and to receive economic benefits, such as governmental allowance and aids.[146] Many minority members in Yunnan had claimed to be of Han descent and denied their affinity with a minority status.[147] Now they adhere to their recognised minority identity to acquire minority privileges.[148] The Zhuang has also been considered to be created, as the groups who now call themselves the Zhuang had no sense of a common ethnic identity when they were identified in the 1950s.[149] Another situation involves groups that have already been assimilated at the time of categorisation. The fixed ethnic identity constantly highlighted ethnic distinction, and they sought to reconstruct their identities. The recent revival and reconstruction of the Manchu culture serves as a good example of this reality.

---

143 Abner Cohen, *Custom and Politics in Urban Africa* (University of California Press, 1969), p. 198.

144 Dru Gladney, supra note 115, at p. 78.

145 Ibid. at p. 93.

146 The Long group in Guangxi province, which has been recognised as Yao *zu*, was an example. See Ma Rong, "Guanyu 'minzu' dingyi [On the Definitions of 'Minzu']", 17:01 *Yunnan Minzu Xueyuan Xuebao* [*Journal of Yunan University of the Nationalities*] (2000), p. 12; Joshua Castellino and Elvira Redondo (eds), supra note 122, at p. 115; Ralph Litzinger, *Other Chinas: the Yao and the Politics of National Belonging* (Duke University Press, 2000), p. 7.

147 Bai in Yunnan as demonstrated by David Y. H. Wu serves as one example. See David Y. H. Wu, supra note 116, at pp. 3, 7–11.

148 Ibid.

149 Katherine Kaup, supra note 31, at pp. 4–5.

4.3.3 *International Obligations of China in Relation to Minority Recognition*

It can be argued that official identification and fixed ethnic status are necessary in order to avoid abuse of minority privileges and allow the establishment of autonomous units and agencies, through which the minorities could pursue political, legislative, and financial autonomy. However, neither official identification nor fixed minority status seems reasonable concerning cultural rights, as culture is not a static concept.[150] Individual cultural preference and identity may change with circumstances. In addition, although the collective rights of China's minorities on legislative and financial affairs under the REA may exclusively derive from the provisions of Chinese law,[151] both domestic law and international law regulate the exercise of the cultural rights. China has undertaken international obligations to protect and promote cultural rights.[152]

There is no international consensus on the definition of minorities. Almost all the attempts to define a minority encompass objective and subjective criteria: the existence of the group with distinct identity and a sense of solidarity.[153] Nor does international law have explicit provisions on minority identification. The existence of minorities does not depend upon the decision of the state but should be established by objective criteria or sufficient elements, as the

150 The Committee on Economic, Social and Cultural Rights (CESCR), General Comment 21: Right of Everyone to Take Part in Cultural Life (Article 15, para. 1 (a), of the ICESCR), 43rd Session, 2009, UN Doc. E/C.12/GC/21, para.11.

151 In terms of the right to culture, language and religion, minority rights in international law are generally formulated from an individualistic perspective. International Covenant on Civil and Political Rights (ICCPR), Article 27; the Human Rights Committee (HRC), General Comment 23: the Rights of Minorities, 50th Session, UN Doc. CCPR/C/21/Rev.1/Add.5, para.3; the HRC, General Comment 31: Nature of the General Legal Obligation Imposed on States Parties to the Covenant, 80th Session, UN Doc. CCPR/C/21/Rev.1/Add.13, para.9.

152 China has ratified, or acceded to, the following instruments on human rights: ICESCR, International Convention on the Elimination of All Forms of Racial Discrimination (ICERD), Convention on the Elimination of All Forms of Discrimination against Women, Convention on the Rights of the Child and two Optional Protocols, Convention on the Rights of Persons with Disabilities, and Convention against Torture and Other Cruel Inhuman or Degrading Treatment or Punishment. China signed the ICCPR in 1998, which has yet to be ratified by the legislature.

153 Francesco Capotorti, Special Rapporteur of the Sub-Commission on Prevention of Discrimination and Protection of Minorities, *Study on the Rights of Persons Belonging to Ethnic, Religious and Linguistic Minorities*, UN Doc. E/CN.4/Sub.2/384/Rev.1 (1979) [the Capotorti Report], para.568; Patrick Thornberry, *International Law and the Right of Minorities* (Clarendon Press, 2001), pp. 164–67; Thomas Musgrave, *Self-determination and National Minorities* (Oxford University Press, 2002), p. 169.

existence of minorities is "a question of fact", not "a question of law".[154] Persons belonging to minorities should also retain the right to choose their own identity.[155] On the other hand, it has been pointed out that the official identification of a minority by the state is essential, as it would facilitate the application of their rights and give the members of the minority a solid basis for effective protection.[156] Amongst the international conventions that China has ratified or acceded to, International Covenant on Economic, Social and Cultural Rights (ICESCR)[157] and International Convention on the Elimination of All Forms of Racial Discrimination (ICERD)[158] are of particular relevance to minority identification.

(1) ICESCR

Article 2 of the ICESCR requires the State Parties to ensure that the rights guaranteed in the Covenant "will be exercised without discrimination of any kind as to race, colour, sex, language, religion, political or other opinion, national or social origin, property, birth or other status".[159] The enjoyment of economic, social and cultural rights (ESCR) without discrimination entails an immediate obligation to eliminate all forms of discrimination.[160] In China, the exclusion of unidentified groups from exercising minority rights and different treatment between minorities with autonomous agencies and minorities without them contravene this provision. Article 15 states that "the States Parties to the present Covenant recognise the right of everyone ... to take part in cultural life ..."[161] Despite the fact that this Article recognises the right of "everyone" to culture, it is relevant in the Chinese context for minority protection as it provides minorities the basis to claim the rights guaranteed by international law. Culture, according to the Committee on ESCR, is a broad, inclusive, and

---

154 Greco-Bulgarian Communities, Advisory Opinion, 1930 P.C.I.J. (ser. B) No.17, at p. 22; the HRC, General Comment 23, para.5.2; the Capotorti Report, ibid, para.61.

155 The CESCR, General Comment 21, paras.15, 55(b); the CERD, General Recommendation 08 concerning the Interpretation and Application of Article 1, paras.1 and 4 of the Convention, A/45/18; the CERD, General Recommendation 32: the Meaning and Scope of Special Measures, CERD/C/GC/32, para. 34.

156 The Capotorti Report, supra note 153, para.62.

157 China ratified the ICESCR in 2001.

158 China acceded to the ICERD in 1981.

159 ICESCR, Article 2.

160 The CESCR, General Comment 20: Non-discrimination in Economic, Social and Cultural Rights, E/C.12/GC/20, para.7; Manisuli Ssenyonjo, *Economic, Social and Cultural Rights in International Law* (Hart Publishing, 2009), pp. 60, 85–86.

161 ICESCR, Article 15.

evolving concept, which encompasses almost every aspect of life.[162] "To take part in" or "participate" in cultural life includes, in particular, the right of everyone, including minorities, "to choose his or her own identity, to identify or not with one or several communities".[163] The minimum core obligations entailed in the Article also require the State Parties to respect the right of everyone to self-identification.[164] Thus, besides the right "to conserve, promote and develop their own culture",[165] minorities should also have the right to identify or not to identify themselves with one or more communities and to change that choice.[166] The Chinese provisions on the determination of ethnic status may constitute a breach.

(2) ICERD

Under the core principle of non-discrimination, the Convention concerning Racial Discrimination requires the uniform application of legislation and governmental actions to all groups, regardless of the racial or ethnic groupings within the territory.[167] The selective application of identification criteria, which leads to the recognition of some and refusal to recognise others, may breach this prohibition.[168] In particular, the identification of an individual as belonging to a minority group, and thus the beneficiary of special measures, "should be based on self-identification by the individual concerned", unless a significant justification exists to permit action to the contrary.[169] Therefore, the Chinese practice of minority identification discussed above would not conform to its obligations under the ICESR and ICERD. The authoritative practice of identifying minorities in China needs to be changed and reformed to equally protect and promote the rights of all ethnic groups without distinction. Even though the communists might prefer a minority definition based on objective criteria, the application of such criteria should be unequivocal and declaratory, and the right of the individuals to identify themselves with one or more groups upheld.

---

162 The CESCR, General Comment 21, paras.11–13.

163 Ibid. para.15.

164 Ibid. para.55(b).

165 Ibid. para.32.

166 Ibid, paras.15, 55(b).

167 The CERD, General Recommendation 24 concerning Article 1 of the Convention, A/54/18, para.2.

168 Ibid, para.3.

169 The CERD, General Recommendation 08; General Recommendation 32, para. 34.

4.4 The Definition of Indigenous Peoples and Indigenous Situation in China

International law has been working on the development of the rights for certain groups that could be categorised as indigenous peoples. Unlike the general individual human rights and the special rights of persons belonging to ethnic, religious or linguistic minorities, the emerging international norms seem to recognise a set of collective rights of indigenous peoples as a group.[170] There are overlapping areas between minority rights and indigenous rights, as both groups are considered to maintain distinguishable identities from other sections in the state. Indigenous peoples may claim rights under Article 27 of the ICCPR,[171] and they are further vested with more rights as indigenous communities. The UN Declaration on the Rights of Indigenous Peoples (UNDRIP) clearly states that "indigenous peoples have the right to self-determination", which enables them to freely determine their political status and to pursue their economic, social and cultural development.[172] It also ensures the rights of indigenous peoples to land, territory, and resources.[173]

The distinctions between minorities and indigenous peoples are blurry for the lack of definition. This may make Chinese minorities potential candidates for claiming status as indigenous peoples. Considering the implications of the right to self-determination in international law and its historical connection with Chinese minorities,[174] the Chinese government denies the existence of indigenous peoples or indigenous issues in China so as to avoid its

---

170 Working Paper on the Relationship and Distinction between the Rights of Persons Belonging to Minorities and Those of Indigenous Peoples (the Working Paper), E/CN.4/Sub.2/2000/10, para.2; the HRC, General Comment 23, para.9; Alexandra Xanthaki, *Indigenous Rights and United Nations Standards: Self-determination, Culture and Land* (Cambridge University Press, 2007), pp. 107–109; Report of the African Commission's Working Group of Experts on Indigenous Populations/Communities, 2005, p. 97; 276/03 Centre for Minority Rights Development (Kenya) and Minority Rights Group (on behalf of Endorois Welfare Council)/Kenya, para.149.

171 Claire Charters, "Chapter 7 Reparations for Indigenous Peoples: Global International Instruments and Institutions", in F. Lenzerini (ed), *Reparations for Indigenous Peoples: International & Comparative Perspectives* (Oxford University Press, 2008), pp. 163–195 at pp. 177–181; Sally Holt, "Family, Private Life, and Cultural Rights", in Marc Weller (ed), *Universal Minority Rights: A Commentary on the Jurisprudence of International Court and Treaty Bodies* (Oxford University Press, 2007), pp. 203–252 at pp. 242–243.

172 The UNDRIP, Article 3.

173 The UNDRIP, Preamble, Articles 26, 32.

174 See Chapters 2, 3.

own minorities claiming indigenous rights.[175] In the Chinese context, whether there are indigenous peoples, or which minorities may claim indigenous rights, depends on how indigenous peoples are defined.

4.4.1 *Criteria for Identifying Indigenous Peoples in International Law*

There is no consensus of the international community on the term "indigenous peoples/populations/communities". Diverse definitions have been developed and advocated by different groups.

(1) Defining "Indigenous"

Article 1 of the ILO Convention 169 presents one example of those definitions. The statement of coverage of the Convention, instead of a definition of indigenous peoples,[176] focuses upon two elements to determine the application of the Convention. Firstly, groups protected by the Convention include:

> (a) tribal peoples in independent countries whose social, cultural and economic conditions distinguish them from other sections of the national community, and whose status is regulated wholly or partially by their own customs or traditions or by special laws or regulations;
> (b) peoples in independent countries who are regarded as indigenous on account of their descent from the populations which inhabited the country, or a geographical region to which the country belongs, at the time of conquestor colonisation or the establishment of present state boundaries and who, irrespective of their legal status, retain some or all of their own social, economic, cultural and political institutions.[177]

In the meantime, self-identification as indigenous and/or tribal constitutes the subjective criterion for determining the groups, to whom the provisions of this Convention apply.[178]

The generally accepted working definition, as suggested by the UN Special Rapporteur Martinez Cobo, has a similar nature, which states:

175 China, the Commission on Human Rights, the 52nd Session, 1995, E/CN.4/1995/WG. 15/2, page 8, para.4; James Summers, *Peoples and International Law (2nd Edition)* (Martinus Nijhoff Publishers, 2014), pp. 259–260.

176 Alexandra Xanthaki, supra note 170, at pp. 70–71.

177 The ILO Convention 169, Article 1.

178 Ibid.

> indigenous communities, peoples and nations are those which, having a historical continuity with pre-invasion and pre-colonial societies that developed on their territories, consider themselves distinct from other sectors of the societies now prevailing in those territories, or parts of them. They form at present non-dominant sectors of society and are determined to preserve, develop and transmit to future generations their ancestral territories, and their ethnic identity, as the basis of their continued existence as peoples, in accordance with their own cultural patterns, social institutions and legal systems.[179]

Indigenousness in those definitions is closely related to the priority of settlement.[180] The historical continuity and attachment to the territory since the pre-invasion and pre-colonisation era, and self-identification as culturally, socially and/or legally distinct from the dominant population in the state, appear to be the fundamental elements for defining indigenous peoples. Many Asian states adhere to this approach. They assert that the issue of indigenous peoples emerged under specific historic circumstances, thus was intimately related to the global colonisation of European countries.[181] Indigenous rights, as argued by India, Pakistan and Indonesia, pertain to:

> peoples in independent countries who are regarded as indigenous on account of their descent from the populations which inhabited the country, or a geographical region to which the country belongs, at the time of conquest or colonisation or the establishment of present State.[182]

Under such a definition, the time of invasion/colonisation/conquest/foreign domination is a decisive factor when identifying indigenous peoples.

Indigenous communities disagree with the objective approach, as the government might use a strict definition to avoid recognising indigenous

179 Martinez Cobo, Study of the Problem of Discrimination against Indigenous Populations, E/CN.4/Sub.2/1986/7/ADD.4, 1986, para.379.

180 Andre Beteille, "The Idea of Indigenous People", 39:02 *Current Anthropology* (1998), p. 188.

181 China, the Commission on Human Rights, the 54th Session, 1997, E/CN.4/1998/106, p. 8, para.37; supra note 175, E/CN.4/1995/WG. 15/2, p. 7, para.3; India, 61 GAOR 2006, Plenary Meetings, 108th mtg., (A/61/pv. 108) p.1; Indonesia, ibid, p.4; Pakistan, ibid, p.4. Bangladesh and Myanmar also made a similar argument. See B. Kingsbury, " 'Indigenous peoples' in International Law: a Constructive Approach to the Asian Controversy", 92 *American Journal of International Law* (1998), p. 434.

182 Ibid.

peoples in the state.[183] They instead argue for a right to identify themselves.[184] This objective/subjective standard argument on the definition, in essence, concerns the delineation of power in regards to indigenous rights: more precisely where the power lies, with the state or with indigenous communities. Many states are in favour of the objective definition as it could enable them to control the application of such rights in their territories. The indigenous communities nevertheless emphasise the subjective element in the definition process. The UNDRIP was eventually adopted without a clear definition or a statement of coverage. It, however, endorsed a weaker form of the principle of self-identification, which leaves states with more discretion.[185] Article 33 (1) provides that "indigenous peoples have the right to determine their own identity or membership in accordance with their customs and traditions".

In contrast to some Asian states that deny the applicability of indigenous rights in Asia by limiting the concept to the colonisation process, the African Commission on Human and People's Rights (ACHPR) developed a broader definition of indigenous peoples so as to ensure the applicability of indigenous rights in Africa. In the African definition, indigenousness is not confined to the priority of settlement. The Report of the African Commission's Working Group of Experts on Indigenous Populations/Communities reveals:

> "indigenous peoples" has come to have connotations and meanings that are much wider than the question of "who came first". It is today a term and a global movement fighting for rights and justice for those particular groups who have been left on the margins of development ... perceived negatively by dominating mainstream development paradigms, whose cultures and ways of life are subject to discrimination and contempt and whose existence is under threat of extinction.[186]

According to the ACHPR Working Group, the concept of indigenous rights is of great importance, as it concerns discrimination, marginalisation and

183 The Report of the African Commission's Working Group of Experts on Indigenous Populations/Communities, 2005, p. 87.

184 James Summers, supra note 175, at pp. 261–262.

185 Article 8 of the Draft Convention explicitly empowers indigenous peoples "to identify themselves as indigenous and to be recognised as such", a similar provision to Article 1(2) of the ILO Convention 169. For a detailed discussion, see James Summers, supra note 175, at p. 262.

186 The Report of the African Commission's Working Group of Experts on Indigenous Populations/Communities, 2005, p. 87.

injustice.[187] It sets out four criteria for identifying indigenous peoples: the occupation and use of a specific territory; the voluntary perpetuation of cultural distinctiveness; self-identification as a distinct collective, as well as recognition by other groups; and an experience of subjugation, marginalisation, dispossession, exclusion or discrimination.[188] Similar to Cobo's definition, the African concept of indigenous peoples recognises the linkage between the peoples and their land and culture. It, however, emphasises the marginalised position of communities for being indigenous, rather than the time of inhabitation. The latter appears to be of little relevance in the African definition.

(2) The Meaning of "Peoples"

Apart from divergent understandings of "indigenous", the meaning of "peoples" is also highly contentious. The collective right of the peoples to self-determination has been well established in international law. In the drafting process of the UNDRIP, the states at first were reluctant to use "peoples" in relation to indigenous groups, and instead proposed "indigenous populations" and "persons belonging to indigenous groups".[189] After the draft declaration adopted the use of "indigenous peoples", many states then attempted to distinguish "indigenous peoples" from "the peoples" in international law, which coincided with Eide's classification of four sets of rights.[190] Indigenous representatives, on the other hand, contended that indigenous peoples should not be treated separately from the concept of "the peoples" in international law.[191]

With a controversy on the interpretation of indigenous "peoples", the UNDRIP further recognised a right to self-determination. The inclusion of such a right was considered as a central component of the Declaration.[192] In the drafting discussion, many states insisted that the exercise of self-determination had to respect territorial integrity and political unity of the sovereign states,

187 Ibid, p. 90.

188 276/03 Centre for Minority Rights Development (Kenya) and Minority Rights Group (on behalf of Endorois Welfare Council)/Kenya, para.150; the Report of the African Commission's Working Group of Experts on Indigenous Populations/Communities, pp. 92–93.

189 James Summers, supra note 175, at p. 258.

190 Ibid, pp. 258–259. According to Eide, these four sets of rights are: the general individual human rights, the additional rights specific to persons belonging to national or ethnic, religious or linguistic minorities, the special rights of indigenous peoples and of indigenous individuals, and the rights of peoples under Article 1 of two Covenants of 1966. See the Working Paper, E/CN.4/Sub.2/2000/10, para.2.

191 James Summers, supra note 175, at pp. 259, 264–265.

192 Alexandra Xanthaki, supra note 170, at p. 109.

and that the draft declaration should be amended accordingly.[193] Argentina suggested on a few occasions the need to modify Article 3 in line with the principle of territorial integrity, which would narrow down the indigenous rights to self-determination into autonomy/self-government or fully participation in the decision-making process.[194] The representatives of indigenous peoples, by contrast, emphasised that self-determination was not a static concept and was continually evolving.[195] They strongly opposed suggestions to alter Article 3 to include the notion of territorial integrity. The UNDRIP eventually incorporated a separate Article 46, which referred to territorial integrity, and linked the exercise of the rights to self-determination with the right to autonomy or self-government in Article 4. However, it failed to clarify the extent or the scope of such a right and its relationship with the well-established norm of the peoples' rights to self-determination as enshrined in the Charter and the 1966 Covenants.[196]

(3) The Definition Advocated by China

The political implications of the principle of self-determination in the formation of modern nation-states may explain the sovereign states' reluctance to associate indigenous peoples with "the peoples" and self-determination. It is possible that indigenous peoples may legitimise their territories in the same way that the nation-states have been legitimised by "nations".[197] In particular, the inherent attachment to land and history as embedded in the concept has been claimed to be one of the most important national ties. Seen from this perspective, China repeatedly pressed for an inclusion of the definition in the Declaration, claiming that without an elaborate definition in the Declaration

193 The Commission on Human Rights, the 56th Session, 1999, E/CN.4/2000/84, Canada, para.50; Brazil, para.53; Ecuador, para.56; Russia, para.61; Argentina, para.63; Guatemala, para73; Venezuela, para.80. The Commission on Human Rights, the 57th Session, 2001, E/CN.4/2001/85, Mexico, para.64, Bangladesh, para.69; Pakistan, para.77; Spain, para.83; New Zealand, para.109.

194 The Commission on Human Rights, ibid, E/CN.4/2000/84, US para.49; Brazil, para.53; Columbia, para.54; Australia 62; Finland, para.70; Norway, para.81. The Commission on Human Rights, ibid, E/CN.4/2001/85, Mexico, para.64; Spain, para.83; Russia para.90.

195 The Commission on Human Rights, ibid, E/CN.4/2000/84, para.47; ibid, E/CN.4/2001/85, paras.58, 61, 87, 94.

196 The Commission on Human Rights, ibid, E/CN.4/2001/85, para.58; James Summers, supra note 175, at pp. 269–274; the Working Paper, E/CN.4/Sub.2/2000/10, para.2.

197 B. Kingsbury, "Chapter 14 The Applicability of the International Legal Concept of 'Indigenous Peoples' in Asia", in Joanne Rauer and Daniel Bell (eds), *The East Asian Challenge for Human Rights* (Cambridge University Press, 1999), pp. 336–377 at p. 348.

was like "building a house without knowing who was going to live in it".[198] It then attempted to link the concept of indigenous peoples with the specific period of colonisation. The Chinese government argued that the question of indigenous peoples was the product of the European countries' pursuit of colonial policies in other parts of the world. European colonisation directly caused indigenous peoples' loss of their ancestral lands and the current status of being discriminated and marginalised in the countries where they live.[199]

China, therefore, suggested that a number of factors should be considered for defining the indigenous peoples:

> … (a) the issue of indigenous people had emerged under specific historic circumstances; it was mainly the result of the colonial policies pursued by the European countries in other regions of the world, particularly in the Americas and Oceania; (b) before the arrival of the colonialists or foreign dominators, the indigenous people had lived for generations in certain countries or geographical regions and had wholly or partly preserved their own social, economic, cultural and political characteristics; (c) indigenous people must not only identify themselves as such, but must also be recognised by the Government and people of the countries in which they resided. With regard to the issue of self-identification, that self-identification should be exercised through certain legal procedures in the context of national legislation.[200]

In this proposal, apart from objective standards and self-identification of the group, state recognition functions as an additional guarantee to make sure that domestic groups are controllable by the states. China further argued that indigenous rights were different from the "historical rights" of ordinary minority nationalities or ethnic groups.[201] To prevent Chinese minorities from claiming such rights might be one of the most important reasons for this stance.

China had a long history of dealing with minorities issues. The treatment of minorities varied in the multiethnic Chinese empires. Different policies were adopted by the ruling regimes. In the process of China's transformation to a modern state, minorities were granted the right to self-determination. In order

198 China, the Commission on Human Rights, the 53rd Session, 1996, E/CN.4/1997/102, para.229.

199 China, supra note 175, E/CN.4/1995/WG. 15/2, pp. 7–8, paras.3, 4.

200 China, supra note 181, E/CN.4/1998/106, p 8, para.37.

201 China, supra note 175, E/CN.4/1995/WG. 15/2, p. 8, para.8.

to secure the territory inherited from the Qing Empire, upon the founding of the PRC, the right of minorities to self-determination was replaced by the collective right to regional autonomy. China's commitment to minorities, in a way, is determined by its history. Indigenous rights, instead, is a relatively new concept. Recognising sections of the population as "indigenous" may suggest the rest are not.[202] Such a connotation is fundamentally contrary to the communist assertion of the pluralistic integration of the Chinese nation. China's policy on minorities is to integrate ethnic groups into the Chinese nation, and at the same time allow them to keep their separate identities. The formulation of minority rights corresponds with this approach, whereas indigenous rights tend to consolidate and strengthen the separateness of the communities from other groups in society, as "being indigenous" is their predominant identity.[203] Indigenous peoples are more likely to claim a separate "nation" from the present state.

In addition, to recognise and protect minority rights in China seems not to be problematic, as minority rights are formulated as individual rights with certain collective nature in international law. The exercise of the collective right to territorial autonomy, therefore, needs to refer to Chinese law, according to which the right to secede is not an option. Indigenous peoples, on the contrary, are equipped with the right to self-determination. The states and indigenous peoples have different opinions on the limits of this right, as it could be read in conjunction with the principle of territorial integrity, or interpreted as the basis of independence. In practice, indigenous peoples have already attempted to claim the right to self-determination under Article 1 of the 1966 Covenants.[204] The distinction between minorities and indigenous peoples is at times not clear-cut. The minorities identified by the Chinese government are likely to have historical affinity to the land, as they are the descendents of ancient native peoples. Seen from this perspective, it is not difficult to understand why China adheres to minority rights and intends to define the indigenous peoples in a way that indigenous rights would not apply to its territory.

202 Andre Beteille, supra note 180, at p. 188; see also Nsongurua Udombana, "Chapter 15 Reparations and Africa's Indigenous Peoples", in F. Lenzerini (ed.), supra note 171, pp. 389–407 at p. 391.

203 The Working Paper, E/CN.4/Sub.2/2000/10, para.23.

204 Claire Charters, supra note 171, at pp. 178–181; Katja Gocke, "The Case of Angela Poma Poma *v.* Peru before the Human Rights Committee: the Concept of Free Prior and Informed Consent and the Application of the International Covenant on Civil and Political Rights to the Protection and Promotion of Indigenous Peoples' Rights", 14 *Max Planck Yearbook of United Nations Law* (2010), pp. 338–370.

4.4.2 *The Applicability of the Concept of Indigenous Rights in China*

(1) The ILO Convention 169

The official position of the Chinese government, to a great extent, adheres to Cobo's definition of indigenous peoples and the standards provided by the ILO Convention 169. The imperial territory varied throughout Chinese history, which led to dynamic ethnic relations. The historical complexity of the Han-minority relation in different imperial dynasties made it very difficult to decide "who came first". By stressing the connection between indigenous rights and the European colonisation, China may successfully argue that there are neither indigenous peoples nor indigenous issues in China, since all ethnic groups lived for aeons on the territory of China and the state [of China] as a whole suffered from imperialist aggression.[205]

Nevertheless, it has been pointed out that there is a possibility to apply Article 1(b) of the ILO Convention 169 to the Chinese situation. Article 1(b) states that indigenous peoples are those whose ancestors inhabited the country at the time of conquest or colonisation or the establishment of present state boundaries.[206] This provision seems to disassociate indigenous history from colonisation, as the identification of indigenous communities depends on the time of the establishment of present state boundaries.[207] However, international law contains no elaborate provisions on the commencement of statehood. This argument may give rise to another uncertainty from the determination of the establishment of present state boundaries. This state boundary could be understood as the boundaries of the PRC, or that of the ROC, or that of the old Chinese empires. China, unlike India or Pakistan who quoted the provision of the ILO Convention 169, has never directly referenced to the Convention. It has used the terms such as "colonists" "foreign dominators" or "colonial policy", but not "the establishment of present state boundaries".

(2) The African Interpretation

The African definition of indigenous peoples may be more applicable in China. First, almost all minorities are of a non-dominant status within the PRC, compared to the Han, the dominant population. Second, although Chinese law recognises ethnic equality and the REA system so as to protect and realise

205 China, supra note 175, E/CN.4/1995/WG. 15/2, p. 8, para.4; Zhou Enlai, supra note 18, at p. 583; China, the Commission on Human Rights, Press Release HR/CN/785 (02/04/1997), pp. 5–6.

206 Wang Shuping, The People's Republic of China's Policy on the Minorities and International Approaches to Ethnic Groups: A Comparative Study, 11 *International Journal on Minority and Group Rights* (2004), p. 178.

207 Ibid.

minority rights, some minorities are in a comparatively marginalised position in practice, which might be the result of historical discrimination of minority cultures.[208] It is also the fact that some minorities possess less bargaining power than others, due to the size of the population, strategic location and political importance.[209] Third, through the Ethnic Identification Project, 55 groups have been recognised as minorities. A set of criteria have been employed in the identification process, including language, culture, customs, mode of production, religion, history, origins, consciousness, and so forth.[210] Many minorities identify themselves as distinctive groups and wish to maintain their separate identities. Also, territorial connection might be found in many cases if taking a closer look of the Ethnic Identification Project.

Therefore, some minorities in China might be considered as "indigenous peoples" under the African definition. The Tibetans, for example, originate from the native people who resided on the Qinghai-Tibet Plateau since ancient times.[211] They have developed a unique social and political system and culture, which are considerably different from the Han. The land, particularly the holy land, is the central aspiration of their identity and culture. The Tibetan group fulfils all the requirements of indigenousness, according to the African definition. The decisive element would be the experience of being subjugated, marginalised, excluded or discriminated in China. The Dalai Lama once claimed that the Tibetans had experienced colonial possession and foreign domination,[212] whilst the CPC contended that the Tibetans enjoyed a wide range of autonomous rights under the REA. The key issue of applying the African definition in China will be the determination of discrimination, marginalisation and injustice, which can be based on solid evidence.

208 Chinese classic literature on occasion derogated minority cultures as "uncivilised" and used discriminatory names to refer to the minorities. During the ROC period, civilisation movements were launched by local governments in the South and Southwest. In the PRC, even though the Central People's Government Council (the predecessor of the State Council) passed decrees to prohibit historical discrimination and insult against the minorities, it was suggested that the social reform in the 1950s included projects to "civilise" minority society. See Chapter 2; Maria Lundberg and Yong Zhou, supra note 6, at p. 282.

209 See Chapter 5, Section 5.2.2. "Financial Autonomy of Sub-provincial Autonomous Units".

210 For the details on the Ethnic Identification Project, see Section 4.3.1.

211 Yang Shengmin and Ding Hong (eds), *Zhongguo minzu zhi* [*the Ethnography of China*] (Zhongyang Minzu Daxue Chubanshe, 2003), p. 226.

212 Statement of HH the Dalai Lama on the Second Anniversary of the Tibetan National Uprising Day (10/03/1961), http://www.dalailama.com/messages/tibet/10th-march-archive/1961, last visited on 28/12/2013.

4.4.3 *Indigenous Peoples in Taiwan*

The constitutional recognition of indigenous peoples in Taiwan poses another challenge. The 1946 Constitution of the ROC simply stated that all racial groups were equal.[213] It further granted Mongolia and Tibet a self-government status and accorded racial groups in frontier regions special legal protection.[214] However, nothing on indigenous rights was reflected in the ROC Constitution until the 1990s. Echoing international movements for indigenous rights, aboriginal peoples in Taiwan initiated campaigns to secure their cultural and political rights in the mid-1980s.[215] In its 1991 Amendment, the ROC Constitution, for the first time, introduced the term—*shanpao* (mountain compatriots), and recognised their rights in national elections.[216] Nevertheless, the term *shanpao* was not accepted by aboriginal communities, as it connoted "primitive" or "condescending", similar to "*fan*" and "*yi*" (traditional Chinese for "barbarians").[217] In response, the Constitution was further amended in 1994 to remove the use of *shanpao*.[218] Instead, the term "indigenous peoples", *yuanzhu min* (the peoples who lived here first),[219] was officially incorporated in the Constitution. A number of laws and regulations on the rights of indigenous peoples have been enacted thereafter, which enshrine a wide range of rights and freedoms for the aborigines in Taiwan.

According to the Indigenous Peoples Basic Law, indigenous peoples have the right to autonomy and self-governance (Article 4). Other rights, such as political participation, fiscal autonomy, education, culture, land and resources, are also recognised and protected.[220] Although the Taiwanese aborigines are entitled to collective rights as a group and to individual rights as indigenous members, the ROC laws on indigenous rights seem not to have provided a similar degree of protection as the international norms do.[221] The legal discourse on indigenous rights adopts a paternalist approach. Most provisions start with

213 The 1946 Constitution of the ROC, Article 5.

214 The 1946 Constitution of the ROC, Articles 26, 64, 91, 119, 120, 168, 169.

215 B. Kingsbury, supra note 181, at pp. 431–432; Huang Guangxue and Shi Lianzhu (eds), supra note 102, at p. 258.

216 The 1991 Constitutional Revision of the ROC, Articles 1, 2. http://lis.ly.gov.tw/lghtml/lawstat/version2/04105/0410580042200.htm, last accessed on 28/10/2015.

217 Huang Guangxue and Shi Lianzhu (eds), supra note 102, at p. 258.

218 The 1994 Constitutional Revision of the ROC, http://lis.ly.gov.tw/lghtml/lawstat/version2/04105/0410583072800.htm, last visited 28/10/2015.

219 B. Kingsbury, supra note 181, at p. 432.

220 The Indigenous Peoples Basic Law of the ROC, Articles 3, 5, 7, 10, 11, 13, 20, 23, 29.

221 Phutoli Chingmak, "Chapter 16 International Law and Reparations for Indigenous Peoples in Asia", in F. Lenzerini (ed), supra note 171, at pp. 462–463.

"the government guarantees/provides/protects …", differing from the international format which emphasises "indigenous peoples have the right to …"

Indigenous peoples in the ROC, are defined as:

> the traditional peoples who have inhibited in Taiwan and are subject to the state"s jurisdiction, including Amis tribe, Atayal tribe, Paiwan tribe, Bunun tribe, Puyuma tribe, Rukai tribe, Tsou tribe, Saisiyat tribe, Yami tribe, Tsao tribe, Kavalan tribe, Taroko tribe and any other tribes who regard themselves as indigenous peoples and obtain the approval of the Executive Yuan through the central indigenous authority upon application.[222]

In this definition, the state approval is one with great significance. The conditions and the procedure to apply for the state approval through the central indigenous authority, however, are not clear so far.[223]

In the PRC context, tribal groups in Taiwan as a whole are referred to as the Gaoshan *zu* (high mountain *minzu*), which was officially recognised by the Beijing regime in 1954.[224] The Gaoshan are generally recorded as *shiju shaoshu minzu* (native minorities). According to Beijing, the Gaoshan people can be further divided into two groups: high mountain tribes and plain tribes (*pingpu zu*).[225] The regime in the mainland claims that, based on archaeological and ethnological evidence, the aborigines in Taiwan are culturally related to the *Baiyue* (Hundred Yue) peoples[226] in the southeast coast of the mainland.[227] It attempts to establish that the Taiwanese aboriginal groups have no differences from the minorities in the southeast, who are also the descendants of the ancient *Baiyue*. The constitutionalisation of indigenous rights in Taiwan, therefore, is particularly challenging. The Han regime/administration in Taiwan is said to be first established during the Ming/Qing dynasty. Taiwan's recognition of indigenous peoples implies that the settlement before the Ming/Qing would

---

222 The Indigenous Peoples Basic Law of the ROC, Article 2.

223 Ibid.

224 Huang Guangxue and Shi Lianzhu (eds), supra note 102, at p. 257.

225 Ibid, pp. 244–247; Wang Xintian and Wu Chunming, "Guanyu Taiwan yuanzhumin yanjiu de jige wenti [Several Issues on the Study of the Aborigines in Taiwan]", 01 *Guangxi Minzu Yanjiu* [*Study of Ethnics in Guangxi*] (2007), p. 30.

226 *Yue*, which could be dated back to the first Millennium BC, was a movable historical collective name given by the Han to the "barbarian" inhabitants of a large tract of territory in southern China and northern Vietnam. See William Meacham, "Defining the Hundred Yue", 15 *Bulletin of the Indo-Pacific Prehistory Association* (1996), pp. 93–99.

227 Wang Xintian and Wu Chunming, supra note 225, at p. 33.

justify the "indigenous" nature. If this is the case, many minority groups, which were incorporated into the Chinese empire during the Ming/Qing or even before, might also argue for their "indigenousness".

4.4.4 *Indigenous Small-numbered Peoples in Russia*

There are a few ethnic/indigenous groups inhabiting the region on the border between China and Russia. Communities on the Chinese side are treated as minorities. The Russian recognition of the same groups as numerically small indigenous peoples may be relevant to the Chinese minority-indigenous argument, as the UNDRIP allows transnational indigenous communities to maintain and develop contacts, relations and co-operations with their own members across international borders.[228]

Russian law identifies four ethnically vulnerable groups: indigenous numerically small peoples, national minorities, small ethnic communities, and small indigenous peoples of the North, Siberia and the Russian Far East.[229] National minorities and ethnic minorities seem to be interchangeable in the context.[230] No clear definitions of national minorities and ethnic minorities could be found in Russian law.[231] Nonetheless, Russia explains in its fourth periodic report to the HRC that national minorities referred to include three types of ethnic communities.[232] Indigenous numerically small peoples, on the other hand, are groups numbering less than 50,000, who live in the territories traditionally occupied by their ancestors, preserve a traditional way of life, economy and trade, and identify themselves as separate ethnic communities.[233] They enjoy extensive rights, including the right to land and the right to maintain traditional activities and way of life.[234] Small ethnic communities, who are entitled to

228 The UNDRIP, Article 36.

229 The Sixth Periodic Report Submitted by Russia under Article 40 of the ICCPR, CCPR/C/RUS/6, para.5.

230 Russia refers to ethnic minorities in its sixth periodic report (CCPR/C/RUS/6, para.5) and in its fifth periodic report under the ICESCR (E/C.12/RUS/5, paras.5, 9). "National minorities" is used in its fourth periodic report under the ICCPR, CCPR/C/84/Add.2, para.290.

231 Vladimir Malakhov and Alexander Osipov, "The Category of 'Minorities' in Russian Federation: a Reflection on Uses and Misuses", in Spiliopoulou Akermark (ed), *International Obligations and National Debates: Minorities Around the Baltic Sea* (Åland Islands Peace Institute, Mariehamn, 2006), pp. 495–542 at pp. 513–519.

232 The Fourth Periodic Report Submitted by Russia under Article 40 of the ICCPR, CCPR/C/84/Add.2, para.296.

233 On the Guarantees of the Rights of Indigenous Numerically Small Peoples of Russia, Article 1.

234 Ibid; see also Bill Bowring, "Chapter 1 Russian Legislation in the Area of Minority Rights", in Oleh Protsyk and Benedikt Harzl (eds), *Managing Ethnic Diversity in Russia* (Routledge, 2012), pp. 15–36 at p. 30.

the protection of traditional living habitat and traditional way of life, have not yet been defined.[235]

However, a clear distinction is drawn between national minorities and numerically small indigenous peoples/small ethnic communities, in spite of the lack of definition. According to the Russian Constitution, "the rights of ethnic minorities confine to the regulation and protection of human and civil rights and freedoms, the rule of law, law and order and the question of nationality as a whole", whilst small indigenous peoples and small ethnic communities are associated with the rights to land and natural resources and with the protection of their traditional habitat and way of life.[236] Without further elaboration, the quantitative requirement of 50,000 is a significant standard that defines indigenous peoples from national minorities and small ethnic minorities in Russia.

Among the Russian list of numerically small indigenous peoples, a few groups have transnational counterparts in China, including the Evenk, Nanai, and Tuvinian-Todzins.[237] Their Chinese counterparts, the Ewenk, Oroqen and Hezhe, have been officially recognised as minorities, and thus are entitled to minority rights prescribed by Chinese law. The relevant Tuvinian community is considered as a subgroup of the Mongol and enjoys autonomous rights by associating with minority Mongols.

(1) The Ewenki Groups

The ancestors of the Ewenk and Oroqen were the native people who lived in the vast land between the Lake Baikal, Amur River and Outer Khingan Mountain. The community depended on hunting, fishing, and reindeer breeding for living.[238] During the Russian-Manchu border conflicts in the 17th century,

---

235 The Russian Constitution, Article 72.

236 The Sixth Periodic Report of Russia, supra note 229, para.5; the Fifth Periodic Report of Russia, supra note 230, para.10.

237 "The 2000 Unified Enumeration of the Indigenous Peoples of Russia", cited in Galina Diatchkova, "Indigenous Peoples of Russia and Political History", 02 *The Canadian Journal of Native Studies XXI* (2001), pp. 225–227.

238 Jiang Yingliang (ed), *Zhongguo minzu shi (xiajuan)* [*the History of China's Nationalities: Volume 3*] (Minzu Chubanshe, 1990), pp. 222, 224; Wang Zhonghan (ed), *Zhongguo minzu shi gaiyao* [*General History of China's Nationalities*] (Shanxi Jiaoyu Chubanshe, 2004), pp. 110–111, 113–114; Zhou Xifeng, "Jianshu Qingdai nenjiang liuyu de Ewenke zu [the Brief Discussion about the Ewenki Nationality of the Nen River Valley in the Qing Dynasty]", 04 *Heilongjiang Minzu Congkan* [*Heilongjiang National Series*] (2002), p. 77; Qi Huijun, "Xunlu Ewenke ren shengtai yimin de minzuxue kaocha [Ethnological Investigation on the Ecological Immigration of Reindeer Ewenki]", 01 *Manyu Yanjiu* [*Manchu Studies*] (2006), pp. 98–99.

many tribes of the ancient Ewenki people migrated south—the current territory of the PRC and gradually developed into two groups, the Ewenk and Oroqen.[239] Various names had been recorded in the classic books regarding those tribes, such as Suolun, Tungus, Yakut, Oroqen, Ewenk, and Tege. Upon the establishment of the PRC, there were mainly five groups that could be linked to those migrated tribes: Suolun, Tungus, Yakut, Oroqen and Bilaer.[240] Even though Suolun, Tungus and Yakut were all recorded in the ethnic self-reported registration in 1951, those groups were classified as the Ewenk (approximately numbering 6178).[241] Oroqen and Bilaer, on the other hand, were recognised as the Oroqen (numbering 949) in 1957.[242]

Compared to the Evenks in Russia who are native inhabitants of the land, the Ewenks and Oroqens on the Chinese side are said to be immigrants from the Qing dynasty. The distinctive Ewenki and Oroqen identity might be the basis to identify them from the Han and other minorities. It, however, seems less sufficient to claim a special connection to the territory. Three or four hundred years is probably not enough to legitimise indigenous claims, if the Han migrants who arrived at Taiwan in the late 17th century are considered to be non-indigenous.

Furthermore, the traditional lifestyle as hunters or reindeer herders has been lost in the integration process. The Yakut Ewenk appears to be the only group that continues an ancient way of living. Tradition, however, is an evolving concept. People who inhabit the same territory may slowly change their tradition and way of living. If the Ewenk people who stay in the ancestral land

239 Ibid. Other scholars classified those groups as *shiju minzu* (native minorities), arguing that they were the descents of ancient groups that had been living there for thousands of years and that they became cross-border nationalities as a result of Russian-Manchu boundary treaties. See Gong Yu, "Ewenke zu feiwuzhi wenhua yichan baohu xianzhuang yanjiu [Investigation on Situation of Ewenki's Non-physical (Intangible) Culture Heritage]", 01 *Manyu Yanjiu* [*Manchu Studies*] (2012), p. 70; Kong Fanzhi, "Shilu Ewenke zu jingji de fazhan yu bianhua [the Economic Development and Changes of the Ewenki Reindeer Herders]", 01 *Heilongjiang Minzu Congkan* [*Heilongjiang National Series*] (1997), p. 40; Chen Yushu, "Luelun Ewenke zu de laiyuan wenti [A Discussion on the Origins of the Ewenks]", Z1 *Zhongguo Minzu* [*China's Ethnic Groups*] (1962), p. 33.

240 Tang Ge, "Elunchun he Ewenke: cong shouliemin dao nongmin de kunjing [Olunchun (Oroqen) and Ewenki: Different Position from Hunter to Farmer]", 01 *Manyu Yanjiu* [*Manchu Studies*] (2008), p. 91; Xu Fangtian and Meng Shuqing, "Elunchun zu yuanliu jianshu [A Brief Discussion on the Origins of the Oroqen]", 04 *Heilongjiang Minzu Congkan* [*Heilongjiang National Series*] (1986), pp. 24, 26.

241 Tang Ge, ibid; Sixty Glorious Years, Statistical Yearbook 1947–2007, Compiled by the Inner Mongolia Autonomous Region Bureau of Statistics, 2007, 1–13 Population of Ethnic minorities, p. 76.

242 Ibid.

are allowed to develop a different mode of production, the possible indigenousness of the Chinese Ewenki groups will not be affected by the transformed productive activities, e.g. animal husbandry, or crops cultivation.

Comparatively, the hunting Oroqen are in a tentative situation, as a hunting ban was passed in 1996 by the Oroqen Autonomous Banner which prohibits all hunting activities in the area.[243] Hunting is considered to be the core value of the Oroqen culture.[244] The hunting ban and the so-called "changing the mode of production" policy would force the Oroqen people to seek a completely different way of living. This involves the determination of "indigenousness" in regard to varying tradition and lifestyle: to what degree the changes are allowed in order to maintain indigenous status. Also, it concerns whether psychological factor would be a crucial element in identifying indigenous peoples in China, when other indicators are not very definitive.

(2) The Hezhe Group

Unlike the "immigrant" groups above, the Hezhe are aboriginal peoples who traditionally lived along the Amur, Sunggari and Ussuri rivers.[245] It has been pointed out that the Hezhe and Manchu had common ancestral origins.[246] The Hezhe communities appeared in the Qing literature as the "dog users" or "fishing Tartars", whilst they called themselves "Nanai" or "Nabei", which in the Hezhe language meant "natives".[247] In the 1990s, according to the structural adjustment policy of the local government, the Hezhe group had successfully transformed their modes of production from traditional fishery to a diversified economic structure—a combination of farming, animal raising, fishery, forestry and tourism.[248] Other characteristics of the Hezhe people,

---

243 It has been pointed out that this hunting ban was not decided by the autonomous authorities. See Maria Lundberg and Yong Zhou, "Hunting-prohibition in the Hunter's Autonomous Area: Legal Rights of Oroqen People and the Implementation of Regional National Autonomy Law", 16 *International Journal on Minority and Group Rights* (2009), pp. 350, 393.

244 Tian Yan, "Hexie shehui linian zhidao xia Elunchun zu wenhua quanli de baohu [Analysing the Protection of Cultural Rights on Elunchun (Oroqen) Ethnic(ity) at the Direction of Harmonious Society]", 05 *Yunnan Daxue Xuebao* [*Journal of Yunnan University*] (2007), pp. 149–153.

245 Tang Ge, supra note 240, at p. 90.

246 Jiang Yingliang (ed), supra note 238, at p. 225.

247 Ibid, pp. 225–226; Wang Zhonghan (ed), supra note 238, at p. 115–116; Yang Shengmin and Ding Hong (eds), supra note 211, at p. 100.

248 Shu Jingxiang, "Woguo Hezhe zu 'jiuwu' qijian shixian le lishixing de kuayue fazhan [the Development of the Historic Span in the Ninth-Five-Year Plan Period of the Hezhens]", 03 *Heilongjiang Minzu Congkan* [*Heilongjiang National Series*] (2001), pp. 40–44; Zhang

such as historical continuity on a specific land, cultural distinctiveness and self-identification as a collective, correspond to essential elements of being indigenous.

(3) The Tuvinians

The Tuvinian communities in China ethnically relate to the Altai Uriankhai. It used to be one of three Uriankhai groups in the Qing Empire, which were later transferred to Russia by the 1864 Russian-Manchu Protocol of Chuguchak (Tacheng).[249] The Tuvinian were the descents of the ancient Turkic people, living life as hunters and fishermen.[250] They used to speak Tuvan, a Turkic language, and practice Shamanism.[251] In the 13th century the Tuvinians were conquered by the Mongols and started their Mongolisation.

The Tuvinian group was not mentioned in the first round of the ethnic identification. The government of the XUAR initiated an ethnic investigation in 1985, though it was not requested by the Tuvinians.[252] The investigation report revealed that: 1) the Tuvininan community used to be a part of the Tuvan people; 2) they had been living together with the Mongols for hundreds of years, and therefore were deeply influenced by the Mongols culturally and economically; 3) they believed in Tibetan Buddhism, intermarried with the Mongols, and considered themselves as the Mongols; 4) other groups, including the Mongols, called them the "Tuvan-speaking Mongols".[253] The Tuvinian group was identified as the Mongols according to the majority will of the Tuvinians. It has been argued that, in the Tuvinian case, the will of the majority was an essential factor in the identification.[254]

Qiwen and Liu Yanhong, "Hezhu zu jingji fazhan de wenti yu duice [Problems and Countermeasures of the Economic Development of the Hezhe Nationality of Heilongjiang Province]", 02 *Heilongjiang Minzu Congkan* [*Heilongjiang National Series*] (2013), pp. 63–66.

249 Zeng Heping, "Zoujin Tuwa ren: Aletai Tuwa ren shehui lishi diaocha (shang) [Approaching the Tuvinian Group: A Social and Historical Investigation of the Altai Tuvans I]", 01 *Xinjiang Difang Zhi* [*Local Chronicles of Xinjiang*] (2011), p. 46; He Jihong, "Tuwa ren kao [the Investigation of the Tuvinians]", 04 *Xinjiang Difang Zhi* [*Local Chronicles of Xinjiang*] (2001), p. 56; Ailiti Shaliyefu, "Tuwa ren jinxi mantan [the Past and Present of the Tuvinians]", 01 *Xinjiang Difang Zhi* [*Local Chronicles of Xinjiang*] (1999), pp. 49–50; Huang Guangxue and Shi Lianzhu (eds), supra note 102, at pp. 219–220.

250 Kang Youming, "Yazhou fudi de Tuwa ren [the Tuvinians in Central Asia]", 02 *Xiyu Yanjiu* [*The Western Regions Studies*] (1994), p. 59.

251 Ibid; Zeng Heping, supra note 249, at pp. 49, 51.

252 Huang Guangxue and Shi Lianzhu (eds), supra note 102, at p. 220.

253 Ibid.

254 Ibid.

Historical connection to the land, identifiable economic life and culture, together with collective consciousness of the group, may form the basis for the Tuvinian communities to claim indigenous status. However, the question in doubt is the Mongolising evolvement of their culture. If the Chinese Tuvivian group intends to claim indigenous status, the establishment of their indigenousness as distinguishable from the Mongols might be a necessary step.

In conclusion, whether there exists indigenous situation in the PRC depends on how indigenous peoples are defined. When the priority of settlement stands as a key criterion, indigenous claims of Chinese minorities might be difficult to justify. All ethnic groups in China have lived in the territory for years and have developed varying extents of interaction and relation throughout history. It is not easy to agree a critical time to determine "who came first". The constitutional recognition of indigenous peoples in the ROC suggests that the settlement before the Ming/Qing dynasty might be a possible ground to identify indigenousness. When indigenous peoples are defined by social/economic/cultural distinctiveness, which intimately associates with historical continuity and attachment to a specific land, some minorities could be viewed as possible candidates for claiming status as indigenous peoples, such as the Tibetans, Mongols and Hezhe. Questions stemming from such a definition include: how important the land is; and to what extent the group need to maintain their traditional lifestyle to be indigenous? It is possible that a community departs from their ancestral land and continues traditional life somewhere else, for example the Ewenks in China. It is also possible that, although the community remains in ancestral land, the lifestyle or the way of living is dramatically changed and the land is no longer the essential part of their life. In either case, the boundaries between indigenous peoples and minorities are vague and ambiguous. Due to the undefined concept, the complexity of the ethnic situation and the reluctance of the Chinese government to grant indigenous rights, the applicability of indigenous rights to Chinese ethnic groups is far from clear.

4.5 Concluding Remarks

The REA system, as an internal arrangement, is adopted to facilitate minority accommodation in China. It is often used as an alternative for minority rights, which enables minorities to establish autonomous areas and exercise autonomy through autonomous agencies. Under the REA system, autonomous areas are established so as to secure regional stability and maintain ethnic balance. Although a concentration of minorities is the prerequisite for establishing an autonomous area, mandatory incorporation of the Han communities in the proposed autonomous area dilutes the minority population percentage. Since the number of the LPC deputies is a proportionate quota based on the size of the population, the minority that is exercising autonomy does not necessarily prevail in the LPC. This means that the right to autonomy might not be effectively exercised through standard democratic procedure, as the Han in many cases constitute the population majority in autonomous areas. The distinctive party-state relationship in China, together with a traditionally strong central government, makes it even more difficult for the minorities to realise autonomous rights through autonomous agencies.

On the other hand, over 400 self-reported groups were officially classified into 55 minorities through the Ethnic Identification Project. This Project took a wide range of factors into consideration, including language, culture, customs, mode of production, religion, history, origins, consciousness, and so forth. The inconsistent application of the identification standards has led to differing treatment of ethnic groups, with some self-identified groups being recognised and others not. Furthermore, as minority status is decided at birth, the fixed ethnic identity imposed creates divisions inside the nation. It potentially fosters ethnic consciousness of the minorities as distinguishable from the Han, although this minority consciousness does not necessarily imply worse relations with the Han.[255] This practice does not facilitate the integration of minorities into a unified multiethnic nation, nor does it fulfil China's obligations under international human rights conventions.

The criteria applied in the ethnic identification process may link some minorities with the developing concept of indigenous peoples. Although the Chinese government constantly denies the existence of indigenous peoples or indigenous issues in China so as to prevent Chinese minorities from claiming such rights, the African definition of indigenous peoples might be applicable, as it concerns discrimination, marginalisation and injustice rather than "who came first". The constitutional recognition of indigenous communities in Taiwan and Russia provides a different perspective of reconsidering the minority-indigenous situation in China. The applicability of indigenous rights in China, to a certain extent, depends on the elaboration of international discourse on indigenous rights. The communist proposition of the Chinese nation, however, is very likely to be challenged by a rising minority consciousness, as well as by possible indigenous claims.

---

255 C. Mackerras, *China's Minorities: Integration and Modernisation in the 20th Century* (Oxford University Press, 1994), p. 267.

CHAPTER 5

Autonomous Rights under the REA System: Legislative and Financial Rights

Chinese law elaborates an array of autonomous powers for the minorities within the framework of the REA system, covering legislation, economic development, finance and taxation, security, resource exploitation, border trade, education, culture, literature, arts, publishing and broadcasting. In general, minority rights under the REA system can be classified into three categories: legislative, financial, and cultural rights. Legislative autonomy and financial autonomy are exclusively derived from Chinese law, while the right of Chinese minorities to culture is governed by domestic law as well as international law. Legislative autonomy has been considered as the most important element under the REA system, as it provides the basis for the effective exercise of other autonomous powers. It reinforces the institutional design of the state, as autonomous legislation can only be passed by the local people's congress (LPC) in autonomous areas. Since the law guarantees minority representation in the LPCs, legislative autonomy would ensure that the interests of minorities will be taken into account in the decision-making process. The right to autonomously manage local finance is likewise essential to independently exercise self-government. Autonomous agencies could adjust governmental balances within autonomous areas according to local conditions and minority characteristics, so as to better protect minority interests. Legislative and financial autonomy directly affect the realisation of minority cultural rights. As will be discussed in the following chapters, legislation concerning the status of minority languages and legal provisions on educational and cultural affairs, together with funds available in local budgets, would facilitate the protection and preservation of minority culture and identity.

The following two chapters focus on the fourth element of the REA system: ethnic autonomous rights. This Chapter examines the rights of the minorities to legislative autonomy and financial autonomy, which are exclusively derived from domestic law. It will first look at autonomous legislative power, adaptation power, and adaptive implementation power and critically appraise how those rights are implemented in practice. It reveals that autonomous legislative right as the core of ethnic territorial autonomy has not been effectively exercised for a number of reasons. Next, the Chapter examines how financial autonomy is exercised through autonomous agencies in the present tax-sharing

 DOI:10.1163/9789004380578_007

system. The centre-oriented national fiscal system and the administration-led taxation reforms have substantially limited the minorities' right to pursue financial autonomy under the REA system.

5.1 Legislative Power of Autonomous Agencies

Some terms in the Chinese legal system need to be clarified before proceeding to legislative autonomy. The law in China, in a broad sense, refers to any provisions or rules that are legally binding. Strictly speaking, national law (*falv*) embraces basic laws and other laws, which are enacted by the NPC and its Standing Committee. Apart from the Constitution—the supreme law, national law prevails over all other sources of Chinese law.[1] Administrative regulation (*xingzheng fagui*) made by the State Council is superior to regional regulation (*difang xing fagui*) and ministerial regulation (*bumen guizhang*).[2] At the local level, regional regulation, which is promulgated by the LPCs and their Standing Committees, overrides regional government regulation (*difang zhengfu guizhang*).[3]

The exercise of legislative power is historically viewed as one of the distinctive features of REA, as only autonomous areas were empowered to enact local legislation at the time. However, the 1982 Constitution expands local legislative power to include provincial units.[4] According to the newly amended Legislation Law, not only the LPCs of provinces and municipalities, as well as their standing committees, could adopt regional regulation, on the condition that it must not contravene the Constitution, national law and administrative regulation, but also the LPCs of sub-districted cities and autonomous prefectures are accorded legislative power on matters concerning "rural and urban construction and management, environmental protection, and preservation of historical heritage and cultural values".[5] Regional regulation, in general, is formulated to implement the provisions of the laws and administrative regulations in accordance with local conditions, or to regulate specific regional matters.[6] Apart from the legislative power that local state institutions are vested

1 The 2015 Amended Legislation Law (the Legislation Law), Articles 7, 87, 88.
2 Ibid, Article 88.
3 Ibid, Article 89.
4 The 1982 Constitution, Article 100.
5 The Legislation Law, Article 72.
According to the 2015 Amendment of the Legislation Law, provinces, autonomous regions, municipalities directly under the central government, sub-districted cities and autonomous prefectures are delegated to enact regional regulations.
6 Ibid, Article 73.

with, autonomous areas also have the right to enact autonomy regulation (*zizhi tiaoli*) and special regulation (*danxing tiaoli*).[7] As prescribed by the Legislation Law and other national laws, autonomy regulation and special regulation can alter (*biantong guiding*) or supplement (*buchong guiding*) the provisions of national law and administrative regulation.[8] Autonomous agencies have the power to alter or cease the implementation of the decisions of state agencies at higher levels, if they do not suit the local conditions.[9]

Therefore, five autonomous regions and autonomous prefectures enjoy two sets of legislative power: to issue regional regulation and regional government regulation as local branches of the state institution, and to enact autonomy regulation and special regulation reflecting local circumstances and minority characteristics as a way of exercising autonomy. The legislative power of the LPCs in autonomous counties is confined to the latter one. By its nature, autonomous areas are granted three categories of legislative autonomy: legislative power, adaptation power and adaptive implementation power.[10]

5.1.1 *Legislative Power*

In compliance with the Constitution, national law and administrative regulation, the autonomous LPCs can adopt regional regulation, autonomy

7 The 1982 Constitution, Articles 115, 116; the Legislation Law, Articles 72, 75.

8 Article 75 of the Legislation Law provides: "[t]he people's congresses of the national autonomous areas have the power to formulate autonomous regulations and separate regulations on the basis of the political, economic and cultural characteristics of the local nationality (nationalities). The autonomous regulations and separate regulations of the autonomous regions shall be submitted to the Standing Committee of the National People's Congress for approval and shall go into effect upon approval. The autonomous regulations and separate regulations of the autonomous prefectures or counties shall be submitted to the standing committees of the people's congresses of the relevant provinces, autonomous regions or municipalities directly under the central government for approval and shall go into effect upon approval". See also the 2001 Marriage Law, Article 50; 2011 Criminal Law, Article 90; 1986 General Principles of Civil Law, Article 151; 2012 Civil Procedure Law, Article 16; 1985 Inheritance Law, Article 35; 1998 Forests Law, Article 48; 1998 Adoption Law, Article 32; Law on the Protection of the Rights and Interests of the Elderly, Article 49 (Article 85 as of the 2012 Draft); 2005 Law on the Protection of Rights and Interests of Women, Article 60.

9 The Law on REA, Article 20.

10 Zhang Dianjun, "Minzu zizhi defang falv biantong de fali fenxi [A Jurisprudential Analysis of Law Accommodation in National Autonomous Areas]", 01 *Guizhou Minzu Yanjiu* [*Guizhou Ethnic Studies*] (2010), pp. 8–17; Song Caifa, "Minzu zizhi defang lifa zizhiquan zai tantao [A Re-examination of Legislative Autonomy in Ethnic Autonomous Areas]", 02 *Faxuejia* [*The Jurist*] (2005), pp. 73–79; Shen Shouwen, "Minzu quyu zizhi defang lifaquan ruogan wenti yanjiu [A Study on Some Problems of Local Legislative Power in Ethnic Autonomous Areas]", 03 *Yunnan Shehui Kexue* [*Social Sciences in Yunnan*] (2007), pp. 75–79.

regulation or special regulation to implement national law and administrative regulation.[11] Except for matters reserved to the NPC and its Standing Committee, they can also legislate on important issues that have not been regulated by higher-level legislative instruments.[12] Regional regulation refers to the rules that are enacted by regional legislatures. Autonomy regulation is defined as "a regulation passed by the people's congress of a national autonomous area that deals with basic issues relating to the autonomy of the autonomous area and to important matters of general concerns there".[13] It is considered to be the most important document within an autonomous area, which has sometimes been named as the "local constitution". Special regulations, on the other hand, may only deal with "one specific area in any particular instrument and thus are more specific in character".[14]

By the end of 2010, 139 autonomy regulations and 777 special regulations have been adopted by 135 autonomous areas.[15] No autonomy regulation, however, could be found in autonomous regions. This does not necessarily mean that the legislative power has never been exercised by autonomous regions. Instead, provisions are passed as regional regulation, as it should only be submitted to the NPC Standing Committee and the State Council for the record.[16] Autonomous legislation enacted by an autonomous region, however, needs to be reviewed and approved by the NPC Standing Committee before entering into force.[17] Although a deposited regional regulation or regional government regulation might be nullified, due to contradiction to higher-level provisions, it remains in force until that nullification occurs. The procedures and criteria of such a scrutiny on regional law are general and vague, and have not been clarified. In practice, thousands of regional regulations and regional government regulations are enacted every year, among which many local authorities fail to report those regulations to the Centre.[18] The NPC Standing Committee

---

11 The Legislation Law, Article 73.

12 Ibid.

13 Quoted in Yash Ghai, Sophia Woodman and Kelley Loper, Is There Space for "Genuine Autonomy" for Tibetan Areas in the PRC's System of Nationalities Regional Autonomy?, 17 *International Journal on Minority and Group Rights* (2010), p. 172.

14 Ibid.

15 Source: http://www.gov.cn/test/2012-06/20/content_2165897_2.htm, last visited on 30/10/2013; Maria Lundberg and Yong Zhou, "Regional National Autonomy under Challenge: Law, Practice and Recommendations", 16 *International Journal on Minority and Group Rights* (2009), p. 313.

16 The Legislation Law, Article 98.

17 The Legislation Law, Article 75; the Law on REA, Article 19.

18 Yash Ghai, Sophia Woodman and Kelley Loper, supra note 13, at p. 171.

and the State Council are rarely found exercising effective supervision on this matter.[19]

At the sub-provincial level, a considerable number of autonomous pieces of legislation are passed, as they only need to be reviewed and approved by the LPC Standing Committee at the provincial level and to be reported to the Centre for the record.[20] This procedural requirement of autonomous legislation being reviewed and approved by a higher-level agency has been interpreted by some scholars as "half legislative power".[21]

Four autonomous regions have generated drafts of autonomy regulation. Mongolia and Guangxi are more active in drafting autonomy regulation than others, as both have drafts submitted to and discussed by the central authority, which are rejected and referred back for further revision.[22] Ningxia and Tibet are working on the 16th draft within their LPCs.[23] Xinjiang is the only autonomous region that has not yet started drafting autonomy regulation.[24] This may suggest that the reluctance of the central authority to allow the XUAR to legislate within the limits of ethnic autonomy is caused by Uyghur's unrest and demand for secession.[25]

The reasons, which explain why the draft autonomy regulation failed to win the central approval, are as follows. First, the dynamic change of the political, economic and legal regime requests for an updated version of autonomy regulation every time.[26] Since the establishment of the PRC, the drafting efforts have been influenced by the Cultural Revolution, the Reform and Opening

19 Ibid.

20 The Legislation Law, Article 75; the Law on REA, Article 19.

21 Wu Zongjin, *Minzu fazhi de lilun yu shijian* [*Theory and Practice of Ethnic Legislation*] (Zhongguo Minzhu Fazhi Chubanshe, 1997), p. 103; Maria Lundberg and Yong Zhou, supra note 14.

22 Pan Hongxiang, "Zizhiqu zizhi tiaoli chutainan de yuanyin fenxi ji duice [Countermeasures and Casual Analysis on Hard Promulating Autonomous Regulations in Autonomous Regions]", 03 *Beifang Minzu Daxue Xuebao* [*Journal of Beifang Ethnic University*] (2009), pp. 55–56; Bai Yongli, "Zizhiqu zizhi tiaoli zhiding yanjiu—yi Neimenggu zizhiqu weili [On the Making of Autonomous Statutes in Autonomous Regions: Taking the IMAR for Instance(as An Example)]", 06 *Meimenggu Shifan Daxue Xuebao* [*Journal of Inner Mongolia Normal University (Philosophy and Social Science)*] (2010), pp. 52–53

23 Pan Hongxiang, ibid.

24 Pan Hongxiang, ibid; He Yunlong, "Xinjiang minzu zizhi defang lifaquan de yunyong fenxi yu duice yanjiu [Suggestions and Analysis on the Exercise of Legislative Power in the XUAR]", 03 *Xinjiang Shehui Kexue* [*Social Science in Xinjiang*] (2006), p. 84.

25 Maria Lundberg and Yong Zhou, supra note 14, at p. 315.

26 Pan Hongxiang, supra note 22, at p. 58; Tan Wanxia, "Guanxi zhuangzu zizhiqu zizhi tiaoli zhi lifa sikao [Legislative Suggestions on Guangxi Autonomous Region's Regulation of Autonomy]", 03 *Guangxi Minzu Yanjiu* [*Study of Ethnics in Guangxi*] (2011), pp. 42–43.

Policy, the transformation from the planned economy to the socialist market economy, and recently by the accession to the WTO. Furthermore, the local party committee is actively engaged in the drafting procedure, which is supposed to be a purely legislative activity.[27] Also, the State Council is involved in the reviewing process of the drafts. This will make it even more difficult to get approved, as the State Council is unwilling to share or to vest their powers with local authorities.[28] Additionally, there has been a lack of clear division of powers between the central government and local authorities since 1949. If autonomy regulation of an autonomous region is approved and the centre-periphery relation is, in a way, legalised, other provincial authorities may claim a greater local autonomy on this basis.[29]

Compared with the procedural limitation on making autonomy regulation and special regulation, it is understandable that autonomous regions prefer to exercise legislative power through making general local regulation. On the matters that have not been regulated by higher-level legislation, a regional regulation or regional government regulation made by an autonomous region reflecting local circumstances and minority characteristics could be viewed as autonomous legislation, though it is not under the name of special regulation.

The legislative power of the LPCs at the prefectural level and below used to be an essential feature of minority autonomy under the REA system, as non-autonomous authorities at the same level are not granted the same right. Hundreds of autonomy regulations and special regulations have been passed at the sub-provincial level. The procedural limitation does not seem to constitute an obstacle for exercising legislative autonomy. The first explanation is that enacting autonomous legislation is the only way to exercise legislative autonomy at the sub-provincial level, as the autonomous LPCs at the prefecture/county level do not have the power to issue regional regulation. The lack of autonomous legislation in an autonomous prefecture or autonomous county might imply an incompetent exercise of autonomous powers. In addition, autonomous legislation at the sub-provincial level would hardly involve the clarification of any fundamental national regime or the delimitation of the centre-periphery relation. For instance, except the TAR, all 10 Tibetan

27 Pan Hongxiang, supra note 22.

28 Pan Hongxiang, supra note 22, at p. 57; Tan Wanxia, supra note 26; Yang Feng, "The Legislation in Autonomous Areas in China: Progress, Limitations and Recommendations", 18:2 *Asian-Pacific Law and Policy Journal* (2017), pp. 70–71.

29 Peter Ferdinand argues that the Law on REA could be used as the administrative and legal basis for the provinces to claim greater autonomy. Peter Ferdinand, *Communist Regimes in Comparative Perspective: the Evolution of the Soviet, Chinese and Yugoslav Systems* (Harvester Wheatsheaf, Barnes & Noble Books, 1991), p. 239.

autonomous prefectures in neighbouring provinces have enacted autonomy regulations. But none of the five autonomous prefectures in the XUAR are governed by their own autonomy regulations. Nevertheless, most autonomy regulations directly take after the constitutional provisions on REA and the Law on REA, which may not manifest local circumstances and ethnic characteristics.[30] Even though autonomous prefectures are delegated to enact regional regulation since 2015, the legislative pattern of autonomous prefectures may remain unchanged as regional regulation is confined to matters concerning "rural and urban construction and management, environmental protection and preservation of historical heritage and cultural values" and subject to the same approval procedure. However, the expansion of regional legislative power would greatly affect the significance of minority legislative autonomy at the sub-provincial level.

5.1.2 *Adaptation Power*

The power of adapting national law and administrative regulation at a higher level to meet the particular needs of the local minorities derives from Article 75 of the Legislation Law, as well as from special clause prescribed in individual national law.[31] Article 75 of the Legislation Law states:

> [a]n autonomy regulation or special regulation may adapt the provisions of national laws and administrative regulations to the particular needs of the minorities of the area, provided that such adaptation must not contradict the basic principles thereof, and must not violate the provisions of the Constitution and the Law on REA, or of other relevant national laws and administrative regulations with particular application to ethnic autonomous areas.[32]

The adaptation power may possibly be viewed as the most important legislative power that only applies to autonomous legislatures. It facilitates the maintenance of the uniformity of the legal system and, in the meantime, serves to respect and preserve the distinctive culture and customs of the minorities.

---

30 Ji Ya and Otguntungga Lag, "Zizhi tiaoli lifa zhidu de queshi yu duice [the Countermeasures and Deletion on the Legislation of the Autonomous Regulation]", 06 *Neimenggu Daxue Xuebao* [*Journal of Inner Mongolia University* (*Humanities and Social Science*)] (2007), p.37.

31 Up to date, 9 national laws contain special clause that allows for minority adaptation.

32 The Legislation Law, Article 75.

The adaptation to national law and administrative regulation at a higher level can be made in the form of autonomy regulation, special regulation, modification rule (*biantong guiding*), or supplementary rule (*buchong guiding*), but not as general regional regulation. The adaptation power, thus, distinguishes legislative autonomy from local legislative power. However, there is no explicit provision on the relationship between autonomy regulation, special regulation, modification rule and supplementary rule. Scholars are divided in this regard.

As autonomy regulation has been widely considered as the fundamental document in an autonomous area, the disagreement centres on the differences between special regulation and modification rule/supplementary rule. Deng Jianmin argues that modification rule/supplementary rule, together with autonomy regulation and special regulation, constitute three basic categories of autonomous legislation, if considering their legislative basis and procedure as well as their legal status.[33] The official sources prefer a format of "autonomy regulation and special regulation as well as modification rule and supplementary rule". In the 2005 White Paper on the Regional Autonomy for Ethnic Minorities in China and the China Ethnic News (a newspaper run by the SEAC), such a format is used.

The second opinion, as Qiao Xiaoyang (the Deputy Secretary General of the 11th NPC Standing Committee) has argued, assumes that there are two types of special regulation in general: one type involves the implementation, modification, and supplementation of national law and administrative regulation; the second concerns the provisions on matters which have not been covered by national legislation, or on matters which are not in the need of national regulation.[34] In other words, the adaptation to alter or supplement a provision that does not conform to minorities' political, economic, and cultural characteristics is embodied as an autonomy regulation or special regulation, and there is no special type of legislation as modification rule/supplementary rule.[35] This argument appears to be more plausible, as modification rule/supplementary

33 Deng Jianmin, "Lun biantong huo buchong guiding yu danxing tiaoli de qubie [Differences between Adaptive Provisions or Supplementary Provision and Specific Regulation]", 07 *Xinan Minzu Xueyuan Xuebao* [*Journal of Southwest University for Nationalities*] (2002), pp. 111–114.

34 Cited in Zhang Dianjun, supra note 10, at p. 10.

35 Ibid. Chen Boli and Xu Xingui also argue that "modification rule" is a general term that does not constitute a separate type of legislative document. But they believe that a special regulation in essence is one type of modification. See Chen Boli and Xu Xingui, "Lifaxue shiye xia de minzu biantong guiding wenti tanxi [A Legislative Discussion of the Ethnic Modification Rule]", 03 *Manzu Yanjiu* [*Manchu Minority Research*] (2007), pp. 8–13.

rule is not the source of Chinese law. Also, neither the Constitution nor the Law on REA has referred to modification rule or supplementary rule. Therefore, modification or supplementation should be made in the form of autonomy regulation or special regulation.

Accordingly, being reviewed and approved by a higher-level legislature is a necessary step for the adaptation to enter into force.[36] This approval requirement may be logically justified on the ground of legislative hierarchy and superiority: adaptation to a superior provision would need the review of the legislature which enacts the original legislation. Nonetheless, some national laws merely request a submission procedure (for the record) for the modification or supplementation to be effective.[37] Such a divergent provision could be explained by lawmaking techniques and the integration of legal system. Article 66 (Article 75 in the 2015 Amendment) of the Legislation Law came into force in 2000. National laws, which are passed after this date, have amended the adaptation provision to comply with the Legislation law.[38] National laws enacted before this date are expected to be revised accordingly.

To date, autonomous areas have adopted over 900 autonomy regulations and special regulations. The adaptation, however, mainly concerns matters relating to marriage, inheritance, adoption, education and language, election, forest, grassland, and land administration.[39] There is still a lack of autonomous legislation on more important issues, such as political, economic, or social affairs.

---

36 The Legislation Law, Article 75.

37 Article 151 of the 1986 General Principle of Civil Law allows for the people's congresses in autonomous areas to adapt the provisions in accordance with the particular needs of the minorities. The adaptation made by the people's congress of the autonomous region should be submitted to the NPC Standing Committee for approval or for the record, whereas the adaptation made by the sub-provincial autonomous legislature only needs to submit to the standing committee of the people's congress at the provincial level for approval.

38 These amendments include: the 2001 Marriage Law, Article 50; 2011 Criminal Law, Article 90; 2012 Civil Procedure Law, Article 16; Law on the Protection of the Rights and Interests of the Elderly, Article 49 (Article 85 as of the 2012 Draft) and 2005 Law of the People's Republic of China on the Protection of Rights and Interests of Women, Article 60. Article 90 of the Criminal Law states: "where the provisions of this Law cannot be completely applied in national autonomous areas, the people's congresses of those autonomous regions or the provinces concerned may formulate adoptive or supplementary provisions based on the political, economic and cultural characteristics of local nationalities and the basic principles stipulated in this Law; and these provisions shall go into effect after they have been approved by the NPC Standing Committee".

39 Song Caifa, supra note 10, at pp. 73–79; Shen Shouwen, supra note 10, at pp. 77–78.

5.1.3 *Adaptive Implementation Power*

Article 20 of the Law on REA further recognises the right to alter or cease the implementation of the decisions of state agencies at higher levels. It reads:

> if a resolution, decision, order, or instruction of a state agency at a higher level does not suit the actual conditions in an ethnic autonomous area, an autonomous agency of the area may report for the approval of that higher level state agency to either implement it with certain alterations or cease implementing it altogether.[40]

In contrast to legislative power discussed above, this clause aims to adapt the implementation of policies and administrative directives of a higher-level agency to suit the local conditions. Such a right is considered by some scholars as a part of administrative autonomy.[41] Not only can the LPC file for an alteration or cease, the LPG may also petition for an adaptation.[42] The LPG could report on their own, if the policy or administrative directive is formulated by the people's government at a higher level, or it could apply for the adaptation, jointly with the LPC, if it is a joint decision made by the people's congress and people's government at a higher level.

It has been suggested that this provision originated from the 1980 CPCCC Meeting on Tibet Affairs.[43] According to the Meeting Memorandum,[44] the first two principles provided that the will of the Tibetans would be taken into account, when making policies concerning Tibet. The third principle allowed the local party committee and state agencies to cease or alter the implementation of guidelines and policies formulated by the CPCCC and its departments, as well as of instructions, notices and decisions that did not suit the Tibetan

40 The Law on REA, Article 20.

41 The Law on REA, Article 20. See also Song Caifa, supra note 10, at pp. 78–79; Wang Yan, "Lun minzu zizhi defang de biantongquan [On Alteration Rights of Autonomous Minority Areas]", 01 *Hubei Minzu Xueyuan Xuebao* [*Journal of Hubei Institute for Nationalities*] (2006), p. 56; Zhang Dianjun, "Minzu zizhi defang biantong zhixing yu tingzhi zhixing falv wenti tanxi [A Study of Implementation with Certain Alterations or Cease Implementing in National Autonomous Areas of China]", 03 *Beifang Minzu Daxue Xuebao* [*Journal of Beifang Ethic University*] (2009), p. 68.

42 Ibid.

43 Maria Lundberg and Yong Zhou, supra note 14, at p. 315.

44 Zhonggong zhongyang guanyu zhuanfa <Xizang gongzuo huitan jiyao> de tongzhi [the 1980 Notice of the CPCCC on Forwarding the Memorandum of the Meeting on Tibet Affairs] (07/04/1980), http://cpc.people.com.cn/GB/64184/64186/66677/4493835.html, last visited on 31/10/2013.

conditions. The adaptation of the implementation of important issues would require permission in advance, whilst the adaptation on general issues only needed to report afterwards. In addition, the CPCCC acknowledged that the Meeting guidelines and principles could also be applied to other autonomous areas.[45]

Those principles, in a way, represented an attempt of the CPC to expand autonomous powers after the Cultural Revolution, in order to correct the past wrongs and to regain minority support.[46] But this new tendency towards "greater autonomy" initiated by the Tibet Meeting was rescinded shortly after ethnic unrest erupted in Xinjiang and Inner Mongolia.[47] Such a change illustrated that the degree of minority autonomy was closely linked with the loyalty of the minorities and regional stability.

A similar principle was later written into the Law on REA (Article 20), with the purpose of according discretion to autonomous agencies to alter higher-level decisions and policies. This provision, however, fails to elaborate a remedial regime against the reply from state agencies at a higher level. The 2001 amended Law on REA incorporated a 60-day mandatory reply period, which, to some extent, enhanced the applicability of this power.[48] Still, the elaboration of a remedial regime has not yet been discussed.

The exercise of adaptive implementation power in practice is very problematic, since a considerable number of key central resolutions, decisions, orders or instructions are jointly issued by the central government and the CPCCC. The right to adapt the implementation of those decisions, though upon the approval from higher-level state agencies, might jeopardise the control of the communists over the state. But if autonomous agencies cannot challenge the implementation of those co-issued decisions, autonomous powers may be substantially limited and incline towards "paper" autonomy. Furthermore, in case an autonomous agency has to work together with the local party committee to petition for an alteration or cease of a co-issued decision, it then turns the constitutional ethnic autonomy into a shared regime: minority-party autonomy. None of these situations would likely to be expected by the CPC. It is difficult to examine the exercise of adaptive implementation power in reality, as few figures have been made publicly available.

45 Ibid.

46 Harbar, "Attempts to Transform CCP's Ethnic Minority Policy in the Early 1980s", 15:02 *The Chinese Historical Review* (2008), pp. 297–298.

47 Ibid, pp. 309–310.

48 Maria Lundberg and Yong Zhou, supra note 14, at p. 317.

5.2 Autonomous Financial Power

As an essential part of REA, the right to autonomously manage local finance is granted by the Constitution and the Law on REA. Autonomous agencies have exclusive rights to manage and use revenues accruing to autonomous areas under the state financial system.[49] According to the Budget Law, draft budgets (*yusuan caoan*) and balances (*juesuan caoan*) of autonomous areas should be compiled by the LPG and its departments, before submitting to the LPC at the corresponding level for examination and approval.[50] An autonomous LPG is responsible for the implementation of the budgets, whilst the LPC and its Standing Committee have supervisory power over the implementation of the budgets and balances at the corresponding level and lower levels.[51] On the compilation of the local draft budget, the LPG has to follow the principles on the division of central-local revenues and expenditures, which are decided by the State Council.[52] Hence, conflicts may arise from the dual accountability of the LPG as an autonomous agency and as the local branch of the State Council.

The national fiscal system has undergone three different phases.[53] The recent change is marked by the establishment of a new taxation distribution system.[54] The taxation reform originates from the 1993 Decision of the State Council on Implementing the Tax Division Management System (the 1993 Decision), which aims to recentralisation and strengthen the central fiscal

49 The 1982 Constitution, Article 117; the Law on REA, Article 32.

50 The Budget Law (amended in 2014), Articles 24, 43.

51 Ibid, Articles 53, 83.

52 Ibid, Article 29.

53 The period of 1950–1979 was the central-dominant period. From 1980 to 1993, the central government continued to further administrative decentralisation. This system divided revenues and expenditures between the central government and local governments and held local governments responsible for balancing their own budgets at different levels. As local budgets were directly linked to local economic growth, local governments were motivated by a desire to promote local economy. Various financial management policies were adopted during this period. Fan and Wan pointed out that such a practice led to a weak central tax system and a strong local tax system. Therefore, a new taxation distribution system has been established and enforced from 1993 onwards. See Liu Zhiguang, "Woguo defang zhengfu caizheng shouru laiyuan jiqi guimo [the Sources and Scale of Local Revenues]", 04 *Difang Caizheng Yanjiu* [*Sub National Fiscal Research*] (2010), pp. 14–15; Peter Ferdinand, supra note 29, at pp. 231–238; Fan Ziying and Wan Guanghua, *The Fiscal Risk of Local Government Revenue in the People's Republic of China, ADBI Working Paper 567*, Tokyo: Asian Development Bank Institute, 2016, p. 6, available at: http://www.adb.org/publications/fiscal-risk-local-government-revenue-prc/, last accessed on 09/04/2018.

54 The 1993 Decision of the State Council on Implementing the Tax Division Management System (the 1993 Decision); the 2014 Budget Law, Article 15.

revenue.[55] According to the 1993 Decision, a tax-sharing system should be established between the central and provincial governments, as well as between the provincial governments and their sub-provincial units.

The current state financial scheme, therefore, is a centre-oriented system established on the decisions of the State Council and its ministry departments. However, the 1993 Decision as the basis of the taxation reform is questionable, as it seems to have gone beyond the power of the State Council. According to the Constitution, the division of functions and powers between the central and local governments is reserved to the NPC.[56] The State Council merely has the power to regulate the detailed division of the centre-periphery functions and powers.[57] The reason for the Constitution to reserve the power of regulating fundamental issues to the NPC is that local deputies could defend regional interests through the congressional procedure. Neither has the NPC explicitly vested such a power with the State Council beforehand.[58] Although the 1994 Budget Law reinstated the establishment of the tax-sharing system based on the 1993 Decision, this subsequent ratification by the NPC was inappropriate, since it may not correct the unconstitutional nature but set an improper precedent.[59] It is unsuitable to classify this overreaching activity of the State Council as an administrative regulation or as a government decision. It has been reported that the legislative attempt to amend the Budget Law started in 2004. But the third review of the draft amendment to the Budget Law by the NPC Standing Committee was not finished until April 2014. The amendment was then approved four months later. This time-consuming amendment procedure is not beyond expectation, considering the significance of the Budget Law as the "economic constitution", which concerns the fundamental question of delimiting the centre-periphery financial power. However, this newly amended Budget Law, again, fails to clarify the centre-periphery relation in the light of fiscal and financial affairs.

In theory, the LPC of an autonomous area can adapt the Budget Law to suit local conditions and minority characteristics. But no such adaptations have been found in public sources so far. Local taxation regulation made by the

55 Fan Ziying and Wan Guanghua, supra note 53, at pp. 3–4.

56 The 1982 Constitution, Articles 62, 89; Ye Bifeng, "Jingji xianfaxue yanjiu de changshi: fenshuizhi juedingquan de xianfa fenxi [A Preliminary Study into Economic Constitution: Constitutional Interpretation of Right of Decision on Adaption of a Tax-sharing System]", 06 *Shanghai Jiaotong Daxue Xuebao* [*Journal of Shanghai Jiaotong University (Philosophy and Social Science)*] (2007), pp. 6–7.

57 Ibid.

58 Ye Bifeng, supra note 56, at pp. 7–8.

59 Ye Bifeng, supra note 56, at pp. 10–11.

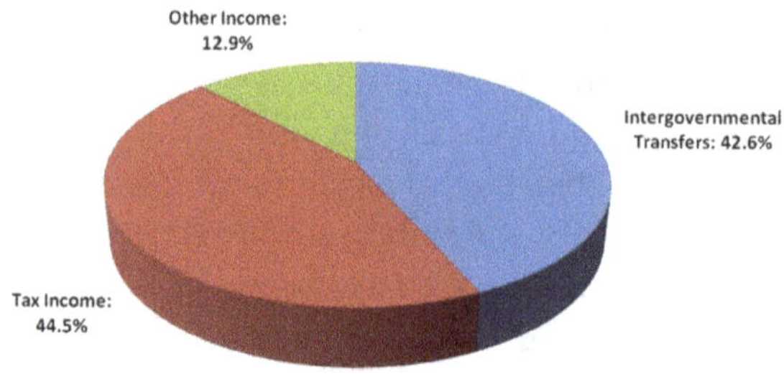

PIE CHART 2 Local General Revenue by Source 2012.

autonomous legislature mainly concerns the implementation of national law and administrative regulation. Without autonomous legislation on financial affairs, the LPG finds no legal basis to autonomously manage local finance. Nor has a petition to alter or cease the implementation of the State Council's decisions been made by autonomous agencies. Hence, autonomous LPGs currently rely upon national law and administrative regulation, as well as the decisions of the central government, to manage local finance. Financial autonomy is considerably limited in this sense.

In general, under the new taxation-sharing system, local revenue mainly comes from three sources: tax benefits, non-tax income, and intergovernmental transfers.[60] (Pie Chart 2.) The general revenue that an autonomous area may receive under the national financial system consists of two sections: the local government's own revenues (*defang benji shouru*), including tax benefits and non-tax income, and intergovernmental transfers.

5.2.1 *Financial Rights of Autonomous Regions*

(1) The Local Government's Own Revenue—Tax Income

Tax income normally constitutes the largest source of the local government's own revenue. The proportion of tax revenue has been declining in recent years. In 2004, tax accounted for 84% in the LPG's own revenue, and the number dropped to 74% in 2016.[61] The remainder of the LPG's own revenue is gathered

60 The 2012 Balance Sheet of the Local Financial Revenues, published by the Ministry of Finance, http://yss.mof.gov.cn/2012qhczjs/201307/t20130715_966217.html, last accessed on 31/09/2017.

61 The proportion of tax income was 84% in 2005, 83% in 2006, 81% in 2007 and 2008, 80% in 2009 and 2010, and 78% in 2011. The statistics from 2004 to 2008 can be found in Jin Wanjun and Fu Guangjun, "Difang caizheng shouru zhong shuishou suozhan bizhong buduan xiajiang [the Decreasing Proportion of Tax Income in Local Fiscal Revenue]", China Taxation Newspaper (08/25/2010), Page 5; the information of 2009–2012 is

from miscellaneous receipts, profits from public ownership, administrative charges and government bonds etc.[62] The following discussion will focus on local tax income.

According to the 1993 Decision, taxes are divided into three categories: central tax, local tax, and shared tax. As exclusive central revenues, custom duties, Value Added Tax (VAT) and consumption tax collected from imported goods, and consumption tax made up to 25.3% of the total tax income in 2012.[63] 75% of domestic VAT and 50% of income tax, which together account for half of the national tax income, also belong to the central revenue income.[64] Therefore, more than half of the national tax income is collected by the central government.

In terms of local taxes at a provincial level, the business tax (15.2% of the national tax income), excluding the business tax from railway services, the headquarters of banks, and head offices of insurance companies, used to be one of the largest sources of the local tax revenue prior to the Business Tax to VAT reform.[65] The estate taxes, land taxes (including urban land use tax, farmland occupying tax and land VAT) and resource taxes, except for the offshore oil tax which is collected by the central government, are exclusively collected

---

summarised from the annual balance sheet of the local financial revenue, published by the Ministry of Finance. The Sheets are available at: http://yss.mof.gov.cn/2016js/201707/t20170713_2648986.html; http://yss.mof.gov.cn/2012qhczjs/201307/t20130715_966217.html; http://yss.mof.gov.cn/2011qgczjs/201207/t20120710_665251.html; http://yss.mof.gov.cn/2010juesuan/201107/t20110720_578445.html; http://yss.mof.gov.cn/2009nianquanguojuesuan/201007/t20100709_327130.html, last visited on 02/11/2013.

62 Ibid.

63 The Ministry of Finance, "2012nian shuishou shouru zengzhang de jiegou xing fenxi [A Structural Analysis of the Increase of Tax Revenue in 2012]", 04 *Zhongguo Caizheng* [*China State Finance*] (2013), pp. 78–79.

64 Ibid. The shared income tax between the central and local authorities comprises the enterprise income tax and individual income tax. However, the income tax collected from railway services, National Post, Industrial and Commercial Bank of China, Agricultural Bank of China, Bank of China, China Construction Bank, China Development Bank, Agricultural Development Bank of China, the Export-Import Bank of China and marine oil and gas enterprises is classified as the central income. The sharing ratio of income tax between the centre and localities, including the enterprise income tax and individual income tax, was 5: 5 in 2002 and 6:4 in 2003. This ratio is to be determined according to the actual situation in the years thereafter. See also Guowuyuan guanyu yinfa suodeshui shouru fenxiang gaige fang'an de tongzhi [the 2001 Circular of State Council on Distributing the Reform Scheme of Income Tax Revenue Sharing], No.37 (2001) of the State Council.

65 The Ministry of Finance, supra note 61; the 1993 Decision. The reform of replacing the business tax with the VAT has been viewed as the most significant tax reform since 1994. For a detailed discussion on China's business tax to VAT reform, see Wei Cui, "China's Business Tax to VAT reform: an interim assessment", 5 *British Tax Review* (2014), pp. 617–641.

by local governments as well.[66] The tax revenue that an autonomous region is entitled to manage in 2012 consists of: the local share of domestic VAT and income tax (35% of the local tax income), business tax (33% of the local tax income), estate taxes and land taxes (27.6%), resource taxes (1.8%) and other taxes (2.6%).[67] As the VAT reform was expanded to all industries in 2016, business tax has been replaced by the value added tax.[68] Although the sharing ratio of the VAT among central and provincial governments is temporarily adjusted to 50-50 during the transitional period (up to 3 years),[69] the local tax income would decrease in the foreseeable future.

The tax classification, tax rate and sharing proportion, which are decided by the central government, equally apply to all provincial units, including five autonomous regions. The uniform implementation leads to regional imbalances between the eastern and western regions, as well as among autonomous areas. Nonetheless, autonomous agencies could be able to remedy the situation by exercising adaptation power. The Legislation Law reserves the right to enact national law on fundamental taxation system to the NPC and its Standing Committee.[70] In the event that no national law has been enacted on fundamental taxation system, the State Council may issue administrative regulation on the matter, upon the authorisation of the NPC and its Standing Committee.[71] This means that the imposition and abolition of tax, tax reduction, tax exemption, tax refund, and payment of delinquent tax should be governed by national law or administrative regulation upon authorisation.[72] Read in conjunction with Article 75 of the Legislation Law, an autonomous legislature, thus, could modify the provisions of existing national law and administrative regulation on taxation to suit the local conditions. However, in practice the autonomous LPCs are found to be inactive in this regard.

---

66 The 1993 Decision.

67 The Ministry of Finance, the 2012 Balance Sheet of the Local Financial Revenues.

68 The Ministry of Finance and the State Administration of Taxation, Guanyu quanmian tuikai yingyehsui gai zengzhishui shidian de tongzhi [the Notice on the Comprehensive Roll-out of the VAT Reform Pilot Program] (2016), Circular [2016] No. 36.

69 The State Council, Guanyu yinfa quanmian tuikai yinggaizeng shidian hou tiaozheng zhongyang yu defang zengzhishui shouru huafen guodu fang'an de tongzhi [the Notice on the Transitional Adjustment of the VAT Income between the Central and Local Government (after the Comprehensive Roll-out of the VAT Reform Pilot Program)] (2016), Circular [2016] No. 26.

70 The Legislation Law, Article 8.

71 The Legislation Law, Article 9.

72 The 2001 Law on the Administration of Tax Collection, Article 3.

For example, the tax reform of crude oil and natural gas, which modified the taxable unit from the volume/quantity produced to the actual sales value,[73] may not substantially benefit the GZAR, as it is deficient in crude oil and natural gas. Instead, the non-ferrous metal ore represents an important pillar industry in the area.[74] Being inspired by the reform on the taxable unit of crude oil and natural gas, the GZAR proposed to tax the extraction of the non-ferrous metal ore on the basis of the sales value so as to balance regional economy and to benefit the people in mining district—a minority concentrated area.[75] This proposal sounded fairly plausible, as it conformed to the general principles under the REA system, as well as to the guidelines of supporting economic and social development of the GZAR with fiscal and taxation policies.[76] The adaptation of taxable unit of the non-ferrous metal ore would not involve the fundamental question of the centre-periphery relation, although it may slightly impair the central tax income.[77] Such an

73 The resource tax, according to the 1993 standards, used to be levied on the basis of taxable volume produced rather than the actual sales value. The tax rate was set at a low range. For example, the resource tax collected from crude oil was 8–30 RMB yuan per ton; natural gas was 2–15 RMB yuan per 1,000 cubic meters; and coal was 0.3–5 RMB yuan per ton. In 2010, a pilot reform of the resource tax was first introduced in the XUAR and then extended to the rest part of the state. The 2011 Amended Interim Regulation on the Resource Tax modified the tax method of crude oil and natural gas from the volume produced to its actual sales value. The adjustment of the resource tax would certainly benefit areas that are rich in crude oil and natural gas. The resource tax income in the XUAR, for example, has doubled in 2011, up to 6.5 billion (1,000,000,000) RMB yuan. Resource tax accounted for 10.52% of the XUAR tax revenue in 2012, where 83% of the taxes were collected from crude oil and gas industries. See the 1993 Interim Regulation on Resource Tax; the 2011 Interim Regulation on Resource Tax, Article 4; Xinjiang Statistical Yearbook 2012, 7–3 "Statistics on Total Government Revenue and Expenditures in Local Finance"; http://www.gov.cn/gzdt/2013-06/04/content_2418804.htm, last accessed on 03/11/2013.

74 The United Task Group, "Guangxi youse jinshu ziyuanshui congjia jizheng gaige yanjiu [A Research on the Reform of the Non-ferrous Metal Ore Resource Tax Based on the Actual Sales Value in Guangxi]", 11 *Difang Caizheng Yanjiu* [*Sub-national Fiscal Research*] (2011), p. 14.

75 The United Task Group, ibid, pp. 16–17.

76 Ibid, p. 21; the State Council, Some Suggestions on Further Promoting the GZAR's Economic and Social Development, 2009.

77 The resource tax is deducted from the taxable enterprise income. The higher the resource tax is, the more the deduction would be. The taxable enterprise income, therefore, would be reduced. But according to the 2016 Notice on the Comprehensive Implementation of the Resource Tax Reform, the resource tax levied on non-ferrous metal ore has been included in the Reform and is, thus, classified into local fiscal income. The Implementing Regulation of the Enterprise Income Tax Law, Article 31; the Ministry of Finance and the State Administration of Taxation, Quanmian tuijn ziyuanshui gaige de tongzhi [the

adaptation of taxable unit could be done through the LPC of the GZAR, which falls within its adaptation power as an autonomous legislature. However, it was the Finance Department of the GZAR that attempted to report to the central government and to receive the approval thereof.[78] The reform proposal, in fact, started with the decision of the Local Party Committee and was formulated by the LPG. It did not involve the LPC and its Standing Committee or the exercise of autonomous legislative power. According to the 2016 Notice of the GZAR Finance Department, the mining of natural resources eventually became taxable on the basis of the sales value.[79] However, this new taxation policy is not the result of exercising autonomous adaptation power. It has been adopted in accordance with the national reform on the resource tax initiated by the Ministry of Finance and the State Administration of Taxation, which authorises the provincial LPG s to determine the rates of the mineral taxes included in the list and to decide new resource taxes and their rates if they are not included in the list.[80]

On the other hand, autonomous legislatures have no discretion to enact regulations on fundamental taxation affairs, for example, imposing new tax, if national law or administrative regulation has not been passed on the matter. As the environmental tax has been imposed in 2018, autonomous areas may be able to claim benefits for their contributions to ecological balance and

---

Notice on the Comprehensive Implementation of the Resource Tax Reform] (2016), Circular [2016] No. 53, Section 2, Subsection 6, Article 1.

78 The Finance Department of the GZAR, http://www.gxcz.gov.cn/newsinfo.asp?id=28901&-CataID=3, accessed on 03/11/2015.

79 The Finance Department of the GZAR, the Notice on the Resource Tax Reform in the GZAR (2016), Circular [2016], No.18.

80 The resource taxes on the list annexed to the Notice include: metals—iron, gold, copper, bauxite, lead and zinc, nickel, tin and other metals or mineral products not listed; non-metals—graphite, diatomite, kaolin clay, fluorite, limestone, pyrite, phosphorus, potassium sulphate, mineral salt, lake salt, salt extracted from subterranean brine by means of solar evaporation, coalbed methane, clay, sand and gravel, other non-metallic mineral products not listed; and sea salt. For the taxes included in the list, the provincial LPG s can propose the tax rates that will be applied within their administrative units from the scope fixed by the list, which are subject to the approval from the Ministry of Finance and the State Administration of Taxation. For mineral extractions not included in the list, the provincial LPG s can freely decide new resource taxes to be imposed and the rates, which are only required to report to the Ministry of Finance and the State Administration of Taxation for the record. The Ministry of Finance and the State Administration of Taxation, the Notice on the Comprehensive Implementation of the Resource Tax Reform, supra note 77, Section 2, Subsection 4, Articles 1–3, http://www.gov.cn/xinwen/2016-05/10/content_5072030.htm, last accessed on 12/11/2017.

environmental conservation through the implementation and adaptation to the Environment Protection Tax Law.[81]

(2) Intergovernmental Transfers

Although the 1993 Decision aimed to clarify and balance central-local financial powers and responsibilities, expenditure responsibilities of a LPG usually outweigh its revenue capacities. Intergovernmental transfer payment, thus, is designed to balance regional economic differences and equalise regional imbalances of basic public services.[82] The eastern provinces, benefiting more from the Opening-up policy, might be able to maintain a financial self-balance. But the Midwest area, where a large number of autonomous areas are located, would certainly depend on the central transfers to restore fiscal balance.[83] The central government, therefore, exerts a tight control over local governments from financial perspective, in particular over autonomous areas. For example in 2012, 4.5 trillion, out of 5.6 trillion, of the central revenue was transferred to local governments.[84] In general, more funds have been transferred from the centre to five autonomous regions than that to other provinces. Over 90% of the local general revenue of the TAR came from the central transfers in 2011, the highest percentage amongst autonomous regions. (Table 5)

After a set of reforms and simplifications, there are mainly three types of intergovernmental transfer payments under the current fiscal system: tax refund (11% in 2012), general financial transfer (47%), and special financial transfer (41%).[85]

81 Article 66 of the Law on REA states that "where autonomous areas that make a contribution to the country's ecological balance and environmental conservation, the State should give them a due benefit compensation". Article 8 of the Provisions on Implementing the Regional Ethnic Autonomy Law also has a similar provision.

82 The 2014 Budget Law, Article 16.

83 Li Jianjun and Wang Dexiang, "Jingji kaifang yu defang caizheng shouzhi fei pingheng [Economic Opening-up and the Imbalance of the Local Budget: A Research Based on the Statistics of Provincial Units]", 01 *Wuhan Daxue Xuebao* [*Wuhan University Journal*] (2012), pp. 108–109, 112; Xu Tao and Lei Lianghai, "Fenshuizhi xia difang zhengfu caizheng shouzhi bupingheng de shizheng fenxi [An Analysis on the Financial Imbalance of Local Governments under the Current Tax Division Management System]", 10 *Jingji Shijiao* [*Economic Vision*] (2011), pp. 16–17.

84 Fan Ziying and Wan Guanghua, supra note 53, at p. 3.

85 According to Article 62 of the Law on REA, autonomous areas are entitled to three financial transfers from higher level governments: general financial transfer, special financial transfer and preferential financial transfer for minority areas. Those transfer categories have been reformed recently. The new general financial transfer embraces old general transfer which now is referred to as equalisation transfer, preferential financial transfer

TABLE 5 Compositions of the Local General Revenue of Autonomous Regions 2011

Unit: Billion (1,000,000,000) RMB yuan

	Own Revenue (Percent in Total Income)	Intergovernmental Transfer (Percent in Total Income)	Total Income
IMAR	178.92 53.5%	155.55 46.5%	334.47
NHAR	41.69 46.8%	47.3 53.2%	88.99
GZAR	126.01 44.5%	157.29 55.5%	283.3
XUAR	104.04 40.9%	150.21 59.1%	254.09
TAR	6.45 8.3%	71.43 91.7%	77.88

SOURCES: CHINA STATISTICAL YEARBOOK 2012, TIBET STATISTICAL YEARBOOK 2012; XINJIANG STATISTICAL YEARBOOK 2012; REPORTS ON THE 2011 BALANCE SHEET OF THE LOCAL FINANCIAL REVENUE AND 2012 BUDGET SHEET OF THE LOCAL FINANCIAL REVENUE BY IMAR, NHAR AND GZAR.

Tax Refund

Under the tax-sharing system, many taxes which used to be the major sources of local tax revenue have become the central income or shared income. As a "compensation" to local governments, the central government utilises the tax refund to facilitate the implementation of the fiscal reform and to motivate local enthusiasm of production.[86] Tax income to be returned from the centre to

for the minorities and other forms of transfers. A few special transfers are merged into the new general financial transfer. See the Ministry of Finance, the 2009 Budget Sheet of the Tax Return and Transfer Payment from the Central Government to Local Governments; the 2012 Balance Sheet of the Tax Return and Transfer Payment from the Central Government to Local Governments.

86 The 1993 Decision; the State Council, Guanyu fenshuizhi caizheng guanli tizhi shuishou fanhuan gaiwei yu ben diqu zengzhishui he xiaofeishui zengzhang lv guagou de tongzhi [the Notice of Linking the Local Tax Refund under the Tax Division Management System with the Growth Rate of Local VAT and Consumption Tax (1994)], Circular [1994], No.47.

provincial governments is calculated through an equation provided by the 1993 Decision, which again applies to all localities in a uniform manner. Using the 1993 tax income as the base figure, taxes to be returned to localities annually are determined by a 1:0.3 indexed ratio of the average growth rate of the corresponding taxes collected nationwide.[87] In other words, the amount of tax refund closely links with the average national growth rate of tax revenues.[88] The faster the average national growth rate grows, the more tax will be refunded to localities; and the more taxes are collected from one region, the more taxes are to be refunded to that particular region. Eastern regions, with a relatively strong economy, obtain more tax refunds from the centre than economically underdeveloped areas.[89] Hence, the tax refund, as a type of intergovernmental transfer, plays a less important role in reducing regional financial disparity and in equalising public services and social welfare across the state.

General Financial Transfer

At the provincial level, the general financial transfer from the central government forms a part of local discretionary revenues, which aims to balance regional fiscal differences and to promote regional equalisation of basic public services.[90] The general financial transfer normally includes 15–17 projects each year. The equalisation transfer as the largest grant, together with wage transfer, welfare transfer and compulsory education transfer, has accounted for over 70% of the general financial transfer since 2009.[91] Favourable treatment of the minorities can be traced in the allocation of general financial transfer. All autonomous units receive financial support under the Transfer Grant for Minority Areas, which makes up 2% of the general financial transfer. Some autonomous areas are also covered by special transfer grants for border areas and old revolutionary districts. In 2012, special grants for minority areas, border areas, and old revolutionary districts totalled 55.9 billion RMB yuan, accounting for

87 Ibid; Wang Shaoguang and Hu Anguang, *The Chinese Economy in Crisis: State Capacity and Tax Reform* (M E Sharpe Inc, 2001), p. 233.

88 Ibid.

89 Xu Bo, "Guanyu fenshuizhi xia shuishou fanhuan wenti de sikao [Some Thoughts on the Issues of Tax Refund under the Tax Division System]", 04 *Caizheng Yanjiu [Public Finance Research]* (2010), pp. 69–70.

90 The 2014 Budget Law, Article 16.

91 The figure is calculated from the Annual Balance Sheets of the Tax Refund and Transfer Payment from the Central Government to Local Governments. 2012 Balance Sheet: http://yss.mof.gov.cn/2012qhczjs/201307/t20130715_966184.html; 2011 Balance Sheet: http://www.gov.cn/gzdt/2012-07/11/content_2181168.htm; 2010 Balance Sheet: http://yss.mof.gov.cn/2010juesuan/201107/t20110720_578421.html; 2009 Balance Sheet: http://yss.mof.gov.cn/2009nianquanguojuesuan/201007/t20100709_327125.html, last visited on 04/11/2013.

2.6% of the general financial transfer.[92] The recent Party decision has specifically called for increasing grants for those areas.[93]

Various formulas have been developed to calculate transfer figures under each grant, after taking different factors into consideration, including the size and density of the population, altitude, temperature, geographic conditions, ethnicity, and so on.[94] The central government is in charge of calculating the transfer amount and allocating those grants to provincial units. Although the State Council is obligated to gradually increase financial transfers to autonomous areas,[95] without detailed provisions on how it would be implemented, autonomous agencies have little influence in the determination process. Many provincial governments use "manage to gain central financial support" in their annual reports.[96] Apart from the calculation equations and actual financial needs, political bargaining power and economic merit are two factors that significantly affect the central decision on the general transfer distribution.[97] Autonomous areas may receive preferential treatment in the transfer allocation because of their minority status. This ethnic element, however, does not function evenly in every case, as the political bargaining power varies from group to group. Different minorities from different localities are likely to be treated differently in the funding allocation process. The central government would pay more attention to the claims of the populous minorities from unstable areas, such as the Tibetans and Uyghurs, and incline to assign them more funds. Minority status may not help to gain more governmental transfers from the centre if a minority group has less bargaining power due to the size of its population or strategic location.

92 Ibid, the 2012 Balance Sheet of the Tax Refund and Transfer Payment from the Central to Local Governments.

93 Zhonggong zhongyang guanyu quanmian shenhua gaige ruogan zhongda wenti de jueding [the CPCCC Decision on "Major Issues concerning Comprehensively Deepening Reforms"], 2013, Section 5 Principle 17.

94 The Ministry of Finance, the 2012 Formulas for Equalisation Transfers from the Central to Local Governments. For the details of the formula, see the 2004 IMF working paper on "Toward More Effective Redistribution: Reform Options for Intergovernmental Transfers in China" (WP/04/98), pp. 11–21.

95 The State Council Provisions on Implementing the Regional Ethnic Autonomy Law, 2005, Article 9. In addition, according to Article 9, the departments of the LPG s at higher levels should also give proper consideration to autonomous areas when allocating special grants.

96 Reports on the 2011 Balance Sheet of the Local Financial Revenue and 2012 Budget Sheets of the Local Financial Revenues from the IMAR, Yunnan, Guizhou, Sh'anxi, Gansu, Qinghai, Xinjiang.

97 Zhan Jing, "Determinants of Central-Provincial Fiscal Transfer: Equity, Bargaining or Efficiency?", 06 *Comparative Economic & Social Systems*, 2011, pp. 73–84.

Special Fund

The special fund, on the other hand, is set up by the central government to cover matters relating to joint responsibilities of the governments at different levels, the responsibilities of the central government which are entrusted with local governments, or certain responsibilities of local authorities.[98] The special transfer payment can only be used for intended purposes, which is also named "a fixed fund for fixed purposes only".[99] The grants under the special financial transfer regime concern a wide range of governmental responsibilities: education, social security and employment, health care, energy saving and environment protection, agriculture, forestry and water conservancy affairs, transport, housing support, and so forth.[100] Once again, the special transfer is calculated and allocated through formulas.[101] Although autonomous status might have been taken into account in the calculation formulas, it is difficult to evaluate to what extent it has secured favourable shares for the minorities in the final distribution.

5.2.2 *Financial Autonomy of Sub-provincial Autonomous Units*

According to the 1993 Decision, a tax-sharing system should also be established within provincial units.[102] The provincial LPG, rather than the LPC, is empowered to carry out the local financial reform, with a reference to the central-provincial model. In practice, regional variances can be found in terms of sub-provincial financial systems. The tax income within a provincial unit can be distributed on basis of tax category or shared in proportion, depending upon local characteristics and actual needs.[103] In the IMAR, the tax income is divided into three sections: tax income of the Region, tax income of the leagues and cities (prefectural level), and shared tax revenues between the Region and the

98 Zhou Meiduo and Yan Xueyong, "Zhongguo zhuanxiang zhuanyi zhifu de zhengzhi luoji: wenti, yuanyin yu chulu [the Political Logic of Specific-Purpose Transfers in China: Problems, Reasons and Solutions]", 09 *Dangdai Caijing* [*Contemporary Finance and Economics*] (2008), p. 36; Xu Mengzhou and Ye Shan, "Lun zhengfujian caizheng zhuanyi zhifu de zhidu anpai [On Institutional Arrangements of Intergovernmental Fiscal Transfer Payment]", 07 *Shehui Kexue* [*Journal of Social Sciences*] (2010), pp. 74–75.

99 Fan Ziying and Wan Guanghua, supra note 53, at p. 6.

100 The 2011 Budget Sheet of the Tax Refund and Transfer Payment from the Central to Local Governments.

101 The Ministry of Finance, the Transitional Method of Financial Transfer Payment, 1999.

102 The 1993 Decision.

103 Ibid; the Minister of Finance, the Notice on Suggestions of Perfecting the Sub-Provincial Tax Division Management System, Circular [1996], No.24; the State Council, the State Council Approval of the Notice of the Minister of Finance on Suggestions of Perfecting the Sub-Provincial Tax Division Management System, Circular [2002], No.26.

leagues and cities.[104] Other provincial administrations have also established a similar system, with varying dividing principles and sharing standards.[105]

Sub-provincial financial transfers also need to be standardised so as to achieve a local financial balance.[106] Under the principle of equality, justice and fairness, reasonable transfer equations reflecting local conditions should be adopted.[107] In terms of the tax refund within a provincial unit, the general equation that has been used at the central-provincial level is widely followed and adapted, provided that the amount of tax to be refunded to the counties is no less than 70% of the total amount received from the central government.[108] One-third of the provincial units have tailored the 1:0.3 indexed ratio to suit the local conditions. The GZAR, IMAR and Qinghai (a Tibetan concentrated province) have all adopted different indexed ratios.[109]

The sub-provincial distribution of general financial transfers has local variances as well. Many provincial governments likewise take objective elements

---

104 The VAT, enterprise income tax and consumption tax collected from regional railway companies, electricity companies, regional branches of banks and insurance companies are the Region's exclusive revenue. Estate taxes and land taxes constitute the fixed income of the leagues and cities. The VAT, enterprise income tax and consumption tax deducting the Region's exclusive portion, individual income tax and resource tax are shared by the Region and the leagues and cities by various ratios, from 10:90 to 65:35. See the People's Government of the IMAR, the Opinion on Improving the Fiscal Management System of the Region and the Leagues and Cities (2011).

105 The People's Government of the TAR, the 2004 Notice on Reforming and Improving the Fiscal Management System; the People's Government of the NHAR, the 1995 Notice on Adjusting Tax Division Management System; the People's Government of the XUAR, the 2004 Notice on Further Improving Tax Division Management System.

106 The State Council, the Approval of the Notice of the Minister of Finance on Suggestions of Perfecting the Sub-Provincial Tax Division Management System, Circular [2002], No.26.

107 Ibid.

108 For the details of the equations, see Wang Shaoguang and Hu Anguang, supra note 87, at pp. 232–233; Christine P. W. Wang and Deepak Bhattasali, *China: National Development and Sub-national Finance: A Review of Provincial Expenditures* (Citic Publishing House, 2003), pp. 35–37. For permissible adjustments at the sub-provincial levels, see the Minister of Finance, the Notice on Suggestions of Perfecting the Sub-Provincial Tax Division Management System, Circular [1996], No.24.

109 It is 1:0.15 in the GZAR, 1:0.5 in the IMAR, 1:0.3 to Hohhot and Baotou, 1:0.21 in Qinghai. See the People's Government of the GZAR, the Decision on Implementing the Tax Division Management System (1994); the People's Government of the IMAR, the Decision of on Implementing the Tax Division System and Deepening the Reform of Fiscal Administration Regime (1994); the People's Government of Qinghai, the Notice on Returning the Growth Amount of "Two Taxes" Collected from the Province-owned Enterprises (2000); see also Wang Dianzhi, "Fenshuizhi zhong de 1:0.3 xishu jiqi liwai [the 1:0.3 Indexed Ratio in the Taxation Division System and its Exceptions]", 05 *Difang Caizheng Yanjiu* [*Sub National Fiscal Research*] (2010), pp. 44–45.

into consideration and allocate sub-provincial general transfers on the basis of provincial overall revenues. The GZAR and IMAR adopt this model.[110] Certain grants are distributed separately, according to the localised distribution models which are based on the central standards of the central-provincial transfers.[111] As special financial transfers are distributed for intended purposes, sub-provincial transfer of such funds would not be an issue, as long as intergovernmental responsibilities are reasonably clarified by the provincial authority. For example, 60.93 billion special financial transfers were assigned to the GZAR and 58.6 billion had been transferred to its sub-provincial divisions in 2011.[112]

The discussion on the sub-provincial financial system above is for general reference. The substantive contents, including a clear division of powers and responsibilities of governments at different levels, a standard intergovernmental transfer regime and the reform of sub-provincial financial system, are far from completed as expected.[113] The statistics revealed in annual fiscal reports of the provincial governments would not reflect the real situation.[114] The centre-periphery financial system has remained in a state of flux since the 1994 reform. The principles on tax classification, tax rate, and sharing proportion between the central and local governments, as well as the standards and forms

110 The Finance Department of the GZAR, the GZAR Transitional Method of Financial Transfers (1996); the Finance Department of the IMAR, the IMAR Transitional Method of Financial Transfers (2001).

111 After the distribution standards of a transfer grant have been passed at the central level, provincial authorities would then produce a local version of them. For example, the Finance Department of the XUAR passed the Method of Financial Transfers for Important Ecological Functions Zone in 2013. The GZAR has been reported to amend the GZAR Method of Financial Transfers for Minority Areas in 2011, after the Ministry of Finance announced the Transfer Method of the Grant for Minority Areas from the Centre to Local Governments.

112 Reports on the 2011 Balance Sheet of the Local Financial Revenue and 2012 Budget Sheet of the Local Financial Revenue of the GZAR.

113 Deng Ziji and Tang Wenqian, "Woguo caishui gaige yu 'dingce sheji'—sheng yixia fenshuizhi caizheng guanli tizhi de shenghua gaige [the Fiscal Reform in China and the Top-down Design—Deepening the Taxation Sivision System at Sub-provincial Level]", 02 *Caizheng Yanjiu* [*Public Finance Research*] (2012), p. 2; Li Jianjun and Xie Xin, "Difang caizheng jiankang yu caizheng fenquan—jiyu Hubei sheng xianji shuju de shizheng fenxi [Local Fiscal Health and Fiscal Decentralisation: An Empirical Study Based on the County-level Data in Hubei Province]", 07 *Dangdai Caijing* [*Contemporary Finance and Economics*] (2011), p. 33.

114 Annual reports of the provincial finance in 2011 are available at the official website of the Ministry of Finance. http://www.mof.gov.cn/zhuantihuigu/2012czysbgjd/bfssysbg/, last visited on 22/12/2016.

of intergovernmental transfers, keep changing. The unstable financial system at the upper level directly affects the establishment of sub-provincial financial regime. The sub-provincial financial system would not be finalised until an explicit and steady regime is established between the central and provincial governments.

Likewise, sub-provincial autonomous agencies may also be able to improve local finance by exercising the adaptation power. Arguably, an autonomous prefecture/county can adapt regional regulations regarding sub-provincial financial arrangements, despite the fact that the Legislation Law only expressly allows for the adaptation to national law and administrative regulation. The logic is that if the adaptation to national law and administrative regulation is legally permitted, then the power to modify regional regulation, which is inferior to national law and administrative regulation, is inherently implied.[115] Article 81 of the Legislation Law appears to approve this reasoning. It states:

> where an autonomous regulation or special regulation varies certain provisions of national laws, administrative regulations or regional regulations, the provisions of the autonomous regulations or special regulations shall prevail in the autonomous areas concerned.[116]

Tension is likely to arise when the regional regulation itself is a type of autonomous legislation passed by the minority who is exercising autonomy at a higher level, for example an autonomous county within an autonomous prefecture which is also a part of an autonomous region. Nonetheless, sub-provincial financial arrangements are mostly decided by the LPGs in the form of governmental decisions/instructions. The legislative power of the LPCs to adapt provisions on financial affairs has not been frequently exercised within a provincial unit. Adaptive implementation of the decisions/instructions of higher level governments could not be found in autonomous prefectures and counties either.

At present, the dominance of the State Council on financial affairs, the changing financial system, and the lack of transparency, together with the undefined centre-periphery relation, render local governments little bargaining power in negotiations with the central government. The LPG dominated financial reform at the provincial level is also inconsistent with the institutional design of minority autonomy. According to the law, it should be the LPCs that

115 Zhang Dianjun, supra note 10, at p. 11.
116 The Legislation Law, Article 90.

have the right to decide on major issues of economic affairs, whilst the LPGs are responsible for managing the economy as a part of its administrative function within a provincial unit.[117] The underlying purposes of vesting the powers with the LPCs and guaranteeing minority representation therein are to ensure that minority characteristics and interests would be taken into account in the decision-making process. Financial autonomy can hardly be achieved in an administration-oriented financial system, as the law does not specify minority representation in people's governments.

A well-functioning people's congress that exercises state power as prescribed by the law would significantly facilitate the realisation of ethnic financial autonomy without any doubts. The 2013 Decision on "Major Issues Concerning Comprehensively Deepening Reforms" of the CPCCC restates the significance of the people's congress in the political system as the representative body, in which the people can exercise state power.[118] It further emphasises the power of the people's congress to review and to supervise the budget and the legalisation of taxation. In the 2018 Decision of the CPCCC on "Deepening Reform of Party and State Institutions", the people's congress is referred to as the "basic political system" for upholding the overall leadership of the Party, the people-centred approach, and the rule of law.[119] However, the question is to what extent the people's congress would be allowed to genuinely exercise its power in the new round of the reform.

5.3 Concluding Remarks

Legislative and financial autonomy are crucial to the exercise of minority rights under REA, as they allow ethnic autonomy to function independently. Legislative autonomy could be viewed as the most critical element under the REA system. It enables the LPCs in autonomous areas to adapt national law and administrative regulation, according to minority political, economic and cultural characteristics. This legislative autonomy is subject to restraints, as the enactment of autonomy regulation and special regulation should be reviewed and approved by higher-level agencies. However, the current legal framework on legislative autonomy is too vague to be implemented and reflects the lack of genuine autonomous legislation in practice. In the case that detailed rules of

117 The Organic Law, Articles 8, 59.

118 The 2013 CPCCC Decision, supra note 93, Section 8 Principle 27.

119 Shenhua dang he guojia jigou gaige fang'an [the CCPCC Decision on "Deepening Reform of Party and State Institutions"] (2018), Section 5, Principle 2.

the reviewing and approval procedure are clarified, and proper remedial measures are adopted for autonomous legislatures to question the review decision, legislative autonomy may operate as the basis to exercise autonomy in other aspects, such as financial and cultural rights.

Financial autonomy also facilitates the effective exercise of local self-government. Independent local finance enables autonomous agencies to make special financial arrangements in accordance with the local conditions and minority characteristics. Although the Constitution and the Law on REA recognise the right of minorities to autonomously manage local financial affairs, the exercise of such a right, in reality, is hardly traceable. The inactive LPCs on financial affairs and the role of the LPGs as local branches of the State Council, rather than as autonomous agencies, have revealed the reality of ethnic financial autonomy. In this regard, the centre-oriented reform and the constantly changing national financial system have contributed to the situation. Simply put, the LPCs in autonomous areas are too weak to effectively exercise constitutional rights and freedoms, as against the powerful Party and the traditionally strong central government. Minority autonomy on financial affairs only exists in legislation at the present stage.

CHAPTER 6

The Cultural Rights of Minorities

Despite the criticism that the REA system is more likely a "paper" or "verbal" autonomy, many observers, including non-Chinese commentators, agree that Chinese minorities are granted by the 1982 Constitution and the Law on REA true autonomy on soft issues, such as culture, language, education, health care, sports, science and technology.[1] In terms of cultural affairs, Chinese minorities can seek protection not only from Chinese law but also from international instruments, under which China as a state party has undertaken obligations to promote and protect minority rights. Thus, this chapter examines the rights of Chinese minorities to culture under Chinese law as well as under binding international conventions. Given the scope and content of the concept of culture, the analysis approaches minority cultural rights through the lens of religion and language, as they are considered to be the fundamental components of minority culture and identity.

This chapter first looks at the obligations that China has undertaken under the International Covenant on Economic, Social and Cultural Rights (ICESCR), the International Convention on the Elimination of All Forms of Racial Discrimination (ICERD) and the International Covenant on Civil and Political Rights (ICCPR) to protect and promote the right of minorities to culture. In comparison with the provisions of Chinese law, this chapter focuses on the rights of Chinese minorities to religious freedom and language. It is argued that although the ethnic autonomy on legislative and financial affairs is not properly implemented due to the inherent flaws of collective autonomy in the authoritarian state of China, the minorities' right to culture is tolerated and encouraged. However, the cultural rights of the minorities are also exercised in a collective manner, which has its own constraints. The collective exercise of cultural rights may conflict with individual human rights. To allow members of the minorities to equally take part in cultural life, regardless of their places of residence, is essential for the realisation of minority rights in China.

1 C. Mackerras, *China's Minorities: Integration and Modernisation in the 20th Century* (Oxford University Press, 1994), pp. 153–159, 164, 265; Binh Phan, "How Autonomous are the National Autonomous Areas of the PRC? An Analysis of Documents and Cases", 32:7 *Issues and Studies* (1996), p. 99; Barry Sautman, "Ethnic Law and Minority Rights in China: Progress and Constraints", 21:03 *Law and Policy* (1999), p. 293; Matthew Moneyhon, "Controlling Xinjiang: Autonomy on China's 'New Frontier' ", 3:01 *Asian-Pacific law & Policy Journal* (2002), p. 151.

 | DOI:10.1163/9789004380578_008

6.1 China's International Obligations Concerning Minority Rights

China has signed and ratified, or acceded to, the following major instruments on human rights: ICESCR, ICERD, the Convention on the Elimination of All Forms of Discrimination against Women (CEDAW), the Convention on the Rights of the Child (CRC) and two Optional Protocols, the Convention on the Rights of Persons with Disabilities, and Convention against Torture and Other Cruel Inhuman or Degrading Treatment or Punishment. In 1998, China also signed the ICCPR, which has not been ratified by the NPC Standing Committee. Among those conventions, the ICESCR, ICCPR and ICERD are particularly relevant to Chinese minorities.

6.1.1 *Commitments under the ICESCR*

The ICESCR became effective for China in 2001 after it was ratified by the NPC Standing Committee. The Covenant concerns general human rights on economic, social and cultural affairs and provides for positive obligations of the state parties to progressively realise the stated rights. Article 2 and Article 15, paragraph 1 (a) are specifically relevant to Chinese minorities.

Article 2 is considered to be of "particular importance to a full understanding of the Covenant",[2] which specifies the general obligations of the state parties. The state members of the ICESCR undertake:

> to take steps, individually and through international assistance and co-operation, especially economic and technical, to the maximum of its available resources, with a view to achieving progressively the full realisation of the rights recognised in the present Covenant by all appropriate means, including particularly the adoption of legislative measures.[3]

According to General Comment 3, deliberate, concrete and targeted actions should be taken, in an active or passive manner, within a reasonably short time after the Covenant entry into force for the states concerned.[4] The state parties have to ensure that the rights guaranteed in the Covenant "will be exercised without discrimination of any kind as to race, colour, sex, language, religion, political or other opinion, national or social origin, property, birth or other status".[5] The obligations under Article 2(1) are not only confined to "obligations

2 The CESCR, General Comment 3, para.1.
3 ICESCR, Article 2 (1).
4 The CESCR, General Comment 3, para.2; Manisuli Ssenyonjo, *Economic, Social and Cultural Rights in International Law* (Hart Publishing, 2009), p. 54.
5 ICESCR, Article 2 (2).

of result", but may also include "obligations of conduct".[6] Although the Covenant aims to achieve progressively the full realisation of ESC rights, the non-discrimination principle is addressed as an obligation of immediate and cross-cutting effect, which is not subject to the availability of resources.[7]

In particular, the Committee on Economic, Social and Cultural Rights (CESCR) was concerned with the reported situation regarding the discrimination against the minorities in China, in the fields of employment, adequate standard of living, health, education and culture.[8] It further called upon China to "undertake necessary measures to ensure that all persons under its jurisdiction enjoy economic, social and cultural rights enshrined in the Covenant without discrimination".[9] The enjoyment of ESC rights without discrimination entails an immediate obligation to eliminate all forms of *de jure* and *de facto* discrimination, including direct and indirect discrimination, as well as systematic discrimination and discrimination in private sphere.[10]

The ICESCR states:

> the States Parties to the present Covenant recognise the right of everyone: (a) to take part in cultural life; (b) to enjoy the benefits of scientific progress and its applications; (c) to benefit from the protection of the moral and material interests resulting from any scientific, literary or artistic production of which he is the author.[11]

Article 15 (1)(a) was initially understood as the guarantee of the enjoyment of the dominant national culture.[12] It has been extended to include the protection of cultural life of minorities and indigenous peoples. This provision recognises the right of individuals or in association with others, as well as a collective right of the community/group, to participate in cultural life.[13] Culture

---

6 Matthew Craven, *The International Covenant on Economic, Social, and Cultural Rights: A Perspective on Its Development* (Clarendon Press Oxford, 1995), pp. 107–108.

7 The CESCR, General Comment 20, para.7; Manisuli Ssenyonjo, supra note 4, at pp. 60, 85, 86.

8 Concluding Observations of the CESCR on the Initial Report of China, UN Doc. E/C.12/1/ADD/107, 2005, p. 5, para.38.

9 Ibid, p. 6, para.45.

10 The CESCR, General Comment 20, pp. 3–5.

11 ICESCR, Article 15, para.1.

12 Sally Holt, "Family, Private Life, and Cultural Rights", in Marc Weller (ed), *Universal Minority Rights: A Commentary on the Jurisprudence of International Court and Treaty Bodies* (Oxford University Press, 2007), pp. 203–252 at p. 218.

13 The CESCR, General Comment 21, p. 3, para.9.

referred to by the Covenant is a broad, inclusive and evolving concept, which is similar to the anthropological definition of culture, encompassing ways of life, language, arts and literature, religion or belief system, methods of production, nature and man-made environments, customs and traditions, and so forth.[14] "Take part in" entitles individual members and the collective to have access to cultural life and to freely participate and actively engage in creating and developing their culture.[15] Free participation involves the right to choose his/her own identity and to identify or not with one or several communities.[16] In addition, minorities also have "the right to conserve, promote and develop their own culture".[17] The rights of minorities guaranteed by Article 15 (1)(a) encompass, *inter alia*, "the right to their cultural diversity, traditions, customs, religion, forms of education, languages, communication media and other manifestations of their cultural identity and membership".[18]

The state parties, on the other hand, undertake obligations to recognise, respect and promote minority cultures as an essential component of the national identity of the states themselves.[19] The nation-building policy, therefore, should be inclusive, constructively integrative and multicultural so as to preserve separate identities of minorities alongside the national culture.[20] The minimum core obligations with an immediate effect imposed upon the states under Article 15, paragraph 1 (a) include: the non-discrimination and equality in participating in cultural life; the right to identify or not with one or more communities; the right to engage in one's own cultural practices in conjunction with other fundamental freedoms; to eliminate barriers that hinder a person's equal access to culture; to allow and encourage the participation of minorities and indigenous peoples in the design and implementation of laws and policies that affect them and to obtain the free and prior consent from the individuals and communities concerned when the preservation of their cultural resources is at risk.[21] The CESCR also urges China to remove restrictions

---

14 Ibid, p. 3, para.11–13.

15 Ibid, p. 4, para.15; Sally Holt, supra note 12, at pp. 221–2; Asbjorn Eide, "Chapter 16: Cultural Rights as Individual Human Rights", in Asbjorn Eide, Catarina Krause and Allan Rosas (eds), *Economic, Social and Cultural Rights: A Textbook* (Martinus Nijhoff Publishers, 2001), pp. 289–301, at p. 293.

16 The CESCR, General Comment 21, p. 4, para.15.

17 Ibid, p. 8, para.32.

18 Ibid.

19 Ibid, p. 6 para.23; p. 8. para.32.

20 Ibid, p. 9, para.33.

21 Ibid, p. 15, para.55; Stephen Hansen, "The Right to Take Part in Cultural Life: Toward Defining Minimum Core Obligation Related to Article 15 (1) (a) of the ICESCR", in Audrey

on freedom of information and expression to enable everyone's right to take part in cultural life.[22]

6.1.2 *State Obligations under the ICCPR*

The ICCPR was signed by the State Council in 1998 and has yet to be ratified by the legislature. It has been reported that relevant competent authorities are in the process of creating conditions for its ratification.[23] The lack of ratification does not mean that China undertakes no obligation in relation to the ICCPR. At least, China is obligated to refrain from acts that would defeat the object and purpose of the Covenant.[24] Furthermore, the provisions of the ICCPR may be considered to reflect customary international law, from which international obligations would also arise. China would be obligated to respect and protect human rights in this regard.

The minority rights clause of the ICCPR might be considered as an international custom.[25] It guarantees the right of ethnic minorities to cultural identity, the right of religious minorities to religion and the right of linguistic minorities to language. Article 27 provides:

> in those States in which ethnic, religious or linguistic minorities exist, persons belonging to such minorities shall not be denied the right, in community with the other members of their group, to enjoy their own culture, to profess and practise their own religion, or to use their own language.[26]

"In those states ... exist" seems to suggest that the clause only concerns those states where minorities exist. During the drafting process, many states, particularly the American states, denied "the existence of minorities on the American continent".[27] The German Democratic Republic asserted that religious minorities did not exist in Germany. It further argued that no state religion was

---

Chapman and Sage Russell (eds), *Core Obligation: Building a Framework for Economic, Social and Cultural Rights* (Intersentia, 2002), pp. 279–303 at pp. 299–300.

22 Concluding Observations of the CESCR on the Initial Report of China, supra note 8, p. 10, para.68.

23 Core Document Forming Part of the Reports of China, UN Doc. HRI/CORE/CHN/2010, Part 2, p. 19.

24 The Vienna Convention on the Law of Treaties, Article 18. China acceded to the Convention in 1997.

25 The HRC, General Comment 24, para.8.

26 ICCPR, Article 27.

27 For instance, Brazil, Chile and Venezuela were of this opinion. See Patrick Thornberry, *International Law and the Right of Minorities* (Clarendon Press, 2001), pp. 154–155.

established in the Republic and religious communities were entitled to manage their own affairs without state interference.[28] However, the states' denial of the existence of minorities should not preclude the application of Article 27 as such.[29] Otherwise, states could avoid their international obligations through the enactment of national laws.[30] On the other hand, the state recognition of a minority in practice is considered to be essential for minority protection, as it "facilitates the application of the principles enunciated in article 27 of the Covenant and give[s] the members of the minority a solid basis for effective protection of the rights guaranteed them at the international level".[31]

General Comment 23 emphasises that "the existence of an ethnic, religious or linguistic minority in a given State party does not depend upon a decision by that State party but requires to be established by objective criteria".[32] The Permanent Court of International Justice states that the existence of [racial minority] communities is "a question of fact", not "a question of law".[33] Capotorti likewise concludes that "the presence of sufficient elements to indicate that a minority exists is sufficient to make applicable the pertinent international rules, and particularly article 27 …"[34] But neither the Human Right Committee (HRC) nor Capotorti further clarifies what those objective criteria/sufficient elements are. Almost all the attempts to define a minority encompass objective and subjective criteria: the existence of the group with distinct identity, and the sense of solidarity.[35] Although there is no international consensus on minority definition, the widely cited Capotorti definition is highly illuminating in understanding the minority concept at the international level, which refers to:

> A group numerically inferior to the rest of the population of a State, in a non-dominant position, whose members-being nationals of the State-possess ethnic, religious or linguistic characteristics differing from those of the rest of the population and show, if only implicitly, a sense of

28 German Democratic Republic, cited in Patrick Thornberry, ibid, p. 158.

29 Capotorti argues that "the fact that international protection of minorities does not depend on official recognition of their existence". Francesco Capotorti, Study on the Rights of Persons Belonging to Ethnic, Religious and Linguistic Minorities, UN Doc. E/CN.4/Sub.2/384/Rev.1, para.61.

30 Patrick Thornberry, supra note 27, at p. 157.

31 Francesco Capotorti, supra note 29, para.62.

32 The HRC, General Comment 23, para.5.2

33 Greco-Bulgarian Communities, Advisory Opinion, the Permanent Court of International Justice, 1930, p. 22.

34 Francesco Capotorti, supra note 29, para.61.

35 Ibid, para.568; Patrick Thornberry, supra note 27, at pp. 165–166; Thomas Musgrave, *Self-determination and National Minorities* (Oxford University Press, 2002), p. 169.

> solidarity, directed towards preserving their culture, traditions, religion or language.[36]

The expression, "persons belonging to such minorities ... in community with the other members of their group", inclines to confer the right on individuals only,[37] though the language of the article itself may suggest certain collective elements. The concern is that, besides historical and political reasons, the collective right of a group as a whole would possibly force individuals to conform to the choice of the majority of the community (minorities within the minority), regardless of individuals' freedom of choice.[38] Also, the sense of belonging is nothing but a personal choice, and it varies from time to time. The individualist nature of minority rights under Article 27 is likely to be understood from this perspective. In *Kitok v. Sweden*, however, the HRC concluded that the right of individual members of minorities might be restricted in order to "protect the rights of the minority as a whole".[39] This decision seems to imply that Article 27 has a collective feature.

The negative formulation, "shall not be denied", suggests a minimum level of obligations placed upon the state parties: not denying the right of minorities to cultural security, religion and linguistic practice. Despite the permissive nature of the language itself, commentators have diverse opinions as to whether the article imposes positive obligations on states to provide special assistance to facilitate the minorities' pursuit. Capotorti argues that, "to enable the objectives of this article to be achieved" and to implement these rights, "it is essential that states should adopt legislative and administrative measures".[40] Thornberry holds a similar opinion.[41] Musgrave, on other hand, asserts that "the obligations contained in Article 27 consist simply of a duty not to interfere with the minority in its enjoyment of its right". Packer argues that the meaningful enjoyment, profession and use may require the engagement of the state, but "the state is not obliged to ensure the result".[42] In General Comment 23, the HRC states:

36 Francesco Capotorti, supra note 29, para.568.

37 The HRC, General Comment 23, para.3.1; General Comment 31, para.9.

38 Francesco Capotorti, supra note 29, paras.207, 209, 573.

39 Kitok *v.* Sweden, Communication No. 197/1985, UN Doc. CCPR/C/33/D/197/1985 (1988), para.9.8.

40 Francesco Capotorti, supra note 29, para.217.

41 Patrick Thornberry, supra note 27, at p. 157.

42 John Packer, "Chapter 6 On the Content of Minority Rights", in Juha Raikka (ed), *Do We Need Minority Rights? Conceptual Issues* (Martinus Nijhoff Publishers, 1996), pp. 121–178 at p. 155.

> … although article 27 is expressed in negative terms, that article, nevertheless, does recognise the existence of a "right" and requires that it shall not be denied. Consequently, a State party is under an obligation to ensure that the existence and the exercise of this right are protected against their denial or violation… Accordingly, positive measures by States may also be necessary to protect the identity of a minority and the rights of its members to enjoy and develop their culture and language and to practise their religion, in community with the other members of the group.[43]

The HRC has recently interpreted this article to include more positive elements, particularly in regard to the rights of indigenous peoples.[44] However, such positive obligations appear to be limited to positive actions of the states to remedy the situation when the rights of minorities are denied or violated.[45] Positive obligations, which are necessary to assist minorities to enjoy culture, to profess religion and to use language, may not be inferred from the article itself. The objection to the inclusion of articles called for state actions to support minorities into the Covenant during the *travaux preparatory* seemed to support such an interpretation.[46]

The concept of culture, according to the HRC, is broad and dynamic. It manifests itself in many forms, including a particular way of life associated with the use of land resources, such as traditional activities of fishing or hunting and the right to live in reserves.[47] In *Kitok v. Sweden* and *Lubicon Lake Band v. Canada*, the HRC has established that the national economic development of the state parties, which interferes with minorities' particular way of life, may amount to a violation of the right to culture.[48] This expansive interpretation does not necessarily prohibit all economic measures of the state parties that may affect minority cultures. The particular way of life, as an essential element of the culture of an ethnic community, must have been first established.[49] Apart from

---

43 The HRC, General Comment 23, paras.6.1, 6.2.

44 Rodolfo Stavenhagen, "Chapter 5 Cultural Rights: a Social Science Perspective", in Asbjorn Eide, Catarina Krause and Allan Rosas (eds), supra note 15, pp. 85–110, at p. 101; Anne-Christine Bloch, "Chapter 20 Minorities and Indigenous Peoples", in Asbjorn Eide, Catarina Krause and Allan Rosas (eds), supra note 15, pp. 373–388, at p. 378.

45 Sally Holt, supra note 12, at p. 224.

46 Patrick Thornberry, supra note 27, at p. 179.

47 The HRC, General Comment 23, paras.3.2, 7.

48 Kitok *v.* Sweden, Communication No. 197/1985 (1988), para.9.2; Lubicon Lake Band *v.* Canada, Communication No. 167/1984 (1990), para.33.

49 Ibid; Sally Holt, supra note 12, at p. 242; Margot Salomon, "Socio-economic Rights as Minority Rights", in Marc Weller (ed), supra note 12, pp. 431–475 at p. 436.

the survival of culture, Article 27 also includes the right of minorities to develop their cultures.[50] The protection of minority livelihood, thus, extends to the adapted and modernised way of life.[51]

The Committee, in *Poma Poma v. Peru*, further distinguishes between state activities that constitute a denial of the right to culture and those that have "certain limited impact on the way of life of persons belonging to minorities".[52] When determining whether the state economic development plans amount to a denial of the cultural rights, the HRC considers, in *Mahuika v. New Zealand*, the procedural participation of affected members or communities—whether they have effectively participated in the decision-making process, as well as the sustainability of the traditional economy of the particular minority—whether they would be able to continue to exercise their cultural rights and to benefit from their traditional life.[53] The requirement of "the effective participation of members of minority communities in decisions which affect them", however, does not equate to prior consent of the affected.[54]

Some commentators, Thornberry,[55] Brownlie,[56] Capotorti,[57] and Wheatley,[58] have considered Article 27 as a rule of general international law, which should be binding upon states who are not parties to the ICCPR.[59] In General Comment 24, the HRC states:

---

50 The HRC, General Comment 23, para.6.2.

51 Sally Holt, supra note 12, at p. 243.

52 Poma Poma v. Peru, Communication No. 1457/2006 (2009), para.7.4; Lansman v. Finland, Communication No. 1023/2001 (2005). See also Margot Salomon, supra note 49, at pp. 437–438.

53 Mahuika et al. v. New Zealand, Communication No. 547/1993 (2000), para.9.5. Margot Salomon, supra note 49, at pp. 438–440; Marc Weller, "Effective Participation of Minorities in Public Life", in Marc Weller (ed), supra note 12, pp. 477–516 at p. 509.

54 Marc Weller, ibid, p. 510; the HRC, General Comment 23, para.7.

55 He argues that there is little evidence in the language itself and the *travaux preparatories* or the subsequent events illustrate the article's status as customary international law. See Patrick Thornberry, supra note 27, at pp. 242–246.

56 Quoted in Patrick Thornberry, supra note 27, at p. 220.

57 In his report, Capotorti emphasises that "this article is not a source of legal obligations for States which have not yet ratified the Covenant, but as the GA of the UN has approved the Covenant, its articles may be considered as having the value of general principles, in the same way as those set forth in solemn UN declarations". Francesco Capotorti, supra note 29, para.327.

58 Steven Wheatley, *Democracy, Minorities and International Law* (Cambridge University Press, 2005), p. 15.

59 According to Thornberry, it's not logical to claim that a state is somehow bound by a general principle of law, if it has consistently rejected that principle as one of customary international law. See Patrick Thornberry, supra note 27, at p. 247.

> ... accordingly, provisions in the Covenant that represent customary international law (and a fortiori when they have the character of peremptory norms) may not be the subject of reservations. Accordingly, a State may not reserve the right to engage in slavery, to torture, to subject persons to cruel, inhuman or degrading treatment or punishment, ...or to deny to minorities the right to enjoy their own culture, profess their own religion, or use their own language. And while reservations to particular clauses of article 14 may be acceptable, a general reservation to the right to a fair trial would not be.[60]

The states parties have divided opinions towards Article 27 and its implementation. Some states simply deny the existence of ethnic groups,[61] or insist that there are no minority problems under their sovereignty as their states are "melting-pots of numerous races".[62] Some other states are of a view that minority questions vary through different continents.[63] The 1979 Capotorti report again reflects diverse attitudes of the state parties towards their minorities.[64] Different levels of protection for minorities can be found in practice. Minorities in some states are entitled to more rights under national regimes than those provided by Article 27. Varying minority arrangements in different states, however, may suggest that no international agreement has been reached in terms of the content of Article 27 in this regard.

Article 27, to a certain extent, may possibly be treated as customary international law, but only within a limited dimension: the general rights of minorities to enjoy culture, to profess religion and to use language should not be denied by the states. It is a weak article due to the lack of specificity, which leaves a wide discretion to the states in its interpretation and implementation.[65] Although the ICCPR is not effective in China at the moment, China, to the least extent, should not deny its minorities the right to enjoy culture, to profess religion and/or to use language.

---

60 The HRC, General Comment 24, para.8.

61 For instance, France stated that it "cannot recognise the existence of ethnic groups, whether minorities or not". Similar assertion could also be found in the statements from Latin American countries. See Francesco Capotorti, supra note 29, paras.66–67.

62 Patrick Thornberry, supra note 27, at p. 155.

63 Ibid.

64 Francesco Capotorti, supra note 29, paras.569, 59–81.

65 Patrick Thornberry, supra note 27, at p. 155; Rodolfo Stavenhagen, supra note 44, at p. 101.

6.1.3 *State Obligations under the ICERD*

China acceded to the ICERD in 1981. The Convention aims to eliminate all forms of discrimination based on race, colour, descent, or national or ethnic origin. Racial discrimination, according to the ICERD, is defined as:

> any distinction, exclusion, restriction or preference based on race, colour, descent, or national or ethnic origin which has the purpose or effect of nullifying or impairing the recognition, enjoyment or exercise, on an equal footing, of human rights and fundamental freedoms in the political, economic, social, cultural or any other field of public life.[66]

The meaning of race in the Convention has not been elaborated yet. One interpretation suggests that, by the definition of racial discrimination, race can be understood as encompassing "colour, descent, and national or ethnic origin".[67] General Recommendation 29, however, states that the term "descent" is the widest, as "descent" in the Convention does not solely refer to "race".[68] It has "a meaning and application which complements the other prohibited grounds of discrimination".[69] Discrimination based on descent also includes discrimination against the members of communities based on forms of social stratification, such as caste.[70] China seems to understand race from the biological perspective, emphasising that the overwhelming majority of the Chinese people are yellow race, with one ethnic group that bears the features of Caucasoid race.[71] The Chinese government contends that the prohibition of discrimination against ethnic groups in China has covered all prohibited grounds of discrimination under the Convention.[72] The ethnic equality provisions in Chinese law, however, in the view of the CERD, do not contain a definition of racial discrimination in full conformity with the Convention, as discrimination

66 ICERD, Article 1 (1).

67 Kristin Hernrard, "Non-discrimination and Full and Effective Equality", in Marc Weller (ed), supra note 12, pp. 75–147 at p. 103.

68 Patrick Thornberry, "Confronting Racial Discrimination: a CERD Perspective", 5 *Human Rights Law Review* (2005), p. 251.

69 The CERD, General Recommendation 29, the Preamble.

70 Ibid.

71 The Chinese government claims that the Russian group belongs to the Caucasoid race. The 13th Periodic Report Submitted by China under Article 9 of the ICERD, CERD/C/CHN/10-13, 2009, p. 4, para.7. A detailed discussion on the evolution of the interpretation of the term "race" in China, see Frank Dikotter, *The Discourse of Race in Modern China* (Hurst and Company, 1992).

72 The 13th Report of China, ibid.

on the grounds of descent and national origin has not been addressed.[73] The Committee, therefore, recommends that China should adopt a comprehensive definition of racial discrimination fully in accordance with Article 1 and enact a comprehensive law to combat all forms of racial discrimination based on race, colour, descent, or national or ethnic origin.[74]

Furthermore, the state parties to the Convention undertake, by all appropriate means and without delay, to condemn racial discrimination in all its forms and to pursue a policy to eliminate racial discrimination and promote understanding among all races.[75] "In all its forms" requires the state parties to ensure the elimination of racial discrimination in domestic laws, policies or other practices by the state authorities and institutions.[76] It also imposes an obligation upon the state parties to prohibit and bring to an end "racial discrimination by any persons, group or organisation".[77]

The principle of non-discrimination protects the equal enjoyment of human rights. This equality principle encompasses *de jure* equality as well as *de facto* equality.[78] To achieve the aim as such, preferential treatment to promote equal enjoyment of human rights is integral to the principle of non-discrimination.[79] The state parties are obligated to take special measures to protect certain racial or ethnic groups and individuals belonging to them, provided that measures taken are appropriate, legitimate, necessary, fair and proportionate and temporary.[80]

On the recognition of racial or ethnic groups in the territory, the Committee emphasises that a set of criteria should be uniformly applied to all groups.[81] According to the CERD, "the application of different criteria in order to

---

73 Concluding Observations of the CERD on the 8th and 9th Reports of China, A/56/18(SUPP), 2001, para.241; Concluding Observations of the CERD on the 10th to 13th Reports of China, CERD/C/CHN/CO/10-13, para.10.

74 Ibid, A/56/18(SUPP), para.241; CERD/C/CHN/CO/10-13, para.11.

75 ICERD, Article 2 (1).

76 Ibid, Article 2 (1) (a)(b)(c).

77 Ibid, Article 2 (1) (d)(e).

78 The CERD, General Recommendation 32, p. 3, para.6.

79 Ibid, p. 6, para.20; the CERD, General Recommendation 14, para.1, 2.

80 Not all differential measures are necessarily temporary. Distinctions should be drawn between special measures and specific rights of certain categories of persons of groups. The latter's rights are permanent, as recognised by international human rights instruments. See the CERD, General Recommendation 32, para.15; Kristin Hernrard, supra note 67, at p. 123. See also ICERD, Articles 1 (4), 2 (2); the CERD, General Recommendation 32, paras.16–18; General Recommendation 14, paras.1, 2.

81 The CERD, General Recommendation 24, para.2.

determine ethnic groups or indigenous peoples, leading to the recognition of some and refusal to recognise others", may give rise to differing treatment among various groups.[82] Persons belonging to such groups should be identified on the basis of self-identification by the individual concerned, unless a justification exists to the contrary.[83]

Article 3, the Apartheid clause, is interpreted in a broad sense so as to address any possible racial segregation in contemporary situation, for example in housing and education.[84] Article 5 of the Convention links the principle of non-discrimination to a non-exhaustive list of human rights, under which the state parties undertake to guarantee the equal enjoyment of those rights.[85] The obligations of states, thus, are confined to the prohibition and elimination of racial discrimination in the exercise of such rights, as the article itself does not create civil, political, economic, social or cultural rights, but assumes the existence and recognition of those rights.[86]

Article 4 targets the propaganda and activities that are based on racial hatred and superiority, requiring the state parties to "declare an offence punishable by law all dissemination of those ideas as well as acts of violence or incitement of such acts".[87] The state parties should also enact special legislation to prohibit and punish "the dissemination of doctrines based on racial superiority and incitement to racial discrimination".[88] In 1997, the amended Criminal Law of the PRC penalises the acts of inciting or disseminating ethnic enmity or discrimination by any persons or organisations, if the circumstances are serious or flagrant.[89] However, the requisite of being "serious or flagrant" for punishing those acts is considered by the Committee as not conforming to the Convention.[90] Consequently, effective remedies in the domestic framework for the victims of racial discrimination are essential and necessary so as to combat racial discrimination.[91] The state parties should also adopt immediate and effective measures, "particularly in the fields of teaching, education,

82 Ibid, para.3.
83 The CERD, General Recommendation 08; General Recommendation 32, para.34.
84 Patrick Thornberry, supra note 68, at p. 252.
85 Ibid, p.253; the CERD, General Recommendation 20, para.1.
86 The CERD, General Recommendation 20, para.1.
87 ICERD, Article 4.
88 Concluding Observations of the CERD on the 2nd Report of China, A/42/18(SUPP), 1987, para.334; Concluding Observations of the CERD on the 3rd and 4th Reports of China, A/45/18(SUPP), 1990, para.116.
89 The Criminal Law of the PRC (last revised in 2015), Articles 249, 250.
90 The CERD, supra note 73, para.242.
91 Ibid; ICERD, Article 6.

culture and information", to combat prejudices and to promote tolerance and understanding.[92]

Apart from the general obligations discussed above, the following issues have also been addressed by the CERD in regard to China's obligations under the Convention. First, the Committee has on many occasions expressed its concerns about the right of minorities to religious freedom, particularly the Tibetans, Hui, and Muslims in Xinjiang, as well as minority party members.[93] The CERD recommends that China should ensure the respect for the rights of minorities to freely profess and practise their religions and review domestic legislation and practice, which may restrict the exercise of such rights.[94] Education is another issue that draws the Committee's attention.[95] The Committee emphasises the equal access of minority members to education, recommending that efforts should be made to implement legislation and policies on bilingual education at all levels.[96] The Chinese government undertakes to respect and guarantee the right of minorities to develop knowledge about their own language and culture.[97] Fair and adequate participation of the minorities in public service and in the decision-making process is also addressed by the Committee. The recommendation of the Committee calls for giving consideration to the inclusion of more minority members in positions of leadership in state agencies and in the CPC.[98]

6.2 The Rights of the Minorities to Culture under Chinese Law

It is difficult to find a universally agreed definition of culture in regard to cultural rights. Various definitions have been developed in different contexts.[99]

92 ICERD, Article 7; Concluding Observations of the CERD on the 5th to 7th Reports of China, A/51/18(SUPP), 1996, para.423.

93 The CERD, A/42/18(SUPP), para.335; A/51/18(SUPP), para.404; A/56/18(SUPP), para.244; CERD/C/CHN/CO/10-13, para.20; CERD/C/SR.1163, para.65; CERD/C/SR.1468, paras.26, 51, 72; CERD/C/SR.1469, para.45; CERD/C/SR.1942, paras.31, 34, 56; CERD/C/SR.1943, para.55.

94 The CERD, A/51/18(SUPP), para.417; A/56/18(SUPP), para.244; CERD/C/CHN/CO/10-13, para.20.

95 The CERD, A/51/18(SUPP), para.407; A/56/18(SUPP), para.245; CERD/C/CHN/CO/10-13, para.22; CERD/C/SR.1163, paras.34, 44, 50, 58; CERD/C/SR.1164, paras.7, 31, 67; CERD/C/SR.1468, paras.17, 23, 42; CERD/C/SR.1942, paras.28, 41, 45, 54, 62, 64; CERD/C/SR.1943, para.54.

96 The CERD, A/51/18(SUPP), para.420; CERD/C/CHN/CO/10-13, para.22.

97 The CERD, A/56/18(SUPP), para.245.

98 The CERD, A/51/18(SUPP), para.414.

99 Janusz Symonides, "Chapter 5 Cultural Rights", in Janusz Symonides (ed), *Human Rights: Concept and Standards* (UNESCO Publishing, 2000), pp. 175–227, at pp. 179–181.

The term "culture" has been used in the strict sense as well as in the general sense. The traditional European notion considers culture as creativity, which is associated with arts, literature, music, dance, and theatre.[100] The second interpretation defines culture as capital, "the accumulated material heritage of humankind in its entirety, or of particular human groups".[101] Culture in the anthropological understanding is a broad concept, which refers to "the sub total of the material and spiritual activities and products of a given social group which distinguishes it from other similar groups".[102] Such a definition, which covers almost all aspects of life,[103] is becoming widely accepted.[104] The CESCR, HRC and UNESCO seem to adhere to this definition.[105]

The Chinese Constitution itself does not explicitly recognise a right of the minorities to culture *per se*. It, instead, guarantees all minorities the right to use and develop their languages, the right to preserve or reform their folkways and customs, and the right to religious freedom.[106] The Law on REA refers to culture a number of times in different contexts. Culture is mostly used in a general sense in relation to the obligations of autonomous agencies to develop local economy and culture.[107] Culture is also presented from a narrow perspective, alongside with minority literature, arts, press, broadcast, cultural heritage, education, science, technology, public health, sports, and so forth.[108] Hence, culture in the Chinese context has two dimensions: as a broad inclusive definition and as a concept in a strict sense. For the purpose of this discussion, culture should be understood as broadly as to cover all aspects of life.

In the Law on REA, the rights of the minorities to languages, folkways and customs, and religion are emphasised separately in Chapter 1 "General Provision".[109] Religion and language are generally viewed as the fundamental

---

100 Stephen Hansen, supra note 21, at pp. 283–284; Rodolfo Stavenhagen, supra note 44, at pp. 88–89.

101 Rodolfo Stavenhagen, supra note 44, at p. 87.

102 Cited in Rodolfo Stavenhagen, supra note 44, at p. 89.

103 Alexandra Xanthaki, *Indigenous Rights and United Nations Standards: Self-determination, Culture and Land* (Cambridge University Press, 2007), p. 207.

104 Janusz Symonides, supra note 99, at pp. 180–181.

105 The CESCR, General Comment 21, paras.11–13; the HRC, General Comment 23, para.7; the UNESCO Mexico City Declaration on Cultural Policies, the Preamble. A further discussion on the UNESCO definition of culture, see Alexandra Xanthaki, supra note 103, at pp. 207–208.

106 The 1982 Constitution, Articles 4, 36.

107 The Law on REA, the Preamble, Article 6.

108 Ibid, Articles 38, 42, 50, 55, 59, 64.

109 The Law on REA, Articles 10, 11.

components of culture and ethnic identity.[110] Distinctive religions and/or languages are the embodiments of minority cultures in China. For example, Tibetan Buddhism is one of the most important features of the Tibetan identity, and the Mongolian language is also essential to the Mongolian culture. The following discussion, therefore, approaches the cultural rights of Chinese minorities from religious and linguistic perspectives.

6.2.1 *Freedom of Religious Belief*

The orthodox Marxist-Leninist theory generally considers religion as "the opium of the people" and "the organs of bourgeois reaction, used for the protection of the exploitation and the stupefaction of the working class".[111] It further claims that the communists should be atheists in nature, maintaining a world view of dialectical and historical materialism and practicing scientific socialism.[112] The attitude of the CPC in regard to religion, however, seems to be inconsistent with this orthodoxy. The Chinese communists have on many occasions stated that the CPC recognises and protects religious freedom. Such a position might be a practical choice, given the political reality in China.

In order to take over the power, the CPC had to mobilise peasants and win support of the minorities. Although the exact number of religious believers was not easy to estimate at the time, a large number of the Han peasants and minorities were religious. Apart from the well-known religions, such as Buddhism and Taoism, many Han people, particularly those in rural areas, had traditional beliefs, worshiping ancestors and spirits. Mao himself believed in Buddha in the early years of his childhood, due to his mother's influence.[113] Apart from minority beliefs, minority groups were also practising Protestantism, Catholicism, Buddhism and Islam.[114]

---

110 Stephen Hansen, supra note 21, at p. 300; Asbjorn Eide, supra note 15; the CERD, A/51/18(SUPP), para.404; CERD/C/SR.1469, para.45; CERD/C/CHN/CO/10-13, para.20.

111 Karl Marx, "Critique of Hegel's Philosophy of Right", in Karl Marx and Friedrich Engels (eds), *On religion* (Scholars Press, 1964), pp. 41–68 at p. 42; V. Lenin, "The Attitude of the Workers' Party to Religion", in Lenin, *On religion* (Progress Publishers), pp. 18–28 at pp. 18–19.

112 V. Lenin, ibid, p. 18; Zhang Zhiyi, "Zhengque renshi he guanche dang de zongjiao xinyang ziyou zhengce [Correctly Understand and Implement the Party's Policy on Freedom of Religious Belief]", 04 *Zhongguo Minzu* [*China's Ethnic Groups*] (1962), p. 3.

113 Mao Zedong, "Childhood Influence (as told to Edgar Snow)", in Donald MacInnis, *Religious Policy and Practice in Communist China* (Hodder and Stoughton, 1972), p. 6.

114 Yang Shengmin and Ding Hong (eds), *Zhongguo minzu zhi* [*the Ethnography of China*] (Zhongyang Minzu Daxue Chubanshe, 2003), pp. 58–434.

When the PRC was established in 1949, according to the official statistics, there were approximately 8,000,000 Muslims, 2,700,00 Catholics and 700,000 Protestants.[115] Almost the whole minority population in Tibet, Inner Mongolia and Liaoning were Buddhists.[116] This number did not include the believers of spirits and magical efficacy, as they were not classified as religion.[117] For the new regime, the critical question would be the accommodation of the minorities into the Chinese nation.[118] Given the actual situation of minority religious practice, the CPC repeatedly propagandised its protective policy in regard to religion in order to unite all the forces that can be united and to mobilise all positive factors that can be mobilised to build a "great socialist country".[119] The communists further pledged that the ongoing social reform would in no way interfere with the long-term policy of religious freedom in minority areas.[120]

Nevertheless, the CPC also held an opinion that religion, in essence, was a historical phenomenon which would endure temporarily.[121] It would naturally disappear when the objective requirements were met. They argued:

115 The Basic Viewpoint and Policy on the Religious Question during Our Country's Socialist Period (Document 19) (1982), Section II. The English translation is available in Donald MacInnis, *Religion in China Today: Policy and Practice* (Orbis Books, 1989), pp. 8–26 at p. 11.

116 Ibid.

117 This kind of beliefs and practices is usually categorised as popular religion or local religion. However, according to the communist standards, it is not a "religion". See Document 19; Adam Yuet Chau, *Miraculous Response: Doing Popular Religion in Contemporary China* (Stanford University Press, 2006); Daniel Overmyer, *Local Religion in Nouth China in the Twentieth Century: the Structure and Organisation of Community Rituals and Beliefs* (Brill, 2009); Stephan Feuchtwang, *Popular Religion in China: the Imperial Metaphor* (Curzon, 2001).

118 Dru Gladney argued that after the founding of the PRC, the real autonomy of the minorities was no longer necessary for garnering support and nationality policy has played an important role in the exercise of power in China. Dru Gladney, *Muslim Chinese: Ethnic Nationalism in the People's Republic* (*2nd Edition*) (Harvard University Press, 1996), p. 90.

119 Zhang Zhiyi, supra note 112, at p. 4; Li Weihan, "Tongyi zhanxian wenti yu minzu wenti [the Question of the United Front and Ethnicities]", quoted in Lin Xianggeng, "Woguo zongjiaojie yu zhongguo gongchandang lingdao de aiguo tongyi zhanxian [China's Religion Circles and the Patriotic United Front Led by the CPC]", 01 *Dangshi Yanjiu yu Jiaoxue* [*Party History Research and Teaching*] (2003), p. 12.

120 Liu Shaoqi, "Zhongguo gongchandang zhongyang weiyuan hui xiang dibaci quanguo daibiao dahui de zheng zhi baogao [Report to the Eighth National Congress of the CPCCC] (15/09/1956)", in Jin Binghao (ed), *Minzu gangling zhengce wenxian xuanbian* [*The Collected Works of the Documents on the National Program and Policy*] (Zhongyang Minzu Daxue Chubanshe, 2006), p. 552.

121 Document 19, Section I; Donald MacInnis, supra note 115, at pp. 10–11; Joshua Castellino and Elvira Redondo (eds), *Minority Rights in Asia: A Comparative Legal Analysis* (Oxford University Press, 2006), p. 120.

> [a]s the genesis and existence of religion is man's oppression by the forces of nature and society, therefore, only when class exploitation has been eliminated from human society and man's power to control nature has been greatly developed, and on this basis man's consciousness and scientific-cultural level have been greatly raised, may religion gradually die out.[122]

Hence, as religion would not die out quickly and a large number of the minority population were religious, the CPC adopted a pragmatic religious policy so as to maintain political stability and territorial integrity.

(1) Religious Freedom before the 1980s

As early as the 1931 Constitution of the Chinese Soviet Republic, the right of workers, peasants and the toiling population to "true religious freedom" was assured in the proposed Soviet Republic.[123] The Common Program reaffirmed the people's freedom of religious belief in 1949.[124] The 1954 Constitution provided that "every citizen of the PRC shall have freedom of religious belief".[125] Religious freedom at the time could be interpreted as follows: the freedom to believe, or not believe, was protected; religious compulsion and discrimination were prohibited; whether to believe in religion and which religion to believe were personal choices that were free from state interference; normal religious practice of the believers and normal activities of the clergy in religious sites were allowed; further measures were to be taken to protect the freedom of religious belief and to facilitate the resolution of the shortage of religious sites.[126]

Only normal religious practice was protected, as safeguarding religious freedom was distinguished from safeguarding "freedom" of counter-revolutionary activities.[127] Counter-revolutionary activities under the disguise of religious practice would not be protected as the right to religious freedom.[128] The term "counter-revolutionary", however, was vaguely defined. Almost anything a person did or did not do might constitute this category.[129]

---

122 Zhang Zhiyi, supra note 112, at p. 3; also quoted in Richard Bush, JR, *Religion in Communist China* (Abingdon Press, 1970), p. 18.

123 The Constitution of the Chinese Soviet Republic, 1931, para.13.

124 The 1949 Common Program, Article 5.

125 The 1954 Constitution, Article 88.

126 Mao Zedong, "On Coalition Government (1945)", in Donald MacInnis, supra note 113, at p. 14; Zhang Zhiyi, supra note 112, at pp. 4–5.

127 Liu Shaoqi, "Report on the Draft Constitution of the PRC (1954)", in Donald MacInnis, supra note 113, at p. 24.

128 Ibid.

129 Richard Bush, JR, supra note 122, at, p. 16.

The CPC also linked religion with feudal oppression and imperialist aggression.[130] The communists claimed that religion had been used by the feudal class and foreign forces as the tool of exploitation and oppression.[131] Hence, guided by the Party and the government, religious followers had to reform and remodel their religious practice so as to abolish feudalist and imperialist elements. For example, the Three-Self Patriotic Movements were launched amongst the Protestant and Catholic churches to eradicate foreign connection and to promote "autonomy, self-support and self-propagation" of the Chinese Christian churches.[132] To the mass believers, the elimination of feudalist and imperialist elements may not significantly affect them. Minority religious leaders, on the other hand, were subject to elusive pressure in the reform campaign, as they used to be labelled as "religious feudal lords" who had exploited and oppressed the people under the cloak of religion in the past.

Furthermore, superstition fell out of the scope of "normal" religious activities. Religious practice was protected, whilst superstitious activities should be abandoned, although differences between the two were not clearly defined. Feudal and superstitious ideas were first construed as the antithesis of the "scientific" new-democratic culture.[133] Superstitious phenomena, as opposed to science, were linked to general beliefs in gods and Shaman-doctors.[134] Under such a definition, religious practices of some minority groups may constitute "superstition", as they involved animist, polytheist and shamanic beliefs. For

130 Zhang Zhiyi, supra note 112, at pp. 4–5; also in Donald MacInnis, supra note 113, at pp. 164–165; Chen Xingyao, "How Did Imperialism Use Religion for Aggression on China? A Historical Survey of Missionary Work in China", cited in Donald MacInnis, supra note 113, at pp. 133–137.

131 Ibid.

132 Zhongguo jidujiao zai xin zhongguo jianshe zhong nuli tujing de xuanyan [the Chinese Manifesto: Direction of Endeavour for Chinese Christianity in the Construction of New China], 10 *Gazette of the People's Government of Henan Province*, 1950, p. 70; Zhao Xiaoyang, "Zhongguo tianzhujiao duli ziban yundong de chucheng [the Initial Formation of Chinese Catholic Independent Self-management Movements]", 04 *Dangdai Zhongguoshi Yanjiu* [*Contemporary China History Studies*] (2012), pp. 107–113; Bishop Zong Huaide, "Zai duli zizhu ziban jiaohui de daolu shang kuobu qianjin [Take Great Strides Along the Road to Independent and Self-reliance Churches]", 01 *Zhongguo Tianzhujiao* [*Catholic Church In China*] (1991), pp. 16–7.

133 The "scientific" new-democratic culture, according to Mao, referred to seeking truth from the facts, the objective truth and the unity of theory and practice. In answer to this thesis, a campaign of "advocating the science and breaking down the superstition" was launched in the Shanxi-Gansu-Ningxia Border Region. See Mao Zedong, "On New Democracy", *Selected Works of Mao Zedong Volume II* (Foreign Language Press, 1965), p. 381.

134 Mao Zedong, "Guanyu Shanganning bianqu de wenhua jiaoyu wenti [On the Question of Culture and Education in the Shanxi-Gansu-Ningxia Border Region] (22/03/1944)", http://cpc.people.com.cn/GB/64184/64185/189963/11567708.html, last visited on 24/12/2013.

example, the Shamans of the Manchu-Tungus and Yi groups performed a variety of functions, including sacrificial ceremonies, cures, and divination, by means of communicating with gods and spirits from another world.[135] However, the eradication of superstitious activities no longer seemed to be the focus of the propaganda after 1949, and the regional bans on the production and sales of "superstitious items" were suspended.[136] The communist theory that superstitious thoughts can be overcome through long-term education may be one of the explanations for this adjournment. The cautious policy in regard to minority religious beliefs might be another reason. On the whole, until the Great Leap Forward, religious practice, customs, and traditions of the minorities were in a way left unaffected.[137]

During the Cultural Revolution, religious beliefs, together with traditional culture and customs, were classified as the "Four Olds" to be destroyed. As a result, temples, churches and mosques were destructed and forcibly closed; religious literature, artefacts and relics were smashed; normal religious activities of the masses were forbidden; some minority customs and practices were prohibited, because of their superstitious nature; the clergy and some religious followers were denounced as the "targets of dictatorship"; and religious believers in some places were even oppressed.[138] It has been suggested that there existed no public practice of religion throughout China until 1971, except for the religious practice of some foreign Muslim visitors.[139]

(2) Religious Freedom in Contemporary China

In 1982, the CPCCC promulgated a directive named "the Basic Viewpoint and Policy on the Religious Question during Our Country's Socialist Period"

135 Xu Wanbang and Qi Qingfu, *Zhongguo shaoshu minzu wenhua tonglun* [*Introduction to Chinese Minority Cultures*] (Zhongyang Minzu Daxue Chubanshe, 1996), p. 276; Yang Shengmin and Ding Hong (eds),supra note 114, at pp. 72, 87–88, 95, 101; Wu Yun-kuang etc, *Bianjiang minzu de guoqu yu xianzai* [*The Past and the Present of the Tribes along the Chinese Border*] (The Orient Cultural Service, 1972), p. 37.

136 Li Xiaochen, "Xin zhongguo jianli qianhou huabei nongcun pochu mixin tanxi [Comments on the Efforts to do (sweep) Away with Superstition in Rural North China around the Founding of New China]", 04 *Zhonggong Dangshi Yanjiu* [*Journal of CPC History Studies*] (2005), p. 90.

137 Luo Zhufeng (ed), Donald MacInnis and Zheng Xi'an (Translators), *Religion under Socialism in China* (M.E. Sharpe, Inc, 1991), pp. 144, 227.

138 For instance, in the 1975 Shadian Incident, the Hui Muslims were suppressed by the PLA for their protests against the forcibly closure of mosques and against the ban on practising Islam. See Document 19; Donald MacInnis,supra note 113, at p. 283; Luo Zhufeng (ed), supra note 137, at pp. 145–146.

139 Donald MacInnis, supra note 113, at p. 283.

(Document 19). It was viewed as the most definitive statement of the CPC on religious affairs.[140] The document restated the nature of religion as a historical phenomenon and its compatibility with socialism, analysed the current religious situation, evaluated the religious policy in the past and set out the guiding principles on religious affairs in China.[141] This document signified religious restoration and revival in the aftermath of the Cultural Revolution. Despite the fact that different party leaders have further elaborated some aspects and proposed their own views on the issue, the essential understanding of the CPC in regard to religion remains unchanged: respect for religious freedom, the separation of state and religion, uniting religious people, the loyalty to the Party and the state, freedom from foreign influence and domination, adapting religions to the socialist society, and managing religious affairs in accordance with the law. Xi Jinping's approach to religion places an emphasis on helping religions adapt to the socialist system, calling for the sinicisation of religions and the legalisation of the management of religious affairs.[142]

The 1982 Constitution again ensures the right to freedom of religion.[143] It prohibits state institutions, public organisations and individuals from compelling citizens to believe, or not believe, in any religion, and from discriminating against citizens for their religious status.[144] However, this freedom of religion is only confined to "normal" religious activities. Furthermore, no-one can use religion to engage in activities that "disrupt public order, impair the health of citizens and interfere with the educational system".[145] Nor shall religious bodies and affairs be subject to foreign domination.[146] The Law on REA reiterates the constitutional provisions on religion, obliging autonomous agencies to guarantee the religious freedom of all citizens within autonomous areas.[147] State officers, who unlawfully deprive of citizens of their freedom to religion or infringe upon the customs and habits of the minorities, will be criminalised, if the circumstances are serious.[148] The Regulation on Religious

140 Luo Zhufeng (ed), supra note 137, at p. xvi.

141 Document 19; Donald MacInnis, supra note 115, at pp. 8–26. A further discussion on the reasons of the persistence of religion and its compatibility with socialism, see Luo Zhufeng (ed), supra note 137, at pp. 85–112, 113–131.

142 Xi Jinping, "Zai quanguo zongjiao huiyi shang de jianghua [Speech at the Conference on Religions] (22–23 April 2016)", 05 *Zhongguo Zongjiao* [*China Religion*] (2016), pp. 6–8.

143 The 1982 Constitution, Article 36.

144 Ibid.

145 Ibid.

146 Ibid.

147 The Law on REA, Article 11.

148 The 2015 Criminal Law, Article 251.

Affairs provides detailed rules regarding the management of religious affairs and the 2017 Revision has incorporated a new principle of "protecting the legal, stopping the illegal, containing the extreme, resisting infiltration, and combating crimes".[149]

In the official context, the religions widely practised in China include Buddhism (Lamaism and Theravada), Daoism, Islam and Christianity (Catholicism and Protestantism, as well as the Eastern Orthodoxy).[150] Minority beliefs, which fall outside of these state-recognised religions, are occasionally referred to as "indigenous" or "primitive" religion.[151] But in most cases, they are not considered to be religions in the general sense. The communists appear to distinguish general beliefs in spirits and gods from the practice of state-approved religions.[152] Luo Zhufeng claims that ideas about spirits and gods are different from normal religious activities, arguing:

> … there are quite a few people in our country who do not believe in a specific religion, but in gods and spirits, worshipping these gods and spirits, and the ancestors, according to traditional customs. This is related to the underdevelopment of science and culture under the semi-colonial and semi-feudal social conditions of our country after entering modern society. We must solve this problem by using education to popularise scientific cultural knowledge and break away from superstition.[153]

Hence, from a religious perspective, the minorities could be divided into two groups: the minorities that practise institutional religions, and the minorities who have minority belief systems. The Tibetan and Mongolian (Lamaism), Dai, De'ang and Blang (Theravada), and Muslims—Hui, Uyghur and Kazak belong to the first category. The minorities in the North and Southwest, for example the Manchu, Ewenk, Oroqen, Miao, Yi and Qiang generally practise minority beliefs, such as Shamanism and the like.

---

149 The Regulation on Religious Affairs (recently revised in 2017), Article 3.

150 The Information Office of the State Council, the White Paper on Freedom of Religious Belief in China (1997), Section 1; the 2nd Periodic Report Submitted by China under Article 9 of the ICERD, CERD/C/126/ADD.1, p. 3, para.10; Joshua Castellino and Elvira Redondo (eds), supra note 121, p. 121.

151 The 2nd Report of China, ibid.

152 Document 19, Section II; Donald MacInnis, supra note 115, at p. 11; the White Paper on Religious Belief, supra note 150, Sections 2 and 3.

153 Luo Zhufeng (ed), supra n.137, at pp. 142–143.

Institutional Religions

In terms of institutional religions, "normal" religious activities are defined as activities that, in accordance with religious customs, take place in designated places of worship or in believers' homes, and are conducted by religious organisations and the believers themselves.[154] Individual worship that takes place in private premises is not subject to too many restraints, as long as the practice does not violate others' rights.[155] Protestant worship services in believers' houses are no longer prohibited, and no prior registration is required for a service.[156] On the other hand, there are more requirements for collective religious activities. First, collective activities should be held at sites registered for religious activities (such as Buddhist monasteries, Taoist temples, mosques, churches and other fixed premises for religious activities). Second, they have to be organised by the sites for religious activities or religious bodies, and be presided over by religious personnel or other persons who are qualified under the prescriptions of the religion concerned. The process of such activities should also be in compliance with religious doctrines and canons.[157]

In order to be registered, a religious site should meet the following conditions: a) it should be established for normal religious activities and in accordance with the principle of independence and self-governance; b) local religious believers have the need to frequently engage in collective religious activities; c) there are eligible religious personnel or other persons who are qualified under the prescriptions of the religions concerned to preside over the religious activities; d) there are necessary funds from lawful sources; and e) it is reasonably located, in accordance with urban planning, without interfering with the normal production and livelihood of the neighbourhood.[158] The religious affairs department of the people's government at different levels takes responsibility for the administration of the registration and operation of religious sites.[159] Put differently, organisations or sites that are not registered for religious purposes should not organise or hold any religious activities.[160] Otherwise, these would be classified as "abnormal" religious activities that are subject to punishment according to the law. For example, religious affairs departments are empowered to close unregistered religious sites and academies,

154 Document 19, Section VI; Donald MacInnis, supra note 115, at pp. 17–8.

155 Ibid.

156 The White Paper on Religious Belief, supra note 150, Section 3.

157 The Regulation on Religious Affairs, Article 40.

158 Ibid, Article 20.

159 Ibid, Articles 21–23, 27, 30, 31, 33, 42.

160 Ibid, Articles 41, 44

confiscate relevant "unlawful" treasuries and revenues or impose a fine, and issue administrative sanctions.[161] Since religious activities are limited to registered sites, religious and theist propaganda or preaching outside of religious sites is considered to be improper or "abnormal", and likewise atheist propaganda in worship places is not allowed.[162] However, outside of religious sites, it seems that only atheist propaganda is legitimate and permissible.

Secondly, apart from venue registration, loyalty to the nation, the government, and the CPC is another inherent part of religious freedom in China.[163] Alongside faith in gods, the clergy and the mass believers are required to retain loyalty to the Party, whose worldview is atheist. This loyalty is indoctrinated through education and media propaganda, as well as through religious measures. In practice, each religion has its own national and local association—the Patriotic Religious Organisation.[164] These religious associations also need to be registered according to the rules that regulate social organisation.[165] The key responsibilities of religious organisations include educating the mass believers and religious personnel about patriotism and assisting the people's governments to implement the laws, regulations and policies.[166] Furthermore, religious academies have to train patriotic personnel who also possess sufficient religious knowledge.[167] The clergy, therefore, should retain loyalty to the Party and fulfil their religious functions under the guidance of the religious association.[168] Otherwise, they may be deprived of their religious status by religious institutions upon the recommendation of the relevant religious affairs departments and subject to administrative or criminal sanctions.[169] For

161 Ibid, Article 69.

162 Document 19, Section VI; Donald MacInnis, supra note 115, at p. 18.

163 It requires that "religious believers, like the people of all nationalities, must support the leadership of the Communist Party, support the socialist system, love their country, maintain the unity of the nation and solidarity of the nationalities, take part in the building of the four modernisations along with all other people, keep up good religious traditions, and do good deeds for socialism". Cited in Luo Zhufeng (ed), supra note 137, at p.141; Joshua Castellino and Elvira Redondo (eds), supra note 121, p. 121.

164 There are eight national patriotic religious organisations, namely the Chinese Buddhist Association, Chinese Taoist Association, Chinese Islamic Association, Chinese Catholic Patriotic Association, National Administrative Commission of the Chinese Catholic Church, Bishops Conference of Catholic Church in China, National Committee of Three-Self Patriotic Movement of the Protestant Churches in China, and China Christian Council.

165 The Regulation on Religious Affairs, Article 7.

166 Luo Zhufeng (ed), supra note 137, at p. 139; Document 19, Section VII; Donald MacInnis, supra note 115, at p. 19; the Regulation on Religious Affairs, Articles 4, 8.

167 Document 19, Section VIII; Donald MacInnis, supra note 115, at p. 20.

168 Ibid; Luo Zhufeng (ed), supra note 137, at p. 138; the CERD, CERD/C/SR.1469, para.14.

169 The Regulation on Religious Affairs, Article 73.

example, Lamas in Tibetan Buddhism and Imams/Akhunds in Xinjiang play decisive roles in connecting the CPC with the followers. Different levels of supervision can be observed in practice for political reasons. The authority exerts closer supervision of Lamas in Tibet than Buddhist monks in the Han concentrated areas. This attempt at control, however, has reportedly been argued not to achieve its objective.[170] In doing this, the CPC can oversee religious beliefs through the clergy and religious associations and control the adaption of religions in accordance with communist values. Seen from this perspective, the separation of state and religion in China requires the non-interference of religion in state affairs, but allows for the government to control religious activities.

Thirdly, reactionary secret societies and pernicious organisations (*xiejiao*) are not protected by the law, as no-one can use religion to disrupt public order, or to impair the health of citizens.[171] According to Article 300 of the criminal law, whoever forms or uses secret societies (superstitious sects), pernicious organisations and/or superstition to undermine the implementation of laws, or to deceive others, may violate the penal code and be punished by judicial bodies.[172] Special interpretive judicial documents were adopted in 1999 and 2001 and *Falun Gong*, in particular, was claimed to be an unauthorised organisation, making use of religion to disturb public order and harm people's lives, property and economic development.[173] The 2017 Joint Judicial Interpretation promulgated by the Supreme People's Court and the Supreme People's Procuratorate defines "evil religion" as illegal organisations established under the guise of religion, qigong, or other illicit forms that deify and worship their leading members, enchant and deceive others by concocting and spreading superstitious

170 Yash Ghai, Sophia Woodman and Kelley Loper, Is There Space for "Genuine Autonomy" for Tibetan areas in the PRC's System of Nationalities Regional Autonomy?, 17 *International Journal on Minority and Group Rights* (2010), p. 178.

171 Document 19, Section X; Donald MacInnis, supra note 115, at p. 22; the White Paper on Religious Belief, supra note 150, Section 2.

172 The Criminal Law (recently revised in 2015), Article 300.

173 The NPC Standing Committee (NPCSC), Decision on Outlawing Heretical Cult Organisations and Preventing and Punishing Heretical Activities, 1999; the Supreme People's Court and the Supreme People's Procuratorate, the 1999 and 2001 Joint Interpretation on Certain Problems in Implementing the Law Applicable to Cases of Organising and Employing Heretical Cult Organisations to Commit Crimes, [Interpretation No. 18] 1999, [Interpretation No. 19] 2001; the Supreme People's Court, Notice on the Implementation of the NPCSC Decision on Outlawing Heretical Cult Organisations and Preventing and Punishing Heretical Activities and the 1999 Joint Interpretation of the Supreme People's Court and the Supreme People's Procuratorate, [No. 29], 1999. See also Joshua Castellino and Elvira Redondo (eds), supra note 121, p. 124.

fallacies and other means, recruit and control their members, and endanger society.[174] However, the distinction between normal religious activities and a cult is not clear cut as some terms in this definition remain vague and broad. It can be argued that the anti-cult legislation is in essence against non-compliance with the established norm of political loyalty.[175] If an organisation incites people to overthrow the government and the CPC,[176] it is very likely to be denounced as *xiejiao*. This is demonstrated by the recent crackdown of the "heretical sect", the Eastern Lightning, which preaches to overthrow the reign of the "evil red dragon". But not all non-registered religious practices would be classified as pernicious organisations to be suppressed. There is a halfway mark between normal religious activities and abnormal cult activities, depending on whether such a practice amounts to a threat to the current regime.

In addition, apart from the general restrictions discussed above, special measures are imposed in the XUAR under the name of preventing terrorism and extremism. The policy of de-extremisation, which aims to combat overseas infiltrations via religious means and prevent ideological infringement by extremists, has been adopted in Xinjiang. A new Regulation on Religious Affairs has been passed by the XUAR People's Congress in the form of regional regulation, rather than special regulation,[177] which is modelled on the national Regulation on Religious Affairs but also incorporates detailed rules on preventing regional radicalisation and combating unlawful religious activities.[178] It defines "unlawful religious activities" as "any activity that is prohibited by the laws, administrative regulations and regional regulations" and "religious extremism" as "distorting religious doctrines and propagating extremism as well as any other extremist thoughts, speeches and activities advocating violence, hostility to society and anti-human".[179] It also explicitly prohibits minors from

174 The Supreme People's Court and the Supreme People's Procuratorate, Joint Interpretation on Certain Problems in Implementing the Law Applicable to Criminal Cases of Organising and Employing Heretical Cult Organisations to Undermine the Implementation of Laws, [Interpretation No. 03], 2017, Article 1.

175 Pitman Porter, "Belief in Control: Regulation of Religion in China", 174 *The China Quarterly* (2003), p. 331.

176 Ibid.

177 Special regulation, as a part of legislative autonomy of autonomous agencies, which can alter or supplement the provisions of national law and administrative regulation, should be reviewed and approved by the NPC Standing Committee before entering into force. Regional regulation, on the other hand, only needs to be submitted to the NPC Standing Committee and the State Council for the record. For the detailed discussion, see Chapter 5, Section 5.1 "Legislative Power of Autonomous Agencies".

178 The 2014 XUAR Regulation on Religious Affairs, Articles 4, 5, 7, 9, 21, 26, 38.

179 Ibid, Articles 65.

participating in religious activities.[180] The religious associations that manage the religious sites and the clergy are obligated to oversee activities involving the secession of the state, the incitement of ethnic hatred, and the propaganda and incitement of terrorism and extremism and to report them to the supervision departments and the police; in return their actions will be rewarded.[181] The religious institutions and personnel in Xinjiang, thus, could be considered to be agencies of the government.

The more controversial regulation is the 2015 Provisions of the Urumqi City to Prohibit the Wearing of Face-masking Robes in Public (the Urumqi Ban), which bans the full face veil (*mengmian zhaopao*) and all other types of clothing, items, or emblems that may propagate religious extremism in public. The breach of those provisions is punishable by a fine (of between 2000 and 5000 RMB), and sanctions provided by laws, including criminal law,[182] and regulations.[183] Although similar bans have been imposed in France and Belgium and have been upheld by the European Court of Human Rights in *S.A.S. v. France* and *Belcacemi and Oussar v. Belgium*, restrictions placed on the exercise of individual freedom to religion shall be prescribed by law, pursue legitimate aim(s), and be proportionate to the aim(s) pursed.[184] The Urumqi Ban is claimed to pursue four aims: maintaining social stability, preventing the infiltration of religious radicalised beliefs, safeguarding public order, and inheriting the Chinese culture and traditions.[185] But it fails to clarify the definition of "face-masking robes" or other extremist clothing/symbols. More importantly, the Urumqi Ban is a regional regulation passed by the LPC of the Urumqi city and approved by the LPC of the XUAR, which becomes effective on 1 February 2015. According to the Legislation law in force at the time, a regional regulation can be adopted by a "comparatively larger city" to govern regional matters or other issues that have not been regulated by national laws and administrative regulations in the light of specific local conditions and actual needs, except for

180 Ibid, Article 37.

181 Ibid, Articles 9, 19, 26.

182 The Criminal Law, Articles 120-(5), "Crimes of Forcing Others to Wear Full-face Coverings".

183 The 2015 Provisions of the Urumqi City to Prohibit the Wearing of Face-masking Robes in Public, Articles 10, 11.

184 France, the Law no. 2010-1192 of 11 October 2010; Belgium, the Law of 1 June 2011; S.A.S. *v.* France, no 43835/11, ECHR 2014, paras.42, 47, 110–113, 123–131, 137–159; Belcacemi and Oussar *v.* Belgium, 37798/13, ECHR 2017, para. 63.

185 The 2015 Provisions of the Urumqi City to Prohibit the Wearing of Face-masking Robes in Public, Article 1.

matters specifically reserved to the NPC and its Standing Committee.[186] Considering the aims pursued by the Urumqi Ban, this veil ban is hardly a regional matter. As there exists no national veil ban, the "specific local conditions and actual needs" of the Urumqi city are likely to be the motive for passing this regional regulation. Such a practice, however, is neither legitimate nor proportionate to justify the limitations to the right to freedom of religion. On 15 March 2015, the new amendment of the Legislation Law becomes effective. It explicitly limits the legislative power of a sub-districted city to regional matters concerning "rural and urban construction and management, environmental protection, and preservation of historical heritage and cultural values".[187] The Urumqi Ban may constitute a regulation *ultra vires* under the newly amended Legislation Law. It, however, remains in force as it has been approved before the adoption of the amendment.[188]

Minority Belief Systems

The religious administration practice suggests that the registration and loyalty requirements discussed above only apply to institutional religions. Minority beliefs are not subject to such restrictions, nor are under the legal protection of religious freedom, since they are not viewed as "religions" by the CPC. Instead, minority

186 According to Article 63 of the 2000 Legislation Law, a "comparatively larger city" is defined as "a city where a provincial or autonomous regional people's government is located or where a special economic zone is located, or a city approved as such by the State Council". Urumqi is the capital city of the XUAR. Article 64 further provides that: "[l]ocal regulations may be formulated to govern the following matters: (1) matters requiring the formulation of specific provisions in light of the actual conditions of an respective administrative area for implementing the provisions of laws or administrative regulations; and (2) matters of local character that require the formulation of local regulations. Except for the affairs provided for in Article 8 of this Law, the provinces, autonomous regions, municipalities directly under the Central Government and the comparatively larger cities may, in light of the specific local conditions and actual needs, first formulate local regulations on all other affairs for which the State has not yet formulated any laws or administrative regulations. Once the laws or administrative regulations formulated on such matters by the State come into effect, the provisions in local regulations which contradict the said laws or administrative regulations shall be null or void, and the organs that have formulated such regulations shall promptly amend or annul the provisions". See the 2000 Legislation Law, Articles 8, 63, 64.

187 The Legislation Law, Articles 72, 73. The new amendment grants sub-districted cities and autonomous prefectures the power to adopt regional regulations. Compared to "comparatively larger city" defined by the 2000 Legislation Law, sub-districted city is a much broader concept that includes "comparatively larger cit[ies]" and other sub-districted cities. See the Legislation Law, Articles 72, 82; and Chapter 5, Section 5.1 "Legislative Power of Autonomous Agencies".

188 The Legislation Law, Article 72.

religious practice can be legalised on the basis of minority folkways, customs and culture.

Compared to institutional religions, minority beliefs are likely to be associated with superstition, as the boundary between religious practice and superstition is not clear cut.[189] The CPC defines religion as an ideology, worldview and cultural phenomenon, which has an established social organisation.[190] Superstition, on the other hand, is referred to as activities performed by sorcerers, witches or other professional superstitious practitioners, which involve communicating with gods, exorcism, cure, divination, fortunetelling, and so forth.[191] Under such a definition, religious activities that are not institutionalised might be labelled as superstition.[192] For example, the Miao group, in general, believe in Animism, worshipping natural spirits, ancestors and ghosts through different rituals.[193] The Shaman (*suni*) of the Yi performs exorcisms and cures disease that cannot be treated by ordinary medicine.[194] The Shamans of the reindeer Ewenks are the spirit medium between the people and gods. They lead worship rituals to call up lost spirits and search for missing reindeers. Minority belief systems, more or less, involve worshipping nature, spirits and gods in an indigenous way, and some of the so-called "feudal superstitious" activities are integral parts of minority cultures.

But minority Shamanism and other indigenous religious practices are not suppressed because of their "superstitious" nature. The CPC now adopts a

---

189 Ka Lina, "Xunlu Ewenk ren de sanmanjiao wenhua [Shamanist Culture of Ewenq People Who Train the Deer]", 02 *Zhongyang Minzu Daxue Xuebao* [*Journal of Central University for Nationalities* (*Philosophy and Social Science*)] (2007), p. 76.

190 The United Front Work Department of the CPCCC, Zongjiao yu mixin shi shenme guanxi [the Relationship between Religion and Superstition], http://www.zytzb.cn/publicfiles/business/htmlfiles/tzb2010/zhishi/200911/574197.html, last visited on 24/02/2013; the CPC, Zongjiao yu mixin de qubie [the Differences Between Religion and Superstition], http://cpc.people.com.cn/GB/64107/65708/66067/66082/4468773.html, last visited on 24/12/2013.

191 Ibid.

192 Adam Yuet Chau, supra note 117, at p. 211; James Miller (ed), *Chinese Religions in Contemporary Society* (ABC-Clio, 2006), p. 57; Christopher Marsh, *Religion and the State in Russia and China: Suppression, Survival and Revival* (Continuum, 2011), p. 218.

193 Lu Qun, "Shilun Miao zu xinyang de shisuxing [On the Secularity of the Miao Religious Beliefs]", 01 *Kaili Xueyuan Xuebao* [*Journal of Kaili University*] (2002), pp. 24–25; "Miaozu yanxu zhijin de wanwu youling xinyang ji yuanyin poxi [On the Last-to-today Beliefs-All Things on Earth Have Sprits-of Miao Nationality]", 04 *Guizhou Minzu Yanjiu* [*Guizhou Ethnic Studies*] (2002), pp. 89–90.

194 Se Yin, "Saman jiao yu nanfang minzu minjian zongjiao bijiao yanjiu [A Comparative Study of Shamanism and Folk Religion in the South]", 03 *Yunnan Shehui Kexue* [*Social Sciences in Yunnan*] (2000), pp. 81–83.

comparatively neutral policy in regard to minority belief systems. Unlike institutional religions, no systematic supervision scheme is adopted to oversee such practices. This policy may be explainable from the following perspectives.

First, Chinese law guarantees the right of the minorities to preserve or reform their folkways and customs.[195] In reality, minority belief systems cannot be easily distinguished from minority folkways and customs,[196] as they affect almost all matters in their life, such as marriage, funeral, festival, and so on.[197] In the Honghe Hani and Yi autonomous prefecture, the majority of the minority villagers believe in ghosts and gods, including cadres and pupils in elementary schools.[198] Religious activities that revolve around the daily life of the Hani and Yi are closely related to folk festivals. The whole village participate in those rituals and festivals, through which the Hani and Yi people worship ancestors and nature.[199] Minority beliefs, thus, are indispensable for preserving minority customs and cultures. The strength of faith, together with traditions and customs, plays an important role in the process of the revival of minority cultures after the Cultural Revolution.

Second, local authorities are reluctant to crack down on "superstitious" activities. They will not gain political credits by doing this, but on the contrary the crack-down may lead to the disapproval and resistance of the minorities.[200] Minority religions, to a certain extent, are commonly associated with the ethnic question.[201] The situation in Tibet and Xinjiang constantly reminds the local authorities to handle minority faiths with extra caution. On the other hand, distinctive minority cultures can serve as tourist attractions, which will benefit the local economy in many ways.[202] According to the economy-oriented policy, local governments have attempted to make eco-cultural tourism that is based on minority belief systems and folkways the pillar industry

---

195 The 1982 Constitution, Article 4; the Law on REA, Articles 6, 10, 37, 38, 50, 55, 64.

196 James Miller (ed), supra note 192, at p. 58.

197 Document 19, Section IX; Donald MacInnis, supra note 115, at, p. 21.

198 Wang Yongzhi, Shi Lina and Ji Yujiao, "Xibu shaoshu minzu qingshaonian zongjiao xinyang zhuangkuang de diaocha yanjiu [An Investigation of the Status of Religious Belief among Minority Teenagers (age 12-17) in the West: Taking the Honghe Hani and Yi Autonomous Prefecture as an Example]", 03 *Shijie Zongjiao Wenhua* [*The World Religious Cultures*] (2012), pp. 71–73.

199 Ibid.

200 Adam Yuet Chau, supra note 117, at pp. 215–217.

201 Document 19, Section II; Donald MacInnis, supra note 115, at p. 11.

202 Adam Yuet Chau, supra note 117, at pp. 215–217; David Y. H Wu, "Chinese Minority Policy and the Meaning of Minority Culture: the Example of Bai in Yunnan, China", 49:01 *Human Organisation* (1990), p. 9.

of the local economy.[203] The official promotion of eco-cultural tourism coincides with the revival of minority cultural and religious traditions.[204]

More importantly, the practice of minority belief systems normally poses no threat to the CPC or the state. Unlike the Tibetans or Muslims in Xinjiang, minority groups that practise minority beliefs are not normally involved in regional unrest or separatist movements. Minority belief systems rarely have a standardised description of the doctrine system and thus may have variations with special regional or group features. The animist beliefs and practices of the Miao, for instance, vary from group to group in different areas.[205] Also, the practice of such beliefs does not involve activities with a considerable number of the followers.

Nevertheless, party members do not enjoy freedom of religion.[206] They can neither believe in religion nor practise it, due to the Marxist atheist philosophy.[207] The CPC, however, allows for exceptions for minority party members at the grass-roots level.[208] The rationale is that some religious beliefs and practices have become an essential part of ethnic traditions and customs. A ban on participating in traditional weddings, funeral ceremonies, or mass festivals that have religious significance, would cut off the close link with the masses and isolate party members from the rest.[209] Put differently, minority party members are not allowed to have religious beliefs, but may attend religious activities as a part of their identities.[210] In the reply to the CERD's question, the Chinese delegate claims that "communism is a religion" and "to hold any other belief would be inconsistent with party membership".[211] However, if communism is a religion, party members should decide freely whether to believe in it or not.

---

203 Wu Xuemei, "Zhuiniuji: cong lishi de jiyi dao xianshi de caoyan [the Drilling-bull Sacrifice: From Historical Reminiscence to Practical Demonstration——Setting Miao Nationality in Xiaomaopuoying Village as An Example]", 04 *Guizhou Minzu Yanjiu* [*Guizhou Ethnic Studies*] (2004), p. 133.

204 David Y. H Wu, supra note 202.

205 Lu Qun, supra note 193; "Shilun Xiangxi Miao zu xinyang de zongzu yishi tezheng [On the Features of Ancestral Consciousness in Which the Miao Nationality Believes in the West of Hunan]", 01 *Hubei Minzu Xueyuan Xuebao* [*Journal of Hubei Institute for Nationalities (Philosophy and Social Science)*] (2001), pp. 46–49.

206 Yash Ghai, Sophia Woodman and Kelley Loper, supra note 170, at p. 182.

207 Document 19, Section IX; Donald MacInnis, supra note 115, at p. 20; C. Mackerras, *China's Ethnic Minorities and Globalisation* (Routledge Curzon, 2003), p. 117.

208 Document 19, Section IX; Donald MacInnis, supra note 115, at p. 21.

209 Ibid.

210 C. Mackerras, supra note 207; the CERD, CERD/C/SR.1469, paras.5, 45, 48.

211 The CERD, CERD/C/SR.1469, para.48.

There has been an apparent trend of religious revival in minority areas since the early 1980s. Community temples and ritual sites have been rebuilt; ancestral and deity tablets have been restored in private households; and religious/cultural festivals have also been promoted.[212] According to the official ideology, religion in the Chinese context only refers to institutional religions, namely Buddhism, Daoism, Islam, Catholicism and Protestantism. "Normal" practice of these religions is strictly regulated by the law. The state control of religion might be explained by the experience from the past. Since the principle of the Mandate of Heaven was the legitimacy foundation of the Chinese empires, religion was claimed in many peasant uprisings as a proper source and inspiration to overthrow the old empire.[213] The "evil cult", such as *Yiguan Dao, Falong Gong* and the East Lightning, and the ethnic unrest in Tibet and Xinjiang reveal, more or less, the potentiality of manipulating religion for political ambitions.

On the other hand, minority belief systems are subject to less restrictions, due to their "non-religious" nature. This type of beliefs has been revived as a part of minority culture. The legal recognition and promotion of minority cultures, together with the strategic emphasis of economic development and eco-cultural tourism, may have contributed to such revivals. However, the arrival of tourists may interrupt the continuation of minority religious traditions, since the practice has been reformed in a way to meet tourist expectations and may lose its religious nature. Climbing the knife ladder, for example, is traditionally performed by the Miao Shaman in the Bull Sacrifice Ritual to reveal his sacredness and privileges as the spirit medium between human and gods.[214] It has now become a profession in some places, which is mainly performed for tourists with no connection to religious sacredness.[215] The tension between

212 Wu Xuemei, supra note 203, at p. 133; Lu Qun, "Miaozu yuanshi zongjiao xinyang de xiandai qiyixing bianhua [the Variety of Modern Deviation in Miao's Primitive Religion and Faith: with an example of Miao in La Dongshan in the West of Hunan Province]", 02 *Zhongyang Minzu Daxue Xuebao* [*Journal of the Central University for Nationalities* (*Philosophy and Social Science*)] (2003), p. 99.

213 From the peasant uprisings in the late Qin dynasty to the Taiping Rebellion, Shamanism, Daoism, Christianity and other forms of folk religions were involved in the resistance to the imperial rule. See also Pitman Porter, supra note 175, at p. 317.

214 Li Mengzhang, "Miaozu zhuiniuji wenhua renleixue chanshi [A Cultural-anthropological Analysis of the 'Drilling-bull' Sacrifice of the Miao]", 09 *Minzu Luntan* [*Minzu Tribune*] (2008), p. 38.

215 Zhao Yuyan, "Lvyou huanjing xia wugu wenhua de bianyi [the Variation of Witchcraft Culture against the Background of Tourism—A Case Study of the Tourism of Miao People in Shanjiang]", 06 *Guangxi Minzu Daxue Xuebao* [*Journal of Guangxi University for Nationalities* (*Philosophy and Social Science*)] (2007), p. 42.

the pursuit of local economic development and the need to preserve minority beliefs and cultures has emerged in many minority areas.

6.2.2 *The Language Rights of the Minorities*

According to Chinese law, spoken and written languages are addressed separately as language and script. Language (*yuyan*) is further distinguished from dialect (*fangyan*).[216] The law recognises a right to language, not to dialect. It has been reported that 56 officially recognised ethnic groups speak more than 80 languages and use over 30 different scripts.[217] The Han have their own language, the Han Language (*hanyu*), which consists of many dialects and subdialects. The remaining 55 minorities speak between 80 to more than 100 mother tongues. Apart from the unified written language of the Han, minority groups use over 30 writing systems.

(1) Linguistic Planning for the Minorities before the 1980s

Upon the establishment of the PRC, the language policy for the minorities had to serve the overall goal of the new regime: to unite the nation and consolidate territorial integrity whilst still properly accommodating the minorities in the Han dominant country. Hence, linguistic equality as a component of the ethnic equality was emphasised by the CPC, which aimed to mobilise and unify the minorities to the greatest extent.[218] The constitutional documents recognised the right of the minorities to develop their own languages and

---

216 There is a slight difference between the Chinese term "*fangyan*" and the English term "dialect". See Maria Kurpaska, *Chinese Languages: A Look Through the Prism of the Great Dictionary of Modern Chinese Dialects* (De Gruyter Mouton, 2010), pp. 1–3.

217 There are different opinions on how many languages are being used. Sun Hongkai argues that there are more than 100 languages being used, whilst other scholars are inclined to go with 80. See Sun Hongkai, "Zhongguo yuyan shibie gongzuo [the Identification of China's Languages]", in Ma Liya et al. (eds), *Zhongguo minzu yuwen zhengce yu falv shuping* [*Review of Policy and Law on Linguistic Minorities in China*] (Minzu Chubanshe, 2007), pp. 31–53 at p. 36; Maria Kurpaska, ibid, at p. 4; Luo Meizhen, *Luo Meizhen zixuan wenji* [*Selected works of Luo Meizhen*] (Minzu Chubanshe, 2007), p. 1. See also Sun Hongkai, "Chapter 10 Theorising Over 40 Years Personal Experiences with the Creation and Development of Minority Writing Systems of China", in Zhou Minglang and Sun Hongkai (eds), *Language Policy in the PRC: Theory and Practice since 1949* (Kluwer Academic Publishers, 2004), pp. 179–199 at p. 181; Jin Xinghua (ed), *Zhongguo minzu yuwen gongzuo* [*the Work on Chinese Ethnic Languages and Scripts*] (Minzu Chubanshe, 2005), p. 19.

218 Mao had on many occasions emphasised respect for minority languages, scripts, customs, traditions, and religions. Mao Zedong, "Zai zhongguo gongchandang diliujie zhongyang weiyuan hui kuoda de diliuci quanti huiyi shang de jianghua [Speech at the 6th Enlarged Meeting of the 6th CPCCC (1938)]", quoted in Jin Xinghua (ed), ibid, p. 25; "On Coalition Government (1945)", in Jin Binghao (ed), supra note 120, at p. 325.

scripts.[219] The 1954 Constitution specifically provided that, in performing their duties, autonomous agencies should employ one or more commonly used languages and scripts in the locality.[220] If one specific group did not know the designated language or script, the language or script of that group should be used when performing state functions.[221]

The Situation of Minority Languages

The linguistic situation of the minorities was not clear when the PRC was established. An extensive linguistic investigation was launched in the 1950s, and 59 minority languages were identified as a result of the investigation.[222] The principles and standards on the language identification and language-dialect classification applied in the investigation were vague as the investigation reports were not made public. From the information revealed in the early 1980s, a number of elements seemed to have been considered: objective standards, the will of the group concerned, and historical, social and political factors.[223]

Apart from linguistic criteria, such as the quantity of vocabulary, pronunciation and grammatical norms, the will of the group played an important role in the investigation process. In particular, an ethnic group was likely to be identified as having a language, rather than a dialect, if it had been recognised as a separate minority, even though the language they spoke may be very similar to other languages.[224] The Buyi language, compared to the Zhuang southern dialect, was more similar to the Zhuang northern dialect.[225] But it was officially classified as a separate Buyi language because of the will of the people concerned.[226] The Xibo group also had its language recognised, despite the linguistic similarity between the Xibo language and the Manchu language.[227]

219 The Common Program, Article 53; the 1954 Constitution, Article 3.

220 The 1954 Constitution, Article 71.

221 The General Programme for the Implementation of REA, Article 15.

222 Sun Hongkai, Hu Zengyi and Huang Xing (eds), *Zhongguo de yuyan* [*the Languages of China*] (Shangwu Yinshu Guan, 2007), pp. 16–18, 21–24; Jin Xinghua (ed), supra note 217, at pp. 38–45.

223 Wang Jun, "Minzu yuwen gongzuo zhong de ruogan renshi wenti [A Few Questions on the Work of Minority Languages and Scripts]", 01 *Minzu Yuwen* [*Minority Lanuages of China*] (1981), p. 5; Hu Mingyang, "Xiandai yuyanxue de fazhan qushi [the Development Trend of Modern Languages]", 00 *Yuyan Yanjiu* [*Studies in Language and Linguistics*] (1981), p. 3; Sun Hongkai, Hu Zengyi and Huang Xing (eds), supra note 222, at pp. 37–41.

224 Sun Hongkai, Hu Zengyi and Huang Xing (eds), supra note 222, at p. 38

225 Wang Jun, supra note 223, at p. 4

226 Ibid.

227 An Jun, "Xibo yuyan wenzi nai manyu manwen de jixu [the Xibo Language and Script are the Continuance of the Manchu Language and Script]", 01 *Manyu Yanjiu* [*Manchu Studies*] (1985), pp. 41–47.

Likewise, a minority group might speak one or more languages since ethnic status was identified on the basis of a set of criteria, within which the language was merely one factor. For example, although the southern dialect and the northern dialect were not mutually intelligible,[228] for political reasons, the Zhuang people as a whole can only have one language. This Zhuang language had a base dialect and standard pronunciation, but in fact consisted of two major dialects. The Yao group, on the other hand, were considered to speak three different languages.[229] Furthermore, when minority A spoke two or more languages and one of these languages was similar to the minority language B, the language used by the sub-group of minority A may, in accordance with the actual situation, be named after the minority language B.[230] Thus, the language used by the Tibetans in the Heishui County, the Aba Tibetan Autonomous Prefecture, was the Qiang language, rather than Tibetan.[231]

On the identification of minority languages, the CPC again employed a flexible and inconsistent strategy so as to establish internal linguistic divisions among the minorities. The CPC's advocacy of minority languages and scripts might partially be explained in such terms. Nonetheless, the classification of the Han language applied a different set of standards. Historically, there was no unified spoken language for the Han. The linguistic unification of the Chinese empires was maintained through the unified script. The majority of the population spoke diverse speeches, according to their geographical locations, although the ruling class and elites spoke a super-dialectal *lingua franca* (known as Mandarin). Regional speeches of the Han language were not mutually intelligible. But the CPC claimed that the Han only had one language which included 7 dialectal groups and many sub-dialects, as those regional speeches "differed most in phonology, less in vocabulary and least in syntax".[232] Apparently, the unified Han language could better serve the unity of the Han, and

228 Li Xulian and Huang Quanxi, "Chapter 13 The Introduction and Development of the Zhuang Writing System", in Zhou Minglang and Sun Hongkai (eds), supra note 217, pp. 239–256 at p. 239.

229 Mao Zongwu, Meng Chaogu and Zheng Zongze (eds), *Yaozu yuyan jianzhi* [*A Brief History of the Yao Language*] (Minzu Chubanshe, 1982), pp. 11–12.

230 Sun Hongkai, Hu Zengyi and Huang Xing (eds), supra note 222, at p. 38.

231 Ibid.

232 Disagreements exist on the classification of dialectical groups of the Han language. Apart from the 7-group classification, the Language Atlas of China divides the Han language into 10 dialectal groups. Some other linguists have different understandings. A detailed discussion on the classification of the Han dialects, see Sun Hongkai, Hu Zengyi and Huang Xing (eds), supra note 222, at pp. 6–9; Language Atlas of China, Longman, 1987, p. A1; and Maria Kurpaska, supra note 216, at pp. 25–90. See also John DeFrancis, "Chapter 7 Language and

the coherence of the Han language would be strengthened by the presence of minority languages and cultures.[233]

Minority Writing Systems

In terms of written language, some minorities had well-established writing systems, for example the Mongolian, Tibetan, Uyghur, Kazakh, Korean, Russian, Kirghiz, Tartar and Xibo.[234] Those groups made up 35% to 40 % of the minority population in the early 1950s.[235] The Yi, Naxi, Miao, Jingpo, Lisu, Lagu and Wa also had their own writing systems, although these scripts were not in common use.[236] The remaining minorities did not have scripts.[237] As a response to the pressing requests of the minorities,[238] the central government launched a campaign to create and reform writing systems for the minorities.

This campaign involved two projects: creating new writing systems and reforming existing minority scripts. During this period, the campaign focused on using Roman or Cyrillic alphabets to create or reform phonetic writing systems

---

Script Reform in China", in Joshua Fishman (ed), *Advances in the Creation and Revision of Writing Systems* (Mouton The Hague Paris, 1977), pp. 121–148 at p. 135.

233 Regie Stites, "Chapter 4 Writing Cultural Boundaries: National Minority Language Policy, Literacy Planning, and Bilingual Education", in Gerard Postiglione (ed), *China's National Minority Education: Culture, Schooling, and Development* (Falmer Press, 1999), pp. 95–130 at p. 96.

234 Zhou Qingsheng, "Zhongsu jianguo chuqi shaoshu minzu wenzi chuangzhi bijiao [A Comparison of the Creation of Minority Writings between the Soviet Union and China]", 06 *Minzu Yuwen* [*Minority Languages of China*] (2002), p. 50; Zhou Minglang, *Multilingualism in China: the Politics of Writing Reforms for Minority Languages 1949–2002* (Mouton de Gruyter, 2003), p. 102; Wang Aiyun, "Zhonggong yu shaoshu minzu wenzi de chuangzhi he gaige [the CPC and the Language Creation and Reform for the Minorities]", 07 *Zhonggong Dangshi Yanjiu* [*Journal of Chinese Communist Party History Studies*] (2013), p. 73.

235 Guanyu bangzhu shangwu wenzi de inzu chuangli wenzi wenti de baogao [the Report on Assisting the Creation of Writing Systems for the Minorities That Did not Have Written Languages] (05/1954), in Jin Binghao (ed), supra note 120, at p. 515.

236 Ibid; Wang Aiyun, supra note 234, at p. 73.

237 Zhou Minglang has noted a distinction between linguistic/functional classification and political categorisation of minority writing systems. He argues that from pure linguistic/functional perspective, minority writing systems include: (1) commonly used writing systems with considerable publications; (2) commonly used writing systems with little publications; and (3) writing systems that were not commonly used, plus languages without writing systems. However, the categorisation at the First National Conference on Minority Education in 1951 was rather political, which divided minority writing systems into (a) commonly used languages; (b) incomplete/simple writing systems and (c) no writing systems. See Zhou Minglang, supra note 234, at p. 102.

238 Zhongyang renmin zhengfu zhengwuyuan guanyu minzu shiwu de jixiang jueding [the Decision of the Central People's Government Regarding the Ethnic work (05/02/1951)], in Jin Binghao (ed), supra note 120, at pp. 445–446.

(*zhuyin wenzi*), rather than using them as phonetic symbols for pronunciation (*zhuyin gongju*), as Romanisation was said to be the future of written language.[239] Mao repeatedly stated that "the Chinese script must be reformed along the common orientation, alphabetisation, of world writing systems" and "characters needed to be abandoned".[240] This campaign on minority written languages also had Soviet influence. Serdyuchenko, as a Soviet advisor and expert, actively engaged in the formulation of the draft plans for minority writing systems.[241]

In the process of creating new writing systems, the selection of the standard language was crucial.[242] Following the Soviet model, the base dialect and the standard pronunciation used by the communities in actual or potential political, economic and cultural centre were to be selected as the standard language.[243] The prestigious pronunciation that had been well accepted by the masses may also be an important factor to be considered.[244]

An example would be the creation of the Zhuang writing system. The Zhuang in the GZAR mainly spoke two dialects, the Northern dialect and the Southern dialect, which were not mutually intelligible.[245] The Zhuang communities had no political, economic and cultural centre, due to their population distribution.[246] Therefore, two writing systems, one for the North and one for the South, were proposed as the first draft.[247] This two-script proposal, however, was allegedly rejected by the Zhuang representatives. They argued that "the coexistence of two writing systems would hinder communication and unity among the Zhuang people".[248] It was finally agreed that only one writing system should be created for the Zhuang. The less diverse Northern dialect, which was used by two-thirds of the total Zhuang population, was selected as the base

239 Fu Maoji, "Bang zhu shaoshu minzu chuangli gaijin he gaige wenzi gongzuo de qingkuang he wenti [the Work of Assisting Minorities to Create, Improve and Reform Their Writing Systems and the Questions Therein]", 02 *Kexue Tongbao* [*Chinese Science Bulletin*] (1956), p. 27; Zhou Qingsheng, supra note 234, at p. 54.

240 Quoted in Zhou Minglang, supra note 234, at p. 199; John DeFrancis, "The Prospects for Chinese Writing Reform", 171 *Sino-Platonic Papers* (2006), p. 2.

241 Fu Maoji, supra note 239, at pp. 22–24; Zhou Minglang, supra note 234, at pp. 171, 177–179, 187–190, 199–201.

242 Zhou Minglang, supra note 234, at pp. 211–212.

243 Fu Maoji, supra note 239, at p. 26; Zhou Minglang, supra note 234, at pp. 212–213.

244 Ibid.

245 Li Xulian and Huang Quanxi, supra note 228, at p. 239.

246 Ibid, p. 241.

247 Ibid.

248 Ibid.

dialect.[249] The Shuanqiao phonological system became the standard pronunciation since it was geographically close to Nanning, the capital of the GZAR.[250] The draft Zhuang script was a hybrid alphabet, consisting of 21 Roman letters, 7 Cyrillic letters, 4 IPA and Arabic letters.[251] The new alphabetic Zhuang writing system quickly obtained the approval from the State Council and became the official written language of the Zhuang in 1957.[252] This new script, however, was not widely accepted in reality.[253] Since the pronunciation was the key in a phonetic writing system, the alphabetic Zhuang script based on the North dialect may sound like a foreign language to the speakers of other dialects.[254]

In the 1950s, 14 new writing systems were proposed for 11 minorities and were approved for experimental use by the State Ethnic Affairs Commission (SEAC).[255] Similar to spoken language, a minority group could also have more than one script.[256] For instance, four writing systems were proposed for the Miao group and different written languages were developed for the Dai and Yi communities in different areas.

Apart from the creation of new scripts for the minorities, some minority scripts were improved or reformed upon the requests of the minorities concerned.[257] The first improvement to the Dai scripts did not make major changes. However, under the advice of Serdyuchenko, the Dai scripts were fundamentally reformed.[258] Also upon aggressive recommendations of the Soviet linguists, the Mongolian, the Arabic writing systems of the Uyghur and Kazakh, and the scripts of the Kirgiz, Tatar, Uzbek and Xibo were reformed on the basis of Cyrillic alphabets.[259]

---

249 Ibid; Fu Maoji, supra note 239, at p. 26; Wei Xinglang, "Pinyin zhuangwen gaige yu xin fangkuai zhuangzi chuyi [Opinions on the Reform of the Zhuang Language Using Phonetic Alphabets and the New Zhuang Block Characters]", 06 *Zhongyang Minzu Daxue Xuebao* [*Journal of Central University for Nationalities* (*Philosophy and Social Science*)] (2012), p. 120.

250 Ibid.

251 Ibid; Wang Jun, "Zhuangwen chuangzhi he xiudingzhong de ruogan wenti [A Few Questions in the Creation and Revision of the Zhuang Writing System]", 05 *Minzu Yuwen* [*Minority Languages of China*] (1982), pp. 11–12.

252 Zhou Qingsheng, supra note 234, at p. 52.

253 Wei Xinglang, supra note 249.

254 Ibid, p. 122; Zhou Minglang, supra note 234, at p. 214.

255 Sun Hongkai, 2004, supra note 217, at p. 181.

256 Zhou Minglang, supra note 234, at p. 212; Zhou Qingsheng, supra note 234, at p. 55.

257 Fu Maoji, supra note 239, at pp. 22–23; Wang Aiyun, supra note 234, at p. 77.

258 A detailed discussion on the improvement of the Dai script, see Zhou Yaowen and Fang Fenghe, "Chapter 11 The Use and Development of Dai and Its Vernacular Writing System", in Zhou Minglang and Sun Hongkai (eds), supra note 217, pp. 201–218.

259 Zhou Minglang, supra note 234, at pp. 178–187; Fu Maoji, supra note 239, at pp. 22–24; Wang Aiyun, supra note 234, at pp. 77–78.

At this stage, the right of the minorities to language was not frequently exercised, as the focus of the minority linguistic work was placed on the creation and reform of minority writing systems. Minority linguistic activities were severely disrupted during the Cultural Revolution: the experimental use of the newly approved scripts was suspended; and the common speech (*Putonghua*)[260] became the only medium of instruction in education.[261]

(2) Language Policy in the New Era

Alongside the full restoration of social and economic orders after the Cultural Revolution, the policy in regard to minority languages and scripts shifted back to linguistic equality. A new round of language research and survey restarted in the late 1980s, and 30 more minority spoken languages were added to the official list.[262] Again, the standards/criteria applied in the identification process of minority languages have not been made publicly available. Meanwhile, traditional scripts of the minorities restored their status and the new writing systems resumed the experimental use in minority areas. Both writing systems were promoted by local governments via media, publication, school education and literacy campaigns. The enactment of the Law on REA and the approval of the Liangshan Yi script (the Sichuan Scheme) as an official writing system also contributed to the boost of minority scripts.[263] Assisting the minorities to create new scripts continued to be the guiding principle at the time,[264]

260 The Common Speech was the unified language that can be used nationwide for communication. It was not only above regional variations of the Han dialects, but also on top of all minority languages. It relied on the Beijing dialect as standard pronunciation, northern Chinese dialect as the base dialect, and modern vernacular classics language as grammatical norms. The promotion of *Putonghua* at first was considered to be the unification the Han language and thus only applied to the Han group, including those lived in minority areas. See the State Council, the Instruction on the Promotion of *Putonghua* (1956).

261 Teng Xing and Weng Yanheng, "Chapter 11 Bilingualism and Bilingual Education in China", in N. Ken. Shimahara, Ivan Z. Holowinsky and Saundra Tomlinson-Clarke (eds), *Ethnicity, Race and Nationality in Education: A Global Perspective* (Lawrence Erlbaum Associates, 2001), pp. 259–277 at p. 261; Hai Lu, "Zhongguo shaoshu minzu xinchuang wenzi de yuyan guihua jiqi shijian [Language Planning and the Practice of Newly Created Writing Systems for Ethnic Minority Languages in China]", 01 *Zhongyang Minzu Daxue Xuebao* [*Journal of Central University for Nationalities* (*Philosophy and Social Science*)] (2012), p. 142.

262 Sun Hongkai, Hu Zengyi and Huang Xing (eds), supra note 222, at p. 26.

263 Pu Zhongliang, "Chapter 14 Policies on the Planning and Use of the Yi Language and Writing System", in Zhou Minglang and Sun Hongkai (eds), supra note 217, pp. 257–275 at p. 259.

264 Ma Xiaoyi, "Shixi minzu yuwen zhengce dui shaoshu minzu xinchuang wenzi de yingxiang [Analysis of the Influence of Minority Language Policy on the New Words Created by Ethnic Minorities]", 04 *Minzu Jiaoyu Yanjiu* [*Journal of Research on Education for Minorities*] (2009), p. 13.

and as a result, two phonetic writing systems were created for the Tu and Qiang.[265]

Some minorities readopted traditional writing systems. In Xinjiang, the Arabic script resumed its status as the official language of the Uyghur and Kazakh. The new Romanised writing system promoted since 1965 was kept as pronunciation assistance.[266] Some other minorities also attempted to resume the use of their traditional writing systems. The Yi group in Sichuan reinvented a new syllabic writing system on the basis of the Classic Yi script and used the Romanised Yi writing system which was created in the 1950s as pronunciation symbols.[267]

However, the resumption of traditional minority scripts is not without problems. The Romanised writing systems have been popularised among the minorities for decades and have already been accepted by the new generations. The People's Congress of the Xishuangbanna Dai Autonomous Prefecture decided to resume the use of the traditional Dai script in 1986.[268] Although the continuous use of the Romanised (reformed) Dai was anticipated by the People's Congress, the complete replacement of the Romanised script by the traditional Dai script was very difficult. This reversal was not widely supported by the Dai communities, as two generations, the young and the middle-aged, received education in the Romanised script. The traditional writing system was completely new to them. It has been suggested that the Romanised Dai language is very likely to become the dominant script in schooling and publication, whilst the usage of the traditional Dai may be limited to Buddhist temples and religious circles.[269]

There seemed to be a policy turn on the minority scripts in the 1990s. The 1991 Decision of the State Council stated that writing systems that were widely accepted by the minorities would be promoted and further developed; as for the

---

265 Boler, "Wenhua ziben lilun shiye xia Tuzu Qiangzu yuyuan jiqi xinchuang wenzi shiyong yu fazhan yanjiu [Languages and New Writing Characters of Tu and Qiang Ethnic Groups: from Cultural Capital Theory]", 04 *Zhongyang Minzu Daxue Xuebao* [*Journal of Central University for Nationalities (Philosophy and Social Science)*] (2008), p. 119.

266 The People's Government of the XUAR, the Notice on Releasing "the Report on the Common Use of Uyghur and Kazak Old Scripts", No.283 [1982], http://www.xjyw.gov.cn/Web/Article.aspx?ArticleId=566, last visited on 25/06/2015.

267 Pu Zhongliang, supra note 263, at pp. 260–261.

268 The People's Congress of the Xishuangbanna Dai Autonomous Prefecture, the Decision of Using the Traditional Dai Writing System (1986), cited in Zhang Xisheng, "Written Language Reform and Regional Autonomy of Dai Nationality in Xishuangbanna", 16 *International Journal on Minority and Group Rights* (2009), p. 425.

269 Zhang Xisheng, ibid, pp. 426, 429–431; Zhou Yaowen and Fang Fenghe, supra note 258, at pp. 209–210, 215–216.

minorities who did not have their own scripts or did not have scripts in common use, they should be encouraged to choose from the commonly used scripts, be it the Han or minority written languages.[270]

In practice, apart from traditionally well established minority scripts, such as the Tibetan, Mongolian, and Arabic, the promotion of the newly created writing systems does not progress as expected. It has been reported that new writing systems created for the Hani, Wa, Miao (Western dialect), Miao (Middle dialect), Miao (Eastern dialect), Dong and Buyi have been widely accepted.[271] But except for the newly created Zhuang script, the performance of other new writing systems is far from satisfactory in the light of cultural function and daily usage. Many literacy campaigns have resorted to commonly used languages; newspapers and broadcasting in minority scripts have been suspended; and minority schools that use new scripts in teaching are confined to a limited extent.[272] Even the popularisation of the Romanised Zhuang script, which has been considered as the most successful new writing system, appears to be not that ideal.[273] It failed to win the support of the speakers of other Zhuang dialects, as the pronunciation is the key of a phonetic writing system.[274] In the new century, fewer documents and efforts have been made in relation to the newly created writing systems.[275]

Legal Provisions on Minority Languages

In the new era, the 1982 Constitution reinstated the right of the minorities to language. Article 4 states that "… all *minzu*(s) have the freedom to use and develop their own spoken and written languages …"[276] However, the Constitution also calls for the promotion, which replaced the term "implementation" in the draft Amendment, of the nationwide use of the Common Speech

270 The State Council, the Circular of the Report of the State Ethnic Affairs Commission on Further Improving Ethnic Language and Script Work, No.32 [1991].

271 Dehong Dai, Jingpo, Zaiwa and Lahu scripts were also welcomed. Sun Hongkai, 2004, supra note 217, at p. 184.

272 Zhao Jincan, "Yuyan taidu yu shaoshu minzu xinchuang wenzii de qianjing [Linguistic Attitude and the Prospect of Ethnic Newly-created Characters]", 05 *Beifang Minzu Daxue Xuebao* [*Journal of Beifang Ethnic University*] (2010), pp. 110–111; Hai Lu, supra note 261, at p. 143.

273 Wei Xinglang, supra note 249.

274 Wei Xinglang, supra note 249, at pp. 120, 122; Lan Liguo, "Tantan Zhuangwen fangan xiudingan zhong de yixie wenti [On the Problems of Emending Zhuang Language System]", 03 *Guangxi Shifan Xueyuan Xuebao* [*Journal of Guangxi Teachers Education University (Social Science)*] (2011), pp. 130–134.

275 Ma Xiaoyi, supra note 264, at p. 14.

276 The 1982 Constitution, Article 4.

(*Putonghua*).[277] According to the Law of the National Commonly Used Language and Script, *Putonghua* and Standardised Chinese Characters (SCC) are the national commonly used language and script.[278] The Law of the National Commonly Used Language and Script further requires the state to popularise the use of *Putonghua* and SCC and provides that it is the right, not obligation, of all citizens to learn and use the national commonly used language and script.[279] It also states that the promotion of *Putonghua* and SCC should not interfere with the right of the minorities to their own languages and scripts, the use of which should also be in accordance with the Constitution, the Law on REA and other laws.[280] Also, it has been argued that China does not have official language(s) (*guanfang yuyan*) as all ethnic languages and scripts are constitutionally equal.[281] The differences between *Putonghua* and SCC and minority languages and scripts lie in the scope of the application. *Putonghua* and SCC are the common languages that are used nationwide, whilst minority languages and scripts are regional languages that are used within particular areas.[282]

Autonomous agencies take the responsibility to guarantee the linguistic rights of the minorities.[283] When performing their duties, autonomous agencies should use one or more languages and scripts, which are designated as commonly used languages and scripts in the localities.[284] Local commonly used languages and scripts are confirmed by autonomy regulations.[285] In case there are two or more commonly used languages and scripts, the language and script of the minority that is exercising regional autonomy is regarded as the main language and script.[286] Hence, on the national level, a monolingual approach—the promotion of *Putonghua* and SCC—has been adopted, and at the regional level, a monolingual, bilingual or multilingual policy could be

277 Ibid, Article 19. See also Gao Jun and Du Xuewen, "'Yutongyin' yu renquan baozhang ['Language Unity' and the Safeguard of Human Rights: the Legal Analysis the Clause of 'Popularising *Putonghua* Nationwide']", 06 *Yanbian Daxue Xuebao* [*Journal of Yanbian University* (*Social Science*)] (2009), p. 155.

278 The Law of the National Commonly Used Language and Script, Article 2.

279 Ibid, Articles 3, 4.

280 Ibid, Articles 2, 3, 4, 8, 9–13.

281 Gao Jun and Du Xuewen, supra note 277, at p. 156.

282 Wang Peiying, "Guanyu yuyan de minzuxing yu shehuixing de guanxi wenti [the Relationship about Language Nationality and Sociality (the Relationship between Ethnic Feature and Social Feature of Languages)]", 01 *Heilongjiang Minzu Congkan* [*Heilongjiang National Series*] (2002), pp. 94–95.

283 The Law on REA, Article 10.

284 Ibid, Article 21.

285 Ibid. In practice, local commonly used languages and scripts are usually recognised by special regulations.

286 Ibid.

pursued, depending on regional provisions on the local commonly used language and script. Most autonomous areas are bilingual or multilingual, using minority language(s) and script(s) as well as *Putonghua* and SCC. In the Yanbian Korean Autonomous Prefecture, the Korean and *Putonghua* and SCC are commonly used.[287] The Korean is further designated as the main language and script in the prefecture.[288]

A few facts are worth noting in regard to the language rights of the minorities. First, as none of the five autonomous regions has passed autonomy regulation, the provisions on local commonly used languages and scripts have been passed as special regulations.[289] Although some autonomous areas have clearly specified minority languages as the local commonly used languages, autonomous agencies can also use *Putonghua* and SCC when performing their duties.[290] In addition, many autonomy regulations and special regulations fail to distinguish the Han language and script from *Putonghua* and SCC. Those documents usually state that the minority languages and the Han language should be used for public purpose.[291]

Not all minority languages and scripts can be designated as local commonly used languages and scripts. There are conditions that need to be met. A local commonly used language must be a language that has been recognised by the state. Dialects, thus, are excluded. Amongst all minority languages, the Mongolian, Tibetan, Uyghur, Kazakh, Korean, Zhuang, and Yi (the Liangshan

287 The Autonomy Regulation of the Yanbian Korean Autonomous Prefecture, 2007, Article 18.

288 Ibid.

289 The XUAR Regulation on the Language and Script Work, 2002; the TAR Regulation on the Study, Use and Development of the Tibetan Language, 2002; the IMAR Regulation on the Language and Script Work, 2004.

290 The TAR Regulation on the Study, Use and Development of the Tibetan Language, Articles 1, 3, 4, 5; the IMAR Regulation on the Language and Script Work, Article 2.

291 From the materials that have been collected, only Tibet and Yunan have used the terms *Putonghua* and SCC in relevant documents, rather than referencing to "the Han language", alongside the minority languages, See the TAR Regulation on the Study, Use and Development of the Tibetan Language, Articles 1, 3–6; the XUAR Regulation on the Language and Script Work, Articles 7–12; the Yunnan Regulation on Minority Language and Script work, 2013, Articles 2, 10,11; the Regulation on Language and Script Work in the Liangshan Yi Autonomous Prefecture, 2009, Articles 2, 4; the Autonomy Regulation of the Liangshan Yi Autonomous Prefecture, 2007, Articles 20, 23; the Regulation on Language and Script Work in the Yanbian Korean Autonomous Prefecture, 2004, Article 2; the Autonomy Regulation of Yanbian Korean Autonomous Prefecture, 2007, Articles 18, 54; the Autonomy Regulation of the Tianzhu Tibetan Autonomous County, 2007, Article 15; the Regulation on Language and Script Work in the Tianzhu Tibetan Autonomous County, 1999, Articles 3, 4; the Regulation on Language and Script Work in the Ebian Yi Autonomous County, 1995, Articles 2, 4.

scheme) seem to be on this prestigious list. Those languages, together with *Putonghua*, become the working languages of the NPC and the National Committee of the Chinese People's Political Consultative Conference.[292] The same recognition requirement also applies to minority scripts. Only official writing systems, which have been approved by the State Council, can be chosen as the local commonly used script. Zhou Minglang argues that minority writing systems can be categorised into three groups: official scripts, experimental scripts and unofficial scripts.[293] Up to date, an estimated list of the official minority scripts includes the Mongolian, Tibetan, Uyghur, Kazakh, Korean, Zhuang, Yi (Liangshan), Dehong Dai, Jingpo, Zaiwa, Hani, Lagu, Miao (Chuandianqian) and Wa.[294] Furthermore, the exercise of the language rights is associated with autonomous agencies, as the status of being "local commonly used language" is established by autonomous legislation. This makes the establishment of an autonomous unit another prerequisite. Therefore, the minorities residing outside of autonomous areas can freely use minority languages and scripts in private life, but may not assert it as a working language in public sectors.

Language Use in Public Service

As discussed above, autonomous agencies should use local commonly used languages and scripts in regard to public service. Local commonly used languages and scripts are also the working languages and scripts of the courts and procuratorates in autonomous areas.[295] Those who are not familiar with local commonly used languages and scripts are entitled to interpreters in court proceedings.[296] Although legal provisions do not specify the minority representation ratio in the people's governments, when recruiting government officials, proper consideration should be given to the members of the minority that is exercising autonomy as well as members of other minorities in the area.[297] The judicial system is required to equip with a reasonable number of personnel

292 Wang Peiying, supra note 282, at p. 95.

293 Zhou Minglang, "Chapter 5 Minority Language Policy in China: Equality in Theory and Inequality in Practice", in Zhou Minglang and Sun Hongkai (eds), supra note 217, pp. 71–95 at pp. 81–84.

294 According to Zhou Minglang, the Russian, Xibo, Uzbek and Tartar were included in the list of commonly used writing systems in the 1950s. However, the status of the Xibo writing system is not clear, as the Chabuchaer Xibo Autonomous County made no regulations on the usage of the Xibo language. See Zhou Minglang, ibid, p. 82; http://www.chinanews.com/cul/2011/05-14/3040728.shtml, last visited on 25/10/2016.

295 The Law on REA, Article 47.

296 Ibid, Articles 21, 47; the 1982 Constitution, Article 139.

297 The Law on REA, Articles 17, 18, 22.

who are proficient in commonly used languages in the locality.[298] Similar provisions can be found in many autonomy regulations and special regulations.[299] In the recruitment of public officials, the TAR gives priority to those who are proficient in the Tibetan and national commonly used language and script.[300] According to the Autonomy Regulation of the Liangshan Yi Autonomous Prefecture, all government departments of the Prefecture should be reasonably equipped with personnel from the Yi or other minorities.[301]

However, the general practice of autonomous agencies suggests a different situation. In the XUAR, only 10% of 2069 official documents issued by three state departments were written in Uyghur in 1993.[302] Recently in Tibet, the government documents issued in SCC have outnumbered those written in Tibetan, due to the shortage of qualified translators.[303] Furthermore, none of the LPCs of five autonomous regions has an official website in the minority script, and only the governments of the XUAR and IMAR maintain separate versions of the official websites in minority languages.

The law further encourages cadres with different ethnic origins to learn each other's languages and scripts.[304] Officers who can proficiently use two or more local commonly used languages and scripts will be awarded.[305] As early as the 1950s, Mao emphasised that the Han cadres working in minority areas must learn local minority languages and scripts and all cadres should learn *Putonghua*.[306] This policy appeared to be welcomed by the Han cadres who worked in minority areas, considering the political and ethnic situation at the

298 Ibid, Article 47.

299 The TAR Regulation on the Study, Use and Development of the Tibetan Language, Articles 5, 10; the Autonomy Regulation of the Liangshan Yi Autonomous Prefecture, Article 18; the Autonomy Regulation of the Yanbian Korean Autonomous Prefecture, Articles 16, 20; the Autonomy Regulation of the Dehong Dai and Jingpo Autonomous Prefecture, Articles 17, 18, 20.

300 The TAR Regulation, ibid, Article 10.

301 The Autonomy Regulation of the Liangshan Yi Autonomous Prefecture, Article 18.

302 Zhou Minglang, supra note 293, at p. 85.

303 Zhou Maocao, "Chapter 12 The Use and Development of Tibetan in China", in Zhou Minglang and Sun Hongkai (eds), supra note 217, pp. 221–237 at p. 233.

304 The Law on REA, Article 49.

305 Ibid.

306 Mao Zedong, Xinjiang yao zuohao jingji gongzuo he zengqiang minzu tuanjie [Xinjiang Should Develop Economy and Enhance National Unity (1963)], http://dangshi.people.com.cn/GB/138903/13241049.html, last visited 25/12/2013. See also Mao Zedong, "Sixty Points On Working Methods (Draft)", cited in Gao Qirong and Li Jiang, "Mao Zedong <gongzuo fangfa liushitiao (caoan)> luelun [A General Discussion of Mao Zedong's Sixty Points On Working Methods (Draft)]", 01 *Dangshi Yanjiu yu Jiaoxue* [*Party History Research & Teaching*] (2008), p. 52; also cited in Sun Hongkai, 2004, supra note 217, at p. 196.

time.[307] Since the 1980s onwards, the enthusiasm of minority cadres to learn *Putonghua* and SCC as their political assets continues, whilst fewer Han cadres are willing to learn minority languages and scripts. Even though it is not an established principle, the top officials in regional Party apparatus, in most cases, are the Han. They are usually reallocated to another place after serving certain time in one locality. The mobility of the party officials objectively prevents them from learning one specific local minority language. The TAR imposes an obligation upon the Han, Tibetan and other minority cadres to learn Tibetan and national commonly used language and script.[308] But the doubts arise in terms of to what extent this provision will be implemented, particularly its applicability to the Han Party members.

Language Use in Education

The implications of the language policy are unclear in terms of minority education, swinging between the integrationism and accommodationism.[309] This might explain why there exist two opposite arguments relating to the purpose of minority education.[310] Some scholars believe that the final purpose of gradually introducing the dominant language as the medium of instruction is to facilitate the integration of minority students into the dominant culture. Others argue that minority education should target preserving ethnic culture and identity, whilst at the same time being proficient in the dominant language. The purpose of minority education in China appears to have adopted an accommodationist approach, as the law emphasises the protection of the rights of minorities to develop and use their languages and scripts as well as the promotion of the general use of *Putonghua* and SCC.[311] The Law on REA, in particular, states:

> [s]chools (classes) and other educational organisations recruiting mostly minority students should, whenever possible, use textbooks in their own languages and use these languages as the media of instruction. Beginning in the lower or senior grades of primary school, the Han language and literature modules shall be taught to popularise *Putonghua* and SCC.[312]

---

307 Sun Hongkai, ibid.

308 The TAR Regulation on the Study, Use and Development of the Tibetan Language, Article 8.

309 Regie Stites, supra note 233, at p. 103.

310 Regie Stites, ibid; Li Ruzhong, "Lun shuangyu jiaoyu de moshi [A Study on the Mode of Bilingual Education in Xinjiang]", 01 *Xinjiang Jiaoyu Xueyuan Xuebao* [*Journal of Xinjiang Education Institute*] (2011), pp. 25–26.

311 Regie Stites, ibid.

312 The Law on REA, Article 37.

By law, all citizens have the right, rather than an obligation, to learn and use national commonly used language and script.[313] Whether a minority student has a choice of avoiding the curriculum modules on the Han language and literature would be the crucial question in practice.

In accordance with the law and state guidelines on education, autonomous agencies reserve the right to manage local educational affairs, including educational plans, educational systems, curricula, establishment of schools, language for instruction, and enrolment procedures.[314] The selection of language for instruction should consider the following factors: the majority will of the population, local linguistic circumstances, the long-term development of the minorities, the improvement of education quality and the promotion of ethnic scientific and cultural exchange.[315] This, therefore, leads to enormous variances from region to region.[316] Bilingual education is the mainstream of compulsory education in minority areas, which involves minority languages and scripts as well as *Putonghua* and SCC as the media of instruction.[317]

In general, there are two school models in autonomous areas: compulsory education is conducted in separate schools for the minorities and the Han; and there is only one school with different classes for the minorities and the Han.[318] Students can freely decide between minority schools/classes and Han schools/classes.[319] Despite the provision that individuals with different ethnic origins are encouraged to learn each other's languages and scripts,[320] bilingual education is, to a certain extent, rather limited in schools/classes for the Han students. For minority schools/classes, learning *Putonghua* and SCC is necessary, whilst learning minority languages and scripts is not compulsory for the Han students.

313 The Law of the National Commonly Used Language and Script, Article 4.

314 The Law on REA, Article 36.

315 The State Education Commission and the State Ethnic Affairs Commission, Guanyu jiaqiang minzu jiaoyu gongzuo ruoggan wenti de yijian [the Opinion on a Few Questions of Enhancing the Ethnic Education Work] (1992), Section 4.

316 Regie Stites, supra note 233, at p. 104.

317 The TAR Regulation on the Study, Use and Development of the Tibetan Language, Article 6; the XUAR Regulation on the Language and Script Work, Articles 18, 19; the Autonomy Regulation of the Yanbian Korean Autonomous Prefecture, Article 54; the Autonomy Regulation of the Dehong Dai and Jingpo Autonomous Prefecture, Article 51.

318 Li Ruzhong, supra note 310, at p. 29.

319 The XUAR Regulation on Language and Script Work, Article 20. See also Pu Zhongliang, supra note 263, at pp. 264–265.

320 The TAR Regulation on the Study, Use and Development of the Tibetan Language, Article 8; the XUAR Regulation on Language and Script Work, Article 17; the Autonomy Regulation of the Yanbian Korean Autonomous Prefecture, Article 55.

Regardless of regional complexity and viability, minority bilingual education shares some features in common. According to the extent of the use of mother tongues and the timing of introducing *Putonghua* into schooling, educational bilingualism can be classified into four types: 1) minority language is used as the main medium of instruction in elementary and secondary schools, plus *Putonghua* and the Han literature as separate modules offered to lower or senior grades in primary schools; 2) some modules are taught in the mother tongues of the minorities, while other modules use *Putonghua* as the language for instruction in compulsory schooling, with varying proportions of the use of two languages; 3) elementary schools start teaching in minority languages while emphasising the learning of *Putonghua*, and then progressively change to *Putonghua* as the medium of instruction in senior grades; 4) *Putonghua* is the language for instruction with separate modules offered on minority languages and scripts.[321]

All four patterns of bilingual education could be found in Xinjiang. In the Hetian area of the XUAR, where the Uyghur account for 96% of the population,[322] some minority schools have traditional classes that use Uyghur as the language for instruction and offer modules on *Putonghua* and SCC.[323] Some other minority schools introduce experimental classes which offer more courses taught in *Putonghua*, but still adhere to the minority language as the main medium of instruction.[324] On the other hand, the Han schools in the cities and towns that have equal enrolment rates of the Han and minority students also include two types of schooling: *Putonghua* as the language for instruction with separate modules on minority languages, and *Putonghua* as the language for instruction with some courses taught in minority languages.[325] However, Gladney notes that although Uyghur has been offered as the language for instruction in elementary and secondary schools, Uyghur history and traditional culture have been downplayed in the state schools.[326]

321 Zhou Qingsheng, "Zhongguo shuangyu jiaoyu leixing [Models of Bilingual Education in China]", 03 *Minzu Yuwen [Minority Languages of China]* (1991), pp. 66–67; Regie Stites, supra note 233, at pp. 107–110; Li Ruzhong, supra note 310, at pp. 29–31; Li Fengjuan et al., "Liangshan Yizu zizhizhou Yi Han shuangyu jiaoxue shixiaoxing tanxi [Analysis of Effectiveness of Bilingual Teaching of Yi and Chinese Languages in the Liangshan Yi Autonomous Prefecture]", 03 *Minzu Jiaoyu Yanjiu [Journal of Research on Education for Ethnic Minorities]* (2011), p. 102.

322 The Xinjiang Statistical Yearbook, 2012, Chapter 3–7.

323 Li Ruzhong, supra note 310, at p. 29.

324 Ibid.

325 Ibid, pp. 29–31.

326 Dru Gladney, *Dislocating China: Reflections on Muslims, Minorities, and Other Subaltern Subjects* (Hurst and Company, 2004), p. 221.

A new policy of bilingual education has been introduced in the XUAR, which explicitly sets out two models for bilingual education in the region. According to the First Model, the core modules for the school entrance examination are taught in *Putonghua* and SCC, and the rest of the courses are taught in minority languages and scripts.[327] In the Second Model, all of the classes are taught in *Putonghua* and SCC, except for the modules on minority language and script.[328] Physical education, music and fine arts can also be taught in minority languages, if the local conditions are not fit. From 2010 onwards, if minority pupils have received bilingual education in pre-school, the Second Model should be adopted in the cities and counties, starting from the first grade of elementary school, unless the conditions are considered not to be fit. In areas where the minorities are concentrated, apart from bilingual education, the department of education at the county level may decide to retain classes using minority languages as the main media of instruction for the students and their parents to choose.

This policy, however, has been revised by the 13th Five-Year Plan for Educational Development of the XUAR, which states that, starting from the 2017 fall semester, *Putonghua* and SCC should be used in the first year of education in elementary and secondary schools.[329] It is not clear to what extent the 13th Five-Year Plan has replaced the previous two models for bilingual education, as it fails to clarify the relationship between bilingual education and "using *Putonghua* and SCC as the media of instruction in full scale".[330] In the meantime, the XUAR has endeavoured to provide full access to bilingual education in pre-schools since 2005, by incorporating pre-school bilingual education into the basic public service system. During the period 2011—2015, the pre-school

327 In elementary schools, the Han literature, mathematics, science, and information technology are instructed in *Putonghua* and SCC; in secondary schools, the Han literature, foreign language, mathematics, physics, chemistry, biology, and information technology are taught in *Putonghua* and SCC; and in high schools, the Han literature, foreign language, mathematics, physics, chemistry, biology, information technology, and General Technology use *Putonghua* and SCC as the medium of instruction. See the People's Government of the XUAR, the XUAR Development Plan of Minority Bilingual Education for Pre-schools, Primary Schools and Middle Schools 2010–2020 (31/03/2011), Section 3, Principle 8, available at http://www.xjedu.gov.cn/xjjyt/jyzt/xqjywlxz/xqsyzc/2013/60171.htm, last accessed on 05/04/2018.

328 Ibid.

329 The 13th Five-Year Plan for Educational Development of the XUAR, 2017, Section 9.

330 Ibid. Section 9 includes three topics: [trans. L.W.] the first is to "improve and enhance the use of *Putonghua* and SCC in teaching"; the second is about "improving the quality of bilingual education"; and the third is to "emphasise the management and leadership of bilingual education".

enrollment rates increased to 74.31%, and the pre-schools that offer bilingual education account for 78.67%.[331] The introduction of a bilingual pre-school programme would promote access to education for members of the minorities, especially to higher education, and facilitate the accommodation of the minorities. The Second Model, however, overemphasises *Putonghua* and SCC in the educational programmes and provides for less access to acquire knowledge of the minority languages and cultures, which would lead to the assimilation of the minorities into the dominant culture. How preserving minority culture and identity while opening up pathways for the participation of the minorities in wider society becomes the central issue in the process of promoting bilingual school systems in the XUAR.[332]

In the Liangshan Yi Prefecture, bilingual education has two models.[333] Model A uses Yi as the language for instruction from primary schools to high schools and merely offers modules on *Putonghua* and SCC. Model B, on the contrary, relies on *Putonghua* for instruction and uses national standard textbooks, offering separate modules on the Yi language and script. Model A is usually promoted in the Yi concentrated areas where Yi is used as the common language, and Model B tends to be found in the cities and towns where *Putonghua* has a popular basis.[334] Students are said to have two opportunities, upon graduation from primary school and secondary school, to choose between Model A and Model B, according to their own needs and preferences.[335]

Bilingual education of the Yi communities in Yunnan and Guizhou mainly adopts Model B.[336] The scattered distribution of the Yi population and the difficulty of learning the Yi script that is based on the standard pronunciation are the possible explanations.[337] Recent research also shows that young people of the

---

331 The 13th Five-Year Plan for Educational Development of the XUAR, 2017, Section 1.

332 Concluding Observations of the CERD on the 8th and 9th Reports of China, A/56/18(SUPP), 2001, para.245; Concluding Observations of the CERD on the 10th to 13th Reports of China, CERD/C/CHN/CO/10-13, para.22; Gay McDougall, Report of the Independent Expert on Minority Issues, Recommendations of the Forum on Minority Issues (2008), A/HRC/10/11/Add.1, para.5.

333 Li Fengjuan et al., supra note 321; Zhu Wenxu and Xiao Xue, "Yizu diqu shaungyu jiaoyu leixing xianzhuang yanjiu [A Study on the Present Situation of Bilingual Education Types in Yi Nationality Areas]", 05 *Minzu Jiaoyu Yanjiu* [*Journal of Research on Education for Ethnic Minorities*] (2005), p. 87.

334 Li Fengjuan et al., ibid, p. 104; Jia Min and Xiong Tingting, "Meiguo yindi'an he woguo Yi zu shuangyu jiaoyu duibi fenxi [A Comparative Study of the Impact of State Language Policy on Bilingual Education of Native American and Chinese Ethnic Yi]", 03 *Mianyang Shifan Xueyuan Xuebao* [*Journal of Mianyang Normal University*] (2008), p. 119.

335 Pu Zhongliang, supra note 263, at pp. 264–265.

336 Zhu Wenxu and Xiao Xue, supra note 333, at pp. 89–90.

337 Ibid.

minorities are inclined to move from rural to urban areas, for education, jobs, or a better life.[338] Hence, the parents of minority students would preferably send their children to the schools/classes that use *Putonghua* as the medium of instruction, considering the future development of their children.[339] The Yi students that enrol in programmes of Model B have outnumbered the students in the schools of Model A.[340] It has been reported that minority schools/classes in the IMAR and XUAR have witnessed a significant decline in the student enrolment.[341] Social and economic factors, such as the opportunities for higher education and job prospects, would indeed affect the educational preference of minority parents.

The annual college entrance examination is available in a limited number of minority languages and scripts, namely the Mongolian, Korean, Tibetan, Uyghur, Kazakh, Kirgiz, and Yi.[342] Except for educational departments or majors in minority languages and scripts, the majority of higher education institutions use *Putonghua* as the language for instruction. In order to promote access to higher education for the minorities, Chinese law provides preferential treatment for minority students.[343] First, the state should set up special institutions for the minorities (*minzu yuanxiao*) or offer them foundation courses (*minzu yuke ban*) in non-minority institutions. Minority students can be recruited from specific areas and then assigned jobs back in those areas after graduation. Second, higher education institutions and secondary technical schools should appropriately adjust admission standards and requirements for minority students. The measures that can be taken include priority admission, quotas for the minorities, and more commonly, awarding minority students extra points in the overall grade. Special consideration should be given to the students from minority groups with less population. The affirmative action policy varies from region to region. It has been suggested that the enrolment of minority students in higher education has increased considerably in recent years.[344] In 2013, the numbers of minority post-graduate and undergraduate students increased to

338 Robyn Iredale and Fei Guo, "Chapter 1 Overview of Minority Migration", in Robyn Iredale, Naran Bilik, and Fei Guo (eds), *China's Minorities on the Move: Selected Case Studies* (M. E. Sharpe, 2003), pp. 3–31 at pp. 15–16.

339 Ibid, pp. 26–27.

340 Li Fengjuan et al., supra note 321, at p. 104.

341 Teng Xing and Weng Yanheng, supra note 261, at p. 269.

342 Pu Zhongliang, supra note 263, at p. 265.

343 The Law on REA, Article 71; Ao Junmei, "Geti pingdeng, yihuo qunti pingdeng [Individual Equality or Groups Equality: Admission Policy for Minority Students in Chinese Higher Education]", 06 *Qinghua Daxue Jiaoyu Yanjiu* [*Tsinghua Journal of Education*] (2006), p. 71.

344 Wang Su, "Chapter 2 Minority Movement and Education", in Robyn Iredale, Naran Bilik, and Fei Guo (eds), supra note 338, pp. 32–50 at pp. 39–40.

1,844,503 and 107,392 respectively.[345] However, the measures of preferential treatment are not evaluated on an individual basis, but are equally applied to all minority students that meet the prescribed conditions. In terms of preferential treatment in higher education, the abuse of such minority benefits by the Han or privileged minority students has also created tensions in practice.[346]

The recruitment tests for national and local civil service are also in SCC, with exceptions in the IMAR and XUAR where the recruitment tests are available in two scripts—Mongolian/Uyghur and SCC.[347] Minority applicants in the XUAR, who use SCC to answer questions during the test, are awarded extra points in the overall grade.[348] In the NHAR, the Hui applicants were entitled to extra 10 points in the recruitment tests, which ensured that the recruitment rate of the Hui was approximately 10 % higher than their application rate.[349] Under the new policy, all minority applicants will be awarded an extra 5 points so as to achieve *de facto* ethnic equality in the public sectors in the NHAR.[350] Although preferential treatment for the minorities in the recruitments tests is common practice,[351] the knowledge of *Putonghua* and SCC in a way constitutes a precondition in the recruitment of civil servants.

Language Use in Business and Other Aspects

Autonomous legislation normally provides that public signs, posters and commercial advertising should be in minority scripts and SCC.[352] This suggests that the sole use of minority scripts in business is not allowed. But in practice, such principles are not strictly applied. In minority cities or towns, bilingual signs,

---

345 The 14th-17th Periodic Reports Submitted by China under Article 9 of the ICERD, CERD/C/CHN/14-17, 2017, p. 13, para.74.

346 Teng Xing and Ma Xiaoyi, "Zhongguo gaodeng jiaoyu de shaoshu minzu youhui zhengce yu jiaoyu pingdeng [China's Preferential Policy to Minority Nationalities in Higher Education and Education Equality]", 05 *Minzu Yanjiu* [*Ethno-National Studies*] (2005), pp. 13, 16.

347 Neimenggu zizhi qu dangzeng qun jiguan he canzhao gongwuyuan fa guanli danwei 2012 nian kaoshi luyong gongwuyuan he gongzuo renyuan jianzhang [the Admission Memorandum of the IMAR Civil Service Recruitment Test (2012)], http://www.impta.com/dangzhengqungwy/2013121113921.asp, last visited on 25/12/2013; the Announcement of the XUAR on Civil Service Recruitment Test, 2013, http://www.xjrs.gov.cn/show_files.asp?ArticleID=8541, last visited on 25/12/2013.

348 The Announcement of the XUAR on Civil Service Recruitment Test, ibid.

349 The NHAR Office for the Recruitment of Civil Servants, Questions and Answers in relation to the Adjustment of the Policy for the Recruitment tests of Civil Servants, Q/As 1 and 5, http://www.nxpta.gov.cn/gwyks/201803/t20180323_4477462.html, last visited on 15/05/2018.

350 Ibid, Q/As 1 and 4.

351 The Law on REA, Article 22.

352 The TAR Regulation on the Study, Use and Development of the Tibetan Language, Articles 11, 12; the XUAR Regulation on Language and Script Work, Article 9; the Regulation on

posters and commercial advertising are used, whilst in less developed areas where the minorities live in concentrated communities, minority script sometimes is the only language that appears in the names or signs of business.

Those autonomous regulations, however, are only effective within autonomous areas. Outside of autonomous areas, according to the Law of the National Commonly Used Language and Script, SCC should be used as the basic characters in the sectors of public service.[353] This national law also allows for the usage of foreign languages in public signs, posters and commercial advertising, if the need for providing public service so requires.[354] Since SCC is not the sole script to be used in the sectors of public service, similar to foreign languages, minority scripts can also be used together with SCC in business and the sectors of public service. The Tibetan street in Chengdu, where both Tibetan and SCC (and sometimes English) are used in business, is a good illustration.

It is the responsibility of autonomous agencies to assist the minorities to develop minority literature, art, publishing, broadcasting, film industry, and other cultural undertakings.[355] The people's governments at all levels are obligated to financially support the compilation, translation and publication of teaching materials and other publications in minority scripts.[356] Radio stations are widely established in minority areas, broadcasting in Korean, Mongolian, Tibetan, Uyghur, Kazakh, Zhuang, Dehong Dai, Lisu, Jingpo, Lagu, Yi, Miao and Buyi.[357] Radio programmes in minority languages have flourished after the Cultural Revolution, with over 200 radio stations using more than 25 minority languages to broadcast.[358] China National Radio has programmes available in Tibetan, Mongolian, Uyghur, Kazakh, Korean, Zhuang, Yi and Dai.[359]

Language and Script Work in the Liangshan Yi Autonomous Prefecture, Articles 23, 24; the Autonomy Regulation of the Liangshan Yi Autonomous Prefecture, Article 20; the Regulation on Language and Script Work in the Yanbian Korean Autonomous Prefecture, Article 9.

353 The Law of the National Commonly Used Language and Script, Articles 13, 14.

354 Ibid, Article 13.

355 The Law on REA, Article 38.

356 Ibid, Articles 37, 38.

357 Bai Runsheng, "Woguo shaoshu minzu yuyan guangbo de lishi yange, diwei yu zuoyong [the Historic Status and Functions of the Broadcasting in Minority Languages]", 17 *Xinwen Aihaozhe* [*Journalism Lover*] (2012), pp. 4–5.

358 Ibid, p. 5.

359 Ibid; Li Qianlan and Wang Handong, "Gaige kaifang yilai zhongguo shaoshu minzu guangbo yingshi shiye de fazhan yu sikao [the Development of Broadcasting and Television Programmes in Minority Languages Since the Reform and Opening Up]", 03 *Hubei Shehui Kexue* [*Hubei Social Sciences*] (2013), p. 191.

Television stations and centres programming in minority languages are also established, although the number of minority languages involved are limited. In 2008, approximately 800, 000, 000 RMB was invested by the state to construct and maintain radio and television networks in minority areas and to translate programmes into minority languages.[360] Furthermore, in the new era of information technology, the standardisation of minority scripts is promoted, focusing on the coding of the widely used and well established minority scripts, such as Tibetan, Mongolian, Uyghur (new and traditional scripts), Kazakh, Kirgiz, Korean, Yi and Dai (Dehong and Xishuang banna).[361] The remaining minority languages, however, have not received equal treatment in terms of state attention and funding.

To summarise, both the law and policy emphasise linguistic equality as a component of ethnic equality in China. According to Chinese law, the minorities have the right to use and develop their spoken and written languages. But the minority language rights are articulated as group rights. Individual right to language appears to be neglected in the authoritative discourse. Put differently, unless a minority group has successfully established its own autonomous authority, they may not be able to claim such rights in the area which is dominated by the Han or other minorities. Also, the bigger the autonomous area is, the easier the language right can be achieved. Such a practice leads to different treatment among the minorities. The minorities that have more bargaining power will receive more privileges in terms of the language rights. Different communities from one minority group may also be treated differently. Conversely, the language policy of the CPC would cause internal divisions within the minorities. The identification of minority languages/dialects and the selection of the standard pronunciation for creating and reforming the scripts can cause linguistic divisions inside the minorities or, in a worse scenario, create internal tension between different communities of one particular minority group. For example, the standard pronunciation of the Bai language, which is based on the Xiguan dialect, has not been accepted by other Bai communities.[362] As *Putonghua* and SCC are widely promoted and accepted nationwide, the national commonly used language and script will possibly be the medium for inter-ethnic and intra-ethnic communication.

---

360 Li Qianlan and Wang Handong, ibid, p. 193.

361 Dai Hong, "Zhongguo shaoshu minzu wenzi xinxi jishu biaozhunhua licheng [the Progress of the Information Technology Standardisation of Chinese Minority Scripts]", 06 *Xinxi Jishu yu Biaozhun Hua* [*Information Technology & Standardisation*] (2011), pp. 8–9.

362 Wang Feng, "Lun yuyan zai zuqun rentong zhong de diwei he biaoxian xingshi [the Role and Expressive Forms of Language in Ethnic Identity]", 04 *Yunnan Shifan Daxue Xuebao* [*Journal of Yunnan Normal University* (*Humanities and Social Sciences*)] (2010), p. 77.

6.3 Concluding Remarks

Chinese law respects for and promotes the right to freedom of religion. Its implementation, however, differentiates institutional religions from other belief systems. Thus, the right of the minorities to profess and practise their beliefs is regulated differently. The minorities who practise institutional religions are subject to many restrictions. "Normal" practice of institutional religions is confined to activities that take place in religious places and are conducted by the clergy and the believers themselves, who are politically loyal to the CPC. Minority belief systems, on the other hand, fall out of the scope of the regulatory supervision scheme, as they are professed and practised as part of minority culture. Such beliefs are practised in a more liberal way. Different treatment of religious minorities apparently does not conform to the obligations that China has undertaken under the ICESR, ICCPR and ICERD in regard to the equal enjoyment of religious rights.[363] In addition, the prohibition of party members to profess and practise religion constitutes an exclusion based on political opinions.[364]

Arguably, the Chinese government has adopted a tolerant attitude towards individual freedom to choose language/dialect and script to express oneself in private life. However, the right to use minority languages in public sectors, such as in education and other aspects, is associated with autonomous agencies. It emphasises the collective nature of the right, and thus neglects the individual rights of minority members to language. Although bilingual education is the mainstream of compulsory education in minority areas, it seems that less attention has been paid to the teaching of minority culture and history.

To sum up, Chinese law recognises the rights of the minorities to religious belief and language.[365] It then obligates autonomous agencies to protect and promote the exercise of such rights.[366] The minorities that do not have their own autonomous authorities are particularly vulnerable to discrimination and denial of fundamental rights and freedoms. Neither the Constitution nor the Law on REA incorporates a meaningful remedial procedure to ensure the implementation of relevant provisions. In the meantime, human rights conventions are not directly enforceable in Chinese courts. Transforming international human rights law into domestic law and amending Chinese law accordingly, thus, would be crucial to the full realisation of the rights recognised.

---

363 ICESR, Articles 2, 15 (1) (a); ICCPR, Article 27; ICERD, Article 5.
364 ICESR, Article 2.
365 The 1982 Constitution, Articles 4, 36.
366 The Law on REA, Articles 10, 11.

Conclusion

This book has examined the rights of China's minorities from the perspective of self-determination. It has considered the definition of "peoples" and the meaning of self-determination in relation to different ethnic groups in China, paying special attention to the REA system as a constitutional arrangement for the minorities to exercise the right to self-determination within the state. The first three chapters dealt with the practice of self-determination in the Chinese context as the basis for an independent statehood. Chapter 1 looked at different definitions of the Chinese nation (people) and their corresponding implications for the minorities in the proposed modern state of China. Chapter 2 examined the application of the political principle of self-determination in China's transformation from a civilisation to a modern state and its influences on the invention of the Chinese nation. Chapter 3 looked at the exercise of the right to self-determination in China, examining the official approach to internal and external self-determination and the rival self-determination claims made by particular groups.

The next three chapters focused on the REA system as the institutional accommodation for China's minorities to exercise internal self-determination. Chapter 4 examined the first three elements of the REA system: regions, minorities, and autonomous agencies. Chapter 5 looked at the legislative and financial autonomy of the minorities as provided by Chinese law, and Chapter 6 dealt with minority cultural rights from religious and linguistic perspectives, through a thorough examination of relevant domestic laws and international norms.

Overall, this study provides an insight into the ethnic issues in contemporary China, by examining the principle of self-determination in shaping China's ethnic grouping and appraising the rights of the minorities and their limits. In doing so, the book has intended to answer the questions of how those policies and laws have come to be, why they are problematic, and what can be done to promote minority rights in China.

1 China's Practice of Self-determination and Minority Rights

Since the 18th century, many theories with diverse origins and focuses have been developed in regard to the political principle of self-determination, among

 | DOI:10.1163/9789004380578_009

which Wilson's and Lenin's conceptions of self-determination were rather influential. Self-determination has played an important role in the creation and dissolution of the states. In international law, the evolution of self-determination can be divided into two stages: the decolonisation process and the post-colonial era. The colonial aspect of the right to self-determination is widely accepted as a part of customary international law, which recognises the right of the dependent peoples to freely determine their own future. The international community, however, has been reluctant to support the self-determination claims by ethnic groups in the colonies, as the emphasis has been placed on respect for the territorial integrity of the colonies as well as the existing states. In the post-colonial era, self-determination is considered to be the right that belongs to the peoples. There is no international consensus on the definition of "peoples". The majority of states, however, indicate no intention to embrace minorities in the notion of the peoples. Differing from the right of the peoples, minority rights are protected by separate regimes in international law, such as Article 27 of the ICCPR and other international human rights instruments regarding minorities. Despite the fact that a number of academics are in favour of the right to secede, arguably international law in general does not entail such a right.

The Chinese concept of the "peoples" and minorities has been shaped by historical experience and political perspectives on the Chinese nationhood. Different theories have been applied and tested in the process of transforming the Chinese Empire into a modern state. Given its unique historical and ethnic background, the creation of a modern state of China has less to do with liberalism and more to do with the invention of a unified national identity. Identifying a particular people in the territory, which has been inhabited by different ethnic groups, has become the central issue.

Sun and the KMT first relied on the principle of nationalism to define the Chinese nation. According to the nationalists, the Chinese nation was interpreted to equate a single Han nation, a five-nations state, and a unified Chinese nation that comprised all ethnicities with common blood and ancestry. The status of the minorities in relation to the Chinese nation therefore changed from being understood as different nations opposed to the Han nation to being understood as subgroups of the unified multiethnic Chinese nation. After the fruitless territorial claim over the Shandong peninsula based on Wilson's idea of self-determination at the Peace Conference, China was, in a way, pushed towards the Soviet Union, as the Western states were not keen to support the Chinese nationalist movements.

After the Soviet-KMT collaboration, self-determination was also asserted by the nationalists under the Soviet influence. The right of racial groups to self-determination in the nationalist context, however, by no means equated to the right to secede, when considering the political reality at the time. Self-determination, according to Sun, could be understood as national independence externally and racial autonomy or self-government internally. In the post-Sun era, Jiang was reluctant to endorse the principle of self-determination, claiming that the Chinese nation was of one stock with the blend of numerous clans. The nationalists, in general, had little genuine support for the right of the minorities to self-determination. The constitutional documents of the ROC, which defined the ROC as the state of the Chinese people and recognised the equality of all Chinese citizens and all ethnic groups, reaffirmed such an interpretation of racial self-determination in the nationalist context.[1] In reality, the KMT adopted an assimilative policy towards the minorities. Except for a few minority groups, including the Manchu, Mongol, Moslem and Tibetan, which were frequently mentioned by the nationalists, other minorities were generally ignored in the nationalists' agenda for nation-building.

The CPC, on the other hand, utilised the communist ideology to mobilise the masses. Despite the communist nature of the Party, certain nationalist traits could be found in its proposition to establish the independent state of China. Mao considered China as a different nation from all other communist nations, and insisted that the CPC could speak for it. The communist definition of Chinese nationhood was also formed on a historical and territorial basis. Meanwhile, the communist documents in the early 1930s recognised the full right of China's minorities to self-determination, including the right to secede. The explicit endorsement of self-determination was possibly formulated under the direct influence of the Comintern. However, the Chinese communists, especially after Mao's seizure of power in the Party, had no intention to acknowledge the right of the minorities to secede. Self-determination was only strategically advocated and interpreted by the CPC to appeal to minority support, in order to compete with the rival KMT and other forces. As the political climate changed, the communists then repudiated the right of the minorities to self-determination and replaced it with the right to regional autonomy within the state. After the establishment of the PRC, the CPC claimed that the Chinese people eventually achieved national independence, and then, based on the Soviet theory of class-struggle, the communists divided the Chinese people into different classes from the inside. Since the class orientation was the barrier that differentiated the people, rather than nationality, such a proposition effectively prevented the regional separatism of ethnic groups. From a legal

1 The 1912 Provisional Constitution of the ROC, Articles 1, 3, 5, 18; the 1931 Provisional Constitution of the Political Tutelage Period, Articles 2, 80; the 1946 Constitution of the ROC, Articles 1, 5.

perspective, the constitutions guaranteed the equality of all groups and provided ethnic territorial autonomy for the minorities as a special arrangement for accommodation.

The Chinese practice of self-determination could be considered as a good illustration of how the concept can be employed to legitimise statehood: in the Chinese case, self-determination had been utilised to appeal to popular support and to achieve national independence. The varying and strategic interpretations of the rights holders, from the minorities to the whole population of the state, reveal the second dimension of the concept: self-determination could also challenge the legitimacy of the state. The main reason that the KMT and the CPC had repudiated the right of the minorities to self-determination was to prevent the minorities from exercising secession, as some minorities had attempted—and still do—to claim self-determination so as to establish states of their own. Such a practice in turn has significantly influenced the invention of the Chinese nation.

Territorial integrity is prioritised in the communist idea of nation-building. As self-determination gradually developed into a legal right of the peoples, any attempt to claim such a right by constituent parts of the PRC, the minorities or not, would be opposed by the Chinese government. Three Chinese territories, Tibet, Hong Kong and Macau, have been involved in the process of decolonisation. The Tibetans first endeavoured to seek independence on the basis of self-determination and raised this issue in the GA. Tibet was not a typical colony in the traditional sense, as it was not geographically separate from China. Thus, it was not generally viewed as a non-self-governing territory under Resolution 1541, Principle IV. However, Tibet was referred to as an example to illustrate that "alien domination" may also exist within sovereign states. Although the right of the Tibetans to self-determination was discussed and three resolutions were adopted by the GA, the lack of international support for Tibetan self-determination or independence could be observed. This reaffirms that the majority of states do not intend to expand colonial self-determination to encompass ethnic groups within the states. The Dalai Lama thereafter revised his demands and argued for the genuine autonomy of the Tibetans within the PRC.

The colonial status of Tibet might have been in doubt; the situation of Hong Kong and Macau, however, was relatively clear, since both were placed on the UN list of non-self-governing territories. Nonetheless, China resumed the exercise of sovereignty in those territories, based on the treaties concluded between the relevant states. The will of the peoples in the territories concerned was not consulted. China claimed that the population of Hong Kong was not a "people" for the purpose of colonial self-determination, whilst the

UK considered this situation to be a "special circumstance". Similar arguments could also be found in the return of Macau. The resumption of the exercise of sovereignty over Hong Kong and Macau, without consulting the will of the peoples concerned, constituted exceptions to colonial self-determination. The application of self-determination in the decolonisation process again proved to be inconsistent.

China holds the opinion that self-determination is limitedly applied to situations of "colonial rule or foreign occupation".[2] Beyond the colonial context, self-determination should be exercised consistently with the principle of territorial integrity, rather than undermined by it, and the right to self-determination is different from the so-called "right of secession", which is not recognised by international law.[3] China's approach to self-determination and minority rights in the post-colonial era can be simplified as follows: the minorities, as a part of the Chinese people, exercise and realise their rights through the political system of people's congress at national and regional levels and the REA system within China's legal framework.

Minority rights are considered to be different from the right of the peoples in international law. The ICCPR incorporates a separate clause, Article 27, regarding minority protection. China signed the ICCPR in 1998, but still has not ratified it. Although the ICCPR is not effective in China at the moment, China is nevertheless bound by Article 27 in the sense that this clause, to a certain extent, could be regarded as customary international law within a limited dimension: the rights of minorities "to enjoy culture, to profess religion and to use language" should not be denied by the state. As well as Article 27, China has also undertaken measures to protect and promote minority rights under the ICESCR and the ICERD. Article 15 of the ICESCR recognises the right of everyone, including minorities, to participate in cultural life, and the ICERD prohibits racial discrimination on the grounds of race, colour, descent, or national or ethnic origin in all its forms. Nonetheless, international norms do not recognise a right to autonomy for minorities. Autonomy is generally seen as an arrangement to accommodate the interests of different groups within the states, and thus has different contents in individual cases.

The REA regime, as the "basic political system" of the state,[4] is often used as an alternative term for minority rights in China. Ethnic territorial autonomy as

2 The Written Statement of the PRC to the ICJ on the Issue of Kosovo, pp. 3–4.

3 Ibid, pp. 5–6.

4 According to the 1984 Law on REA, ethnic territorial autonomy was "an important political system", whereas in the amended 2001 Law on REA, it has become the "basic political system" of the state. Therefore, there are three basic political systems in China: the People's Congress, the People's Political Consultative Conference, and the REA.

a restricted form of self-determination has been constitutionally established since the founding of the PRC in 1949. Four elements are highlighted in the REA system: regions, minorities, autonomous agencies and autonomous rights. The first three elements have been discussed more fully in Chapter 4.

Not all non-Han ethnic groups in China are the minorities. Only those who have been officially recognised by the central government as *shaoshu minzu* can claim minority rights. Groups who identify themselves as a separate ethnicity but fail to acquire official recognition cannot claim minority status, and thus are effectively denied minority rights. The term "minority", in the Chinese context, has a strong political and administrative nature.[5] The minority status of ethnic groups has been confirmed through the Ethnic Identification Project. Various elements have been applied in this Project, and the self-identification of the group is merely one element among many. Objective criteria, such as historical origin, mode of production, language, customs and tradition, culture and religion, are also taken into account. It is difficult to detect the decisive element(s) in ethnic identification, as the application of the same standards can lead to diversified results, with some self-identified groups being recognised and others not. Such a practice constitutes a breach of China's obligations under the ICESCR and ICERD, which require the equal protection of the law and further provide the right of everyone to self-identification.[6]

Furthermore, China's minorities are essentially ethnic minorities. Minorities may be recognised on linguistic and/or religious grounds, but language and/or religion are not the sole reason for being identified as such. Put differently, China's minorities might be linguistic or religious groups under Article 27, whilst linguistic and religious groups are not necessarily the minorities (*shaoshu minzu*) that can claim minority rights in China.

The way that the minorities have been identified may make those groups potential candidates for claiming status as indigenous peoples. The non-existence of indigenous peoples or indigenous issues in China, as claimed by the Chinese government, is questionable, as some minority groups, such as the Tibetan, Mongol and Hezhe, do have indigenous features. The denial of the existence of indigenous peoples in China may also be challenged by the constitutional

5 Wang Wenguang and You Weiqiong, "Xin zhongguo chengli yilai Yunnan minzu shibie de renshi yu fansi [the Identification of Yunnan's Ethnic Groups since the Founding of the PRC and Its Enlightenment]", 02 *Yunnan Minzu Daxue Xuebao* [*Journal of Yunnan Nationalities University* (*Social Sciences*)] (2010), p. 10.

6 ICESCR, Articles 2, 15; the CESCR, General Comment 21, E/C.12/GC/21, p. 15, para.55(b); ICERD, Article 1; the CERD, General Recommendation 24, paras.2, 3; General Recommendation 08; General Recommendation 32, para.34.

recognition of indigenous peoples in the ROC and Russia. However, there is no international consensus on the definition of indigenous peoples. The UNDRIP includes no clear definition, whilst the definition under the ILO Convention 169 is not applicable in China, as it focuses on the priority of settlement and is closely related to European colonialism. Indigenous peoples have been linked to the right to self-determination in international law. This might be another reason, apart from contentious definitions of indigenous peoples, for China's objection to the application of the concept in China. Due to the undefined terms, the complexity of the ethnic situation, and the reluctance of the Chinese government to grant indigenous rights, the applicability of such rights in the Chinese context remains unclear. Whether a Chinese minority could claim indigenous rights may depend on the elaboration of international discourse on indigenous rights.

Despite the law stating that autonomous units should be established in areas where the minorities live in concentrated communities, without further explanation, standards for establishing autonomous areas or changing their administrative boundaries are not clearly provided by the law. A concentration of minority communities is the prerequisite for establishing an autonomous area, but this does not necessarily imply that the minorities account for the majority of the local population. It has been pointed out that the minorities fail to form a population majority in more than 70% of the autonomous areas.[7] This directly affects the exercise of autonomous rights through autonomous agencies. Nonetheless, the inclusion of the Han communities in autonomous areas is mandatory. Historical administrative division is another factor that has been employed by the CPC to decide upon the establishment of autonomous areas. Those standards are flexibly applied to maintain the Han-minority and minority-minority balances in the locality. Political considerations, such as territorial integrity and national defence, may also have played an essential role in the process of establishing autonomous areas.

The collective right to territorial autonomy is exercised through the LPC and the LPG of an autonomous area. According to the institutional design, the LPC is the body in which local people can exercise state power within its administrative division. Meanwhile, the LPG is the executive agency of the LPC at the corresponding level as well as the local branch of the state administration. The LPC, in theory, should be the most important and powerful institution within which the minorities can exercise autonomous rights. The law introduces a proportionate quota model to select the LPC deputies. In general, the LPC

7 Maria Lundberg and Yong Zhou, Regional National Autonomy under Challenge: Law, Practice and Recommendations, 16 *International Journal on Minority and Group Rights* (2009), p. 304.

deputies are elected according to the average representation ratio, based on the size of the population. The minorities may receive favourable treatments in terms of the deputy quota allocation, and thus would elect more deputies than the average proportionate ratio in the locality. But this favourable allocation of minority deputies is confined to situations when a minority makes up less than 30% of the local population. So the minorities may not be able to secure a decisive vote in the LPC, because of the size of the population. To allocate deputy representatives on the basis of the population size of ethnicities may guarantee general participation of the minorities in the LPC, but the inherent disadvantage of this practice is not difficult to see. It is very likely that the minorities cannot secure their interests in the LPC, due to the "majority rule" applied in the decision-making process. Seen from this perspective, a special consultation procedure on matters that affect the minorities should be introduced into Chinese law as a useful complement to remedy the outvoted problem of minority deputies in the LPC.

In the autonomous LPG, the chief executive of the government has to be a citizen from the minority that is exercising autonomy. The ability of the chief executive of autonomous areas to appoint the component personnel of his own office, however, is constrained by the *nomenklatura* system. Indeed, the CPC exerts a firm control over the state institution. It is difficult to distinguish the policies/decisions of the state from those of the CPC. Though there are proportionate minority party members, it is the fact that the minorities are underrepresented in the political centre of the Party. Although special arrangements are made for the minorities in the recruitment of state officers and the minorities are not excluded from accessing public services, the lack of minority members in important posts in the state and party apparatus cannot be denied.

Legislative and financial autonomy exclusively derive from the provisions of domestic law. Legislative autonomy could be viewed as the most critical element under the REA system. It allows autonomous legislature to make regional rules or to adapt national laws and administrative regulations at higher levels to suit the local conditions. Autonomous legislation, however, only becomes effective after being reviewed and approved by the high-level agency. Autonomous agencies also have the right to alter or cease the implementation of the state agencies' decisions at higher levels. In reality, autonomous legislation is usually found in sub-provincial autonomous units. Neither is legislative autonomy exercised in an independent way. Most autonomous regulations merely reinstate the provisions of the law on REA or other laws. Legislative adaptation, in general, concerns soft issues, such as marriage, inheritance, adoption, education and language, election, forest, grassland, and land administration.

The minorities also have the right to autonomously manage local financial affairs. Due to the dominant role of the State Council on financial affairs and the constantly changing national financial system, ethnic financial autonomy has rarely been exercised. Little space is left for autonomous units to improve local financial situations through taxation. The intergovernmental transfers are allocated by the central government or provincial LPGs. Although ethnicity is one of the elements that may affect funding allocation, autonomous areas at lower levels would by no means control it. In terms of financial affairs, the LPGs in autonomous areas mainly act as local branches of the State Council, rather than as autonomous agencies.

Culture is a broad and inclusive concept. Therefore, the cultural rights of China's minorities are evaluated from the perspectives of religion and language in Chapter 6. The minorities can be divided into two groups in terms of religion: the minorities that practise institutional religions and the minorities who have minority belief systems. The practice of institutional religions is subject to many restrictions prescribed by the law. On the contrary, minority belief systems are not viewed as "religions", but as part of minority culture. Compared to the restrictions conferred on institutional regions, the exercise of minority cultural rights is usually favoured and encouraged. Different treatment of religious practices apparently do not conform to the fundamental principle of ethnic equality and non-discrimination provided by Chinese law and by international human rights conventions, to which China is a signatory. According to the international obligations that China has undertaken, registration and other requirements placed on institutional religions may substantially restrict the exercise of religious rights and freedoms.

Arguably, China's minorities can freely use minority language and script in private life and retain the right to interpreters in public sectors. However, the promotion of minority language and script as official working language and script could only be achieved through autonomous agencies. This implies that unless a minority group has successfully established its own autonomous authority, they might not claim such rights in a Han or other minority dominant area. This shows the constraints of exercising the cultural rights in a collective manner. The individualist aspect of minority rights is somehow neglected in the Chinese context. Such practices again lead to different treatment amongst the minorities or amongst the communities within one minority group in the light of minority linguistic rights.

In conclusion, the rights holders of self-determination in China have varied as the political climate has changed. Although minority groups were once granted the right to self-determination, it is now down to the Chinese people as a whole to exercise such a right. China's minorities, on the other hand, are entitled to a collective right to regional autonomy as the means for exercising internal self-determination. The constitutional design of the REA system could have worked as the mechanism to guarantee the general participatory rights of the minorities and to preserve their separate identities. Nonetheless, minority legislative and financial autonomy are currently not effectively enforced through autonomous agencies, whilst autonomous management of cultural affairs seems to be tolerated and encouraged. Despite the Chinese government's argument that minority rights have been protected and promoted through China's comprehensive legal system,[8] in reality, differences do exist between the legal provisions and the actual enforcement and implementation of such provisions.

2 Prospects for Ethnic Territorial Autonomy in China

A rising minority consciousness may challenge the communist definition of the unified Chinese nation. But the protection and promotion of minority rights continue to be a matter of state interest. China is undertaking international obligations to promote human rights and is indeed making efforts to improve its human rights conditions. Yet in the light of minority rights, China still needs to further amend its domestic law in order to comply with its international obligations.

Although the Chinese government claims that the comprehensive legal system of China, particularly the constitutional recognition of ethnic equality and the REA system, has effectively protected and promoted the rights of minorities,[9] there are disparities, as observed by the CESCR,[10] between China's domestic law and its obligation to protect minority rights under international law. The Constitution has no provisions on the status of international treaties in the Chinese legal system and treaties are not considered as a source of Chinese law.[11] It has been suggested that human rights treaties need to be transformed into domestic law to be enforceable in China.[12] So far, those human

8 China, the Initial Report Submitted by China under Articles 16 and 17 of the ICESCR (2003), E/1990/5/Add.59, pp. 5–6, para.6; the 2nd Periodic Report Submitted by China under Articles 16 and 17 of the ICESCR (2010), E/C.12/CHN/2, p. 5.

9 The 10th, 11th, 12th, and 13th Periodic Reports Submitted by China under Article 9 of the ICERD (2008), CERD/C/CHN/10-13, p. 5, para.12; the CERD, Summary Record of the 1943rd Meeting, 75th Session, 2009, CERD/C/SR.1943, p. 2, para.3.

10 The CESCR, Concluding Observations on the 2nd Periodic Report of China (2014), E/C.12/CHN/CO/2, p. 3, para.9.

11 The Legislation Law, Article 2.

12 In the 1990s, the Chinese government stated in its reports to the Committee Against Torture and the CESCR that the instrument, once approved by the NPC Standing Committee, was "binding under the Chinese law and China must honour the corresponding obligations"

rights treaties have not been transformed into Chinese law, nor have they been directly invoked by the Chinese courts.[13] On the other hand, the constitutional provisions are not directly enforceable in Chinese courts, unless there exists ordinary legislation through which the Constitution is implemented.[14] The

and that "no further special legal transformation is required to turn it into domestic law". Thus, the provisions of the UN Convention against Torture would take precedence over the conflicting domestic law. The Chinese delegation also explained, in response to the questions put by the members of the Committee on the Elimination of Racial Discrimination, that international conventions were directly applicable without further incorporation and would supersede domestic law in any case of conflicts, unless China made a reservation to a specific provision. In 2005, China's position has subtly changed to: "the International Covenant on Economic, Social and Cultural Rights is enforceable and the requirements of Covenant could be fulfilled by invoking domestic laws which largely correspond to the Covenant obligations". In its second periodic report to the CESCR in 2010, the official position on the applicability of the treaty has changed to the transformation approach. The Chinese government indicates that "in accordance with the conventional practice of applying international treaties in China, such treaties do not directly function as the legal basis for the trial of cases in Chinese courts, and international human rights treaties are no exception; rather, they are applied after being transformed into domestic law through legislative procedures". The application of international treaties within the Chinese legal system, human rights instruments in particular, still depends on the constitutional clarification. At the moment, the judicial practice and administrative opinions seem to have adopted a dualist approach on the application of human rights treaties in China. See the Core Document Forming Part of the Reports of State Parties, HRI/CORE/1/ADD.21/REV.2, Part 1, p. 14, para.51; the CAT, Summary Record of the 51st Meeting, 4th Session, 1990, CAT/C/SR.51, p. 2, para.2; the CERD, Summary Record of the 1469th meeting, 59th Session, 2001, CERD/C/SR.1469, paras.4, 47; Replies of China to the List of Issues, 2005, CESCR/NONE/2004/10, p. 2, para.1; the 2nd Periodic Report of China, supra note 8, p. 9; Replies of China to the List of Issues, 2014, E/C.12/CHN/Q/2/Add.1, p. 6, para.18.

13 Huang Yao, "Guoji renquan fa yu guonei fa de guanxi [the Relationship between International Human Rights Law and National law]", 03 *Waiguo fa Yiping* [*Global Law Review*] (1999), p. 77; Chen Lihu and Huang Jianqiu, "Guoji renquan gongyue yu renquan baohu [International Human Rights Treaties and Human Rights Protection: an Analysis of the Implementation in Domestic Judicial System]", 03 *Xiandai Guoji Guanxi* [*Contemporary International Relations*] (2003), p. 27.

14 In QI Yuling *v.* CHEN Xiaoqi (2001), the High People's Court of Shandong Province directly applied Article 46 of the Constitution to protect the Plaintiff's right to education. However, this attempt was quickly halted by the Supreme People's Court of China. The Constitution remains unenforceable in the Chinese courts. In addition, the judgments issued by the people's courts shall, in accordance with law, cite relevant laws, regulations and other normative legal documents as the ruling basis, and the Constitution cannot be cited as the basis of such decisions. The Provisions of the Supreme People's Court on the Citation of Laws, Regulations, and Normative Legal Documents in the Judgments, Interpretation No. 14 [2009] of the Supreme People's Court, Preamble, Articles 1, 2, 3, 4, 5; the Notice of the Supreme People's Court on Issuing the Specifications for Preparing Civil Judgments by the People's Courts, No. 221 [2016] of the Supreme People's Court, Section 3 Subsection (7)(4). See also Albert Chen, as quoted in Yash Ghai, *Hong Kong's New Constitutional*

Law on REA could be viewed as the legislation to implement the constitutional right of the minorities to territorial autonomy. But its provisions are very declaratory and more concerned with the collective exercise of ethnic territorial autonomy through autonomous agencies, rather than the individual human rights of the minorities. Furthermore, the Law on REA does not provide for a remedy mechanism against violations. Put differently, the Law on REA may not operate as an arguable basis of individual claims in courts. China is thus obligated to fully incorporate the provisions of human rights treaties into domestic law and adopt appropriate measures, including access to effective remedies, to promote the realisation of minority rights.

In particular, the ICESCR, ICERD and other international instruments call for immediate action to ensure the enjoyment of human rights and freedoms without discrimination in any form or in any sphere. Discrimination against China's minorities or individuals belonging to them in regard to their cultures can nevertheless still be found in many aspects of social life. Although ethnic hatred and discrimination has been penalised, the Chinese criminal code only deals with ethnic discrimination in very specific forms, i.e. inciting ethnic hatred or discrimination with serious or flagrant circumstances and publishing materials that involve discriminating against or insulting the minorities with flagrant circumstances and serious consequences.[15] Discrimination against the minorities in other forms and in other spheres, which is explicitly prohibited by the Constitution and the Law on REA, may not be redressed, due to the lack of actionable remedies.[16] The introduction of a comprehensive definition of discrimination in the form of a separate anti-discrimination law,[17] which incorporates corresponding remedial procedures, including civil, administrative and criminal means, could be viewed as a good starting point to guarantee and promote minority rights in China. The enactment of a comprehensive anti-discrimination law would also facilitate the enjoyment of the right to equality of all individuals and groups.

Order: the Resumption of Chinese Sovereignty and the Basic Law (Hong Kong University Press, 1999), p. 89.

15 The Criminal Law (amended in 2015), Articles 249, 250.

16 There is no actionable claim in the Chinese courts if the substantive law does not reference a specific right. For instance, as the Constitution can only be enforced through the implementing legislation, the most important implementing legislation in regard to the right to culture is the Law on REA. Therefore, the Han, the minorities residing outside of the autonomous areas, and unidentified groups may not be able to claim the equal right to culture before the court.

17 The CERD, Report of the CERD, 2001, A/56/18(SUPP), p. 45, para.241; the CESCR, supra note 10, p. 4, para.14.

The exercise of minority cultural rights is regulated by domestic law as well as by international law. Chinese law tends to emphasise the collective nature of minority rights. But the collective way of exercising minority rights through autonomous agencies has its own constraints. It may conflict with the rights of individual members of the minorities. More importantly, the autonomous rights guaranteed by the REA system are only available to minority groups who manage to establish autonomous areas. Those who are scattered outside of these autonomous areas or throughout the country, who account for approximately one third of the total minority population,[18] have no effective means of realising autonomous rights. Considering the complexity of the ethnic situation in China, the individualist theory of human rights enshrined in international instruments as an alternative would significantly promote the full realisation of cultural rights. It would provide members of the minorities with equal opportunities to take part in cultural life, regardless of their place of residence. Emphasising the individualist aspect of minority rights is essential for the minorities who are scattered throughout the country or outside of the autonomous areas. Furthermore, as discussed in Chapter 4, no new minority has been identified since 1979 and the completion of the ethnic identification process was announced in the 1990s. An individualistic approach to minority rights, therefore, implies that the authoritative practice of the ethnic identification needs to be changed and reformed to equally protect and promote the rights of all ethnic groups without distinction. A clear and explicit legal definition of the minorities is necessary if the Chinese government is to maintain the identification criteria, and it must in turn be applied to all groups equally. The individual members concerned should have the liberty to identify themselves with one or several groups, and more importantly to access effective remedies in the form of legal and administrative procedures in order to maintain the validity of any system imposed.

In the meantime, as discussed in Chapter 1, economic development has become the top priority in communist nation-building since the 1980s. However, the overemphasis on economic growth is one of the major contributors to ethnic tension. Conflicts mainly arise from the uneven distribution of economic benefits and the impacts of economic development upon the minorities and their cultures. The disparities in economic development between the Han and minority areas could, possibly, be adjusted through national policies and fiscal planning. The tension, however, exists between economic success as the

18 China, the 14th-17th Periodic Reports Submitted by China under Article 9 of the ICERD (2017), CERD/C/CHN/14-17, p. 10, para.46.

fundamental prerequisite of maintaining a unified China[19] and the unavoidable impacts of the economic plans upon minority cultures. A further clarification of the relationship between national economic development and minority protection is of great importance. As minority cultural heritage, traditional culture, and environmental interests are often affected by business activities in autonomous areas, the CESCR, by adopting General Comment 24, specifically emphasises the obligation of State parties to respect, protect and fulfil economic, social and cultural rights in respect to infringements in the context of business activities.[20] This also suggests that economic development should be pursued in conformity with the rights of the minorities. The Chinese government should revisit its paternalist approach in relation to the treatment of the minorities and respect for their free will. To do this, the inclusion and participation of the minorities in the law making process may be presented as an option. Furthermore, since the minorities fail to form the majority of the population in more than 70% of the autonomous areas, the incorporation of a special consultation procedure for affected members or communities under Article 15 of the ICESCR, the ICERD, and Article 27 of the ICCPR into Chinese law would help to accommodate minority interests in relation to economic development. New provisions, mandating consultations with minority members and communities, prior to the commencement and at all stages of any economic and business development project that may affect their interests, should be inserted into the Law on REA. Special attention should also be paid to the effective remedies that are available in the case of violations of minority rights, particularly those arising from private business activities.

Amongst all of the rights of China's minorities, the collective right to legislative and financial autonomy is exclusively exercised according to Chinese law. The implementation of such rights is also greatly affected by the Chinese political situation, since it concerns not only the Han-minority relation but also the party-state relation and the central-local relation. The building of a state under the rule of law, together with a legalised centre-periphery relation, could serve as the basis for the minorities to genuinely exercise their rights through autonomous agencies. A well-functioning people's congress that exercises state power on behalf of the electorate as prescribed by the law would be the central institution to fully realise minority rights in China.[21] The ongoing

19 C. Mackerras, *China's Minorities: Integration and Modernisation in the Twentieth Century* (Oxford University Press, 1994), p. 260.

20 The CESCR, General Comment 24, paras.10–24.

21 It has been argued that the development since the 1980s has revealed a growing importance of the NPC as a political institution. See Joshua Castellino and Elvira Redondo (eds),

reform advocated by the CPCCC[22] may, to a certain extent, improve the situation. It aims to strengthen the rule of law and the role of the people's congress at all levels of state life.[23] More radical reforms in the realm of the Chinese political system, however, may still need time. Considering the political reality in China, consideration should be given to the inclusion of more minority members in positions of leadership, not only in the government but also in the Party and other institutions.[24] Temporary measures, e.g. special policies for the recruitment and promotion of minority representatives and party members, are necessary to improve the minorities' representation in the political centre of the state and the Party, so as to secure minorities' interests in the decision-making process.

Minority Rights in Asia: A Comparative Legal Analysis (Oxford University Press, 2006), pp. 132–133,143–144.

22 Zhonggong zhongyang guanyu quanmian shenhua gaige ruogan zhongda wenti de jueding [the 2013 CPCCC Decision on Major Issues Concerning Comprehensively Deepening Reforms]; Shenhua dang he guojia jigou gaige fang'an [the 2018 CPCCC Decision on Deepening Reform of Party and State Institutions].

23 The 2013 CPCCC Decision, ibid, Section 1, para.2; Section 8, para.27; Section 9; the 2018 CPCCC Decision, ibid, Sections 2 and 5.

24 The CERD, Concluding Observations on the 5th, 6th, and 7th Periodic Reports of China (1996), CERD/C/304/Add.15, p. 4, para.24.

References

Adler, Joseph A, Chinese Religions, Laurence King Publishing Ltd, London, 2002.

Ailiti Shaliyefu, Tuwa ren jinxi mantan [The Past and Present of the Tuvinians], *Xinjiang Difang Zhi* [*Local Chronicles of Xinjiang*], 1999, No.1, pp. 48–51.

An, Zhimin, Shilun wenming de qiyuan [A Discussion on the Origin of Civilisation], *Wenwu* [*Archaeology*], 1987, No. 5, pp. 453–457.

An, Zhimin, Tantan zhongguo wenming de qiyuan [The Origin of Chinese Civilisation], *Henan Shifan Daxue Xuebao* [*Journal of Henan Normal University*], 1991, No. 3, pp. 67–72.

Anderson, Benedict, Imagined Communities: Reflections on the Origin and Spread of Nationalism (Revised Edition), Verso, 1991.

An, Jun, Xibo yuyan wenzi nai manyu manwen de jixu [The Xibo Language and Script Are the Continuance of the Manchu Language and Script], *Manyu Yanjiu* [*Manchu Studies*], 1985, Issue 01, pp. 41–47.

Angle, Stephen, Human Rights and Chinese Thoughts: a Cross-cultural Inquiry, Cambridge University Press, 2002.

Anghie, Antony, Imperialism, Sovereignty and the Making of International Law, Cambridge University Press, 2005.

Ao, Junde, Guanyu minzu quyu zizhi fa de liangge jiben wenti [Two Fundamental Questions About Autonomy of Ethnic Regions—in Commemoration of the 20th Anniversary of the Promulgation of the Law of Ethnic Regions Autonomy], *Guizhou Minzu Xueyuan Xuebao* [*Journal of Guizhou University for Ethnic Minorities(Philosophy and Social Sciences)*], 2004, Issue 06, pp. 39–43.

Ao, Junmei, Geti pingdeng, yihuo qunti pingdeng [Individual Equality or Groups Equality: Admission Policy for Minority Students in Chinese Higher Education], *Qinghua Daxue Jiaoyu Yanjiu* [*Tsinghua Journal of Education*], 2006, No.6, pp. 70–74.

Bai, Runsheng, Woguo shaoshu minzu yuyan guangbo de lishi yange, diwei yu zuoyong [The Historic Status and Functions of the Broadcasting in Minority Languages], *Xinwen Aihaozhe* [*Journalism Lover*], 2012, No.17, pp. 3–7.

Bai, Yongli, Zizhiqu zizhi tiaoli zhiding yanjiu—yi Neimenggu zizhiqu weili [On the Making of Autonomous Statutes in Autonomous Regions: Taking the IMAR for Instance (as An Example)], *Neimenggu Shifan Daxue Xuebao* [*Journal of Inner Mongolia Normal University (Philosophy and Social Science)*], 2010, No.6, pp. 52–57.

Barelli, Mauro, Shaping Indigenous Self-determination: Promising or Unsatisfactory Solutions?, *International Community Law Review*, 2011, No. 13, pp. 413–436.

Sir Bell, Charles, Tibet Past and Present, Oxford At The Clarendon Press, 1968.

Bergere, Marie-Claire, "Chapter 12 The Chinese Bourgeoisie, 1911–37", in Fairbank, John K (ed), The Cambridge History of China: Volume 12, Cambridge University Press, 1983, pp. 722–826.

Beteille, Andre, The Idea of Indigenous People, *Current Anthropology*, 1998, Volume 39, No. 2, pp. 187–192.

Bianco, Lucien, translated by Bell, Muriel, Origins of the Chinese Revolution 1915–1949, Stanford University Press, 1971.

Bloch, Anne-Christine, "Chapter 20 Minorities and Indigenous Peoples", in Eide, Asbjorn, Krause, Catarina, and Rosas, Allan (eds), Economic, Social and Cultural Rights: A Textbook, Martinus Nijhoff Publishers, 2001, pp. 373–388.

Bodde, Derk, "Chapter 1 The State and Empire of Chin", in Twitchett, Denis, and Fairbank, John K. (eds), The Cambridge History of China: Volume 1, Cambridge University Press 1986, pp. 20–102.

Bodin, Jean, On Sovereignty: Four Chapters from the Six Books of the Commonwealth, Cambridge University Press, 1992.

Boler, Wenhua ziben lilun shiye xia Tuzu Qiangzu yuyuan jiqi xinchuang wenzi shiyong yu fazhan yanjiu [Languages and New Writing Characters of Tu and Qiang Ethnic Groups: From Cultural Capital Theory], *Zhongyang Minzu Daxue Xuebao [Journal of Central University for Nationalities (Philosophy and Social Science)]*, 2008, No. 4, pp. 118–124.

Bovingdon, Gardner, "Chapter 4 Heteronomy and Its Discontents—'Minzu Regional Autonomy' in Xinjiang", in Rossabi, Morris (ed), Governing China's Multiethnic Frontiers, University of Washington Press, 2004, pp. 117–154.

Bowring, Bill, "Chapter 1 Russian Legislation in the Area of Minority Rights", in Protsyk, Oleh, and Harzl, Benedikt (eds), Managing Ethnic Diversity in Russia, Routledge, 2012, pp. 15–36.

Brandt, Conrad, Schwartz, Benjamin, and Fairbank, John K. (eds), A Documentary History of Chinese Communism, London: George Allen & Unwin Ltd, 1952.

Breuilly, John, Nationalism and the State, Manchester University Press, 1993.

Buchanan, Allen, "Chapter 2 Democracy and Secession", in Moore, Margaret (ed), National Self-determination and Secession, Oxford University Press, 1998, pp. 14–33.

Buchanan, Allen, Justice, Legitimacy and Self-determination: Moral Foundations for International Law, Oxford University Press, 2004.

Buchheit, Lee, Secession: the Legitimacy of Self-determination, Yale University Press, 1978.

Bush, Richard, JR, Religion in Communist China, Abingdon Press, 1970.

Cassese, Antonio, "Chapter 4 The Self-determination of Peoples", in Henkin, L. (ed), The International Bill of Rights: the Covenant on Civil and Political Rights, Columbia University Press, 1981, pp. 92–113.

Cassese, Antonio, Self-Determination of Peoples: A Legal Reappraisal, Cambridge University Press, 1995.

Castellino, Joshua, International Law and Self-determination: the Interplay of the Politics of Territorial Possession with Formulations of Post-colonial 'National' Identity Developments in International Law, Martinus Nijhoff Publishers, 2000.

Castellino, Joshua, The Protection of Minorities and Indigenous Peoples in International Law: A Comparative Temporal Analysis, *International Journal on Minority and Group Rights*, 2010, No. 17, pp. 393–422.

Castellino, Joshua, and Gilbert, Jeremie, Self-determination, Indigenous Peoples and Minorities, *Macquarie Law Journal*, 2003, No. 03, pp. 155–178.

Castellino, Joshua, and Redondo, Elvira (eds), Minority Rights in Asia: A Comparative Legal Analysis, Oxford University Press, 2006.

Capotorti, Francesco, Study on the Rights of Persons Belonging to Ethnic, Religious and Linguistic Minorities, UN Doc. E/CN.4/Sub.2/384/Rev.1.

Chan, C.W., Human Rights and Democracy with Chinese Characteristics?, *Human Rights Law Review*, 2013, Volume 13, Issue 4, pp. 645–689.

Chang, Hao, "Chapter 5 Intellectual Change and the Reform Movement, 1890–8", in Fairbank, John K, and Liu, Kwang-Ching (eds), The Cambridge History of China: Volume 11, Cambridge University Press, 1980, pp. 274–338.

Chang, Gee-Yuen, A Study on the Chinese Ethnology, The Commercial Press, 1929.

Chang, Kwang-chih, "Chapter 1 China on the Eve of the Historical Period", in Loewe, Michael, and Shaughnessy, Edward L (eds), The Cambridge History of Ancient China, Cambridge University Press, 1999, pp. 37–73.

Charters, Claire, "Chapter 7 Reparations for Indigenous Peoples: Global International Instruments and Institutions", in Lenzerini, F. (ed), Reparations for Indigenous Peoples: International & Comparative Perspectives, Oxford University Press, 2008, pp.163–195.

Chau, Adam Yuet, Miraculous Response: Doing Popular Religion in Contemporary China, Stanford University Press, 2006.

Chen, Boli, and Xu, Xingui, Lifaxue shiye xia de minzu biantong guiding wenti tanxi [A Legislative Discussion of the Ethnic Modification Rule], *Manzu Yanjiu [Manchu Minority Research]*, 2007, Issue 03, pp. 8–16.

Chen, Chao, Zhongguo xingzheng quhua yange shouce [The History of Administrative Divisions in China], Zhongguo Ditu Chubanshe, 2000.

Chen, Jianyue, Duo minzu guojia hexie shehui de goujian yu minzu wenti de jiejue—ping minzu wenti de 'qu zhengzhihua' yu 'wenhuahua' [The Construction of a Harmonious Society in a Unified Multi-ethnic State: Comments on the Depoliticalisation and Culturalisation of the Ethnic Question], *Shijie Minzu [Journal of World Peoples Studies]*, 2005, No. 05, pp. 1–13.

Chen, Liankai, Lun zhonghua wenming qiyuan jiqi zaoqi fazhan de jiben tedian [On the Origin of Chinese Civilisation and the Chief Characteristics of Its Early-stage Development], *Zhongyang Minzu Daxue Xuebao [Journal of Central University for Nationalities (Philosophy and Social Science)]*, 2000, No.5, pp. 22–34.

Chen, Lihu, and Huang, Jianqiu, Guoji renquan gongyue yu renquan baohu [International Human Rights Treaties and Human Rights Protection: An Analysis of the Implementation in Domestic Judicial System], *Xiandai Guoji Guanxi [Contemporary International Relations]*, 2003, No. 03, pp. 23–28.

Chen, Xinlin, Zuqun lilun yu zhongguo de zuqun yanjiu [Ethnic Group's Theory and Nationalities Research in China], *Guizhou Minzu Yanjiu [Guizhou Ethnic Studies]*, 2005, No. 06, pp. 1–5.

Chen, Xingyao (Hsieh Hsing-yao), "How Did Imperialism Use Religion for Aggression on China? A Historical Survey of Missionary Work in China", in Macinnis, Donald (ed), Religious Policy and Practice in Communist China, Hodder and Stoughton, 1972, pp. 133–137.

Chen, Yangyong, Gongtong gangling yu xinzhongguo sanda zhengzhi zhidu de queli [The Common Programme and the Establishment of Three Fundamental Policies in the New China], *Dangde Wenxian [Literature of Chinese Communist Party]*, 2009, No.4, pp. 19–26.

Chen, Yuping, Minzu wenti nengfou 'qu zhengzhihua' zhenglun zhi wojian [Whether the Ethnic Question Could Be De-politicalised], *Xinan Minzu Daxue Xuebao [Journal of Southwest University for Nationalities]*, 2008, No. 07, pp. 1–7.

Chen, Yushu, Luelun Ewenke zu de laiyuan wenti [A Discussion on the Origins of the Ewenks], *Zhongguo Minzu [China's Ethnic Groups]*, 1962, No. Z1, pp. 32–38.

Chen, Yushu, Guanyu Elunchun zu de laiyuan [On the origins of the Oroqens], *Wenshizhe [Journal of Literature, History and Philosophy]*, 1962, No. 4, pp. 59–62.

Chen, Yunhua, Dui dangdai Xinjiang shaoshu minzu wenzi biange huodong de huigu yu sikao [A Review of the Reform on Minority Writing Systems in Xinjiang], The Collection of Papers From the Third Annual Academic Conference on National History, 2003, pp. 485–494.

Chen, Yunhua, and Wang, Chunyan, Dangdai Xinjiang liangci zhongda wenzi gaige chuyi [On Two Reforms of Writing System in Xinjiang], *Yuyan Yu Fanyi [Language and Translation]*, 2002, No. 1, pp. 27–30.

Chen, Zhi, Yixia xinbian [The Early Concepts of Chineseness and Barbarism], *Zhongguoshi Yanjiu [Journal of Chinese Histocial Studies]*, 2004, No.1, pp. 3–22.

Cheng, Aihua, Minzu diqu caizheng zhuanyi zhifu wenti yanjiu—yi Guangxi zhuangzu zizhiqu huanjiang Maonan zu zizhixian de diaocha weili [Research on the Subprovincial Fiscal Transfer System in Autonomous Areas], *Yunnan Shehui Kexue [Social Science in Yunnan]*, 2010, No.4, pp. 120–124.

Chiang, Kai-shek, China's Destiny and Chinese Economic Theory, London: Dennis Dobson Ltd., 1947.

Ching, Julia, Chinese Religions, Macmillan, 1993.

Chingmak, Phutoli, "Chapter 16 International Law and Reparations for Indigenous Peoples in Asia", in Lenzerini, F. (ed), Reparations for Indigenous Peoples: International & Comparative Perspectives, Oxford University Press, 2008, pp. 409–465.

Cobban, Alfred, The National State and National Self-determination, Collins, The Fontana Library, 1969.

Cohen, Abner, Custom and Politics in Urban Africa, University of California Press, 1969.

Cobo, Martinez, Study of the Problem of Discrimination Against Indigenous Populations, UN Doc. E/CN.4/Sub.2/1986/7/ADD.4, 1986.

Connor, Walker, The National Question in Marxist-Leninist Theory and Strategy, Princeton University Press, 1984.

Cooney, Sean, Why Taiwan Is not Hong Kong: A Review of the PRC's "One Country Two Systems" Model for Reunification with Taiwan, *Pacific Rim Law & Policy Journal*, 1997, Volume 6, No. 3, pp. 497–548.

Craven, Matthew, The International Covenant on Economic, Social, and Cultural Rights: A Perspective on Its Development, Clarendon Press Oxford, 1995.

Crawford, James, The Creation of States in International Law (2nd Edition), Clarendon Press, Oxford, 2006.

Crawford, James, The Right of Self-determination in International Law: Its Development and Future, in Alston, Philip (ed), Peoples' Rights, Oxford University Press, 2001, pp.7–67.

Crawford, James, State Practice and International Law in Relation to Secession, *British Year Book of International Law*, 1998, Volume 69, Issue 01, pp. 85–117.

Curry, Roy Watson, Woodrow Wilson and Far East Policy 1913–21, Bookman Associates (New York), 1957.

Dai, Hong, Zhongguo shaoshu minzu wenzi xinxi jishu biaozhunhua licheng [The Progress of the Information Technology Standardisation of Chinese Minority Scripts], *Xinxi Jishu yu Biaozhun Hua* [*Information Technology & Standardisation*], 2011, No.6, pp. 7–9.

Dagati, Patricia A., Hong Kong's Lost Right to Self-Determination: A Denial of Due Process in the United Nations, *New York Law School Journal of International and Comparative Law*, 1992, No. 13, pp. 153–179.

Dalai Lama's Appeal to the Secretary General of the United Nations (09/09/1959), in Shiromany, A. A. (ed), The Spirit of Tibet: Universal Heritage--Selected Speeches and Writings of HH the Dalai Lama XIV, Allied Publishers, 1995, pp. 26–28.

Davis, Clarence B., and Gowen, Robert J., The British at Weihaiwei: A Case Study in the Irrationality of Empire, *Historian*, 2000, Volume 63, Issue 1, pp. 87–104.

DeFrancis, John, "Chapter 7 Language and Script Reform in China", in Fishman, Joshua (ed), Advances in the Creation and Revision of Writing Systems, Mouton The Hague Paris, 1977, pp. 121–148.

DeFrancis, John, The Prospects for Chinese Writing Reform, *Sino-Platonic Papers*, 2006, No.171, pp. 1–26.

Deng, Jianmin, Lun biantong huo buchong guiding yu danxing tiaoli de qubie [Differences between Adaptive Provisions or Supplementary Provision and Specific Regulation], *Xinan Minzu Xueyuan Xuebao* [*Journal of Southwest University for Nationalities*], 2002, No.7, pp. 111–114.

Deng, Xiaoping, Selected Works Volume 2: The Present Situation and the Tasks before Us (16/01/1980), http://english.peopledaily.com.cn/dengxp/vol2/text/b1390.html.

Deng, Xiaoping, Selected Works, Volume 3: An Idea for the Peaceful Reunification Of the Chinese Mainland and Taiwan (26/06/1983), http://english.peopledaily.com.cn/dengxp/vol3/text/c1120.html.

Deng, Xiaoping, Selected Works Volume 3: Opening Speech at the 12th National Congress of the Communist Party of China (01/09/1982), http://english.peopledaily.com.cn/dengxp/vol3/text/c1010.html.

Deng, Xiaoping, Selected Works, Volume 3: Our Basic Position On the Question of Hong Kong (24/09/1982), http://english.peopledaily.com.cn/dengxp/vol3/text/c1040.html.

Deng, Xiaoping, Selected Works Volume 3: Unity Depends on Ideals and Discipline, (07/03/1985), http://english.peopledaily.com.cn/dengxp/vol3/text/c1350.html.

Deng, Xiaoping, The Question of Minority Nationalities in the Southwest (21/07/1950), in Policy Research Office of the State Ethnic Affairs Commission (ed), Zhonguo gongchandang zhuyao lingdaoren lun minzu wenti [The Comments on Ethnicity Questions from the Main Leaders of the CPC], Minzu Chubanshe, 1994, pp. 51–64.

Deng, Ziji, and Tang, Wenqian, Woguo caishui gaige yu 'dingce sheji'—sheng yixia fenshuizhi caizheng guanli tizhi de shenghua gaige [The Fiscal Reform in China and the Top-down Design—Deepening the Taxation Division System at Sub-provincial Level], *Caizheng Yanjiu* [*Public Finance Research*], 2012, Issue 02, pp. 2–6.

Di, Chengguang, Deng Xiaoping 'yiguo liangzhi' gouxiang de xingcheng yu fazhan [Formation and Development of Deng Xiaoping's 'One Country Two Systems' Conception]", *Anhui Shixue* [*Historical Research in Auhui*], 2007, Issue 03, pp. 69–76.

Diatchkova, Galina, Indigenous Peoples in Russia and Political History, *The Canadian Journal of Native Studies XXI*, 2(2001), pp. 217–233.

Dikotter, Frank, The Discourse of Race in Modern China, Hurst and Company, 1992.

Dreyer, June, China's Forty Millions: Minority Nationalities and National Integration in the Peoples' Republic of China, Harvard University Press, 1976.

Dreyer, June, China's Political System: Modernisation and Tradition, Paragon House, 1993.

Driest, Simone Van Den, Remedial Secession: A Right to External Self-determination As A Remedy to Serious Injustices?, Intersentia, 2013.

Driest, Simone Van Den, Crimea's Separation from Ukraine: An Analysis of the Right to Self-determination and (Remedial) Secession in International Law, *Netherlands International Law Review*, 2015, Volume 62, pp. 329–363.

Du, Yonghao, Huaxia-Han zu, zhonghua minzu yu zhonghua renmin [Huaxia-Han Nationality, Chinese Nation and Chinese People], *Heilongjiang Minzu Congkan [Heilongjiang National Series]*, 2010, No. 01, pp. 8–16.

Du, Zhongwu, Cong 'yigang simu' dao 'yiguo liangzhi': zhonggong sandai lingdao jiti yu wodang duitai zhengce [The Policy of the Three Leadership Collectives and the Party to Solve Taiwan Problem: From 'One Guiding Principle and Four Contents' to 'A state, Two Systems'], *Zhonggong Yunnan Shengwei Dangxiao Xuebao [The Journal of the CCP Yunan Provincial Committee School]*, 2001, Volume 2, No. 4, pp. 16–19.

Eastman, Lloyd E., "Chapter 3 Nationalist China During the Nanking Decade 1927–1937", in Fairbank, John K., and Feuerwerker, Albert (eds), The Cambridge History of China: Volume 13, Cambridge University Press, 1986, pp. 116–167.

Eide, Asbjorn, "Chapter 16: Cultural Rights as Individual Human Rights", in Eide, Asbjorn, Krause, Catarina, and Rosas, Allan (eds), Economic, Social and Cultural Rights: A Textbook, Martinus Nijhoff Publishers, 2001, pp. 289–301.

Eide, Asbjorn, "In Search of Constructive Alternatives to Secession", in Tomuschat, Christian (ed), Modern Law of Self-determination, Martinus Nijhoff Publishers, 1993, pp. 139–176.

Eide, Asbjorn, Working Paper on the Relationship and Distinction Between the Rights of Persons Belonging to Minorities and Those of Indigenous Peoples, UN Doc. E/CN.4/Sub.2/2000/10.

Elliot, Mark, The Case of the Missing Indigene: Debate Over a "Second-Generation" Ethnic Policy, *The China Journal*, 2015, No. 73, pp. 186–213.

Elliot, Mark, and Hua, Li, (Translator), Qingdai manzhouren de minzu zhuti yishi yu manzhouren de zhongguo tongzhi [Manchu National Consciousness and Manchu Rule in China During the Qing Dynasty], *Qingshi Yanjiu [Studies in Qing History]*, 2002, Vol. 4, pp. 86–93.

Emerson, Rupert, From Empire to Nation: the Rise of Self-assertion of Asian and African peoples, Harvard University Press, 1962.

Engels, Frederick, The Origin of the Family, Private Property and the State, The Camelot Press, 1940.

Engers, J. F., From Sacred Trust to Self-determination, *Netherlands International Law Review*, 1977, Vol. 24, Issue 1–2, pp. 85–91.

Erie, Matthew, China and Islam: The Prophet, the Party, and Law, Cambridge University Press, 2016.

Espiell, H. Gros, The Right to Self-Determination: Implementation of United Nations Resolutions, UN Doc E/CN.4/Sub.2/405/Rev.1, 1980.

Fairbank, John K., "Introduction: the Old Order", in Fairbank, John K. (ed), The Cambridge History of China: Volume 10, Cambridge University Press, 1978, pp. 1–34.

Fairbank, John K., "Chapter 5 The Creation of the Treaty System", in Fairbank, John K. (ed), The Cambridge History of China: Volume 10, Cambridge University Press, 1978, pp. 213–263.

Fan, Ziying, and Wan, Guanghua, The Fiscal Risk of Local Government Revenue in the People's Republic of China. *ADBI Working Paper 567*, 2016, available at http://www.adb.org/publications/fiscal-risk-local-government-revenue-prc/.

Fei, Xiaotong, Guanyu woguo minzu de shibie wenti [Ethnic Identification in China], *Zhongguo Shehui Kexue* [*Social Science in China*], 1980, Issue 1, pp. 147–162; English version: Ethnic Identification in China, *Social Science in China*, 1980, Issue 1, pp. 94–107.

Fei, Xiaotong (ed), Zhonghua minzu duoyuan yiti geju [The Pluralistic Unity of the Chinese Nation], Zhongyang Minzu Xueyuan Chubanshe, 1989.

Fei, Xiaotong, Zhonghua minzu duoyuan yiti geju [The Pluralistic Unity of the Chinese nNation], in Fei, Xiaotong and Lin, Yaohua (eds), Zhongguo minzu xue dangqian de renweu [the Current Task of the Ethnology in China], Minzu Chubanshe, 1957.

Fei, Xiaotong, and Lin, Yaohua, Zhongguo minzu xue dangqian de renweu [the Current Task of the Ethnology in China], Minzu Chubanshe, 1957.

Ferdinand, Peter, Communist Regimes in Comparative Perspective: the Evolution of the Soviet, Chinese and Yugoslav Systems, Harvester Wheatsheaf (Barnes & Noble Books), 1991.

Feuchtwang, Stephan, Popular Religion in China: the Imperial Metaphor, Curzon, 2001.

Fitzgerald, John, The Nationless State: the Search for a Nation in Modern Chinese Nationalism, *The Australian Journal of Chinese Affairs*, 1995, No.33, pp. 75–104.

Fletcher, Joseph, "Chapter 2 Ch'ing (Qing) Inner Asia *c.* 1800", in Fairbank, John K. (ed), The Cambridge History of China: Volume 10, Cambridge University Press, 1978, pp. 35–106.

Foster, Caroline, Articulating Self-determination in the Draft Declaration on the Rights of Indigenous Peoples, *European Journal of International Law*, 2001, Volume 21, pp. 141–157.

Franck, Thomas, The Emerging Right to Democratic Governance, *American Journal of International Law*, 1992, Volume 86, pp. 46–91.

Francis, John De, Nationalism and Language Reform in China, Princeton University Press, 1950.

Fromherz, Christopher, Indigenous Peoples' Courts: Egalitarian Juridical Pluralism, Self-determination, and the UN Declaration on the Rights of Indigenous Peoples, *University of Pennsylvania Law Review*, 2008, Volume 156, pp. 1341–1381.

Fu, Maoji, Bang zhu shaoshu minzu chuangli gaijin he gaige wenzi gongzuo de qingkuang he wenti [The Work of Assisting Minorities to Create, Improve and Reform Their Writing Systems and the Questions Therein], *Kexue Tongbao* [*Chinese Science Bulletin*], 1956, No. 2, pp. 20–31.

Fu, Sinian, Yixia dongxi shuo [The Hypothesis of the Yi in the East and Xia in the West], in Liu, Mengxi (ed), Zhongguo xiandai xueshu jingdian: Fu Sinian juan [Chinese Modern Academic Classics: Fu Sinian Volume], Hebei Jiaoyu Chubanshe, 1996, pp. 187–240.

Fung, Edmund S. K., Anti-Imperialism and the Left Guomindang, *Modern China*, 1985, Vol.11, pp. 39–76.

Gao, Hong, Wei Yuan yu haiguo tuzhi [Wei Yuan and Illustrated Treatise on the Maritime Kingdoms], Liaohai Chubanshe, 1997.

Gao, Jun, and Du, Xuewen, "Yutongyin" yu renquan baozhang ["Language Unity" and the Safeguard of Human Rights: the Legal Analysis the Clause of Popularising *Putonghua* Nationwide], *Yanbian Daxue Xuebao* [*Journal of Yanbian University (Social Science)*], 2009, No. 6, pp. 154–159.

Gasster, Michael, "Chapter 9 The Republican Revolutionary Movements", in Fairbank, John K, and Liu, Kwang-Ching (eds), The Cambridge History of China: Volume 11, Cambridge University Press, 1980, pp. 463–534.

Gerbillon, Jean-François, (Zhang Cheng), "A Summary of the Historical Investigation of the Grand Tartar", in Du, Wenkai (ed), Qingdai xiren jianwen lu [The Travelogue of Foreigners During the Qing Dynasty], Zhongguo Renmin Daxue Chubanshe, 1985, pp. 85–122.

Ghai, Yash, "Autonomy as A Participatory Right in the Modern Democratic State: Public Participation, Autonomy and Minorities", in Skurbaty, Zelim (ed), Beyond A One-dimensional State: An Emerging Right to Autonomy?, Martinus Nijhoff Publishers, 2005, pp. 3–45.

Ghai, Yash, Woodman, Sophia, and Loper, Kelley, Is There Space for 'Genuine Autonomy' for Tibetan Areas in the PRC's System of Nationalities Regional Autonomy?, *International Journal on Minority and Group Rights*, 2010, Issue 17, pp. 137–186.

Ghai, Yash, The Basic Law of the Special Administrative Region of Macau: Some Reflections, *International and Comparative Law Quarterly*, 2000, Volume 49, No. 1, pp. 183–198.

Ghanea, Nazila, and Xanthaki, Alexandra (eds.), Minorities, Peoples and Self-Determination Essays in Honour of Patrick Thornberry, Martinus Nijhoff Publishers, 2005.

Giddens, Anthony, The Nation-State and Violence, Volume 2: A Contemporary Critique of Historical Materialism, Polity Press, 1985.

Gilbert, Geoff, Autonomy and Minority Groups: A Right in International Law?, *Cornell International Law Journal*, 2002, Volume 35, pp. 307–353.

Gladney, Dru, Dislocating China: Reflections on Muslims, Minorities, and Other Subaltern Subjects, Hurst and Company, 2004.

Gladney, Dru, Muslim Chinese: Ethnic Nationalism in the People's Republic (2nd Edition), Harvard University Press, 1996.

Gray, Jack (ed), Modern China's Search for a Political Form, Oxford University Press, 1969.

Gocke, Katja, The Case of Angela Poma Poma v. Peru before the Human Rights Committee: the Concept of Free Prior and Informed Consent and the Application of the International Covenant on Civil and Political Rights to the Protection and Promotion of Indigenous Peoples' Rights, *Max Planck Yearbook of United Nations Law*, 2010, Volume 14, pp. 337–370.

Goldstein, Melvyn C., A History of Modern Tibet Volume 1: the Demise of the Lamaist State, 1913–1951, University of California Press, 1992.

Goldstein, Melvyn C., A History of Modern Tibet Volume 2: the Calm before the Storm, 1951–1955, University of California Press, 2007.

Goldstein, Melvyn C., The Snow Lion and the Dragon: China, Tibet and the Dalai Lama, University of California Press, 1997.

Gong, Yu, Ewenke zu feiwuzhi wenhua yichan baohu xianzhuang yanjiu [Investigation on Situation of Ewenki's Non-physical (Intangible) Culture Heritage], *Manyu Yanjiu* [*Manchu Studies*], 2012, No.1, pp. 70–74.

Grunfeld, A. Tom., The Making of Modern Tibet, An East Gate Book, M. E. Sharpe, Inc, 1996.

Guo, Yingjie, Cultural Nationalism in Contemporary China, Routledge Curzon, 2004.

Gunn, Geoffrey C., Qin, Chuanan (Translator), Aomen shi 1557–1999 [Encountering Macau: A Portuguese City-state on the Periphery of China 1557–1999], Zhongyang Bianyi Chubanshe, 2009.

Gyatso, Tenzin, The Fourteenth Dalai Lama of Tibet, Freedom in Exile: the Autobiography of His Holiness The Dalai Lama of Tibet, A John Curtis Book, Hodder & Stoughton, 1990.

Harbar, Attempts to Transform CPC's Ethnic Minority Policy in the Early 1980s, *The Chinese Historical Review*, 2008, Volume 15, No.2, pp. 296–314.

Hai, Lu, Zhongguo shaoshu minzu xinchuang wenzi de yuyan guihua jiqi shijian [Language Planning and the Practice of Newly Created Writing Systems for Ethnic Minority Languages in China], *Zhongyang Minzu Daxue Xuebao* [*Journal of Central University for Nationalities* (*Philosophy and Social Science*)], 2012, No. 1, pp. 141–146.

Han, Zhongtai, Yizhong zicheng, sange minzu: dui Huangnihe youan buyi zuqun minzu shibie de zaidiacha [A Restudy of the Ethnic Identification of the Buyi Ethnic Group on the Right Bank of the Huangni River], *Yunnan Minzu Daxue Xuebao* [*Journal of Yunnan Nationalities University* (*Social Sciences*)], 2012, No. 3, pp. 5–10.

Hannikainen, Lauri, "Self-determination and Autonomy in International Law" in Suksi, Markku (ed), Autonomy: Applications and Implications, Kluwer Law International, 1998, pp. 79–95.

Hannum, Hurst, Autonomy, Sovereignty, and Self-determination: the Accommodation of Conflicting Rights (Revised Edition), University of Pennsylvania Press, 1990.

Hannum, Hurst, "Territorial Autonomy: Permanent Solution or Step Towards Secession?", in Skurbaty, Zelim A. (ed), Beyond A One-dimensional State: An Emerging Right to Autonomy?, Martinus Nijhoff Publishers, 2005, pp. 153–159.

Hansen, Stephen, "The Right to Take Part in Cultural Life: Toward Defining Minimum Core Obligation Related to Article 15 (1) (a) of the ICESCR", in Chapman, Audrey, and Russell, Sage (eds), Core Obligation: Building A Framework for Economic, Social and Cultural Rights, Intersentia, 2002, pp.279–303.

Hao, Shiyuan, Goujian shehui zhuyi hexie shehui yu minzu guanxi [Relations among Nationalities and the Building of A Harmonious Society of Socialism], *Minzu Yanjiu* [*Ethno -National Studies*], 2005, No. 03, pp. 1–13.

Hao, Shiyuan, Meiguo shi zhongguo jiejue minzu wenti de bangyang ma?—ping "dierdai minzu zhengce" de guoji jingyan jiaoxun shuo [Is the US a Model for Solving China's Ethnic Problems? A Critique of the Notion of Lessons of International Experience in the "Second-Generation Ethnic Policy"], *Shijie Minzu* [*Journal of World Peoples Studies*], 2012, No. 02, pp. 1–15.

Hao, Shiyuan, Zhongwen "minzu" yu "shaoshu minzu" de yingyi wenti [The English Translation of "Minzu" and "Shaoshu Minzu"], *Zhonguo Minzubao* [*China Ethnic News*], Mar. 22, 2013, at p. 5.

Hao, Yen-p'ing, and Wang, Erh-Min, "Chapter 3 Changing Chinese Views of Western Relations, 1840–95", in Fairbank, John K. and Liu, Kwang-Ching (eds), The Cambridge History of China: Volume 11, Cambridge University Press, 1980, pp. 142–201.

Harding, Harry, "The Chinese State in Crisis", in Twitchett, Denis, and Fairbank, John (eds), The Cambridge History of China Volume 15, Cambridge University Press, 1991, pp. 107–217.

Harrell, Stevan, (Bamo, Ayi and Qumo, Tiexi, Translators), Tianye zhong de zuqun guanxi yu minzu renting [Field Studies of Ethnic Identity: Yi Communities of Southwest China], Guangxi Renmin Chubanshe, 2008.

Harrison, Henrietta, China, Arnold, 2001.

He, Baogang, "China's National Identity: A Source of Conflict Between Democracy and State Nationalism", in Leong H. Liew and Shaoguang Wang (eds), Nationalism, Democracy and National Integration in China, Routledge Curzon, 2004, pp. 170–195.

He, Husheng, and Ma, Xueyang, Xinshiqi dang de zongjiao gongzuo jiben fangzhen he zhuyao zhengce yanjiu [Research on the Basic Policy and Guiding Principles of the CPC on Religious Work in the New Era], *Zhongguo Tese Shehui Zhuyi Yanjiu* [*Studies on Socialism with Chinese Characteristics*], 2012, Issue 01, pp. 51–58.

He, Jihong, Tuwa ren kao [The Investigation of the Tuvinians], *Xinjiang Difang Zhi* [*Local Chronicles of Xinjiang*], 2001, No. 4, pp. 42–44.

He, Shutao, *Dui ershi shiji zai zhongguo zuiyou yingxing de sanda minzu dingyi de jianyao fenxi* [Comments on Three Influential Definitions of Nation in the 20th Century China], *Heilongjiang Minzu Congkan* [*Heilongjiang National Series*], 2009, Issue 04, pp. 14–18.

He, Yunlong, Xinjiang minzu zizhi defang lifaquan de yunyong fenxi yu duice yanjiu [Suggestions and Analysis on the Exercise of Legislative Power in the XUAR], *Xinjiang Shehui Kexue* [*Social Science in Xinjiang*], 2006, No.3, pp. 82–86.

Heberer, Thomas, China and Its National Minorities: Autonomy or Assimilation, M. E. Sharpe, Inc., 1989.Heintze, Hans-Joachim, "On the Legal Understanding of Autonomy", in Suksi, Markku (ed), Autonomy: Applications and Implications, Kluwer Law International, 1998, pp. 7–32.

Heintze, Hans-Joachim, "Territorial Autonomy and International Stability: Pros and Cons from the Viewpoint of International Law", in Skurbaty, Zelim A. (ed), Beyond A One-dimensional State: An Emerging Right to Autonomy?, Martinus Nijhoff Publishers, 2005, pp. 47–62.

Hernrard, Kristin, "Non-discrimination and Full and Effective Equality", in Weller, Marc (ed), Universal Minority Rights: A Commentary on the Jurisprudence of International Court and Treaty Bodies, Oxford University Press, 2007, pp. 75–147.

Hershey, Amos S., The Shantung Cession, *American Journal of International Law*, 1919, Volume 13, pp. 530–536.

Higgins, Rosalyn, "Self-determination and Secession", in Dahlitz, Julie (ed), Secession and International Law, The United Nations, 2003, pp. 21–38.

Hilpold, P., Self-determination in the 21st Century – Modern Perspectives for An Old Concept, *Israel Yearbook on Human Rights*, 2005, Volume 36, pp. 247–288.

His Holiness the Dalai Lama's Press Statements on the 'Agreement'—Statement Issued in Tezpur (18/04/1959): http://www.tibet.net/en/index.php?id=186&rmenuid=11.

Ho, David Y.F., "Chapter 11 Filial Piety and Its Psychological Consequences", in Bond, Michael H. (ed), The Handbook of Chinese Psychology, Oxford University Press, 1996, pp. 155–165.

Hobsbawm, Eric, and Ranger, Terence, (eds.), The Invention of Tradition, Cambridge University Press, 1983.

Holt, Sally, "Family, Private Life, and Cultural Rights", in Weller, Marc (ed), Universal Minority Rights: A Commentary on the Jurisprudence of International Court and Treaty Bodies, Oxford University Press, 2007, pp. 203–252.

Hooijmaijers, Marcel, Hong Kong and the Right of Self-determination, *Tilburg Foreign Law Review*, 1997, Volume 6:197, pp. 197–226.

Hornbeck, S. K., "Chapter IV Part II Shantung at the Peace Conference", in Temperley, H. W. V. (ed), A History of the Peace Conference of Paris Volume VI, Henry Frowde and Hodder & Stoughton, 1924, pp. 368–390.

Horowtiz, Donald, "Chapter 9 Self-determination: Politics, Philosophy and Law", in Moore, Margaret (ed), National Self-determination and Secession, Oxford University Press, 1998, pp.181–214.

Hsu, Cho-yun, "Chapter 8 The Spring and Autumn Period", in Loewe, Michael, and Shaughnessy, Edward L, (eds), The Cambridge History of Ancient China, Cambridge University Press, 1999, pp. 545–586.

Hsu, Immanuel C.Y., "Chapter 2 Late Ch'ing Foreign Relations, 1866–1905", in Fairbank, John K, and Liu,Kwang-Ching (eds), The Cambridge History of China: Volume 11, Cambridge University Press, 1980, pp. 70–141.

Hu, Angang, and Hu, Lianhe, Dierdai minzu zhengce: cujin minzu jiaorong yiti he fanrong yiti [A Second-Generation Ethnic Policy: Advancing a Single Body of Ethnic Integration and Prosperity], *Xinjiang Shifan Daxue Xuebao* [*Journal of Xinjiang Normal University*], 2011, Volume 35, No. 05, pp. 1–12.

Hu, Mingyang, Xiandai yuyanxue de fazhan qushi [The Development Trend of Modern Languages], *Yuyan Yanjiu* [*Studies in Language and Linguistics*], 1981, No.00, pp. 1–8.

Huang, Guangxue, and Shi, Lianzhu (eds), Zhongguo de minzu shibie [China's National Identification: the Origins of 56 Nationalities], Minzu Chubanshe, 2005.

Huang, Hongzhao, Aomen shi [The History of Macau], Fujian Renmin Chubanshe, 1999.

Huang, Jilian (ed), The Collection of Historical Records of Chinese-Japanese Negotiation on the Twenty-one Demands 1915–23, Anhui University Press, 2001.

Huang, Xianhong, Lun wanshan xingzheng shouzhang fuzezhi [The Perfection of the Chief Executive Responsibility System], *Zhongguo Faxue* [*China Legal Science*], 1999, Issue 03, pp. 98–103.

Huang, Yao, Guoji renquan fa yu guonei fa de guanxi [The Relationship between International Human Rights Law and National law], *Waiguofa Yiping* [*Global Law Review*], 1999, No. 03, pp. 73–79.

Huang, Ze, Yunnan weishibie qunti yuanjiu de zuqun lilun yiyi [The Significance of the Research about the Unidentified Ethnic Groups in Yunnan], *Guangxi Minzu Xueyuan Xuebao* [*Journal of Guangxi University for Nationalities (Philosophy and Social Science)*], 2001, No. 2, pp. 26–31.

Huang, Zhu, Zhongguo gongchandang minzu zhengce de zhongda zhuanbian [A Great Transformation of the CPC's Policy towards Nationalities—from Federalism to Regional Autonomy of Ethnic Groups], *Zhongnan Minzu Daxue Xuebao* [*Journal of the South-Central University for Nationalities (Humanities and Social Sciences)*], 2003, Volume 23, No. 4, pp. 5–6.

Hughes, Christopher R., Chinese Nationalism in the Global Era, Routledge, 2006.

Hui, Victoria Tin-bor, War, State Formation and Citizenship Rights: an Comparison of Ancient China and Early Modern Europe, *World Economics and Politics*, 2008, Volume 9, pp. 6–20.

Ichiko, Chuzo, "Chapter 7 Political and Institutional Reform, 1901–11", in Fairbank, John K, and Liu, Kwang-Ching (eds), The Cambridge History of China: Volume 11, Cambridge University Press, 1980, pp. 375–415.

IMF Working Paper on "Toward More Effective Redistribution: Reform Options for Intergovernmental Transfers in China", Working Paper No. 04/98, 2004.

International Commission of Jurists, The Question of Tibet and the Rule of Law—A Preliminary Report, Geneva, 1959.

International Commission of Jurists, A Report to the International Commission of Jurists by Its Legal Inquiry Committee on Tibet: Tibet and the Chinese People's Republic, Geneva, 1960.

Iredale, Robyn, Naran, Bilik, and Guo, Fei (eds), China's Minorities On the Move: Selected Case Studies, M. E. Sharpe, 2003.

Jacobs, Dan N., Yin, Gang (Translator), Bao Luoting: Sidalin paidao zhongguo de ren [Borodin: Stalin's Man in China], Shijie Zhishi Chubanshe, 1989.

Jakubowski, Andrzej, Cultural Rights As Collective Rights: An International Law Perspective, Martinus Nijhoff Publishers, 2016.

Jansen, Marius, "Chapter 6 Japan and the Chinese Revolution of 1911", in Fairbank, John K, and Liu, Kwang-Ching (eds), The Cambridge History of China: Volume 11, Cambridge University Press, 1980, pp. 339–374.

Ji, Ya, and Otguntungga, Lag, Zizhi tiaoli lifa zhidu de queshi yu duice [The Countermeasures and Deletion on the Legislation of the Autonomous Regulation], *Neimenggu Daxue Xuebao* [*Journal of Inner Mongolia University* (*Humanities and Social Science*)], 2007, No.6, pp. 36–40.

Jia, Min, and Xiong, Tingting, Meiguo yindi'an he woguo Yi zu shuangyu jiaoyu duibi fenxi [A Comparative Study of the Impact of State Language Policy on Bilingual Education of Native American and Chinese Ethnic Yi], *Mianyang Shifan Xueyuan Xuebao* [*Journal of Mianyang Normal University*], 2008, No. 3, pp. 115–120.

Jiang, Lihong, Shangjunshu zhuizhi [General Comments of the Book of Lord Shang], Zhonghua Shuju, 1986.

Jiang, Yingliang (ed), Zhongguo minzu shi (xiajuan) [The History of China's Nationalities Volume 3], Minzu Chubanshe, 1990.

Jing Binghao (ed), Zhongguo gongchandang minzu gongzuo fazhan yanjiu dier bian: xinjiang xizang [Research on the Developments of the CPC's Ethnic Work Volume 2: Xinjiang and Tibet], Zhongyang Minzu Daxue Chubanshe, 2007.

Jin, Binghao (ed), Minzu gangling zhengce wenxian xuanbian [The Collected Works of the Documents on the National Program and Policy], Zhongyang Minzu Daxue Chubanshe, 2006.

Jin, Binghao, Bi, Yueguang and Han, Yanwei, Minzu yu zuqun: shi gainian de hubu haishi dianfu [The Differences and Similarities between Ethnic Group and Minzu]?, *Heilongjiang Minzu Congkan* [*Heilongjiang National Series*], 2012, No. 02, pp. 4–15.

Jin, Binghao, Sun, Jun and Xiao, Rui, Minzu wenti 'qu zhengzhihua"wenhuahua': xin silu haishi lao taolu [The De-politicalisation and Culturalisation of the Ethnic Question: A New Approach or An Old Scheme]?, *Heilongjiang Minzu Congkan [Heilongjiang National Series]*, 2012, No. 03, pp. 8–16.

Jin, Binghao, and Xiao, Rui, Jianchi zhongguo tese shehui zhuyi shehui minzu lilun zhengce—pingxi 'dierdai minzu zhengce' shuo [On Maintaining Socialism Ethnic Theory and Policy with Chinese Characteristics—Analysis of Second-generation Ethnic Policy], *Xibei Minzu Daxue Xuebao [Journal of Northwest Southwest University for Nationalities]*, 2012, No. 04, pp. 12–19.

Jin, Xinghua (ed), Zhongguo minzu yuwen gongzuo [The Work on Chinese Ethnic Languages and Scripts], Minzu Chubanshe, 2005.

Johnson, Chalmers A., Peasant Nationalism and Communist Power, Stanford University Press, 1963.

Johnston, Reginald F., Confucianism and Modern China, Victor Gollancz Ltd (London), 1934.

Kalina, Xunlu Ewenk ren de sanmanjiao wenhua [Shamanist Culture of Ewenq People Who Train the Deer], *Zhongyang Minzu Daxue Xuebao [Journal of Central University for Nationalities (Philosophy and Social Science)]*, 2007, No. 2, pp. 76–80.

Kang, Youming, Yazhou fudi de Tuwa ren [The Tuvinians in Central Asia], *Xiyu Yanjiu [The Western Regions Studies]*, 1994, No.2, pp. 59–62.

Kaup, Katherine Palmer, Creating the Zhuang: Ethnic Politics in China, Lynne Rienner Publishers, 2000.

Keatings, Michael, and McGarry, John (eds), Minority Nationalism and the Changing International Order, Oxford University Press, 2001.

Keightley, David N,. "Chapter 4 The Shang: China's First Historical Dynasty", in Loewe, Michael, and Shaughnessy, Edward L (eds), The Cambridge History of Ancient China, Cambridge University Press, 1999, pp. 232–291.

Kingsbury, B., "Chapter 14 The Applicability of the International Legal Concept of 'Indigenous Peoples' in Asia, in Rauer, Joanne, and Bell, Daniel (eds), The East Asian Challenge for Human Rights, Cambridge University Press, 1999, pp. 336–377.

Kingsbury, B., " 'Indigenous Peoples' in International Law: A Constructive Approach to the Asian Controversy", *American Journal of International Law*, 1998, No. 92, pp. 414–457.

Kirby, William, The Internationalisation of China: Foreign Relations at Home and Abroad in the Republican Era, *The China Quarterly*, 1997, Volume 150, pp. 433–458.

Klabbers, Jan, The Right To Be Taken Seriously: Self-determination in International Law, *Human Rights Quarterly*, 2006, Volume 28, pp. 186–206.

Knop, Karen, Diversity and Self-determination in International Law, Cambridge University Press, 2002.

Koo, V. K. Wellington, The Institute of Modern History of the Chinese Academy of Science (Translator), Wellington Koo Memoir Volume I, Zhonghua Shuju, 1983.

Kong, Fanzhi, Shilu Ewenke zu jingji de fazhan yu bianhua [The Economic Development and Changes of the Ewenki Reindeer Herders], *Heilongjiang Minzu Congkan* [*Heilongjiang National Series*], 1997, No. 1, pp. 40–42.

Koskenniemi, Martti, National Self-determination Today: Problems of Legal Theory and Practice, *International and Comparative Law Quarterly*, 1994, Volume 43, pp. 241–269.

Kuo, Ting-Yee, "Chapter 10 Self-strengthening: the Pursuit of Western Technology", in Fairbank, John K. (ed), The Cambridge History of China: Volume 10, Cambridge University Press, 1978, pp. 491–542.

Kurpaska, Maria, Chinese Languages: A Look Through the Prism of the Great Dictionary of Modern Chinese Dialects, De Gruyter Mouton, 2010.

Kuyper, P. J., and Kapteyn, P. J. G., "Chapter 22 A Colonial Power as Champion of Self-Determination: Netherlands State Practice in the period 1945–1975", in Panhys, H. F. van, et al (ed), International Law in the Netherlands, Sijthoff &Noordhoff Oceana, 1980, pp.149–218.

Lan, Liguo, Tantan Zhuangwen fangan xiudingan zhong de yixie wenti [On the Problems of Emending Zhuang Language System], *Guangxi Shifan Xueyuan Xuebao* [*Journal of Guangxi Teachers Education University* (*Social Science*)], 2011, No. 3, pp. 130–134.

Language Atlas of China, Longman, 1987.

Lenin, V., "The Attitude of the Workers' Party to Religion", in Lenin, On Religion, Progress Publishers, pp. 18–28.

Lenin, V., "The Revolutionary Proletariat and the Right of Nations to Self-determination", Collected Works of Lenin Volume 21, Lawrence & Wishart London.

Lenin, V., "Theses on the Socialist Revolution and the Right of Nations to self-determination", Collected Works of Lenin Volume 22, Lawrence & Wishart London.

Lenin, V., The Compilation Bureau of the Central Committee of the CCP on the Works of Marx, Engels, Lenin and Stalin (Translator), "Note to the Theses on the Socialist Revolution and the Right of Nations to Self-determination", Liening quanji [Collected Works of Lenin Volume 27], Renmin Chubanshe, 1990.

Lewis, Mark Edward, China Between Empires: the Northern and Southern Dynasties, the Belknap Press of Harvard University Press, 2009.

Li, Fengjuan, Jiabamujia, Ma, Jinwei, and Alimorizha, Liangshan Yizu zizhizhou Yi Han shuangyu jiaoxue shixiaoxing tanxi [Analysis of Effectiveness of Bilingual Teaching of Yi and Chinese Languages in the Liangshan Yi Autonomous Prefecture], *Minzu Jiaoyu Yanjiu* [*Journal of Research on Education for Ethnic Minorities*], 2011, No. 3, pp. 101–106.

Li, Jianjun, and Wang, Dexiang, Jingji kaifang yu defang caizheng shouzhi fei pingheng [Economic Opening-up and the Imbalance of the Local Budget: A Research Based on the Statistics of Provincial Units], *Wuhan Daxue Xuebao* [*Wuhan University Journal*], 2012, No.01, pp. 106–112.

Li, Jianjun, and Xie, Xin, Difang caizheng jiankang yu caizheng fenquan—jiyu Hubei sheng xianji shuju de shizheng fenxi [Local Fiscal Health and Fiscal Decentralisation: An Empirical Study Based on the County-level Data in Hubei Province], *Dangdai Caijing* [*Contemporary Finance and Economics*], 2011, No.7, pp. 33–42.

Li, Lianjiang, The Empowering Effect of Village Elections in China, *Asian Survey*, 2003,Volume 43, pp. 648–662.

Li, Mengzhang, Miaozu zhuiniuji wenhua renleixue chanshi [A Cultural-anthropological Analysis of the 'Drilling-bull' Sacrifice of the Miao], *Minzu Luntan* [*Minzu Tribune*], 2008, No.9, pp. 38–39.

Li, Ruzhong, Lun shuangyu jiaoyu de moshi [A Study on the Mode of Bilingual Education in Xinjiang], *Xinjiang Jiaoyu Xueyuan Xuebao* [*Journal of Xinjiang Education Institute*], 2011, No.01, pp. 25–34.

Li, Qianlan, and Wang, Handong, Gaige kaifang yilai zhongguo shaoshu minzu guangbo yingshi shiye de fazhan yu sikao [The Development of Broadcasting and Television Programmes in Minority Languages Since the Reform and Opening Up], *Hubei Shehui Kexue* [*Hubei Social Sciences*], 2013, No.3, pp. 190–194.

Li, Xiaochen, Xinzhongguo jianli qianhou huabei nongcun pochu mixin tanxi [Comments on the Efforts to Do (Sweep) Away with Superstition in Rural North China around the Founding of New China], *Zhonggong Dangshi Yanjiu* [*Journal of CPC History Studies*], 2005, Issue 04, pp. 86–92.

Li Xulian, and Huang Quanxi, "Chapter 13 The Introduction and Development of the Zhuang Writing System", in Zhou, Minglang, and Sun, Hongkai (eds), Language Policy in the PRC: Theory and Practice since 1949, Kluwer Academic Publishers, 2004, pp. 239–256.

Li, Xueqin (ed), Shisanjing zhushu: Liji Zhengyi [The Thirteen Classics Explanatory Notes and Commentaries: the Book of Rites], Beijing Daxue Chubanshe, 1999.

Li, Xuezhi, Minyuan guoqi zhizheng [The Debate Over the National Flag of the Republic of China in 1912], *Shixue Yuekan* [*Journal of Historical Science*], 1998, No. 01, pp. 46–50.

Li, Yunxia, Manwen de qiyuan jiqi fazhan yanbian [The Origin and Development of Manchu Characters], *Manyu Yanjiu* [*Manchu Studies*], 2003, No. 1, pp. 63–67.

Liang, Hong-Ming, "China", in Herb, Guntram H, and Kaplan, David H (eds), Nations and Nationalism: A Global Historical Overview, Volume 2, 1880–1945, ABC-CLIO Inc., 2008, pp. 787–795.

Liew, Leong H., and Wang, Shaoguang (eds.), Nationalism, Democracy and National Integration in China, Routledge Curzon, 2004.

Lin Xianggeng, Woguo zongjiaojie yu zhongguo gongchandang lingdao de aiguo tongyi zhanxian [China's Religion Circles and the Patriotic United Front Led by the CPC], *Dangshi Yanjiu yu Jiaoxue* [*Party History Research and Teaching*], 2003, Issue 01, pp. 10–16.

Lin, Yaohua, Zhongguo xinan diqu de minzu shibie [Ethnic Identification in Southwest China], *Yunnan Shehui Kexue* [*Social Science in Yunan*], 1984, Issue 02, pp. 1–5.

Litzinger, Ralph, Other Chinas: the Yao and the Politics of National Belonging, Duke University Press, 2000.

Liu, E, "Chapter 1 Minzu yici de hanyi jiqi fazhan guilv [The Definition of Minzu and Its Development]", in Huang, Guangxue, and Shi, Lianzhu (eds), Zhongguo de minzu shibie [The Ethnic Identification in China], Minzu chubanshe, 2005, pp. 1–25.

Liu, Lydia H, The Clash of Empire: the Invention of China in Modern World Making, Harvard University Press, 2004.

Liu, Shaoqi, "Report on the Draft Constitution of the PRC 1954", in Macinnis, Donald (ed), Religious Policy and Practice in Communist China, Hodder and Stoughton, 1972, pp. 23–24.

Liu, Shaoqi, "Report to the Eighth National Congress of the CCP (05/09/1956)", in Jin Binghao (ed), Minzu gangling zhengce wenxian xuanbian [The Collected Works of the Documents on the National Program and Policy], Zhongyang Minzu Daxue Chubanshe, 2006, pp. 551–553.

Liu, Shaoqi, "Various Questions Concerning Fundamental Policies in Anti-Japan Guerrilla Warfare (16/10/1937)", in Jin, Binghao (ed), Minzu gangling zhengce wenxian xuanbian [The Collected Works of the Documents on the National Program and Policy], Zhongyang Minzu Daxue Chubanshe, 2006, pp. 205–209.

Liu, Zhiguang, Woguo defang zhengfu caizheng shouru laiyuan jiqi guimo [The Sources and Scale of Local Revenues], *Difang Caizheng Yanjiu* [*Sub National Fiscal Research*], 2010, No. 04, pp. 14–19.

Lloyd-Jones, Stewart, and Pinto, Antonio Costa (eds), The Last Empire: Thirty Years of Portuguese Decolonisation, Intellect, 2003.

Lu, Qun, Shilun Xiangxi Miao zu xinyang de zongzu yishi tezheng [On the Features of Ancestral Consciousness in Which the Miao Nationality Believes in the West of Hunan], *Hubei Minzu Xueyuan Xuebao* [*Journal of Hubei Institute for Nationalities (Philosophy and Social Science)*], 2001, No. 1, pp. 46–49.

Lu, Qun, Shilun Miao zu xinyang de shisuxing [On the Secularity of the Miao Religious Beliefs], *Kaili Xueyuan Xuebao* [*Journal of Kaili University*], 2002, Issue 01, pp. 24–25.

Lu, Qun, Miaozu yanxu zhijin de wanwu youling xinyang ji yuanyin poxi [On the Last-to-today Beliefs-All Things on Earth Have Sprits-of Miao Nationality], *Guizhou Minzu Yanjiu* [*Guizhou Ethnic Studies*], 2002, No. 4, pp. 88–92.

Lu, Qun, Miaozu yuanshi zongjiao xinyang de xiandai qiyixing bianhua [The Variety of Modern Deviation in Miao's Primitive Religion and Faith: with an example of Miao in La Dongshan in the West of Hunan Province], *Zhongang Minzu Daxue Xuebao [Journal of the Central University for Nationalities (Philosophy and Social Science)]*, 2003, No. 2, pp. 96–99.

Luard, Evan, Britain and China, Chatto & Windus, 1962.

Lundberg, Maria, and Zhou, Yong, Hunting-prohibition in the Hunter's Autonomous Area: Legal Rights of Oroqen People and the Implementation of Regional National Autonomy Law, *International Journal on Minority and Group Rights*, 2009, Volume 16, pp. 349–397.

Lundberg, Maria, and Zhou, Yong, Regional National Autonomy under Challenge: Law, Practice and Recommendations, *International Journal on Minority and Group Rights*, 2009, Volume 16, pp. 269–327.

Luo, Gang, The Factual Account of Dr. Sun Yat-sen, Volume 5, *Zhengzhong Shuju*, 1988.

Luo, Meizhen, Luo Meizhen zixuan wenji [Selected Works of Luo Meizhen], Minzu Chubanshe, 2007.

Luo, Zhufeng (ed), MacInnis, Donald, and Zheng, Xi'an (Translators), Religion under Socialism in China, M.E. Sharpe, Inc, 1991.

Lustgarten, Laurence, Legal Control of Racial Discrimination, The Macmillan Press, 1980.

Ma, Rong, Guanyu 'minzu' dingyi [On the Definitions of 'Minzu'], *Yunnan Minzu Xueyuan Xuebao [Journal of Yunan University of the Nationalities]*, 2000, Volume 17, No. 1, pp. 5–13.

Ma, Rong, Lijie minzu guanxi de xin silu – shaoshu zuqun de "qu zhengzhihua" [A New Approach to Understanding Minority Group Relations: the "De-politicisation" of the Ethnic Question], *Beijing Daxue Xuebao [Journal of Peking University (Philosophy and Social Science)]*, 2004, No. 06, pp. 122–133.

Ma, Rong, A New Perspective in Guiding Ethnic Relations in the 21st Century: 'De-politicisation' of Ethnicity in China, *Asian Ethnicity*, 2007, Volume 08, No. 03, pp. 199–217.

Ma, Xiaoyi, Shixi minzu yuwen zhengce dui shaoshu minzu xinchuang wenzi de yingxiang [Analysis of the Influence of Minority Language Policy on the New Words Created by Ethnic Minorities], *Minzu Jiaoyu Yanjiu [Journal of Research on Education for Minorities]*, 2009, No. 4, pp. 10–16.

Mackerras, C., China's Minorities: Integration and Modernisation in the 20th Century, Oxford University Press, 1994.

Mackerras, C., China's Minority Cultures: Identities and Integration since 1912, Longman, 1995.

Mackerras, C., China's Ethnic Minorities and Globalisation, Routledge Curzon, 2003.

MacInnis, Donald, Religion in China Today: Policy and Practice, Orbis Books, 1989.

Malakhov, Vladimir, and Osipov, Alexander, "The Category of 'Minorities' in Russian Federation: a Reflection on Uses and Misuses", in Åkermark, Sia Spiliopoulou (ed),

International Obligations and National Debates: Minorities Around the Baltic Sea, Åland Islands Peace Institute, Mariehamn, 2006, pp. 495–542.

Mao, Zedong, Mao Zedong wenji [The Writing of Mao Zedong: Volume 4], Zhongyang Wenxian Chubanshe, 1996.

Mao, Zedong, "Childhood Influence (as Told to Edgar Snow)", in Macinnis, Donald (ed), Religious Policy and Practice in Communist China, Hodder and Stoughton, 1972, pp. 6–7.

Mao, Zedong, "On Coalition Government 1945", in Mao Zedong, Selected Works of Mao Tse-Tung, Volume III, Pergamon Press, 1965, pp. 205–270.

Mao, Zedong, "The Question of Independence and Initiative within the United Front(05/11/1938)", in Selected Works of Mao Zedong Volume 2, http://cpc.people.com.cn/GB/64184/64185/66616/4488931.html; English translation is available at http://www.marxists.org/reference/archive/mao/selected-works/volume-2/mswv2_11.htm.

Mao, Zedong, "The Chinese Revolution and the Chinese Communist Party (12/1939)", Selected Works of Mao Zedong Volume II, Pergamon Press, 1965, pp. 305–334.

Mao, Zedong, "On Coalition Government (1945)", in Macinnis, Donald (ed), Religious Policy and Practice in Communist China, Hodder and Stoughton, 1972, p.14.

Mao, Zedong, "On New Democracy", in Selected Works of Mao Zedong Volume II, Foreign Language Press, 1965, pp. 339–384.

Mao, Zedong, "On the New Stage (10/1938)", in Jin Binghao (ed), Minzu gangling zhengce wenxian xuanbian [The Collected Works of the Documents on the National Program and Policy], Zhongyang Minzu Daxue Chubanshe, 2006, pp. 221–226.

Mao, Zedong, "On the Ten Major Relationships (25/04/1956)", in Jin, Binghao (ed), Minzu gangling zhengce wenxian xuanbian [The Collected Works of the Documents on the National Program and Policy], Zhongyang Minzu Daxue Chubanshe, 2006, pp. 540–541.

Mao, Zedong, "Sixty Points On Working Methods (Draft)", in Gao, Qirong and Li, Jiang, Mao Zedong 'gongzuo fangfa liushitiao (caoan)' luelun [A General Discussion of Mao Zedong's Sixty Points On Working Methods (Draft)], *Dangshi Yanjiu yu Jiaoxue* [*Party History Research & Teaching*], 2008, No. 01, pp. 50–55.

Mao, Zedong, "Overthrowing the Clan Authority of the Ancestral Temples and Clan Elders, the Religious Authority of Town and Village Gods, and the Masculine Authority of Husbands (1927)", in Macinnis, Donald (ed), Religious Policy and Practice in Communist China, Hodder and Stoughton, 1972, pp. 7–10.

Mao, Zedong (Author), Kau, Michael Y. M., and Leung, John K. (eds), The Writing of Mao Zedong, 1949–1976: Volume 1 September 1949-December 1955, M.E. Sharpe, Inc, 1986.

Mao, Zongwu, Meng, Chaogu, and Zheng, Zongze (eds), Yaozu yuyan jianzhi [A Brief History of the Yao Language], Minzu Chubanshe, 1982.

Marsh, Christopher, Religion and the State in Russia and China: Suppression, Survival and Revival, Continuum, 2011.

Marx, Karl, "Critique of Hegel's Philosophy of Right", in Marx, Karl, and Engels, Friedrich, On religion, Scholars Press, 1964, pp. 41–68.

May, Stephen, Language and Minority Rights: Ethnicity, Nationalism, and the Politics of Language (2nd Edition), Routledge, 2012.

Meacham, William, Defining the Hundred Yue, *Bulletin of the Indo-Pacific Prehistory Association,* 1996, Volume 15, pp. 93–100.

Memorandum on Genuine Autonomy for the Tibetan People, http://tibet.net/important-issues/sino-tibetan-dialogue/memorandum-on-geniune-autonomy-for-the-tibetan-people/.

Mccorquodale, Robert, Negotiating Sovereignty: the Practice of the United Kingdom in Regard to the Right of Self-determination, *British Yearbook of International law,* 1995, Volume 66, pp. 283–331.

McGregor, Richard, The Party: the Secret World of China's Communist Rulers, Allen Lane, 2010.

Miller, David, On Nationality, Clarendon Press, 1995.

Miller, James (ed), Chinese Religions in Contemporary Society, ABC-Clio, 2006.

Mitter, Rana, The Manchurian Myth: Nationalism, Resistance, and Collaboration in Modern China, University of California Press, 2000.

Moneyhon, Matthew, Controlling Xinjiang: Autonomy on China's 'New Frontier', *Asian-Pacific law & Policy Journal,* 2002, Volume 3, Issue 01, pp. 120–152.

Morgan, Rhiannon, Transforming Law and Institution: Indigenous Peoples, the UN and Human Rights, Ashgate Publishing, 2011.

Moseley, George, The Consolidation of the South China Frontier, University of California Press, 1973.

Minzu shibie he genggai minzu chengfen gongzuo yi jiben wancheng [Ethnic Identification and the Alteration of Ethnic Identity Have Completed—An Interview with Huang Guangxue, the Vice Director of the SEAC], *Zhongguo Minzu* [*China's Ethnic Groups*], 1987, Issue 02, pp. 16–17.

Mullaney, Thomas, Coming to Terms with the Nation—Ethnic Classification in Modern China, University of California Press, 2011.

Musgrave, Thomas, Self-determination and National Minorities, Oxford University Press, 2002.

Naran, Bilik, Minzu yu minzu gainian bianzheng [Dialectic of Minzu and the Minzu Concept], *Minzu Yanjiu* [*Ethno-National Studies*], 1990, Issue 05, pp 11–17.

Naran, Bilik, Minzu yu minzu gainian zai bianzheng [Another Dialectic of Minzu and Minzu Concept], *Minzu Yanjiu* [*Ethno-National Studies*], 1995, Issue 03, pp. 9–15.

Naran, Bilik, Minzu bainian huimou [A Historical Review of Minzu], *Guangxi Minzu Yanjiu* [*Study of Nationalities in Guangxi*], 2000, No. 02, pp. 17–23.

Nivison, David Shephed, "Chapter 11 The Classical Philosophical Writing", in Loewe, Michael, and Shaughnessy, Edward L (eds), The Cambridge History of Ancient China, Cambridge University Press, 1999, pp. 745–812.

O'Brien, Kevin J., Villagers, Elections, and Citizenship in Contemporary China, *Modern China*, 2001, Volume 27, pp. 407–435.

O'Brien, Kevin J., and Li, Lianjiang, Accommodating "Democracy" in a One-Party State: Introducing Village Elections in China, *The China Quarterly*, 2000, Volume 162, pp. 465–489.

Oliverira, de Adolfo (ed), Decolonising Indigenous Rights, Routledge, 2009.

Overmyer, Daniel, Local Religion in Nouth China in the Twentieth Century: the Structure and Organisation of Community Rituals and Beliefs, Brill, 2009.

Packer, John, "Chapter 6 On the Content of Minority Rights", in Raikka, Juha (ed), Do We Need Minority Rights? Conceptual Issues, Martinus Nijhoff Publishers, 1996, pp. 121–178.

Pan, Hongxiang, Zizhiqu zizhi tiaoli chutainan de yuanyin fenxi ji duice [Countermeasures and Casual Analysis on Hard Promulating Autonomous Regulations in Autonomous Regions], *Beifang Minzu Daxue Xuebao* [*Journal of Beifang Ethnic University*], 2009, No. 3, pp. 55–60.

Pan, Jiao, "Zuqun" yu minzu gainian de hubu haishi dianfu [On the Differences and Similarities between Ethnic Group and Ethnos], *Yunan Minzu Daxue Xuebao* [*Journal of Yunnan Nationalities University* (*Social Sciences*), 2009, Volume 26, No. 01, pp. 22–28.

Pastor, Robert A., and Tan, Qingshan, The Meaning of China's Village Elections, *The China Quarterly*, 2000, Volume 162, pp. 490–512

Pepper, Suzanne, "Chapter 13 The KMD-CCP Conflict 1945–1949", in Fairbank, John K., and Feuerwerker, Albert (eds), The Cambridge History of China: Volume 13, Cambridge University Press, 1986, pp. 723–788.

Phan, Binh, How Autonomous Are the National Autonomous Areas of the PRC? An Analysis of Documents and Cases, *Issues and Studies*, 1996, Volume 32: 7, pp. 83–108.

Philpott, Daniel, "Chapter 5 Self-determination in Practice", in Moore, Margaret (ed), National Self-determination and Secession, Oxford University Press, 1998, pp.79–102.

Pomerance, Michla, Self-determination in Law and Practice: the New Doctrine in the United Nations, Martinus Nijhoff Publishers, 1982.

Pomerance, Michla, The United States and Self-determination: Perspectives on the Wilsonian Conception, *American Journal of International Law*, 1976, Volume 70, pp. 1–27.

Porter, Pitman, Belief in Control: Regulation of Religion in China, *The China Quarterly*, 2003, Volume 174, pp. 317–337.

Powers, John, History as Propaganda: Tibetans Exiles Versus the People's Republic of China, Oxford University Press, 2004.

Pu, Zhongliang, "Chapter 14 Policies on the Planning and Use of the Yi Language and Writing System", in Zhou, Minglang, and Sun, Hongkai (eds), Language Policy in the PRC: Theory and Practice since 1949, Kluwer Academic Publishers, 2004, pp. 257–275.

Qi, Huijun, Xunlu Ewenke ren shengtai yimin de minzuxue kaocha [Ethnological Investigation on the Ecological Immigration of Reindeer Ewenki], *Manyu Yanjiu* [*Manchu Studies*], 2006, No. 1, pp. 98–105.

Qin, Naichang, Makesi zhuyi minzu lilun zhongguohua de zhongda shijian [Ethnic Edentification: Great Practice of the Localisation of Marxist Ethnic Theory in China], *Guangxi Minzu Yanjiu* [*Study of Ethnics in Guangxi*], 2009, No.2, pp. 20–28.

Quane, Helen, The United Nations and the Evolving Right to Self-determination, *International and Comparative Law Quarterly*, 1998, Volume 47, No.03, pp. 537–572.

Raic, David, Statehood and the Law of Self-determination, Kulwer Law International, 2002.

Ren, Qiang, and Yuan, Xin, "Chapter 5 Impacts of Migration to Xinjiang since the 1950s", in Iredale, Robyn, Naran, Bilik, and Guo, Fei (eds), China's Minorities On the Move: Selected Case Studies, M. E. Sharpe, 2003, pp. 89–104.

Report of the African Commission's Working Group of Experts on Indigenous Populations/Communities, 2005.

Richardson, H. E., Tibet and Its History, London Oxford University Press, 1962.

Riedel, Eibe, Giacca, Gilles, and Golay, Christophe (eds), Economic, Social, and Cultural Rights in International Law: Contemporary Issues and Challenges, Oxford University Press, 2014.

Rossabi, Morris, Governing China's Multiethnic Frontiers, University of Washington Press, 2004.

Salomon, Margot, "Socio-economic Rights as Minority Rights", in Weller, Marc (ed), Universal Minority Rights: A Commentary on the Jurisprudence of International Court and Treaty Bodies, Oxford University Press, 2007, pp. 431–475.

Sautman, Barry, Ethnic Law and Minority Rights in China: Progress and Constraints, *Law and Policy*, 1999, Volume 21, Issue 03, pp. 283–314.

Sautman, Barry, Scaling Back Minority Rights? The Debate About China's Ethnic Policies, *Stanford Journal of International Law*, 2010, Volume 46:01, pp. 51–120.

Sautman, Barry, and Dreyer, June (eds), Contemporary Tibet: Politics, Development, and Society in a Disputed Region, M.E. Sharpe, 2006.

Schmitt, Carl, Political Theology: Four Chapters on the Concept of Sovereignty, The University of Chicago Press, 2005.

Schram, Stuart, "Chapter 14 Mao Tse-tung's Thought to 1949", in Fairbank, John K., and Feuerwerker, Albert (eds), The Cambridge History of China: Volume 13, Cambridge University Press, 1986, pp. 789–870.

Scharf, Michael, Earned Sovereignty: Juridical Underpinnings, *Denver Journal of International Law and policy*, 2004, Volume 31, No.03, pp. 373–387.

Schrecker, John, The Reform Movement, Nationalism and China's Foreign Policy, *The Journal of Asian Studies*, 1969, Volume 29, No. 1, pp. 43–53.

Schwartz, Benjamin, Chinese Communism and the Rise of Mao, Harvard University Press, 1966.

Se, Yin, Saman jiao yu nanfang minzu minjian zongjiao bijiao yanjiu [A Comparative Study of Shamanism and Folk Religion in the South], *Yunnan Shehui Kexue* [*Social Sciences in Yunnan*], 2000, Issue 03, pp. 80–84.

Seton-Watson, Hugh, Nations and States—An Enquiry Into the Origins of Nations and the Politics of Nationalism, Methuen London, 1977.

Shao, Chuan Leng, and Palmer, Norman D., Sun Yat-Sen and Communism, Thames and Hudson (London), 1961.

Shaughnessy, Edward L, "Chapter 5 Western Zhou History", in Loewe, Michael, and Shaughnessy, Edward L (eds), The Cambridge History of Ancient China, Cambridge University Press, 1999, pp. 292–351.

Shen, Jianming, Sovereignty, Statehood, Self-Determination, and the Issue of Taiwan, *American University International Law Review*, 2002, Volume 15, Issue 5, pp. 1101–1161.

Shen, Shouwen, Minzu quyu zizhi defang lifaquan ruogan wenti yanjiu [A Study on Some Problems of Local Legislative Power in Ethnic Autonomous Areas], *Yunnan Shehui Kexue* [*Social Sciences in Yunnan*], 2007, Issue 03, pp. 75–79.

Shi, Yilong, Ethnic Group buneng zuowei Minzu de yingwen duiyi [Minzu Should Not Be Translated as Ethnic Group], *Shijie Minzu* [*World Ethno-National Studies*], 1999, No. 04, p. 79.

Shi, Zhe, Zai lishi juren shenbian—Shizhe huiyi lu [At the Side of the Giant in History: Shi Zhe's Memoirs], Zhongyang Wenxian Chubanshe, 1991.

Shi, Zongren, Miaozu yu chuguo guanxi xinlun [New Interpretation to the Relation of Miao People and the State of Chu], *Zhongyang Minzu Daxue Xuebao* [*Journal of the Central University for Nationalities (Philosophy and Social Sciences)*], 1994, Volume 6, pp. 23–26.

Shiromany, A. A. (ed), The Spirit of Tibet: Universal Heritage--Selected Speeches and Writings of HH the Dalai Lama XIV, Allied Publishers, 1995.

Shu, Jingxiang, Woguo Hezhe zu "jiuwu" qijian shixian le lishixing de kuayue fazhan [The Development of the Historic Span in the Ninth-Five-Year Plan Period of the Hezhens], *Heilongjiang Minzu Congkan* [*Heilongjiang National Series*], 2001, No. 3, pp. 40–44.

Sima, Qian, Han, Zhaoqi (Chief Translator), Shi Ji [Records of the Grand Historian: Volume I, Annals of the Zhou Dynasty], Zhonghua Shuju, 2008.

Simpson, George, and Yinger, J., Racial and Cultural Minorities: an Analysis of Prejudice and Discrimination (4th Edition), Harper and Row Publisher, 1972.

Skurbaty, Zelim A., "Introduction", in Skurbaty, Zelim A. (ed), Beyond A One-dimensional State: An Emerging Right to Autonomy?, Martinus Nijhoff Publishers, 2005, pp. xxxi–lviii.

Smith, Anthony, The Ethnic Origins of Nations, Basil Blackwell, 1986.

Smith, Anthony, National Identity, Penguin Books, 1991.

Smith, Anthony, Nationalism: Theory, Ideology, History, Polity Press, 2001.

Song, Caifa, Minzu zizhi defang lifa zizhiquan zai tantao [A Re-examination of Legislative Autonomy in Ethnic Autonomous Areas], *Faxuejia* [*The Jurist*], 2005, Issue 02, pp. 73–79.

Spence, Jonathan, "Chapter 3 The K'ang-hsi Reign", in Peterson, Willard J (ed), The Cambridge History of China: Volume 9, Cambridge University Press, 2002, pp. 120–182.

Sprenkel, Sybille Van Der, "Chapter 7: The Role of Law in the Changing Society", in Gray, Jack (ed), Modern China's Search for A Political Form, Oxford University Press, 1969, pp. 225–267.

Ssenyonjo, Manisuli, Economic, Social and Cultural Rights in International Law, Hart Publishing, 2009.

Stalin, Joseph, "Marxism and the National Question", in Franklin, Bruce (ed), The Essential Stalin: Major Theoretical Writings 1905–52, Croom Helm London, 1973, pp. 54–84.

Statement Issued at the Press Conference Held at Mussoorie (20/06/1959), in Shiromany, A. A. (ed), The Spirit of Tibet: Universal Heritage--Selected Speeches and Writings of HH the Dalai Lama XIV, Allied Publishers, 1995, pp. 10–14.

Statistics Department of the Government of XUAR, Xinjiang Statistical Yearbook 2012.

Stavenhagen, Rodolfo, "Chapter 5 Cultural Rights: A Social Science Perspective", in Eide, Asbjorn, Krause, Catarina, and Rosas, Allan (eds), Economic, Social and Cultural Rights: A Textbook, Martinus Nijhoff Publishers, 2001, pp. 85–110.

Stavenhagen, Rodolfo, Ethnic Conflicts and the Nation-state, The Macmillan Press, 1996.

Stites, Regie, "Chapter 4 Writing Cultural Boundaries: National Minority Language Policy, Literacy Planning, and Bilingual Education", in Postiglione, Gerard A. (ed), China's National Minority Education: Culture, Schooling, and Development, Falmer Press, 1999, pp. 95–130.

Straumann, Benjamin, Early Modern Sovereignty and Its Limits, *Theoretical Inquiries in Law*, 2015, Issue 16, pp. 423–446.

Su, Bingqi, and Yin, Weizhang, Guangyu kaoguxue wenhua de quxi leixing wenti [The Region, System and Type of Culture in the Archaeology], *Wenwu* [*Archaeology*], 1981, No. 5, pp. 10–17.

Summers, James, Peoples and International Law, Martinus Nijhoff Publishers, 2007.

Summers, James, Peoples and International Law (2nd Edition), Martinus Nijhoff Publishers, 2014.

Sun, Hongkai, "Chapter 10 Theorising Over 40 Years Personal Experiences with the Creation and Development of Minority Writing Systems of China", in Zhou, Minglang, and Sun, Hongkai (eds), Language Policy in the PRC: Theory and Practice since 1949, Kluwer Academic Publishers, 2004, pp. 179–199.

Sun, Hongkai, "Zhongguo yuyan shibie gongzuo [The Identification of China's Languages], in Ma, Liya et al. (eds), Zhongguo minzu yuwen zhengce yu falv shuping [Review of Policy and Law on Linguistic Minorities in China], Minzu Chubanshe, 2007, pp.31–53.

Sun, Hongkai, Zhongguo shaoshu minzhu yuyan huoli paixu yanjiu [Ranking of the Chinese Ethnic Languages in Terms of Their Vitality], *Guangxi Minzu Daxue Xuebao* [*Journal of Guangxi University for Nationalities (Philosophy and Social Science)*], 2006, No. 5, pp. 6–10.

Sun, Hongkai, Hu, Zengyi, and Huang, Xing (eds), Zhongguo de yuyan [The Languages of China], Shangwu Yinshuguan, 2007.

Sun, Yat-sen, "Chapter 10 The Principle of Nationalism", in Kedourie, Elie (ed), Nationalism in Asia and Africa, Weidenfeld and Nicolson, 1971, pp. 304–317.

Sun, Yat-sen, The Three Principles of the People: San Min Chu I, China Publishing Co.

Sun, Yat-sen, Sun Yat-sen's Collected Works Volume 1, Zhonghua Shuju, 1981.

Sun, Yat-sen, Sun Yat-sen's Collected Works Volume 2, Zhonghua Shuju, 1982.

Sun,Yat-sen, Sun Yat-sen's Collected Works Volume 5, Zhonghua Shuju, 1985.

Sun, Yat-sen, Sun Yat-sen's Collected Works Volume 9, Zhonghua Shuju, 1986.

Suksi, Markku, "Autonomy, Minorities and Self-determination—the Protection of the Rights of Minorities by Means of Autonomy: the Cases of the Aland and Kosovo", in Skurbaty, Zelim A. (ed), Beyond A One-dimensional State: An Emerging Right to Autonomy?, Martinus Nijhoff Publishers, 2005, pp. 379–399.

Symonides, Janusz, "Chapter 5 Cultural Rights", in Symonides, Janusz (ed), Human Rights: Concept and Standards, UNESCO Publishing, 2000, pp.175–227.

Tan, Qixiang (ed), Zhongguo lishi ditu ji [The Historical Atlas of China Volume VIII: the Qing Dynasty Period, Zhongguo Ditu Chubanshe, 1996.

Tan, Zhaoyi, Minguo shiqi xingguixi de minzu zhengce pingshu [A Comment on the Policy Concerning the Ethnic Nationalities by Neo-Guangxi Regime During 1911–1949 Period in China], *Guangxi Shifan Daxue Xuebao* [*Journal of Guangxi Normal University*], 2005, Volume 41, No. 2, pp. 133–137.

Tan, Wanxia, Guanxi zhuangzu zizhiqu zizhi tiaoli zhi lifa sikao [Legislative Suggestions on Guangxi Autonomous Region's Regulation of Autonomy], *Guangxi Minzu Yanjiu* [*Study of Ethnics in Guangxi*], 2011, Issue 03, pp. 40–46.

Tang, Ge, Elunchun he Ewenke: cong shouliemin dao nongmin de kunjing [Olunchun (Oroqen) and Ewenki: Different Position From Hunter To Farmer], *Manyu Yanjiu* [*Manchu Studies*], 2008, No. 1, pp. 89–94.

Teng, Xing, and Ma, Xiaoyi, Zhongguo gaodeng jiaoyu de shaoshu minzu youhui zhengce yu jiaoyu pingdeng [China's Preferential Policy to Minority Nationalities in Higher Education and Education Equality], *Minzu Yanjiu* [*Ethno-National Studies*], 2005, No. 5, pp. 10–18.

Teng, Xing, and Weng, Yanheng, "Chapter 11 Bilingualism and Bilingual Education in China", in Shimahara, N. Ken., Holowinsky, Ivan Z., and Tomlinson-Clarke, Saundra (eds), Ethnicity, Race and Nationality in Education: A Global Perspective, Lawrence Erlbaum Associates, 2001, pp. 259–277.

Tian, Yan, Hexie shehui linian zhidao xia Elunchun zu wenhua quanli de baohu [Analysing the Protection of Cultural Rights on Elunchun (Oroqen) Ethnic(ity) at the Direction of Harmonious Society], *Yunnan Daxue Xuebao* [*Journal of Yunnan University*], 2007, No.5, pp. 147–153.

The Compilation Committee on the Local History of Weihai City, The History of Weihai, Shandong Renmin Chubanshe, 1986.

The Ethnic Affair Commission of Guizhou Province, Fifty Years of Ethnic Work in Guizhou, Guizhou Minzu Chubanshe, 1999.

The State Council, The White Paper: Freedom of Religious Belief in China, 1997.

The State Council, The White Paper: The Taiwan Question and Reunification of China, 1993.

The State Council, The White Paper: The One-China Principle and the Taiwan Issue, 2000.

The State Council, The White Paper: Regional Ethnic Autonomy in Tibet, 2004.

The Research Center of General Office of the Standing Committee of the National People's Congress (ed), Zhongguo jindai bupingdeng tiaoyue huiyao [The Collection of the Unequal Treaties in Modern History of China], Minzhu Fazhi Chubanshe, 1996.

The United Front Work Department of the CPC Central Committee (ed), Minzu wenti wenxian huibian [The Collection of Documents on the National Question (July 1921– September 1949)], Zhonggong Zhongyang Dagnxiao Chubanshe, 1991.

The Writing Group of the Overview of the Dali Bai Autonomous Prefecture, Dali Baizu zizhizhou gaikuang [Overview of the Dali Bai Autonomous Prefecture], Yunnan Minzu Chubanshe, 1986.

Thornberry, Patrick, Confronting Racial Discrimination: A CERD Perspective, *Human Rights Law Review*, 2005, Volume 5, pp. 239–269.

Thornberry, Patrick, "Images of Autonomy and Individual and Collective Rights in International Instruments on the Rights of Minorities", in Suksi, Markku, (ed), Autonomy: Applications and Implications, Kluwer Law International, 1998, pp. 97–124.

Thornberry, Patrick, International Law and the Right of Minorities, Clarendon Press, 2001.

Tilly, Charles, The Formation of National States in Western Europe, Princeton University Press, 1975.

Tombs, Robert (ed), Nationhood and Nationalism in France: From Boulangism to the Great War 1889–1918, HarperCollins Academic, 1991.

Tomuschat, Christian, "Chapter 1 Secession and Self-determination", in Kohen, Marcelo (ed), Secession: International Law Perspective, Cambridge University Press, 2006, pp. 23–45.

Townsend, James, Chinese Nationalism, *The Australian Journal of Chinese Affairs*, 1992, No. 27, pp. 97–130.

Tsang, Steve, A Modern History of Hong Kong, I.B. Tauris & Co Ltd, 2007.

Tuohutasen, Batehan, Xinjiang minzu yuyan wenzi gongzuo dashiji [Chronology of the Events of Xinjiang Ethnic Language and Script Work], *Yuyan yu Fanyi* [*Language and Translation*], 1995, No. 1, pp. 5–12.

Udombana, Nsongurua, "Chapter 15 Reparations and Africa's Indigenous Peoples", in Lenzerini, F. (ed), Reparations for Indigenous Peoples: International and Comparative Perspectives, Oxford University Press, 2008, pp. 389–407.

Ulanfu, Report on the Establishment of Guangxi Zhuang and Ningxia Hui Autonomous Region at the Fourth Session of the First National People's Congress, (07/07/1957), http://www.npc.gov.cn/wxzl/gongbao/2000-12/23/content_5328393.htm.

UNESCO Ad Hoc Expert Group on Endangered Languages, Language Vitality and Endangerment, 2003.

US, Department of State, The China White Paper: August 1949, Volume 1, Stanford University Press, 1967.

Wakeman, Frederic, "Chapter 4 The Canton Trade and the Opium War", in Fairbank, John K. (ed), The Cambridge History of China: Volume 10, Cambridge University Press, 1978, pp. 163–212.

Wang, Aiyun, Zhonggong yu shaoshu minzu wenzi de chuangzhi he gaige [The CPC and the Language Creation and Reform for the Minorities], *Zhonggong Dangshi Yanjiu* [*Journal of Chinese Communist Party History Studies*], 2013, No. 07, pp. 71–81.

Wang, Christine P. W., and Bhattasali, Deepak, China: National Development and Sub-national Finance: A Review of Provincial Expenditures, Citic Publishing House, 2003.

Wang, Dianzhi, Fenshuizhi zhong de 1:0.3 xishu jiqi liwai [The 1:0.3 Indexed Ratio in the Taxation Division System and Its Exceptions], *Difang Caizheng Yanjiu* [*Sub National Fiscal Research*], 2010, Issue 05, pp. 41–46.

Wang, Feng, Lun yuyan zai zuqun rentong zhong de diwei he biaoxian xingshi [The Role and Expressive Forms of Language in Ethnic Identity], *Yunnan Shifan Daxue Xuebao* [*Journal of Yunnan Normal University* (*Humanities and Social Sciences*)], 2010, No. 4, pp. 72–78.

Wang, Huanlu, Mozi jigu [Commentaries on Mozi]: Volume 1, Shanghai Guji Chubanshe, 2005.

Wang, Jianlang, Zhongguo feichu bupingdeng tiaoyue de lishi kaocha [A Historical Investigation of the Abolition of Unequal Treaties in China], *Lishi Yanjiu* [*Historical Research*], 1997, Issue 05, pp. 5–19.

Wang, Jun, Minzu yuwen kexue taolunhui [The Scientific Symposium on National Languages], *Kexue Tongbao* [*Chinese Science Bulletin*], 1956, Issue 01, pp. 96–99.

Wang, Jun, Minzu yuwen gongzuo zhong de ruogan renshi wenti [A Few Questions on the Work of Minority Languages and Scripts], *Minzu Yuwen* [*Minority Lanuages of China*], 1981, Issue 01, pp. 1–7.

Wang, Jun, Zhuangwen chuangzhi he xiudingzhong de ruogan wenti [A Few Questions in the Creation and Revision of the Zhuang Writing System], *Minzu Yuwen* [*Minority Languages of China*], 1982, No. 05, pp. 7–15.

Wang, Junhua, and Zhou, Zhenfan, Dalai yonghu "guanyu heping jiefang xizang banfa de xieyi" de dianbao [The Telegram from the Dalai Lama to Validate the 17 Points Agreement], *Zhongguo Dang'an* [*China Archives*], 2009, Volume 3, pp. 76–77.

Wang, Junmin, Shoulie jingji wenhua leixing de dangdai bianqian [The Contemporary Change of the Hunting Economy], *Zhongyang Minzu Daxue Xuebao* [*Journal of the Central University for Nationalities (philosophy and social science)*], 2005, No. 6, pp. 57–64.

Wang, Peiying, Guanyu yuyan de minzuxing yu shehuixing de guanxi wenti [the Relationship about Language Nationality and Sociality [The Relationship between Ethnic Feature and Social Feature of Languages)], *Heilongjiang Minzu Congkan* [*Heilongjiang National Series*], 2002, No. 01, pp. 93–95.

Wang, Shaoguang, and Hu, Anguang, The Chinese Economy in Crisis: State Capacity and Tax Reform, M E Sharpe Inc, 2001.

Wang, Shuping, The People's Republic of China's Policy on the Minorities and International Approaches to Ethnic Groups: A Comparative Study, *International Journal on Minority and Group Rights*, 2004, Volume 11, pp. 159–185.

Wang, Su, "Chapter 2 Minority Movement and Education", in Iredale, Robyn, Naran, Bilik, and Guo, Fei (eds), China's Minorities On the Move: Selected Case Studies, M. E. Sharpe, 2003, pp. 32–50.

Wang, Wenguang, and You, Weiqiong, Xinzhongguo chengli yilai Yunnan minzu shibie de renshi yu fansi [The Identification of Yunnan's Ethnic Groups Since the Founding of the PRC and Its Enlightenment], *Yunnan Minzu Daxue Xuebao* [*Journal of Yunnan Nationalities University (Social Sciences)*], 2010, No. 2, pp. 95–99.

Wang, Xiaoming, and Wang, Yongxi, Elunchun yu Ewenke zu tongyuan kao [Research on the Common Origin of Oroqen and Ewenk], *Heilongjiang Minzu Congkan* [*Heilongjiang National Series*], 1987, No. 1, pp. 44–50.

Wang, Xintian, and Wu, Chunming, Guanyu Taiwan yuanzhumin yanjiu de jige wenti [Several Issues on the Study of the Aborigines in Taiwan], *Guangxi Minzu Yanjiu* [*Study of Ethnics in Guangxi*], 2007, No. 01, pp. 30–37.

Wang, Yan, Lun minzu zizhi defang de biantongquan [On Alteration Rights of Autonomous Minority Areas], *Hubei Minzu Xueyuan Xuebao* [*Journal of Hubei Institute for Nationalities*], 2006, No. 1, pp. 55–59.

Wang, Yongzhi, Shi, Lina, and Ji, Yujiao, Xibu shaoshu minzu qingshaonian zongjiao xinyang zhuangkuang de diaocha yanjiu—yi Yunnan sheng Honghe Hani zu yizu zizhizhou qingshaonian zongjiao xinyang xianzhuang weili [An Investigation of the Status of Religious Belief Among Minority Teenagers (Age 12–17) in the West: Taking the Honghe Hani and Yi Autonomous Prefecture as An Example]", *Shijie Zongjiao Wenhua* [*The World Religious Cultures*], 2012, No. 3, pp. 68–74.

Wang, Zhonghan (ed), Zhongguo minzu shi gaiyao [General History of China's Nationalities], Shanxi Jiaoyu Chubanshe, 2004.

Wang, Zhonghan (ed), Zhongguo minzu shi [The National History of China], Zhongguo Shehui Kexue Chubanshe, 1994.

Wang, Zuoan, Tantan zongjiao gongzuo jiben fangzhen [On the Basic Policy on Religious Work], *Zhongguo Zongjiao* [*China Religion*], 2009, Issue 02, pp. 8–11.

Weatherley, Robert, Making China Strong: the Role of Nationalism in Chinese Thinking on Democracy and Human Rights, Palgrave Macmillan, 2014.

Wei, Xinglang, Pinyin zhuangwen gaige yu xin fangkuai zhuangzi chuyi [Opinions on the Reform of the Zhuang Language Using Phonetic Alphabets and the New Zhuang Block Characters], *Zhongyang Minzu Daxue Xuebao* [*Journal of Minzu University of China (Philosophy and Social Science)*], 2012, No. 6, pp. 120–125.

Welhengama, Gnanapala, Minorities' Claims: From Autonomy To Secession—International Law and State Practice, Ashgate, 2000.

Weller, Marc, "Effective Participation of Minorities in Public Life", in Weller, Marc (ed), Universal Minority Rights: A Commentary on the Jurisprudence of International Court and Treaty Bodies, Oxford University Press, 2007, pp. 477–516.

Weller, Marc, Escaping the Self-determination Trap, Martinus Nijhoff Publishers, 2008.

Weller, Marc, "Settling Self-determination Conflicts: An Introduction", in Weller, Marc, and Metzger, Barbara (eds), Settling Self-determination Disputes: Complex Power-sharing in Theory and Practice, Martinus Nijhoff Publishers, 2008, pp. xi–xvii.

Wells, Audrey, The Political Thought of Sun Yat-sen: Development and Impact, Palgrave, 2001.

Wheatley, Steven, Democracy, Minorities and International Law, Cambridge University Press, 2005.

Williams, Craig, International Human Rights and Confucianism, *Asia-Pacific Journal on Human Rights and the Law*, 2006, Volume 7:1, pp. 38–66.

Wright, Arthur F., "Chapter 2 Sui Dynasty", in Twitchett, Denis (ed), The Cambridge History of China: Volume 3, Cambridge University Press, 1979, pp. 48–149.

Woodside, Alexander, "Chapter 5 The Ch'ien-Lung Reign", in Peterson, Willard J (ed), The Cambridge History of China: Volume 9, Cambridge University Press, 2002, pp. 230–309.

Wu, David Y. H., Chinese Minority Policy and the Meaning of Minority Culture: the Example of Bai in Yunnan, China, *Human Organisation*, 1990, Volume 49, No.1, pp. 1–13.

Wu, Xuemei, Zhuiniuji: cong lishi de jiyi dao xianshi de caoyan [The Drilling-bull Sacrifice: From Historical Reminiscence to Practical Demonstration——Setting Miao Nationality in Xiaomaopuoying Village as An Example], *Guizhou Minzu Yanjiu* [*Guizhou Ethnic Studies*], 2004, No. 4, pp. 130–134.

Wu, Yun-kuang, etc, Bianjiang minzu de guoqu yu xianzai [The Past and the Present of the Tribes along the Chinese Border], The Orient Cultural Service, 1972.

Wu, Zongjin, Minzu fazhi de lilun yu shijian [Theory and Practice of Ethnic Legislation], Zhongguo Minzhu Fazhi Chubanshe, 1997.

Wusipanuofu, Kuerbanali, Huiyi Yili Kazakh zizhizhou chengli de guochneg [Recalling the Founding Process of the Yili Kazakh Autonomous Prefecture], http://www.xjyl.gov.cn/Article/ShowArticle.aspx?ArticleID=8333.

Xanthaki, Alexandra, Indigenous Rights and United Nations Standards: Self-determination, Culture and Land, Cambridge University Press, 2007.

Xiao, Ping, and Li, Xiaowu, Xingzheng shouzhang fuze zhi de gengxin yu fazhan [Renewal and Development of Chief Executive Responsibility System], *Nanchang Daxue Xuebao* [*Journal of Nanchang University* (*Humanities and Social Sciences*)], 2002, Issue 02, pp. 48–52.

Xie, Youxian, Hu, Xianghua and Tian, Mengqing, "Qiangxian kuoquan", "caizheng sheng zhiguan xian" zhixia de zizhizhou diwei wenti yanjiu [A Study on the Status of Autonomous Prefecture in the Process of "Power Expansion of Strong Counties" and "Province Directly Administrate Counties" Reform], *Heilongjiang Minzu Congkan* [*Heilongjiang National Series*], 2012, No. 03, pp. 21–27.

Xu, Bo, Guanyu fenshuizhi xia shuishou fanhuan wenti de sikao [Some Thoughts on the Issues of Tax Refund under the Tax Division System], *Caizheng Yanjiu* [*Public Finance Research*], 2010, No. 04, pp. 69–71.

Xu, Chongde, Lun "yiguo liangzhi" dui shixian guojia tongyi de yiyi [The Strategic Importance of "One Country, Two Systems" to the Realisation of National Unity], *Zhongguo Faxue* [*China Legal Science*], 1990, Issue 02, pp. 13–20.

Xu, Chongde, Zhonghua renmin gongheguo xianfa shi [The Constitutional History of the People's Republic of China], Fujian Renmin Chubanshe, 2003.

Xu, Fangtian, and Meng, Shuqing, Elunchun zu yuanliu jianshu [A Brief Discussion on the Origins of the Oroqen], *Heilongjiang Minzu Congkan* [*Heilongjiang National Series*], 1986, No. 4, pp. 24–27.

Xu, Mengzhou, and Ye, Shan, Lun zhengfujian caizheng zhuanyi zhifu de zhidu anpai [On Institutional Arrangements of Intergovernmental Fiscal Transfer Payment], *Shehui Kexue* [*Journal of Social Sciences*], 2010, Issue 07, pp. 69–79.

Xu, Tao, and Lei, Lianghai, Fenshuizhi xia difang zhengfu caizheng shouzhi bupinghheng de shizheng fenxi [An Analysis on the Financial Imbalance of Local Governments under the Current Tax Division Management System], *Jingji Shijiao* [*Economic Vision*], 2011, No.10, pp. 16–17.

Xu, Wanbang, and Qi, Qingfu, Zhongguo shaoshu minzu wenhua tonglun [Introduction to Chinese Minority Cultures], Zhongyang Minzu Daxue Chubanshe, 1996.

Xu, Xinxi, Shilun Shang Zhou shenquan zhengzhi de goujian yu zhenghe [On the Construction and Integration of Shangzhou Theocracy], *Yindu Xuekan* [*Yindu Journal*], 2006, Volume 1, pp. 10–14.

Yan, Qiyan, Guizhou weishibie minzu renkou de fenbu tedian he lishi chengyin [The Historical Causes and Distribution Characteristics of the Unidentified Ethnic Groups in Guizhou], *Minban Jiaoyu Yanjiu* [*Private Education Research*], 2009, No. 2, pp. 27–31.

Yang, Bojun, Mengzi yizhu [Mencius with Comments], Volume 1 and 2, Zhonghua Shuju, 1960.

Yang, Feng, The Legislation in Autonomous Areas in China: Progress, Limitations and Recommendations, *Asian-Pacific Law and Policy Journal*, 2017, Volume 18:2, pp. 46–82.

Yang, Shengmin, and Ding, Hong (eds), Zhongguo minzu zhi [The Ethnography of China], Zhongyang Minzu Daxue Chubanshe, 2003.

Yang, Yonghong, Sovereignty in China's Perspective, Peter Lang Academic Research, 2017.

Yang, Yuqing, Guojia liyi: su'e dui zaihua hezuozhe de xuanze [State Interests: the Choice of the Soviet Union on Its Alliance in China]", *Lishi Yanjiu* [*Historical Research*], 1999, Volume 4, pp. 140–154.

Ye, Bifeng, Jingji xianfaxue yanjiu de changshi: fenshuizhi juedingquan de xianfa fenxi [A Preliminary Study into Economic Constitution: Constitutional Interpretation of Right of Decision on Adaption of a Tax-sharing System], *Shanghai Jiaotong Daxue Xuebao* [*Journal of Shanghai Jiao Tong University (Philosophy and Social Science)*], 2007, No. 6, pp. 5–14.

Ye, Jianying, *Guanyu Taiwan huigui zuguo shixian heping tongyi de fangzhen zhengce de jianghua* [Elaborations on Policy concerning the Return of Taiwan to the Motherland and Peaceful Reunification], *Gazette of the State Council*, 1981, Issue 22, pp. 687–688.

Ye, Zhangyu, Zhonggong diyidai zhongyang lingdao jiti jiejue xianggang wenti zhanjue juece de lishi kaocha [A Historical Investigation of the Strategic Decision on the Settlement of the Question of Hong Kong by the First Generation of Collective Leadership of the CPC Central Committee], *Dangdai Zhongguoshi Yanjiu* [*Contemporary China History Studies*], 2007, No. 03, pp. 46–52.

Yee, Herbert S., and Lo, Sonny S. H., Macau in Transition: the Political Decolonisation, *Asian Survey*, 1991, Volume 31, No. 10, pp. 905–919.

Yu, Lingyun, Guoqi de xianfa yiyi [The Constitutional Significance of the National Flag], *Faxue Pinglun* [*Law Review*], 2015, No. 03, pp. 20–23.

Yu, Mengyuan (Yolanda), Instrumental Autonomy, Political Socialisation, and Citizenship Identity: A Case Study of Korean Minority Citizenship Identity, Bilingual

Education and Modern Media Life in the Post-Communism Transitioning China, Springer, 2017.

Yu, Ying-Shih, "Chapter 6 Han Foreign Relations", in Twitchett, Denis, and Fairbank, John K (eds), The Cambridge History of China: Volume 1, Cambridge University Press, 1986, pp. 377–462.

Yu, Ying-Shih, Qian Mu yu zhongguo wenghua [Qian Mu and Chinese Culture], Shanghai Yuandong Chubanshe, 1994.

Yue, Qianhou, Gu Weijun yu kangri waijiao [V. K. Wellington Koo and Anti-Japanese Diplomacy], Hebei Renmin Chubanshe, 1998.

Yujiro, Murata, Sun Zhongshan yu xinhai geming shiqi de "wuzu gonghe" lun [Sun Yatsen and the Theory of 'Five Nations' Republic During the Period of the 1911 Revolution], *Guangdong Shehui Kexue* [*Social Sciences in Guangdong*], 2004, Issue 5, pp. 121–128.

Zeng, Heping, Zoujin Tuwa ren: Aletai Tuwa ren shehui lishi diaocha (shang) [Approaching the Tuvinian Group: A Social and Historical Investigation of the Altai Tuvans I], *Xinjiang Difang Zhi* [*Local Chronicles of Xinjiang*], 2011, No. 1, pp. 45–51.

Zhang, Dianjun, Minzu zizhi defang falv biantong de fali fenxi [A Jurisprudential Analysis of Law Accommodation in National Autonomous Areas], *Guizhou Minzu Yanjiu* [*Guizhou Ethnic Studies*], 2010, No. 1, pp. 8–17.

Zhang Dianjun, Minzu zizhi defang biantong zhixing yu tingzhi zhixing falv wenti tanxi [A Study of Implementation with Certain Alterations or Cease Implementing in National Autonomous Areas of China], *Beifang Minzu Daxue Xuebao* [*Journal of Beifang Ethic University*], 2009, No. 3, pp. 66–71.

Zhang, Dinghuai, and Li, Yanchao, Shijian lixing: "yiguo liangzhi" zhengce de lilun jichu [The Theoretical Basis for the 'One Country Two Systems' Policy], *Dangdai Zhongguo Zhengzhi Yanjiu Baogao* [*Research Reports on the Politics of Contemporary China*], 2011, Issue 00, pp. 314–340.

Zhang, Jinfan, Zhongguo xianfa shi [Chinese Constitution History], Jilin Renmin Chubanshe, 2004.

Zhang, Qianfan, The Constitution of China: A Contextual Analysis, Hart Publishing, 2012.

Zhan, Jing, Zhongyang dui sheng caizheng zhuanyi zhifu de jueding yinsu: gongping, yijia haishi xiaoyi? [Determinants of Central-Provincial Fiscal Transfer: Equity, Bargaining or Efficiency?], *Jingji Shehui Tizhi Bijiao* [*Comparative Economic & Social Systems*], 2011, No. 6, pp. 73–83.

Zhang, Qiwen, and Liu, Yanhong, Hezhu zu jingji fazhan de wenti yu duice [Problems and Countermeasures of the Economic Development of the Hezhe Nationality of Heilongjiang Province], *Heilongjiang Minzu Congkan* [*Heilongjiang National Series*], 2013, No. 2, pp. 62–66.

Zhang, Minggeng, and Zhang, Mingjv, Zhongguo lidai xingzheng quhua [The History of Administrative Divisions in China: 221 BC to 1991], Zhongguo Huaqiao Chubanshe, 1996.

Zhang, Yong, Cong "shiba xingqi" dao "wuse qi" [From the Eighteen–star Flag to Five-colour Flag], *Beijing Daxue Xuebao* [*Journal of Peking University* (*Humanities and Social Sciences*)], 2002, Volume 39, No. 2, pp. 106–114.

Zhang, Zhiyi, Zhengque renshi he guanche dang de zongjiao xinyang ziyou zhengce [Correctly Understand and Implement the Party's Policy on Freedom of Religious Belief], *Zhongguo Minzu* [*China's Ethnic Groups*], 1962, Issue 04, pp. 2–5.

Zhang, Xisheng, Written Language Reform and Regional Autonomy of Dai Nationality in Xishuangbanna, *International Journal on Minority and Group Rights*, 2009, Issue 16, pp. 423–432.

Zhao, Jincan, Yuyan taidu yu shaoshu minzu xinchuang wenzii de qianjing [Linguistic Attitude and the Prospect of Ethnic Newly-created Characters], *Beifang Minzu Daxue Xuebao* [*Journal of Beifang Ethnic University*], 2010, No. 5, pp. 110–114.

Zhao, Suisheng, A Nation-State by Construction: Dynamics of Modern Chinese Nationalism, Stanford University Press, 2004.

Zhao, Xiaoyang, Zhongguo tianzhujiao duli ziban yundong de chucheng [The Initial Formation of Chinese Catholic Independent Self-management Movements], *Dangdai Zhongguoshi Yanjiu* [*Contemporary China History Studies*], 2012, Issue 04, pp. 107–114.

Zhao, Xuexian, Peng, Qian, and Yang, Wenshun, (eds), Zhongguo guomin dang minzu lilun yu minzu zhengce yanjiu [The Study on the National Theory and Policy of the GMD], Zhongyang Minzu Daxue Chubanshe, 2010.

Zhao, Yuyan, Lvyou huanjing xia wugu wenhua de bianyi [The Variation of Witchcraft Culture Against the Background of Tourism—A Case Study of the Tourism of Miao People in Shanjiang], *Guangxi Minzu Daxue Xuebao* [*Journal of Guangxi University for Nationalities* (*Philosophy and Social Science*)], 2007, No. 6, pp. 37–42.

Zhonguo jidujiao zai xinzhongguo jianshe zhong nuli tujing de xuanyan [The Chinese Manifesto: Direction of Endeavour for Chinese Christianity in the Construction of New China], *Gazette of the People's Government of Henan Province*, 1950, Issue 10, p. 70.

Zheng, Yongnian, Discovering Chinese Nationalism in China: Modernisation, Identity, and International Relations, Cambridge University Press, 1999.

Zheng, Yongnian, The Chinese Communist Party as Organisational Emperor: Culture, Reproduction and Transformation, Routledge, 2010.

Zhou, Enlai, "A Few Questions on the Policy Towards Ethnicities in China (04/08/1957)", in the Policy Research Office of the State Ethnic Affairs Commission (ed), Zhonguo gongchandang zhuyao lingdaoren lun minzu wenti [The Comments on Ethnicity Questions from the Main Leaders of the CCP], Minzu Chubanshe, 1994, pp. 162–189;

"Ethnic Regional Autonomy Contributes to National Unity and Common Progress (05/03/1957)", pp. 146–159; "The Work in Regard to the Ethnicities in the Northwest (26/06/1950)", pp. 47–50.

Zhou, Enlai, "On a Few Questions of the Chinese People's Political Consultative Conference (07/09/1949)", in Jin, Binghao (ed), Minzu gangling zhengce wenxian xuanbian [The Collected Works of the Documents on the National Program and Policy], Zhongyang Minzu Daxue Chubanshe, 2006, pp. 407–409.

Zhou, Enlai, "The Liberation of Taiwan is Achievable", in Zhou Enai Xuanji [Selected Works of Zhou Enlai Volume 2], Renmin Chubanshe, 1984.

Zhou, Guolin, Ershisi shi quanyi [Serials of Twenty Four Histories (Interpretation)]: Book of Wei, Hanyu Dacidian Chubanshe, 2004.

Zhou, Qingsheng, Zhongguo shuangyu jiaoyu leixing [Models of Bilingual Education in China], *Minzu Yuwen* [*Minority Languages of China*], 1991, No. 3, pp. 65–69.

Zhou, Qingsheng, Zhongsu jianguo chuqi shaoshu minzu wenzi chuangzhi bijiao [A Comparison of the Creation of Minority Writings between the Soviet Union and China], *Minzu Yuwen* [*Minority Languages of China*], 2002, No. 6, pp. 47–57.

Zhou, Maocao, "Chapter 12 The Use and Development of Tibetan in China", in Zhou, Minglang, and Sun, Hongkai (eds), Language Policy in the PRC: Theory and Practice since 1949, Kluwer Academic Publishers, 2004, pp. 221–237.

Zhou, Meiduo and Yan, Xueyong, Zhongguo zhuanxiang zhuanyi zhifu de zhengzhi luoji: wenti, yuanyin yu chulu [The Political Logic of Specific-Purpose Transfers in China: Problems, Reasons and Solutions], *Dangdai Caijing* [*Contemporary Finance and Economics*], 2008, No. 9, pp. 35–40.

Zhou, Minglang, "Chapter 5 Minority Language Policy in China: Equality in Theory and Inequality in Practice", in Zhou, Minglang, and Sun, Hongkai (eds), Language Policy in the PRC: Theory and Practice since 1949, Kluwer Academic Publishers, 2004, pp. 71–95.

Zhou, Minglang, Multilingualism in China: the Politics of Writing Reforms for Minority Languages 1949–2002, Mouton de Gruyter, 2003.

Zhou, Shengchun, Cao, Jiangang, and Hu, Qian, Zhongguo lishi shang de nongben gongshangmo sixiang yu zhengfu zhengce de shanbian [Development of Agriculture-oriented Ideology and Corresponding Government Policies in the Chinese History], *Zhejiang Daxue Xuebao* [*Journal of Zhejiang University* (*Humanities and Social Sciences*)], 2004, Volume 2, pp. 13–22.

Zhou, Xifeng, Jianshu Qingdai nenjiang liuyu de Ewenke zu [The Brief Discussion about the Ewenki Nationality of the Nen River Valley in the Qing Dynasty], *Heilongjiang Minzu Congkan* [*Heilongjiang National Series*], 2002, No. 4, pp. 77–81.

Zhou, Yaowen, and Fang, Fenghe, "Chapter 11 The Use and Development of Dai and Its Vernacular Writing System", in Zhou, Minglang, and Sun, Hongkai (eds), Language

Policy in the PRC: Theory and Practice since 1949, Kluwer Academic Publishers, 2004, pp. 201–218.

Zhu, Suli, "Federalism" in Contemporary China: a Reflection on the Allocation of Power Between Central and Local Government, *Singapore Journal of International & Comparative Law*, 2003, Volume 7, pp. 1–14.

Zhu, Wenxu, and Xiao, Xue, Yizu diqu shaungyu jiaoyu leixing xianzhuang yanjiu [A Study on the Present Situation of Bilingual Education Types in Yi Nationality Areas], *Minzu Jiaoyu Yanjiu* [*Journal of Research on Education for Ethnic Minorities*], 2005, No. 5, pp. 87–92.

Zong, Daoyi, Deng Xiaoping yu zhongying xianggang wenti de tanpan [Deng Xiaoping and the Talks on the Question of Hong Kong between China and the United Kingdom], *Dangdai Zhongguoshi Yanjiu* [*Contemporary China History Studies*], 2007, Volume 13, Issue 3, pp. 53–59.

Zong, Huaide, Bishop, Zai duli zizhu ziban jiaohui de daolu shang kuobu qianjin [Take Great Strides Along the Road to Independent and Self-reliance Churches], *Zhongguo Tianzhujiao* [*Catholic Church In China*], 1991, Issue 01, pp. 16–17.

Index

www.ingramcontent.com/pod-product-compliance
Lightning Source LLC
LaVergne TN
LVHW020000031026
849161LV00021B/691